NEW SOCIOLOGY LIBRARY

No. 5

General Editor: Professor NORBERT ELIAS

Department of Sociology, University of Leicester

The Sociology of Community

NEW SOCIOLOGY LIBRARY

The Sociology of Community

A Selection of Readings

Edited and Introduced by
Colin Bell and Howard Newby
Department of Sociology, University of Essex

With a foreword by
Professor Norbert Elias

FRANK CASS AND CO. LTD.

First published 1974 in Great Britain by
FRANK CASS AND COMPANY LIMITED
67 Great Russell Street, London WC1B 3BT, England

and in United States of America by
FRANK CASS AND COMPANY LIMITED
c/o International Scholarly Book Services Inc.
P.O. Box 4347, Portland, Oregon 97208

ISBN 0 7146 2970 7

Library of Congress Catalog No. 72–92975

Made and printed in Great Britain by
WILLIAM CLOWES & SONS, LIMITED
London, Beccles and Colchester

Contents

PART VII

Towards a Theory of Communities*
Norbert Elias

Colin Bell and Howard Newby have reaped a rich harvest from the sociological field of community studies. The selection from the work in that field presented here should satisfy readers of many different tastes and interests. Specialists in the sociology of community studies will find the authors' brief, informative and succinct survey of the field and the introductory summaries to each chapter as useful for their own teaching and research as the comprehensive selection of articles itself. All those concerned with the welfare of people, whether social workers and nurses or magistrates and local authorities, will find here information about the community aspects of peoples' lives which all too often still fails to find a place in their professional training. If one is interested in sociological theories one will find here evidence of the scope as well as the limitations of the functionalist-structuralist schools of sociological theory. The authors point out, very rightly I think, that the theoretical aspects of community studies are less advanced than the empirical work in that field. It may be helpful to consider why that is the case. Also, I thought it may perhaps be useful if I show, in broad outline, that this need not be so. Sociological theories need not be built high into the air in such a manner that their relevance for empirical sociological investigations is negligible.

The key problem with which one is confronted by the variety of contemporary community studies is straightforward and relatively simple. The figurations of people which are investigated today under the name 'community' vary a great deal. The term community can refer to villages with some characteristics of a state in relatively undifferentiated agrarian societies. It can refer to a backwater village of a more or less urbanized nation state. It can be used with reference to a suburban community, a neighbourhood region or an ethnic minority of a large industrial city. Especially in America a whole town can be studied as a community. One could prolong the list. The problem evidently is: what links these different groupings to each other as objects of community studies? In former days one

---

* I have discussed this paper with Brian S. Martin, University of Leicester and am indebted to him for his help.

might have expected to find an adequate answer simply in the form of a definition. But on its own a definition can be of little help in this case. It would have to be a generalizing abstraction built so high in the air that its relevance for detailed empirical investigations and thus its propensity for being tested would be negligible. What cognitive value could a definition of the term 'animal' have on its own unrelated to the testable theoretical model of the developmental order in which more and more differentiated and complex animals have evolved from simpler and less complex organisms? A similar question can be asked with reference to the changeable groupings which men form with each other, among them, to communities. A definition indicating what all communities have in common can have little cognitive value unless it is connected with an overall model indicating how and why the characteristics of communities change when societies become more differentiated and more complex. That is what I am going to show. I hope it may be useful for understanding the way communities function in different societies.

But before one can set about this task one has to clear away a number of obstacles. Some of the older connotations obstinately cling to the community concept. They cling in the same way to the concept of a development of human societies. It is better to bring them into the open. An example is the pertinacity with which the community concept is associated with the folk pole of a folk-urban continuum. In terms of our own time this implies that communities are a form of group life which can only be found in 'traditional' as distinct from 'modern', in mainly agrarian as distinct from urbanized and industrialized societies. However, static polarities such as that represented by the 'folk-urban' continuum or by the reduction of all societies to two types 'traditional' and 'modern', are highly inadequate conceptual devices which evade the main issue: they leave no room for the understanding and explanation of the continuous process, of the development in the course of which one type of society transformed itself into another, and still transforms itself into another under our very eyes: largely agricultural, pre-industrial into more urbanized, more differentiated and complex societies, more 'traditional' into more 'modern' societies. They develop from one stage to another without any absolute break. Static typologies which associate communities with less differentiated societies nostalgically preserve a use of the term community which helped to launch it on its career, but which has long been overtaken by the advance in the field of community studies, as one can see in this volume. It may be expedient to remember the older meaning of the community concept. Then it will be easier to cut oneself loose from it.

The germinal concept, the concept 'Gemeinschaft', was introduced into the sociological literature by the German sociologist Tönnies. A sample of his writings is included here. As one can see from it, Tönnies used the conceptual representation of a formerly predominant manner of life and contrasted it with another concept representing the present manner of living, with 'Gesellschaft', usually translated in this context as 'association'. The latter referred in Tönnies' version to a kind of social life which is cold, impersonal and fragmented. 'Association', as he saw it, lacks cohesion; human beings are relatively isolated; friction and strife occur frequently. Life in communities, by contrast, is warmer, more homely and affectionate. Solidarity and harmony, unity of purpose and co-operation, ensured by a firm tradition are greater. The community-association polarity, in other words, like the folk-urban polarity, has romantic undertones. It reflects, at least in its initial version, the discontent and suffering connected with increasing urbanization and industrialization; it betrays a certain longing for a reversal of the trend, for a return to an earlier stage in the development of societies where life was simpler and appeared to possess all those desirable qualities that are missed in the present. For a time, 'community' became the symbol of these qualities.

The elevation of aspects of an earlier stage of development to the status of a cherished ideal by men of the following stage is nothing new. It is a recurrent feature of European and perhaps of other societies. There are many examples. The relatively autarkous land-owning knight of the earlier middle ages became a subject of romantic longing in the later middle ages when the power ratio of kings and princes in relation to that of the mass of the nobles increased. Cervantes provided a great deal of fun for his own and later genera-tions by satirizing in his Don Quixote this romancing about the past beauties of chivalry. A little later aristocratic ladies and gentlemen imprisoned in the golden cage of a large royal Court and alienated from the countryside, were enraptured by the dreamlife of simple shepherds and shepherdesses conjured up before them by pastoral lyrics and novels which followed a tradition of court and city life that went back to antiquity. The decline of the handicrafts in the period of increasing mechanization created for a while the fashion (of which Wagner's 'Meistersinger' is an example) of presenting the life of the old craftmasters with a nostalgic but ennobling patina.

Tönnies' use of the term 'community' shows a similar type of sentiment. Community was for him the symbol of a past and a better age. By telescoping the long and gradual development of societies into a static dichotomy 'community', symbol of a better past, and 'association', symbol of a disturbed and disturbing present, he gave expression to a growing trend of his time. The book in which he put forward this theoretical scheme was published late in the nineteenth century. It was a time of transition when the previously dominant social belief of the rising middle classes of Europe, the belief in the better future to come, in the necessary progress of human societies, became gradually weaker and the opposite belief that the present times are worse, that the good times lay in the past, once more gathered momentum.

One can perhaps gain a better understanding of this turning point and with it of the early meaning of the term community, if one compares Tönnies' dichotomy 'community' and 'association' with Durkheim's dichotomy 'mechanical solidarity' and 'organic solidarity'. The latter was used as a theoretical framework in Durkheim's book on the division of labour which was published six years after Tönnies book.[1] At that time Durkheim's confidence in the progress of society was still fairly firm even though some doubts had crept in. Like Tönnies, Durkheim was concerned with two different ways in which people can be bonded to each other. He, too, treated these different patterns of bonding as characteristics of the former and the present condition of European societies. Both men, in other words, reduced the continuous long-term process of social change to two static types though Durkheim provided at least a partial answer to the problem of the movement between them by linking the two types of bonding to each other as different stages of the division of labour.

However, the underlying sentiment, the implied value attached to the two types of bonding was in Durkheim's case exactly the opposite from that which Tönnies had infused into his conceptual dichotomy. In fact Tönnies complained firstly that Durkheim who had reviewed his book briefly but not unfavourably and who, he felt, had evidently learned something from it, never mentioned the fact in his book, and secondly that Durkheim had put the whole scheme upside down. According to Tönnies' hypothesis the older conditions of society were, in his own words 'quasi-organic', the more modern conditions 'quasi-mechanical',[2] while Durkheim called the former 'mechanical' and the latter 'organic'. One encounters here an almost paradigmatic example of a controversy which on the face of it centres on a disagreement about social structures, while it is in fact a disagreement due to different social beliefs, to different extraneous values attached to these structures and therefore to different ways of perceiving them. The contrast between Tönnies' and Durkheim's typology, in other words, is symptomatic of one of the main sources of confusion in sociology—to the fusion of statements about structures and statements about ideals in sociological theories.

The community concept has suffered for a long time from this confusion. One encounters it strongly marked already here at the inception of the term as a sociological concept. While on the face of it Tönnies' distinction between 'Gemeinschaft' and 'Gesellschaft', between 'community' and 'association' simply referred to specific differences in the structure of human bonding, these differences were in his exposition so inextricably interwoven with his beliefs and ideals that the cognitive value of his theory was gravely impaired. It would be interesting to pursue the question whether the social success of his book would have been the same without this fusion of structure and ideal. What one can regard as fairly certain is the fact that the sentiment which helped the community concept on its way was symptomatic of a rising trend both of feeling and of thinking in society at large which gathered strength from the later part of the nineteenth century on. Up to that time the belief that advances in industry, science and technology were the harbingers of progress and a better life had been fairly widespread and dominant among the literati and the reading public of European societies. As industrialization and urbanization advanced the tide began to turn. The feeling that industry, science and urban life were a kind of Pandora's box, a source of evils, gained the ascendancy over the belief in progress. At that stage Tönnies' book which represented life in the small communities of less developed societies compared with that in large industrial cities as the good life, as a better world which was lost, could not fail to have a fairly wide appeal. It sailed with the wind. Ever since, the use of the term community has remained to some extent associated with the hope and the wish of reviving once more the closer, warmer, more harmonious type of bonds between people vaguely attributed to past ages.

Yet at the same time, considerable progress has been made by sociologists specially concerned with community studies in disentangling in their studies structure and sentiment. To some extent one can follow in this volume the transformation of the community concept from its use as a word of praise for a seemingly unvarying condition of a better past, into a better fitting and in this sense more realistic code word for specific structures of human bonding whose common features change in a characteristic manner according to the stage of development of a society. How they change I shall try to show.

However, the transformation of the community concept from a term where sentiment dominated the vision of structure to a term aimed at giving structure priority over sentiment was a slow and arduous process. In many cases the change in that direction came about as a result of controversies about short-term issues between social scientists who perceived communities differently because they approached their problems under the guidance of extraneous values or biases which were different and antagonistic.

I thought it might be helpful to refer briefly to a controversy of this kind. It is a well known episode in the development of community studies and illuminates as a classic, an almost paradigmatic example some of their basic problems. I refer to the exploration of the same Mexican village community by Robert Redfield, and seventeen years later, by Oscar Lewis. The striking differences in what they perceived and reported, as both authors recognized, were not so much due to factual changes which the community had undergone in the interval between the two visits, as to differences in the basic outlook with which the two authors approached their task. Lewis' summing up of some of the differences between Redfield's and his own picture of the same community (from: *Life in a Mexican Village, Tepoztlan Restudied*, Illinois, 1951, pp. 428ff.) shows this very clearly:

> The impression given by Redfield's study of Tepoztlan is that of a relatively homogeneous, isolated, smoothly functioning and well-integrated society made up of a contented and well adjusted people. His picture of the village has a Rousseauan quality which glosses lightly over evidence of violence, disruption, cruelty, disease, suffering and maladjustment. We are told little of poverty, economic problems or political schisms. Throughout his study we find an emphasis upon co-operation and unifying factors in Tepoztecan society. Our findings, on the other hand, would emphasize the underlying individualism of Tepoztecan institutions and character, the lack of co-operation, the tensions between villages within the municipio, the schisms within the village and the pervading quality of fear, envy and distrust—in interpersonal relations.

Redfield acknowledged (in *The Little Community, Viewpoints for the Study of a Human Whole*, Chicago, 1955, p. 134) that Lewis' summary was on the whole just. Yet he made this statement in a book which was very unambiguously devoted to his belief that the 'little community' or, in terms of the folk-urban continuum, the 'folk-community' possesses a 'wholeness', a homogeneity, a solidarity and is representative of a 'good life'—all of which are lost as one gets nearer to the urban pole of the continuum. It is a memorable example of the fact that a strongly held extra-scientific belief used as guiding matrix of sociological or anthropological research makes its holder impervious to the absorption of facts which run counter to it—which is of course as true of a dogmatic belief in the better life of the past as of that in the better life of the future.

Is it possible to move beyond a condition of community research in which untested conventions and beliefs determine what one perceives as significant? At present, community research, as the editors of this volume very rightly point out, lacks a firm theoretical basis. That undoubtedly is the main reason for the uncertainties that still beset much of the research in this field. The question is why that is the case. I have given a good deal of thought to this problem first in connection with a community study in Leicestershire which I undertook, together with J. L. Scotson, some years ago, and again, when reading other community studies among them those represented here. Some suggestions for a theoretical model which occurred to me in that context, I thought, might be interesting to discuss here.

The term 'community' is used today in a wider sense than that in which it was used by Redfield when he spoke of the 'little community'. It referred then and can still refer to villages of pre-industrial and predominantly agricultural societies. It can refer to villages in the less developed regions of more advanced industrial and urban societies. The studies from southern Italy in this volume are examples. But it can also refer, as one can see here, to suburban groups and estates of large cities in highly industrialized and urbanized societies. It can be applied to neighbourhood groups, to groups of hippies, to religious or ethnic minorities, to student communities and to many other types of grouping even within the metropolitan cities. It is perhaps not entirely easy to discover the connecting links between different types of communities with which community research in general and this volume in particular are concerned. They move into one's field of vision only if one recognizes that the structural characteristics of communities are a function of the developmental stage of the social field to which they belong. Communities which form part of societies at comparable levels of social development have basic structural characteristics in common and differ in specific ways from communities of societies at different stages of development though one has to take account of the fact that societies do not develop in all areas at an even rate.

In order to understand both the relatedness and the differences of different types of communities, therefore, one requires a developmental framework. The prevailing lawlike theories which abstract from the succession of changes that societies undergo in the sequence of time are of little use if one is confronted with problems of this kind. One can work toward their solution only by developing process-theories which do not abstract from the long-term diachronic dimension of social change and which represent in the form of a model the structure, the sequential order of change itself and set out to explain it.

For some time now sociologists have moved away from long-range process theories. They have tried to make do with lawlike theories of the middle-range (so-called). These are usually little more than short- and narrow-range generalizations abstracted from selected aspects of their own relatively differentiated societies; they leave out of account less differentiated societies of the past and of their own time as well as the whole movement of the structured sequence of changes leading from the long process of the past through the short present towards a future. A peculiar distortion has followed from this foreshortening of the sociologists' field of vision. Under the name 'modern' the short-term problems of the sociologists' own societies and high level generalized abstractions from them stand in the centre of the field almost in isolation. The long process of past developments has shrunk into a single type of society called 'traditional' and the future appears as a largely quantitative projection of short-term trends of the present.

The foreshortening of the perspective from a long- and wide-range to a short- and narrow-range vision has been by no means entirely unproductive. It has led to an experimentation with empirical sociological research into a great variety of contemporary problems unequalled in any previous phase of the development of sociology. But it has remained almost entirely sterile at the theoretical level. In fact one may doubt whether any of the lawlike systems of abstractions with a short- and narrow-range perspective which have been put forward as sociological theories in the second half of the twentieth century deserve to be called theories. Almost all of them lack at least two indispensable qualifications of scientific theories which are closely connected with each other: They are untestable, they can neither be confirmed nor refuted by empirical research. Nor can they serve as stepping stones for suggesting new problems and for the development of further theories which go beyond them. There is a coming and going of short-lived theoretical fashions in sociology, most of them semi-philosophical in character, i.e. with an uncertain position halfway between a philosophy of society and a science of society. As such they can neither assist in the indispensable cross-fertilization of the empirical and the theoretical levels of research nor ensure the continuity of advance of knowledge on both levels—which in spite of all innovatory revolutions is one of the principle characteristics, and one of the principle social functions, of theories of the older sciences.

In more than one respect the swing of the pendulum from the long-range sociological process-theories of the nineteenth century to the lawlike short-range sociological theories of recent times has been rather extreme. Now, in a spiral movement which is not uncharacteristic of early scientific processes of this kind, one can move once more towards long-range theories on a new level where theories can be enriched by the wealth of new evidence worked out at the empirical level and can be at the same time systematically tested by, and guide, the research at that level.

Taking up at a new level of the spiral the lost thread of the older theories, however, also requires a re-orientation in another respect. It requires a return from the prevailing interaction theories and the whole idiom of speaking and thinking rooted in them to the inter-dependence theories of the earlier period, to a theory of human bonding. Tönnies and Durkheim were concerned with differences in the pattern of bonding. So was Marx when he spoke of the changing relations of production. The great pioneers of that period had no occasion to explain in general terms the distinguishing characteristics of interdependence theories and especially the differences between interdependence and interaction theories. For the latter did not exist at the time. But in this context it is necessary to bring these differences into the open. Otherwise one cannot work towards a theoretical framework for community studies; one cannot get the differences and the relationship between communities at different stages sharply into focus without enquiring into the structure of interdependencies which bind members of communities to each other and to people without. Moreover, as the structure of these bonds change in a highly specific manner when less differentiated and less complex develop into more differentiated and more complex societies, the concept of social development itself becomes clearer if one determines the distinguishing characteristics of different types of communities as characteristics of different developmental stages. The questions one has to answer, therefore, are firstly: What are the specific interdependencies between people who form with each other that kind of figuration which we call a community as distinct from those between people forming other types of figurations? And secondly: How and why do these characteristic community bonds change when the structure of the wider society changes?

It will require some further elaboration before it can become apparent what kind of assistance one may expect for community research and community work from a dynamic theory of social bonding. At present one of the main obstacles to such an approach is the relative looseness, not to say vagueness, of many of the technical terms currently used in the sociological and anthropological literature if one refers to the way people are linked to each other in societies. Many of these terms suffer from a characteristic socio-logical disease: they are shrouded in a voluntaristic twilight. They blur the distinction between human bonds that can be made and unmade at will by those concerned, and human bonds which cannot be made and unmade at will. Durkheim's use of the term 'organic solidarity' is a good example of this twilight. It suggests that people are functionally interdependent like organs in an organism and that solidarity is arrived at, and in this sense people become inter-dependent, as a result of their moral decision. More recent examples are concepts like 'role', 'interaction' and the ubiquitous 'human relations'. Their use can easily give the impression that the central task of sociology is to study how individual people act or behave when they make contact or form relations with each other. The implications appear to be that human beings are always free to act, to interact, to form relationships as they like. In actual fact their ability to do this is limited and sociological studies are very much concerned with the problem of how limited it is and why.

Enquiries into the interdependencies which bind people to each other provide some of the answers. For the fact that men are dependent on each other in a great variety of ways limits the scope of their choices and their actions. The concept of interdependence, in other words, conveys as the others do not the peculiarly compelling nature of human bonds. It enables one to distinguish between interdependencies which people can bring about, up to a point, voluntarily and deliberately, as is sometimes the case when people marry, choose an occupational training or form a team for research purposes, and interdependencies by which they are bound but which they cannot individually enter or break at will. Thus people of feudal societies who were bonded to each other as serfs, vassals and feudal lords could perhaps, in a limited way, move within that particular scheme of social bonds, also known as 'social structure', but they could not at will reshuffle the pattern of their inter-dependencies and become bonded instead as followers and leaders of parliamentary parties or as industrial workers and managers. Although it is certainly possible for men to bind themselves to each other with due deliberation and by their own choice, the whole groundwork of interdependencies which bind people to each other at a given developmental phase has not been planned or willed by those who form it and are bound by it. Even the term 'social structure', which is often used as a technical term for this groundwork and which conveys something of the compelling nature of inter-human bonds, is open to misunderstandings because one tends to use it as if it referred to something that exists outside and above human beings. One is apt to forget that it refers to specific patterns of interdependencies between people, to the varying ways in which human beings are bonded to each other, e.g. in the form of communities, of social classes, of metropolitan cities, of nation states or groups of nation-states.

In recent times the chains of interdependencies between people have become almost visibly more far-flung and more closely knit. One can hardly fail to notice. So many millions of human beings are in one way or the other dependent on each other that the chains of interdependencies appear impersonal although they are nothing but dependencies of persons, mostly unevenly reciprocal, on each other. Yet although these and many other changes are nothing but changes in the bonding of people, none of the people involved in them has actually planned or willed these changes. By moving out of the voluntaristic twilight one is able, as one shall see, to determine the direction of such changes with a high degree of certainty and precision.

One other preliminary observation is necessary. Then the stage is fairly set for a clarification and explanation of the changes which communities undergo within such a wider framework. It may be useful to state explicitly that interdependencies between people are completely neutral features of communities or societies—neutral in terms of co-operation and conflict: they can give rise to either. A very simple example can show that. If one rents a flat and the walls are thin, oneself and one's neighbours become interdependent in certain respects. They may be noisy when one wants to go to sleep or vice versa. One may suffer in silence or may try to do something about it. One may come to an agreement or engage in a prolonged battle of noises as a test of power. Co-operation and conflict in other words are ways of handling problems that arise when people become interdependent or more interdependent or in different ways than before. Seen as stationary conditions, conflict and co-operation appear as antagonistic and incompatible. Seen as episodes in a process of changing reciprocal dependencies, they emerge as different ways of handling problems, particularly of power problems, inherent in that process.[3]

Some of the common properties of communities, in the traditional sense of the word, can be stated very briefly. A community, one can say, is a group of households situated in the same locality and linked to each other by functional interdependencies which are closer than interdependencies of the same kind with other groups of people within the wider social field to which a community belongs. Specific reciprocal dependencies of people having their home in relatively close propinquity within certain visible or invisible boundaries form, as it were, the primary common ground which relates communities of all kinds to each other. In almost all cases these dependencies are unevenly reciprocal, that is to say, there are power differentials; and they include forms of personal and affective interdependencies represented in their simplest form by common gossip circuits, by the exposure of the community members to the pressures of praise and blame gossip and to their emotional involvement in gossip tensions and battles which are often the prelude or the symptoms of power struggles by other means.

One can distinguish between communities of different types shading into each other because the structure and pattern of interdependencies between people who have their home in the same locality change with the development of societies. They change in a manner which is as clearly structured as the development of the societies where these community changes occur. Otherwise there would be nothing to discover.

In predominantly agrarian communities within relatively undifferentiated societies the interdependencies binding those who form these communities to each other tend to be all-embracing. Using our differentiated vocabulary with reference to the structural characteristics of these communities, and using it therefore somewhat inappropriately,[4] one can say, people who form these communities are usually interdependent in most aspects of their lives—with regard to military, economic, religious, sexual, political, medical, educational aspects of their lives as well as to others of which our conceptualization is still poor, such as sociability, leisure, identity or gossip. In most of these respects community members are more closely bonded to each other than to outside groups. The chains of interdependencies which link communities of simpler societies to groups outside are comparatively short, undifferentiated and small in number. Among them interdependencies due to the exposure to physical violence, to the possible involvement in physical struggles with other groups is one of the strongest if not the strongest determinant of the structure of communities in these earlier stages of differentiation and integration when durable and effective monopolies of physical power have not yet formed themselves, or have broken down. As a dominant type of interdependence it is closely linked with others which to some extent can modify its operation, such as interdependencies due to common intercommunal traditions of kinship and culture including ties of language and religion as determinants of group identities.

What we call 'economic' interdependencies of communities with outside groups play, by comparison, a lesser part. Most of the means for satisfying consumption needs have to be found locally: so also, to a large extent, do the means for coping with internal conflicts and for protecting community members from intra-communal violence, threats or constraints, as far as they are protected from such dangers.

What binds community members most strongly to each other, apart from common defense needs in relation to the violence potential of other groups, is the overriding need to assure the communal survival not simply by preserving or acquiring a sufficiency of impersonal means of food production, such as land, cattle or fish, but above all by a steady replacement of the old by the young who can take care of production as well as defense, by preventing destruction through violent internal conflicts, by handing on the basic orientation and skills of one generation to another and with it the communal sense of identity. Thus, common traditions, such as ancestor worship and (closely connected) the use of common land, where it exists, common rituals and festivals, involvements in communal balance of power tensions and conflicts and in common gossip circuits, are some of the other interdependencies binding community members more closely to each other than to outsiders at this stage.

Thus, the range of social functions which have to be performed within communities of less differentiated societies, is much wider than it is in communities which form part of more differentiated societies and which are integrated together with many other groups into a relatively durable state. But although the range is wider, these various social functions are not, or are only to a very small extent, performed by different specialized groups. Food producing, educational, military, governmental, juridical, religious, medical and many other social functions may all be performed by the same people when the occasion arises. They may have an intermittent, not a permanent character. A lesser degree of differentiation of functions—of 'division of labour' as we call it—is not necessarily identical with the absence of these functions. Their performance may not have the character of a specialized occupation but it may be that corresponding social functions are known and performed as distinct functions perhaps even with distinct names.

Moreover, social functions which with increasing differentiation of societies and the corresponding lengthening of the chains of interdependencies assume a highly impersonal and perhaps a semi-public or public character, and which we accordingly represent by means of depersonalizing concepts such as 'economic', 'political', 'social' or 'professional' are often hardly divorced from those which with increasing differentiation of societies assume a more purely private or personal character, such as family, household or leisure functions. One might say: what we call private or personal affairs of people are more public and public affairs more personalized at this stage.

Also, communities of simpler societies which must rely to a much greater extent on their own resources, come up more frequently against problems which require decisions at the community level than communities of more differentiated societies. They can range from problems of communal defense and attack to problems arising from food shortages, from a feud between two families, from a funeral of an important person or from a stranger's wish to attend the ceremonial sacrifice to a local god.[5] These communities in other words still fulfil for their members many of the functions which in more differentiated and complex societies with a greater number of hierarchically ordered levels of integration are vested in higher level authorities such as governments and the state organization which they control.

One of the indicators of this state-like structure of what we generically call 'tribes' or, in less misused and more specific terms, villages and towns of simpler societies, is the distinguishing character of their leading positions. Although the reasons are not usually analysed, names in these cases are applied to the heads of villages or small urban communities which are different from those normally used for the heads of village or small town communities within more differentiated state societies. The latter may be called mayor; the former chiefs, elders or kings. The different names are symptomatic of the different nature of the positions and of the different structural characteristics of the communities where these positions occur. They are symptomatic of the fact that communities of less differentiated societies have more self-ruling functions than those of more differentiated societies. It would not be inappropriate to speak in such cases of *village states*. In fact, village state is in many cases a more suitable conceptualization of the evidence than tribe or tribal community.

Until fairly recent times one could still find many examples of village states in Africa. One may still find them today. The autonomy of these village communities, like that of higher level state units, is never absolute. It depends on the extent to which the communities have to fulfil and can fulfil effectively for their members their function as self-reliant and self-regulating defense and survival-units. Their relative autonomy is thus closely connected with the structure of the whole social field of which they form part. It varies with the extent to which state formation processes have got under way there or, in other words, with the degree, the effectiveness and permanence of the control at higher levels of state integration. The coming of the colonial regimes, for example, and even more the formation of independent African states have brought about in many sectors of that social field a more lasting and effective higher level centralization than ever before. Hence decisions on a host of problems are increas-

ingly taken at higher levels of integration and above all at governmental level; this is in contrast to previous stages at which they were
taken more or less autonomously at the level of villages and small
urban communities, or perhaps of loosely knit federations of such
communities and of early dynastic states comprising a number of
them which still left each community with a good many self-ruling
functions.

These integration—or state formation—processes, in Africa as
elsewhere, produce specific tensions and conflicts which are highly
significant for the structure of these processes. With great regularity
the reduction or loss of relative autonomy at the lower levels and
the consequent defunctionalization of many lower level positions,
e.g. the positions of chiefs and elders or of kings and their courts,
entail a severe retrenchment of their representatives' power resources
and status. They threaten whole groups, which the rise of a higher
level integration relegates to the position of lower level integrations,
with dependence on former outsiders and, therefore, with a loss of
identity, pride and meaning. Hence the change is hardly ever
accepted without resistance. Tensions and conflicts between those
favoured by the rise in functions of a higher level of integration and
control, and those affected by the decline in function and power of
what now become lower level integrations, and competition for the
occupation of the emergent higher level positions are recurrent
structural features of state formation processes and, in fact, of
integration processes of all kinds.

At present one is apt to perceive such tensions and conflicts
merely as symptoms of individual rivalries between particular
persons or groups and in that sense simply as historical occurrences.
A theoretical model of state formation processes[6] showing the
structure of long-term processes of this type can help to transform
the historical into a sociological mode of perception. But the
transformation has not yet permeated public thinking sufficiently:
one cannot yet assume that integration conflicts can be easily
recognized as structured social conflicts *sui generis* in the same way
as, for example, class conflicts are recognized as such. If this were
the case it would be easier to perceive the so-called tribal conflicts
in the nascent African nation states as integration conflicts
characteristic of a state formation process. It would be possible to
study them, and perhaps to handle the recurrent problems better,
as symptoms of a particular phase in such a process. One could learn
a good deal from systematic comparisons with corresponding
phases of long-term state formation processes elsewhere. One of the
main clues, perhaps even *the* main clue to the differences in the long-
term development of African and European societies lies in the high

instability and the consequent discontinuities of most past state integration processes in Africa and the comparatively high continuity and stability of many state formation processes in Europe. Seen in this wider context the relationship and the differences between African and European communities become more accessible to one's understanding. Many tribal communities, many village- and small town-states in Africa are not simply, as they may appear today, lower level integrations of a process of state formation at the level of nation states, but also products of disintegration processes, of the break-up of former state integrations usually at the level of early dynastic states. European communities of whatever kind, on the other hand, usually show in their constitution the traces of the long, and in many cases, fairly continuous state formation processes which are, by and large, characteristic of European societies. As a rule these communities have been disempowered much longer. Also, the incipient formation of a higher level integration above that of the nation state in Europe may in this context become more easily recognizable as a later phase of the same type of process, of which the integration of pre-national village and early dynastic states into national states, especially in Africa south of the Sahara represents an earlier phase. The integration quarrels and conflicts between nations in Europe are the counterpart of those between tribes in Africa. Modified in accordance with the characteristics of a supra-national level of integration, the basic problems repeat themselves. All these social changes bear the hallmark of processes with a recognizable structure. In the course of such a process relatively independent social units become interdependent or more interdependent or interdependent in different ways from before. Almost invariably the threatened loss of function and power of social units on the verge of becoming a lower level of integration leads to struggles of dominance, to balance of power struggles of a specific kind. In contemporary sociology, the concept of a *structure of social change* still implicit in many sociological theories of the nineteenth-century pioneers, has gone out of fashion. Explicitly and on a new level, this is an example of its usefulness.

This does not mean that tribal communities with the structural characteristics of village states are havens of harmony and co-operation until they are dragged into the whirlpool of a higher level centralization and state formation process. That the internal interdependencies binding members of village communities in simpler societies more closely to each other than to outsiders include many areas of their lives which in communities of more differentiated societies are excluded from community interdependencies, in no way implies the predominance of co-operation and the absence of conflicts in the former. All these communities consist of a number of recognizably different social groups. Men and women form such groups. So do the generations. They are bound to each other; but their bonds are usually strongly ambivalent. Tensions between these basic social groups, latent or overt, arise because tradition sanctions as a rule very pronounced patterns of dominance and subordination. Tensions become stronger and may flare up as open conflicts whenever these traditional patterns are threatened or change. The same can be said of groups of different wealth and status, e.g. chiefly groups and commoners, or of groups of different origin and traditions, settled in different quarters of a village or a town. These differences, too, tend to engender tensions, perhaps simmering and below the surface, perhaps flaring up in the form of acute struggles and even of violent conflicts. In a number of village states of southern Ghana in former days different subgroups, living in different quarters, had their own military companies formed by the younger generation or perhaps by all commoners of fighting age. They often competed and occasionally fought with each other. But they also on occasions, joined forces in fighting external enemies of their village or town including the colonial government.[7] With the progress of the state formation process at the higher level of integration these Asafo companies changed their functions. They ceased to be fighting forces and became largely ceremonial, ritual and social institutions, sometimes with political functions within the community.

The example throws light on the direction of the transformation which communities undergo with the formation of higher level states comprising a greater number of towns, villages or homesteads and represented by a specialized and permanent central government as the highest controlling and decision-taking body, with its own specialized and permanent sub-agencies at the lower level and with its own centrally controlled armed forces.

In less differentiated societies, thus, a community can be the highest, and is certainly one of the highest *effective* levels of integration of people. Village states illustrate that condition. As societies become more differentiated and the hierarchy of levels of integration grows in size and complexity, communities develop into one of the lower levels of integration. The range of decisions which can and must be taken at the community level decreases with the upward development of societies towards greater differentiation and complexity, just as it increases whenever an upward development goes into reverse and changes into a downward development. While members of communities in the form of villages or towns within a non-mechanized agrarian social field must and can take decisions among themselves for a wide range of problems, the scope for decisions at the community level shrinks in proportion to the growth and the effectiveness of integration and control at higher state levels. Communities of less differentiated societies, in other words, have many, those of more differentiated societies, by comparison, few self-ruling functions:[8] if the former have to rely largely on self-help, on the mobilization of their own communal resources in the case of outside attacks, of internal conflicts and acts of violence or of natural catastrophes, the latter are in these, as in many other cases, dependent on state authorities and their local agents to a much greater extent.

Nor are the members of communities in more differentiated societies any longer bonded to each other more closely than to outsiders by the need for organizing (through rivalries and struggles, through conflict management and co-operation) the distribution of scarce resources within their reach. As the units of integration grow in size with regard to territory and population and the inter-dependency chains which bind first producers to last consumers become longer and more differentiated, not only the use of physical force, but also the production and exchange of goods and the services become increasingly subject to the control and supervision of higher level authorities, which in turn are reciprocally linked to advances in differentiation, in the production and distribution of goods.

Are there any functions left which still give a locality the character of a community when societies transform themselves into more and more urbanized nation-states where work is increasingly done with the help of machines driven by men-made energies? Are there, in other words, specific functional interdependencies which can bind, in these societies too, residents of the same locality more closely to each other than to groups outside?

One cannot answer these questions and, in fact cannot adequately understand both the sociological and the social problems of communities without attending to yet another aspect of the advancing differentiation of societies. It is an aspect of social differentiation which as such has been sociologically neglected perhaps because tradition confines the sociologists' attention to the 'division of labour' and thus deflects attention from the many aspects of social differentiation not covered by that narrow concept. I refer to the increasing differentiation of peoples' impersonal public and their personal private functions for each other. This aspect of social differentiation is of crucial significance for any enquiry into the residual community functions which localities can still retain when societies become more differentiated and the levels of integration above the community level increase.

In communities of less differentiated societies, as I have indicated, private and public functions play a part, as it were rolled into one. They are less distinguishable. As the bonds between first producers and last consumers become longer and more differentiated and the decision-making machinery becomes an affair of many levels with many feed-backs, private and public aspects of people's functions and lives become more highly and more firmly differentiated. Commodities and services are provided by means of long chains of interdependent and hierarchically-ordered specialized occupations with a strongly *impersonal and public* character even if they retain the form of a private enterprise. The functions of this type of occupation *for their occupants*, in other words, have to be increasingly subordinated to their functions *for others*—to their impersonal functions within this wide and far-flung nexus of functions. Even the highest co-ordinating and integrating functions, even governmental occupations have become enmeshed in this increasingly complex nexus of interdependent social functions. Even they have lost their character of personal and hereditary possessions of certain families; for thousands of years in dynastic states these functions were performed by, or were in the gift of, ruling houses or families. Instead, they have become occupations for paid functionaries whose public office and private life have to be kept strictly apart—if anything with a subordination of the latter under the former. The bonding of more and more people in increasingly longer and more complex interdependency chains, thus, imposes upon occupational positions of all kinds an increasingly impersonal and public character. The divorce of peoples' occupational from their sparetime and especially from their private and leisure activities becomes more pronounced. Hence if there are any bonds left which in highly differentiated societies attach residents of the same locality more closely to each other than to people elsewhere, they are usually confined to people's private lives. Common dependencies on educational, medical, religious, consumption and sociability needs can still be considerable and the response to social requirements of this type can still give a locality, an estate, a suburb, a village or a neighbourhood, to a greater or lesser extent the character of a community.

In the case of women and children, until a short time ago, the division of their lives into a public and a private sphere was still less pronounced than in that of men. The dominance of private and personal concerns in the lives of women was noticeably stronger. In so far as that is still the case therefore, women, by comparison with their men, tend to be more closely bonded by community ties. They are more likely to become involved in the network of personal relationships with emotive undercurrents of liking and disliking, respect and disrespect, sympathies and antipathies which is a structural characteristic of all localities with the character of communities. The emotional undercurrents running through this network may be kept at a temperate level or express itself more openly in standing quarrels and feuds between local families and factions. Whichever it is, emotive undercurrents of this kind, both positive and negative, play a significant part in communities everywhere as a specific layer of human interdependencies. They satisfy sociability needs for human bonds beyond the family level and the ambivalent stimulation which goes with them. In communities of less differentiated societies, however, these emotive currents tend to permeate a very wide range of communal bonds, including those arising from economic, religious, political, sociability interdependencies and others for which we have no clear conceptual label, such as the interdependencies due to differentials of physical strength and agility. By contrast, in communities of more differentiated societies these currents are usually confined to interdependencies of people's private lives.

One of the most ubiquitous manifestations of these emotive aspects of community bonds is the community grapevine. As shown elsewhere,[9] it is structured in accordance with the structure of the community itself and particularly with its distribution of power chances—usually uneven. Sub-groups of stratified communities may use gossip as a means of keeping others in their place. These on their part may retaliate if their power ratio allows it. One of the tests one can use in order to ascertain the extent to which an estate, a village, an urban neighbourhood or a town within an advanced industrial nation-state has retained or acquired community characteristics is the examination of the extent to which the people who live there, as families or individually, are involved in the gossip-flow of their locality and form part of its gossip circuits. The question is: How far are they susceptible to the pressure of gossip as an instrument of communal integration and control? For people who remain wholly aloof, who are emotionally wholly unaffected by communal blame— and praise—gossip and its pressure for conformity stand outside the community level of integration. A locality ceases to have the character of a community if the interdependence of the people who live there is so slight, if their relative independence is so great that they are no longer involved in the local gossip flow and remain indifferent to any gossip control or, for that matter, to any other form of communal control.

One further move in the process of change in the structure of human bonding becomes clearer and more accessible to a sociological diagnosis if one uses as a guide this model of the changing

functions of communities as they gradually unfold themselves. What
it brings into focus, broadly speaking, is an increasing defunctionalization of communities until all that is left from the wide
range of binding functions of communities in less differentiated
societies are a community's functions for the private lives of those
who form it. These become more accentuated when others recede.
However, as one follows the development further, one discovers that
some of these functions, too, become eroded.

The evidence used in *The Established and the Outsiders* has already
suggested that the extent to which the bonding of people's private
lives within their locality surpasses their bonds of the same type
with non-locals is class-specific. It emerged that members of an
old working class community were much more firmly bonded to
each other in their private lives than members of an adjoining
middle-class neighbourhood. The former had acquired a fairly high
degree of cohesion and even of self-sufficiency with regard to the
satisfaction of sociability needs. As one saw before, functions
for the satisfaction of sociability needs and, in a wider sense, of
leisure needs, can promote a measure of integration even in localities
of highly differentiated state societies and can endow them with
community characteristics. These functions too, however, tend to
decline when the transport mobility of a locality's residents increases
and when they can afford to satisfy some or most of their sociability
and their leisure needs outside their place of residence. This was
certainly one of the reasons why an old working-class locality had a
much higher cohesion and more pronounced community characteristics than an adjoining middle-class neighbourhood.

However, the development of relatively cheap means of long-
distance transport within reach of large sections of the lower middle-
and of the working classes, has immensely increased their spacial
mobility. Until fairly recent times the poorer social strata usually
walked everywhere. Today that is no longer the case to the same
extent. The coming of railways, cars and aeroplanes, has initiated
yet another significant change in the bonding of people which
affects the community character of localities. Many more groupings
outside the locality where people live cater for those personal needs
of people which have remained and which, in varying degrees still
remain, the mainstay of the community characteristics of a locality
in highly differentiated societies. Residential localities have not
entirely lost their advantages. It is still often easier, cheaper and
more convenient for people to seek in their own neighbourhood
satisfaction for the various extrafamilial needs of their personal
lives, including the need for company and good cheer, in familiar
surroundings where they can feel at home. But the price to be paid

for what is sometimes called the 'community spirit' is not inconsiderable. The pleasure is apt to be dulled by routinization. It tends to be blunted by the narrowness of the community circles, by the sameness of conversations and gestures. Devoid of any other functions than that which they have for some personal needs of their members, communities in differentiated societies can easily fail to provide for their members the looked for personal satisfactions, and enforce a pattern of life which continuously hovers on the margins of boredom; and the whole syndrome is reinforced by the pressure and inescapability of the social control which community members tend to exercise upon each other.

Transport mobility has made it less inescapable. By opening opportunities outside people's communities for the satisfaction of needs which many people previously had to find within them, it contributes to a further loss of community functions of the localities where people live. Increasingly commercial organizations, e.g. holiday camps, offer services with some community functions for which one has to pay and which for that reason can be avoided if they do not provide the expected satisfactions. Transport mobility, in other words, has greatly increased the scope of people's choice. Many voluntary organizations which are not confined to a single locality, such as charity and party organizations, associations of people with the same hobbies or the same causes, church organizations and sectarian movements, can pursue their overtly legitimizing aims and tasks by providing some community functions, such as a network of extrafamilial personal bonds with power differentials, gossip channels and sociability functions. But community functions of this personal type play a part and are even sometimes explicitly fostered in organizations and institutions with an unambiguous dominance of impersonal public functions and interdependencies, such as public and private enterprises, universities or hospitals. Because of the dominance of impersonal, public interdependencies and functions, organizations of this type are sometimes labelled as formal organizations. But this is a vacuous term. The distinction made before between social positions where people's functions for others predominate and those where the main function is for the holders themselves, gives a clearer picture. In the former type of positions the functions for the occupants themselves are subordinate to those they have to perform for others, but they are never absent. Hence all these impersonal and public organizations are full of personal undercurrents. Whatever their impersonal and public functions are, they often also have, in varying degrees, the character of undercover communities; they are beehives of personal groupings and interdependencies full of bonds of sympathy and antipathy, affection and emotional loathing, with a gossip flow and gossip struggles structured in accordance with the power differentials and many other characteristics of residential communities.

It is not surprising, therefore, that Colin Bell and some of his colleagues in the field of community research have come to the conclusion that this type of research should no longer be confined to groupings of people who are residents of the same locality. The theoretical framework which I have tried to provide for community studies, as one can see, gives some support to this demand. However, it still remains a question of conceptual economy and precision whether or not it is advisable to extend the concept of community in this way. If sociologists who specialize in community research wish to bring into their net the wider problem area they will have to distinguish between local and non-local, between residential and non-residential communities; they will have at the same time to account for their use of the term 'community' in both cases. In this respect, too, a dynamic theory of social bonding, which pays attention, as has been done here, to the emotional, as well as to the power aspects of social bonding may be of help. For these are among the main links between the type of locality-bound communities encountered in highly industrialized and integrated nation states where the main community functions of localities are functions for people's personal lives, and the type of 'communities' which are not locality-bound. Otherwise one might prefer to open up as a specialized field of sociological studies the whole field of sociable groupings, of sociability, as a still largely unexplored aspect of the sociology of leisure.

It may be helpful to add that the terms 'social interdependencies' and 'social bonds' are used here interchangeably. 'Social bonds' appears to me a useful term. But at present it still has voluntaristic undertones: it tends to be misunderstood as an idealizing expression for positive bonds of affection and love between people. As used here, it is an entirely neutral concept. Like interdependencies, social bonds between people can give rise to conflict as well to co-operation and compromise. They can induce hostility and hatred as well as affection and sympathy. Whichever it is, the changes in people's interdependencies, in their bonds, which one can observe if one compares communities at different stages of the development of societies, show, I think, very impressively the firmness of the structure of long-term social processes.

One can summarize in a fairly simple way the overall direction of the process of change in the structure of human interdependencies and, more particularly, of communities which has been shown here. One can say: The scope and differentiation of functions at the

community level decreases as those at other levels of integration
increase. Or simpler still: Communities become less differentiated
as societies become more differentiated. These formulae provide a
general orientation, but the neatness of the language may conceal
a certain oversimplification of the process to which the words refer.
They do not for instance bring out clearly enough that the great
variety of functions which are performed at the community level
in less differentiated societies have not, or have only to a very small
extent, the character of occupational specialities performed by
different groups of people. Thus it would be more correct to say that
in less differentiated societies many more functions are performed
at the community level than in more highly differentiated societies
and that communities lose functions to higher levels of social
integration which develop, sooner or later, in conjunction with an
increasing differentiation of social functions. The nexus of interdependencies at the community level in other words, changes in a
clearly recognizable way together with that of the nexus of interdependencies in the wider social field of which a community forms
part. In accordance with the phase of development of societies and
in the light of this development these changes can be explained. The
corrections make it easier to understand that the summary formulae
at the beginning of this paragraph are not descriptive lawlike
statements, but abbreviated didactic representations of an explanatory
process theory.

As such they indicate in a nutshell the shortcomings of any
unilinear developmental theories which give the impression that the
sequential order of the development of society has the character of
a structural change in one direction only. They draw attention to
the fact that increasing differentiation usually goes hand in hand
with a de-differentiation of varying degrees. The emergence of new
social functions or the greater occupational differentiation of previously undifferentiated functions has its counterpart in the decay
of older functions and of the social positions whose occupants
perform them. A spurt towards closer integration or towards the
emergence of a new level of integration goes hand in hand with a
spurt towards partial disintegration. At any given moment, in
other words, one can observe in the development of societies trends
in opposite directions, one of which may be dominant. For a long
time the dominant trend in the development of the commonwealth
of men has been, with fluctuations, a trend towards increasing
differentiation of social functions and the corresponding increase in
the levels of integration. But any theoretical model of this development would be deficient if it failed to include the counter-trends and
the many whirls and eddies which the simultaneous operation of

opposite trends engenders within the developmental flow—in the form of tensions and conflicts between groups which lose and groups which gain from these changes. The loss of functions of communities which goes hand in hand with the emergence of higher levels of integration to which these functions accrue is an illuminating example of the dialectic character of the development of societies.

It may be worth mentioning in this context a similar pattern of long-term change not unconnected with this: that of the level of integration to which one refers as 'the family'. As integration and differentiation of functions advance in society at large, families, too, lose ruling, producing and other functions while their always present functions as consumption units, as people bonded by and for the satisfaction of what have now become more distinctly private and personal needs are increasingly accentuated. The similarities in the direction of changes which families and communities undergo when societies become more differentiated and integration more comprehensive is more than a coincidence. Within the wider development of societies these two strands are closely connected. They are in fact inseparable. As far as one can go back, one encounters family-like groupings which form or which have formed with others, groups or clusters of families. A community is a grouping of this kind. If one envisages both as part of an uninterrupted inter-generational flow it is as difficult to imagine a family in the singular as it is to imagine a community in the singular.

Among specialists for the study of these two types and levels of integration, one encounters from time to time the tendency to consider them as 'basic' units of societies presumably because they are among their smallest constituent parts. However, neither of these two types of human groupings are unchanging universals of the development of societies. Families may appear as such because their animalic functions are biological universals. But the social ordering and control of these biological functions to which the term 'family' refers are not. If one is able to perceive both families and communities as levels of integration within an uninterrupted inter-generational flow, one discovers soon enough that the observable groupings of people to which one attaches these names undergo structural changes in connection with state formation processes, advancing division of labour and other structural changes in the wider social field. The atomistic mode of explanation derived from older physical models which enjoins us to explain the properties of larger composite units in terms of those of their smallest constituent parts is inappropriate to studies of highly integrated units.[10] One can see it here. So far as societies are concerned, the structure of the smaller units such as families or communities, changes as it were in the slipstream of changes of the larger units as they emerge and develop. In this field the atomistic tradition—according to which the key to the understanding of larger units lies in analysis and dissection of larger composite units into smaller component parts and in the exploration of the properties of the latter in isolation as a means of understanding the properties of the former—is inappropriate and unproductive. If one is concerned with the study of large composite units representing a closely woven flow of functional interdependencies, the most productive procedure is often almost the opposite from that prescribed by the atomistic and mechanistic models represented by classical physics. Instead of attempting to gain from the exploration, and particularly from the measurement of artificially isolated part units and their purely additive assembly a picture of the larger composite unit so that analysis leads the way, one has to proceed in an almost opposite manner. Analysis yields the lead to synthesis. The emergent image of the larger composite unit indicates where to insert the analyst's dissecting knife and helps to show how the provisionally isolated smaller part units fit into, and are determined by, the more or less closely-woven larger nexus of functional interdependencies of which they form part. In such a field analysis and isolation on their own as means of research are apt to remain sterile.

Yet more often than not, communities are studied in isolation. Anthropologists and sociologists still conform to a tradition of community research which focuses attention on a single community or perhaps on a small group of communities of common descent as if they existed in a vacuum. As a rule little attention is paid to the structural differences of communities at different levels of social development. Lack of such a theoretical frame of reference and of systematic comparisons which it makes possible is one of the reasons why at present criteria for the selection of data in community studies are generally uncertain, subject to passing fashions and often arbitrary, dictated by personal sentiments and the social ideals of the investigators. More and more details about more and more communities are assembled without the help of a unifying theoretical frame of reference as a guide in the framing of problems and the selection of evidence, as an explicit and shared means of orientation which can be put to the test and, if necessary, revised and expanded in the light of the result of further empirical researches.

A brief quotation from a community study where such a wider theoretical framework has been used may help to place it into stronger relief. It is taken from Anton Blok's study of a Sicilian village with special regard to the problems of the Mafia:[11]

Before Unification, the population of Genuardo lived most of their lives within the boundaries of their village. Discussing Bourbon times Brancato[12] notes:

'Separated from other villages through the absence of reciprocal relationships, each community developed its own life. The more it was located towards the interior of the island the less it was open to external influences. Even in language, accent, and expression each community distinguished itself from others . . . Neither was the sense of their isolation absent from the consciousness of the inhabitants; and for that reason the territory of the various communities were called *stato* (state) . . .'

It must not be assumed, however, that the isolation of villages like Genuardo was ever complete. Also before 1860 local markets established regular contacts between the various towns in the interior of the island. Agricultural labourers travelled southward to the coastal areas to assist in the grain harvest, to return to the hills and mountains where wheat ripened a month or so later. Furthermore, those who held supervisory offices on the large estates maintained relationships with landowners living in Palermo or elsewhere. Finally men of learning as, for example, priests and civil servants spent some years in the city for their training.

These patterns of contact between Genuardo and the larger society gradually extended after the inception of the Italian state in 1861. Military service, large-scale emigration to overseas countries, the two world wars, and recent migrant labour to northern Europe widened the horizon of many villagers. Yet the relations between the village and the nation-state remained precarious. For the majority of the Genuardesi . . . national roles, as opposed to local roles were not readily accessible . . .

The Italian nation-state only slowly encased the village without ever integrating it completely. . . . As we know from other areas in Europe, the process of centralization evolved in close connection with a growing differentiation, with the development of regional and national markets among other things. This increasing complexity required the operation of central institutions for their co-ordination. For example, the transfer of goods over longer distances requires an adequate network of roads as well as a certain degree of public safety.[13] Given the relative isolation of communities like Genuardo in Sicily of the nineteenth and early twentieth centuries, there were few things which required and thus helped to facilitate central control. On the contrary, their orientation toward self-sufficiency entailed a proper power structure alien to any over-arching control. . . .

The process of state formation at the nation state level has the same general direction everywhere. To mention two of the directional changes at this level: The web of human interdependencies becomes more differentiated and more closely knit than it has ever been before, and the scope of the specialized co-ordinating and controlling functions of central governments and their agencies grow accordingly. In particular, the internal pacification of a country at the nation state level, the means which accrue to central governments for improving the effectiveness of controlling violence throughout the country increase.

But while the general direction of state formation processes at this level is the same in all countries, in details the pattern of development of different nation states vary greatly; and so does, therefore, the extent to which villages, towns or estates retain or give up ruling functions of violence and conflict control, etc. The example of the Sicilian community, as shown by Anton Blok, is one of many instances which bring this relationship between community development and state formation processes into fuller relief. The transition from a dynastic into a nation state does not automatically ensure that the web of what we call 'economic' and 'political' interdependencies becomes more differentiated and closely knit at an even rate throughout all the territories whose inhabitants are nominally integrated in the form of a nation. Nor does it ensure automatically the ability of a central government to assert its monopoly of physical power and to establish effective violence and conflict control within the boundaries of the nation state. Thus the use of physical violence and to some extent its regulation and control at a local level, of which the Mafia is an example, is symptomatic of the specific pattern of the development of the Italian nation state. To quote once more:

> I have tried to convey the idea that the rise and development of the Sicilian *mafia* should be understood as an incidence in the long-term processes of centralization and national integration of Italian Society . . . In the absence of a relatively impersonal central control over the means of violence, the notion of a State or nation with which people could identify themselves remained completely unknown. Long after the so-called unification of Italy in 1861, people saw themselves primarily as subjects of, and identified themselves with, powerful local and regional strong-men, called *pezzi grossi* upon whom they in fact depended for their living and their security.[14]

For reasons into which one need not go here the growth of an interdependency network equivalent to that of some of the older nation states, and the building up of an effective organization for the control of violence unlicensed by the Italian central government remained difficult so far as Sicily was concerned. Hence villages and towns there retained many community properties characteristic of an earlier stage in a state formation process. It would be interesting to compare, say, West African village communities in the early stages of their integration into the emergent national states with Sicilian communities at a comparable level of state development.

It is fairly easy to show that in England, too, social functions were still performed at the community level, i.e. at the level of the parish, during the nineteenth century, though to a slowly diminishing extent, which in course of time came under the control of a more centralized state organization. But in this case as in many others communities did not have the egalitarian character often implicitly associated with the concept of a 'community'. In accordance with the overall structure of English society during the eighteenth and part of the nineteenth centuries representatives of the gentleman class were more or less firmly in control at the community level. The observation of an English magistrate may illuminate the point. In 1811 W. Mainwaring made a speech to his fellow-magistrates in which he admonished them, amongst others, to stimulate the initiative of parishes in looking after the security of their members. In this context he, too, mentioned that a community has in some respects the character of a state:[15]

> Let it be remembered that every parish is a little independent state in this respect, that it has power to regulate and direct how the nightly watch shall be kept in its own district. In almost every parish there are some gentlemen who take an interest and active interference in their parochial concerns—would they meet and seriously consider this important subject, surely there can be little doubt but that the present mode of watching the night, so evidently defective, might be improved. ... Gentlemen, at this particular time, when surrounding nations are looking upon this great and powerful country with admiration, and fleeing to it from all quarters for safety and protection, is it not most disgraceful that the peaceful inhabitant of its great metropolis cannot lie down at night to rest, without the apprehension that his house may be ransacked and his most valuable property taken from him before the morning.

It must be enough to indicate with the help of such examples how the theoretical model briefly outlined here can help in empirical studies and how empirical studies in turn can serve as a testing ground for the model.[16] For what has been done here, the brief representation of the structure of specific directional long-term changes, has been designed in such a way that it can be revised and further developed in the light of empirical studies. Like every other theoretical synthesis in a scientific field it is a step on a road, not an end in itself. Synthesis is geared to analysis so that analysis can be geared to synthesis. Theory is geared to empiry so that empiry can be geared to theory. These are the conditions for gaining greater certainty in the study of societies as in all other scientific studies.

At a time when uncertainty prevails and an exuberance of wild theorizing threatens to swamp the even development of sociological teaching and research, one may perhaps count that as a gain.

One of the functions of such a theory is that of bringing into focus the often neglected links between community studies as a sociological speciality and other sociological specialities. The development of communities, as one can see, goes hand in hand with state formation processes as well as with the process rather narrowly conceptualized as 'division of labour' and more comprehensively as 'differentiation of social functions' or, briefly, as 'social differentiation'. One can gain a better understanding of communities as of other figurations of people if one does not move backwards in one's imagination, i.e. backwards from one's own level of social integration and differentiation and of conceptual differentiation, towards less differentiated units of integration as if one's own level represented the immutable centre of the social universe. One can gain a more accurate picture if one imagines instead the conditions of less differentiated and smaller social units with fewer levels of integration. That requires a greater effort of distancing oneself, but a more accurate picture is gained. For that is how more differentiated societies have become what they are. In this way one can reconstruct in the form of a testable model the line of development leading from the former to the latter.

If extended, such a model can serve as a gauge for determining the many stages that lie between, say, a community with the characteristics of a village stage in a relatively undifferentiated agrarian social field and a community of one of the types characteristic of the developed industrial nation states. Like other groupings which interdependent people form with each other or (to use the much-needed generic term) like other figurations of men, communities have structural characteristics which bear the stamp of the specific societies within which they form themselves. Hence a theory which can be of help in empirical enquiries into communities has to take account of this wider development. It cannot be a theory of communities alone. It should enable those who are concerned with community problems to compare one community with others and to recognize differences and similarities in their structure. It should provide students of communities with a sociodynamic gauge which enables them to determine and to explain the specific functional interdependencies which at a given stage bind those who form a community more closely to each other than to those who do not belong, and at the same time those other interdependencies binding them, individually and communally, to others outside.

The pattern of this whole web of internal and external bonds,

which is the matrix of co-operation and conflict and of all that lies
between them, changes in the course of the development of societies
in a clearly structured manner which one can determine with a
growing degree of precision and thus with increasing certainty.
Hence the working out and the use of such a model can help to
allay the uncertainties with regard to the selection of evidence from
the mass of observable data and the reconstruction of their connections which one frequently encounters at present during the conduct
of community studies. It can help to lessen the risk that selection of
evidence and reconstruction of connections in any particular
investigation of this kind are *dominated* by personal sentiment or
by passing professional fashions and ideologies.

It is an additional gain that by means of such an approach one
can begin to counteract the tendency towards increasing fragmenta-
tion of sociology—its break-up into a number of professionalized
specialities whose connections with each other threaten to become
more and more tenuous. The significance of community research as
a sociological speciality is not impaired—it is rather enhanced if
one becomes aware that communities cannot be adequately studied
as isolated units and that this type of enquiry, in order to be fully
productive, needs to take into account the structure of the wider
social field and its changes. The structure of the wider social
field in turn is illuminated, as one can see in this volume, through
the study of communities.

NORBERT ELIAS. 1973

NOTES

1 F. Tönnies, *Gemeinschaft und Gesellschaft*, Berlin, 1887. E. Durkheim, *De
la Division du Travail Sociale*, Paris, 1893.

2 Sorokin wrote in Contemporary Sociological Theories, London 1928, p. 491:
'One cannot help thinking that Durkheim intentionally gave his social types
names which were opposite to those given by Tönnies.' This however, is not
certain. One can only say with certainty that the perception of both and,
therefore, their theoretical schemes were influenced by different sentiments
about the value of past and present times. A useful discussion of some of
these problems can be found in Marica, Émile Durkheim, *Soziologie und
Soziologismus*, Jena 1932 Introduction, part 2.

3 One may add—by way of clarifying the concept of dependencies—that the
scope for decisions about the two alternative solutions of such problems
called summarily co-operation and conflict can vary widely. It is very small
if the survival, the resources or even identity and pride of two groups or two
people depend on either of them getting something which both need or covet,
but which can only satisfy the needs or wishes of one of them. The conflict
potential of that kind of figuration is very great whether the groups who form

it are village communities, class organizations or states, whether the persons who form it are husband and wife or partners in business. The nature of their interdependence as competitors for the same scarce chances of satisfaction narrows their scope of decision with regard to co-operation or conflict in favour of the latter.

4 The implicit assumption that the classificatory divisions which one applies to one's own society secure precision and clarity of thought if applied to other societies irrespective of the level of their development is a rationalist fallacy. Precision and clarity of thought in the study of societies can only be gained if one is able to conceptualize as less differentiated or as more differentiated that which testable evidence demonstrates as such or in other words if one uses a clearly worked out developmental framework for one's observation of details. At present such a framework, as one can see, is just beginning to emerge. One can see here one of the difficulties produced by this inadequacy of our theoretical equipment. The concepts used in the text, concepts such as 'military', 'economic', 'religious', etc., refer directly or indirectly to recognizably different groups of occupational specialisms performed by different groups of people. But in less differentiated societies the social functions to which these terms can refer are usually not performed as separate occupations by different groups of specialists. Also, their performance often has an intermittent and not a permanent character. As long as a fully developmental idiom of speaking, writing and thinking has not established itself—or re-established itself on the new level—it is useful to be aware of the distortions that are inherent in the use of the idiom of more differentiated societies for the exploration of less differentiated societies.

5 I made this request to the head of a village community while doing fieldwork with my students in Southern Ghana. As it happened, he was chief and priest at the same time. I asked to be allowed to be present at the sacrifice to a local god for two reasons. Firstly because animal sacrifices tend to disappear with increasing differentiation and state integration of societies as part of a civilizing process (in the structural sense of the word). I had for a long time hoped to take part in a ritual of this kind and to experience it first hand and not only as a literary event through books from antiquity or about antiquity. Secondly I regarded my request as an experimental approach which would help me to understand better the structure, and particularly the power structure, of the village community. It would lead too far here to report the results of my request. But what followed, especially the calling together of the village council and the long discussions which took place there had in many respects the character of state actions. It gave me a much clearer picture of the way one arrived at decisions which might affect the wellbeing of the community, and of the high debating and diplomatic abilities of the people concerned in such decisions.

6 A blueprint of such a process can be found in *Über den Prozess der Zivilisation*, Bern and Munich, 1969, vol. II.

7 For further details see Terence J. Johnson, 'Protest, Tradition and Change: Southern Gold Coast Riots 1899–1921', *Economy and Society*, I, 2 May 1972, pp. 164–193.

8 'Self-ruling functions' are characteristic of the structure of communities at that level of social development regardless as to whether these functions are vested in the positions of kings or chiefs or in those of councils and assemblies, regular or occasional, of all or most of the members of a community. A conceptual problem arises only in the case of 'communities' such as feudal estates where the mass of the community members are permanently relegated to the condition of unfree serfs or slaves.

9 N. Elias and J. L. Scotson, *The Established and the Outsiders*, Frank Cass, London, 1965, p. 89ff.

10 The limitations of the atomistic tradition of thinking have been discussed more fully in N. Elias, 'The Sciences,' in R. Whitley, ed., *Social Processes of Scientific Development*, London and Boston, 1974, pp. 21–42.

11 Anton Blok, *The Mafia of a Sicilian Village (1860–1960)*, Amsterdam, 1972, pp. 19–22.

12 Francesco Brancato, *La Sicilia nel Primo Ventennio del Regno d'Italia*, Bologna, 1956, pp. 22, 30.

13 N. Elias, *Über den Prozess der Zivilisation*, Bern and Munich, 1969, vol. II, pp. 222ff. and N. Elias, *Was ist Soziologie*, Munich, 1970, pp. 154–159.

14 Anton Blok, *The Mafia of a Sicilian Village*, Amsterdam, 1972, p. 239.

15 W. Mainwaring, 'An Address to the Grand Jury at the opening of the General Session, etc., etc.', December 2, 1811, in *The European Magazine*, London, 1812, vol. 61, p. 107.

16 It is not difficult to see that the model of changing patterns of human inter-dependencies briefly outlined here represents a continuation on a new level of the exploration of problems raised and discussed by Durkheim and Tönnies in the books mentioned before. Such a development on the theoretical level in connection with the vast extension of relevant knowledge on the empirical level, I think, is long overdue. It would have lengthened this introductory essay unduly had I tried to discuss here explicitly in what way my theory constitutes a continuation and in what way a revision and rejection of the older theories. I reserve the discussion of these and of a number of connected problems for a book on the deep structure of history which will also embody as a chapter some parts of this essay.

In a recent publication entitled *Human Societies*, ed. G. Hurd, my name has been associated with a type of developmental and comparative sociology said to have been developed under the leadership of Professor I. Neustadt. As I do not know of any work he has done and has published in that field nor of any innovatory thought he has contributed to it, I cannot judge the merits of that claim. But I wish to state publicly that my name has been associated with this book by the editor without my knowledge and consent. It is true that its plan is based on that of one of my lecture courses and that it uses to some extent the developmental and comparative approach which I have introduced or re-introduced to sociology and of which this paper is one example. However as some, though not all contributions to this book, particularly the editor's introduction, distort this approach and represent a lowering of its intellectual level, I find it necessary to say quite clearly that I had nothing to do with it.

Introduction

Over the past fifty years there have accumulated literally hundreds of community studies. They are, at one and the same time, some of the most appealing and infuriating products of modern sociology. They are appealing because they present in an easily accessible and read-able way, descriptions and analyses of the very stuff of sociology, the social organization of human beings; and infuriating because they are so idiosyncratic and diverse as to steadfastly resist most attempts to synthesize their findings. Community studies, however, continue to be widely read, offering in particular an access to sociology for many new students of the subject and continue to provide an apparently inexhaustible pool of 'social facts' upon which theorists may draw in order to buttress their arguments. Yet out of community studies, there has never developed a theory of community, nor even a satis-factory definition of what community is. The concept of community has been the concern of sociologists for more than two hundred years, but even a satisfactory definition of it in sociological terms appears as remote as ever.

This failure to define what is community is not due to any lack of interest. Indeed the problem is rather that there are, if anything, too many rather than too few attempts at defining the term. It is com-pounded by the place of 'community' in the social thought of Western industrialized culture since the beginning of the nineteenth century. In the reaction to industrialization the concept of community was elevated to an almost deistic status and almost all intellectuals were prepared to pay homage before it. The reason why community could unite the respect of virtually the whole political and philosophical spectrum was that it was itself so amorphous and so malleable. Community simply stood for what an almost endless group of thinkers—including some of sociology's most eminent founding fathers[1]—believed to be what society *should* consist of. It was, in other words, the Good Life, and even though different individuals' conceptions of the Good Life varied very considerably indeed, the fact that they could all be included under the label 'community', meant that they could all unite in their praise of it. The emotive over-tones contained in the use of community continue to this day. Every-one, it seems, wishes to live in a community. Feelings may be more equivocal concerning life in collectivities, groups, networks or societies, but the desire to live in a *community* is something that unites even violently conflicting groups in a deeply divided society. Sociologists have not been immune to these subjective feelings which community conjures up. Their definitions of community have also incorporated their ideas of the Good Life. The result has been a confusion between what community *is* (empirical description) and what the sociologists have felt it *should be* (normative prescription).

The definitional debate over the nature of community therefore hides a deeper conceptual problem. As some of the following contributions to this volume show, community sociologists have reacted to this problem in two ways. There has been an attempt to discontinue the use of the term 'community' and replace it by another which avoids the incorporation of value judgements—'locality' for example. 'Community studies' should therefore become 'locality studies', the study of the inter-relationship of social institutions within a territorially defined area.[2] The alternative to this has been to abjure the community as an object of sociological study at all, but to use it instead as a *method* of obtaining data. The sociologist's only interest in the community as such should be to provide him with usable data to test his hypotheses. The community, or the locality, is therefore analogous to the laboratory of the physical scientist.[3] In this respect, the dividing line between a community study and any other empirical study virtually ceases to exist, and indeed what is and is not considered a community study is frequently an arbitrary decision and rests primarily upon custom.

These disputes over the nature of community and community studies have not, however, prevented community studies from being carried out. After all, as Hillery has rightly observed,[4] the significant question concerns the nature of social groups, not whether yet another definition of community is possible. And there can be no doubt that community studies, for all their imperfections, have contributed towards the answering of this question. For the value of this contribution subsequent community sociologists must acknowledge a considerable debt to the pioneer modern community study, Robert and Helen Lynd's study of *Middletown*.[5] The Lynds, in their study of Muncie, Indiana, in the early 1920's, set the style for future community studies, and, while few would unquestioningly accept their techniques today, their contribution was nevertheless a seminal one. Their study was, as John Madge points out, 'the first scientific and ostensibly uncritical, objective description of small-town life. Here for the first time, without reformist overtones and without dramatization, was a mirror held up to the ordinary American.'[6] Their approach, techniques and analysis have been followed remarkably closely by many later sociologists of the community and the problems which the Lynds encountered and to which they posed solutions are the same, in many cases, as those faced by all community sociologists.

The Lynd's study did not emerge out of an intellectual vacuum, however. Though the study itself was something of a historical accident, the particular form it took was moulded by the Lynd's own anthropological orientation. The Lynds were working in a small institute of social and religious research which decided to survey religious provisions and practices in a small American town, but they found it was impossible to study religion in isolation without relating it to other social institutions in the locality. As they sought a suitable frame of reference in which to put their study, they were attracted by the work of American social anthropologists, particularly Clark Wissler and W. H. R. Rivers, who both presented classifications under which the activities of any 'culture' could be classified. The Lynds found that the methods and approach of social anthropology to the study of primitive tribes could legitimately be applied to contemporary American community. Their success paved the way for further anthropologically-oriented studies of American communities during the inter-war years.

The most notable exponent was Lloyd Warner, who with his numerous research associates, carried out the extensive survey of Newburyport or 'Yankee City' during the 1930's.[7] It was Warner's ambition to 'compare . . . the other societies of the world with one of our own civilization, and . . . to accommodate our techniques, developed by the study of primitive society, to modern groups . . .'[8] The Yankee City study was part of a grandiose plan to develop a taxonomy of all societies, including the Australian aboriginal society whose study preceded that of Yankee City, and the social organization of the Irish peasantry, which was subsequently carried out by two research workers from the Yankee City project.[9] Yankee City is taken, for the purposes of this taxonomy, to typify American society. The community is variously called a 'convenient microcosm for field study' and a 'laboratory' by Warner—'a microscopic whole representing the total American Community'[10]. His view of the community was, however, strongly influenced by the classical structural-functionalism of Malinowski and Radcliffe-Brown, and Warner admits that 'the analogy of the organism was in our thinking when we looked at the total community of Yankee City and the various parts of its internal structure.'[11] Elsewhere the community is called a 'working whole in which each part had definite functions which had to be performed, or substitutes acquired, if the whole society was to maintain itself.'[12]

Such a functionalist approach has remained until fairly recently the primary perspective for the study of communities, both in the United States and elsewhere. As far as British community studies are concerned, Arensberg and Kimball's study of County Clare, *Family and Community in Ireland*, appears to be the most direct means by which the influence of functionalist anthropology has become established. Equally influential, however, has been a somewhat inward-looking Welsh school of anthropology which began with Alwyn Rees' pioneering study of a Montgomeryshire parish, *Life in a Welsh Countryside*.[13] Over the next fifteen years, the prefaces of most British studies acknowledged a debt to him, and the number of studies of Welsh communities (not all of which have been published) remains considerable.[14] The influences of Warner and Rees unite in the work of W. M. Williams, who was a student under Rees but whose analysis of Gosforth[15]—in particular its status system—was clearly influenced by Warner's investigations in Yankee City. In so far as there can be said to be *any* common theoretical perspective underlying British community studies, therefore, that of classical functionalist anthropology is paramount.

The holistic approach of anthropology and the heavy reliance on participant observation as a research method are together responsible for the non-comparability of many community studies. The idiosyncracies of some studies are notorious: some undoubtedly tell one as much about the researcher as about the community which he purports to study. Participant observation is always a potentially rewarding, but also problematic relationship between the fieldworker and his data, but there are dangers, too, of which researchers have not always been aware. Frequently, the values of the observer cannot be disentangled from his data and there is no guarantee that another investigator would produce similar results. In short, there must be some question about the scientific validity of the results gathered from many community studies. In too many cases, the style of research—of direct observation and reporting—has been little above that found in many newspapers and magazines. We should beware of calling this social science.

It should not be concluded from these remarks, however, that it is totally impossible to compare and synthesize in the field of community studies. We would argue, though, that the inter-relationship of theory, method and substance in community studies is so close and so complex that any synthesization must take account of the first two categories as well as the third. Elsewhere[16] we have delineated six streams or approaches to community studies, more than one of which may be contained in any particular monograph, but each of which will determine which particular aspects of a community are the focus of attention.

1. *The Ecological Approach*. The most carefully developed and comprehensive statement of the ecologist's position is contained in Amos Hawley's, *Human Ecology: A Theory of Community Structure*. In it he wrote that, 'The community has often been likened to an individual organism. So intimate and so necessary are the interrelations of its parts . . . that any influence felt at one point is almost immediately transmitted throughout. Further, not only is the community a more or less self-sufficient entity, having inherent in it the principle of its own life process, it has also a growth of natural history with well-defined stages of youth, maturity and senescence'[17]. The solidarity and shared interests of community members are regarded as a function of their *common residence*. Hence the distinctive aspect of the ecological approach is the stress on the *spatial* consequences of social organization. There is often great emphasis placed on the physical nature of the localities with which they deal, so much so that it is occasionally difficult to remember, as Don Martindale has pointed out, that social life is a 'structure of interaction, not a structure of stone, steel, cement and asphalt, etc.'[18]

The principal exponents of the ecological approach have been the 'Chicago School' of community sociologists whose series of monographs appeared in the 1920's and 1930's. Their manifesto and programme for research was outlined by Robert Park in a paper in the American Journal of Sociology of 1916.[19] He related what he called 'local organization' to the city plan of Chicago and introduced the term 'natural areas' for areas of 'population segregation'. Each of these 'natural areas'—for instance the 'Gold Coast', the 'Ghetto', 'Little Sicily'—became the locale for specific studies. Park believed that he could study Chicago with the 'same patient methods of observation that anthropologists . . . had expended on the life and manner of the North American Indian'.[20] But Park also began the collection of statistical data relating to the city and this began the trend that culminates in the 'neo-ecology'—of Schnore, Otis Dudley Duncan, Shevky and Bell.

Human ecology at its finest provides sharp and accurate descriptions of the spatial aspects of communities. However, the pursuit of this approach seemed almost to stop after the early 1930's. It was gradually realized that common location in the physical structure of a community could only be a starting point for an investigation and few sociologists could treat this factor as the sole independent variable. More recently, however, the classical ecological approach has been combined with other approaches, such as that of Weber on social class, to provide more satisfying sociological explanations of spatial patterns and processes in an urban environment. The most notable example is Rex and Moore's recent study of Sparkbrook in

Birmingham.[21] An unusual example of the ecological approach applied to a rural community is the study by John and Dorothy Keur of the Dutch village of Anderen in *The Deeply Rooted*.[22]

2. *Communities as Organizations*. The organic emphasis of the ecological approach reflects the heavy reliance on analogies with biological organization. Communities have also been treated as organizations in the sociological sense, however. This consideration of the community as a social arrangement for the achievement of specific goals has appealed in particular to those who wish to study the political aspects of a community, especially community power. The specification of individual and group goals in a community is, however, an extremely troublesome task, as the debate on community power in the United States has shown all too clearly.[23] Nevertheless, the notion of collective goals has been incorporated into a number of definitions of community.[24] In addition, the concentration of power in a few hands, usually in small geographically isolated, rural communities, has led even casual observers to compare them with total institutions. Like them a community has been regarded as 'a social system that not only tended to regulate the total lives of the inmates, but which also set barriers to social interaction with the outside'.[25] Hillery has examined this idea in his book, *Communal Organizations: A Study of Local Societies*. Hillery, however, concludes that the total institution is a different *kind* of entity from the community, primarily because the community has no goal. This would seem to disqualify the community from being considered as *any* type of organization. In certain circumstances, however, the community might profitably be considered as such for the testable hypothesis which could be derived from such a model.

3. *Communities as Microcosms*. Many sociologists are drawn to the study of communities not simply because they are seen as being of interest in their own right, but because of what can be learned from them about wider societal processes. Here communities are not only objects of study, but *samples* of the culture in which they are located. Community sociologists are therefore concerned to establish the representativeness of the localities they study. Occasionally, this is taken to excess, such as in the claim that 'all America is in Jonesville'[26] or that 'Yorkshire might be claimed as a microcosm of England.'[27] It must be apparent, however, that no community study is representative in any statistical sense of the wider society. But this is not to say that community studies can contribute nothing to a science of society: what is of chief concern is that the community level is the correct level of analysis for the particular sociological problem. These strictures not only apply to attempts to study societal problems in a community context, but also to attempts to generalize

from community studies about macro-social processes. Stein's, *The Eclipse of Community*, for example, attempts to assess the consequences of increasing urbanization, industrialization and bureaucratization on the autonomy of local communities in American society through a consideration of the major American community studies. Stein uses them as 'case studies showing the ways in which large-scale social processes shaped human affairs in local settings'.[28] Exercises like this, however, can only be involved in the data at second hand and whilst no one would deny the need for the synthesization of the detailed knowledge contained in community studies, there is the danger which Stein does not entirely avoid, of confusing selective descriptions of communities with the communities themselves. Any approach to a community which considers it a microcosm of society is therefore fraught with difficulties.

4. *Community Study as Method.* This approach to community studies views the community as neither an object of study, nor a sample of society, but simply as a source of data. The community study is therefore a form of sociological research. This approach to community studies leads the sociologist to ask a different series of questions in and of the community from those which are asked when the community is treated as an object of study. As Arensberg and Kimball, the principal proponents of this view, put it, the community study is merely a means of 'getting to grips with social and psychological facts in the raw'.[29] As a method, the community study is just one of a number of observational techniques, central to which is the 'massive immersion' (again to use Arensberg and Kimball's words) of the researcher in his data. Community study therefore concerns the study of human behaviour *in* communities. What the field worker needs to know is not 'everything' about a community, but how the data which he collects are related to his theory before, during and after his 'massive immersion'.

Within the field of community studies the dispute over whether the community is a legitimate object of sociological studies is a continuing one. Elaborations of both points of view are found in this volume.

5. *Communities as Types.* Treating communities as types is the closest to the classical tradition of Tönnies. When dealing with communities we are dealing centrally with the rural-urban continuum, for all others have taken this as their starting-point, either to present some variation on it or to set themselves up against it. This typological approach to communities is also a theory of social change— the aim is not merely to classify communities, but to say something about the nature and direction of social processes. Apart from Tönnies, the central figure in this tradition is Robert Redfield, whose

somewhat arcadian view of community led him to use his community studies to test the general thesis that the more urban a community became the greater the degree of social disorganization.[30] In the tradition of the classical writers on community, Redfield's 'folk society'[31] is riddled with value judgements, yet errors in his conceptualization of rural and urban communities need not rule out *any* form of rural-urban differences from consideration.

The main point against the rural-urban continuum is that it locates *social* relationships in a specific *locale*—a problem which has been presented to, but never reconciled by, the human ecologists. Recent research has shown that neither the rural nor the urban 'end' of the continuum is a single type of unchanging entity.[32] Thus, 'while some are born "urban" and others achieve urbanization, none can be said to have urbanization thrust upon them'.[33] Gans has maintained that class and family cycle are of greater value in the explanation of behaviour in communities than ecological or typological considerations—class is the best indicator of the ability of individuals to *choose* and the stage reached in the family cycle determines the area of choice which is most likely. Gans concludes that 'ways of life do not coincide with settlement type'[34] and implies that no sociological definition of any settlement type can be formulated. If this is true—and it is an open empirical question, since settlement type may affect the way of life of those *within* the group who *cannot* choose—it would destroy notions of a rural-urban or any other continuum of community based upon patterns of settlement.

6. *Community and Networks.* Out of the disenchantment with the typological approach to communities there has emerged a desire to investigate the interaction of particular social groups which may be found in all communities. In particular, there has been an emphasis on what Warren[35] has called the 'vertical' and 'horizontal' dimensions of the local social system—the study of nationally and locally-oriented groups. The analytical tool for delineating and analysing these groups is the 'social network', first conceived by Barnes for use in his study of a Norwegian fishing community.[36] Networks for some people are locality bound, for others less so. Traditional notions of community may be subsumed under the label of 'locality bound, close-knit network'. One of the changes that may be occurring for many, but not all, social groups is not so much the 'eclipse of community' as that their social networks are becoming less locality bound and less close-knit. Detailed empirical investigations of such problems will only be advanced by painstaking elaborations of the concepts concerned in network analysis; such as those of Mitchell and his colleagues[37] who have carefully distinguished between the structural characteristics and the content of networks. When a satisfactory

way of recording social networks has been carried out, there is every hope that we shall be well on the way to having comparable and theoretically relevant data on community studies.

Examples of each of these approaches can be found in the selections included in this volume. We have made no attempt, however, to achieve a uniform coverage of the field of community studies, neither geographically nor theoretically—given the limitation on the number of selections we can make, this would have been an impossible task. Instead we have selected certain substantive topics which illustrate some of the problems and issues that preoccupy community sociologists. In this way we hope that each section will achieve an internal coherence that is otherwise difficult to achieve in a selection of readings that includes extracts rather artificially removed from the context of the parent studies. For this reason, and also because we believe it is a more appropriate purpose for a reader, we have concentrated more on the 'sociology' of the field of community studies rather than substantive findings. We are concerned more with the theoretical and methodological problems underlying community studies than with the analysis of individual localities. For this purpose, the original studies must be consulted. Indeed, we wish to stress that the reading of this book should in no way be regarded as a substitute for a reading of the original community studies from which the majority of the selections have been taken.

COLIN BELL AND HOWARD NEWBY. 1973

NOTES

1 See Nisbet, R., *The Sociological Tradition* (London: Heinemann, 1967), ch. 3.
2 See the paper by Margaret Stacey in this volume.
3 See the final paper of this volume by Arensberg and Kimball.
4 Hillery, G. A., *Communal Organizations: A Study of Local Societies* (Chicago: Chicago University Press, 1969), p. 4.
5 Lynd, R. S., and Lynd, H. M., *Middletown: A Study in Contemporary American Culture* (New York: Harcourt Brace, 1929). They also undertook an important restudy, *Middletown in Transition* (New York: Harcourt Brace, 1937).
6 Madge, J., *The Origins of Scientific Sociology* (London: Tavistock, 1963), p. 128.
7 The completed study is contained in five volumes. Warner has abridged the series into one volume, *Yankee City* (New Haven: Yale University Press, 1963). Extracts reprinted in this volume.
8 Warner, W. L., and Lunt, P. B., *The Social Life of a Modern Community* (New Haven: Yale University Press, 1941), p. 4.
9 Arensberg, C. H., and Kimball, S. T., *Family and Community in Ireland* (Cambridge, Mass.: Harvard University Press, 1940). Extracts reprinted in this volume.
10 Warner, W. L., *Structure of American Life* (Edinburgh: Edinburgh University Press, 1952), p. 33. Extracts reprinted in this volume.
11 Warner, W. L., and Lunt, P. S., op. cit., p. 12.

12 Ibid., p. 14.
13 Rees, A. D., *Life in a Welsh Countryside* (Cardiff: University of Wales Press, 1950).
14 An up-to-date list is found in Lewis, G. J., 'A Welsh Rural Community in Transition', *Sociologia Ruralis*, vol. X, 2, 1970, pp. 143–161.
15 Williams, W. M., *The Sociology of an English Village: Gosforth* (London: Routledge and Kegan Paul, 1956).
16 Bell, C., and Newby, H., *Community Studies* (London: Allen and Unwin, 1972), Ch. 2. A more extended discussion of many of the points outlined in this Introduction can be found in this book.
17 Hawley, A., *Human Ecology: A Theory of Community Structure* (New York: Ronald, 1950), p. 50.
18 See his 'Introduction' to Max Weber's *The City* (New York: Free Press, 1958), p. 29.
19 Reprinted in Park, R. E., *Human Communities: The City and Human Ecology* (New York: Free Press, 1952).
20 Ibid.
21 Rex, J., and Moore, R., *Race, Community and Conflict* (London: Oxford University Press, 1967). Paper by Rex reprinted in this volume.
22 Keur, D., and Keur, J., *The Deeply Rooted* (Washington, Seattle: University of Seattle Press, 1955).
23 See Bell, C., and Newby, H., op. cit., ch. 7.
24 See, for instance, Sussmann, M. B. (ed.), *Community Structure and Analysis* (New York: Crowell, 1959). Pp. 1–2; Kaufman, H. F., 'Toward an International Conception of Community', *Social Forces*, vol. 38, 1959, pp. 8–17; Sutton, W. A., and Kolaja, J., 'The Concept of Community', *Rural Sociology*, vol. 25, 1960, pp. 197–203.
25 Hillery, G. A., op. cit., p. 14.
26 Warner, W. L., *Democracy in Jonesville* (New York: Harper and Row, 1949) p. ix.
27 Dennis, N., Henriques, F., and Slaughter, C., *Coal is our Life*, Social Science Paperback edition (London: Tavistock, 1969), p. 11.
28 Stein, M., *The Eclipse of Community* (New York: Harper Row, 1964), p. 1.
29 Arensberg, C. M., and Kimball, S. T., *Community and Culture* (New York: Harcourt Brace, 1965), p. 30.
30 Redfield, R., *The Folk Culture of Yucatan* (Chicago: University of Chicago Press, 1961).
31 Redfield, R., 'The Folk Society', *American Journal of Sociology*, vol. 52, 1947.
32 See, for instance, Lewis, O., *Life in a Mexican Village: Tepoztlan Restudied* (Urbana: University of Illinois Press, 1951); Avila, M., *Tradition and Growth*, (Chicago: University of Chicago Press, 1969); Mayer, P., 'Migrancy and the Study of Africans in Towns', *American Anthropologist*, vol. 64, 1962; Gusfield, J., 'Tradition and Modernity: Misplaced Polarities in the Study of Social Change', *American Journal of Sociology*, vol. 72, 1967; Pahl, R. E., 'The Rural-Urban Continuum', *Sociologia Ruralis*, vol. IV, 1966.
33 Mayer, P., op. cit., p. 591.
34 Gans, H. J., 'Urbanism and Suburbanism as Ways of Life' in Rose, A. M. (ed.), *Human Behaviour and Social Processes* (London: Routledge and Kegan Paul, 1952), p. 643.
35 Warren, R., *The Community in America* (Chicago: Rund McNally, 1963).
36 Barnes, J., 'Class and Community in a Norwegian Island Parish', *Human Relations*, vol. 7, 1954.
37 Mitchell, J. C. (ed.), *Social Networks in an Urban Situation* (Manchester: Manchester University Press, 1969).

PART I

Theoretical Preliminaries
to the
Study of Community

CHAPTER 1

Theoretical Preliminaries to the Study of Community

INTRODUCTION

One of the main problems concerning the study of community is that it has little or no substantive sociological theory of its own. A branch of sociology called 'the community' cannot be considered in the same way as, say, 'the family', 'stratification', 'organizations', and so on—we can only concern ourselves with a number of community *studies*. This reflects the non-cumulative nature of most community studies: whilst it might justly be said that they have contributed a a good deal to sociology, they have nevertheless contributed very little to each other. Thus we cannot draw upon a body of theory of the community—rather we must fall back upon a list of individuals who have written about the concept of community itself.

Such a list is a very lengthy one. Exhortations to 'define your terms' have been taken to heart in this case and most sociologists who have undertaken community studies—and not a few others—have attempted to provide an acceptable definition of community. The difficulties involved in this task have already been alluded to—most definitions of community reflect not so much what community *is* but what it *should be*. Normative prescription has overridden empirical description in most cases. Not surprisingly, there is little agreement to be found among the various existing definitions of the term. Hillery's analysis of 94 definitions of community showed that the only common element in them was the fact that they all dealt with people: 'Beyond this common basis, there is no agreement.'[1] More recently, however, there have been some encouraging attempts to break through this apparent impasse, as some of the contributions below show.

Much of the confusion surrounding the concept of community derives from the use made of it by Ferdinand Tönnies. Tönnies' book, *Gemeinschaft und Gesellschaft*, first published in 1887, has provided a constant source of ideas for those who have dealt with the community ever since.[2] Tönnies' greatest legacy was the typological usage of community, a typology usually expressed in terms of a dichotomy. The 'community-society' dichotomy along with 'authority-power', 'status-class', 'sacred-secular' and 'alienation-progress', have been represented by Nisbet as the unit ideas of the sociological tradition. They are, as he wrote, 'the rich themes in nineteenth century thought. Considered as linked antitheses, they form the very warp of the sociological tradition. Quite apart from their conceptual significance in sociology, they may be regarded as epitomizations of the conflict between tradition and modernism, between the old order made moribund by the industrial and democratic revolutions, and the new order, its outlines still unclear and as often the cause of anxiety as of elation and hope.'[3] Value judgements were thus incorporated by Tönnies into the very substance of his analysis. Equally pervasive, however, has been his conferring of the term community on a specific *locale* (see Part II). It is this territorial reference which has led to a dichotomy in community studies between those which focus, to put it crudely, on the people, and those which focus on the territory.

Parsons, though, avoids forcing a choice between these two approaches. His tentative definition of community (which should be treated as such) is as follows: '. . . that aspect of the structure of social systems which is referable to the territorial location of persons . . . and their activities.' There follows an important qualification: 'When I say "referable to" I do not mean determined exclusively or predominantly by, but rather *observable and analysable with reference to location as a focus of attention* (and of course a partial determinant).'[4] As Parsons states, the territorial reference is central, though it is necessary to stress, with him, that the primary concern is with 'persons acting in territorial locations' and, in addition, 'since the reference is to *social* relations, persons acting in relation to other persons in respect to the territorial location of both parties . . . The *population*, then, is just as much a focus of the study of community as is the territorial location.' The Parsonian pattern-variables, breaking down as they do the solidary concepts of *Gemeinschaft* and *Gesellschaft*, have opened the way to analysis along these lines. Recent detailed work on communities has shown that, far from there being an exclusive continuum from *Gemeinschaft* to *Gesellschaft*, relationships of *both* types are found in the *same* community.

A different reaction to the confusion over what constitutes a community has been to abandon it as an object of study and instead to view community studies as a *method* of elucidating data illustrative of some wider generalization. Such a view is echoed by Havighurst and Jansen in their 'trend report' on Community Research published as an edition of *Current Sociology* in 1967: 'A community study is not a branch of sociology, such as ecology, demography and social psychology. Rather it is a form of sociological research that is useful for a variety of research purposes.'[5] Margaret Stacey's paper, reprinted below, is a spirited defence of 'community' as an object worthy of study. If institutions are locality based *and* interrelated there may well be, she argues, a *local social system* that deserves sociological study. She does not want to call this local social system a 'community' for the latter, she feels, is a non-concept. In other words, Stacey claims that the definitional debate about community is something more—it represents a much more serious *conceptual* disagreement. Instead sociologists should concentrate on institutions and the interrelations in specific localities.

The concept for analyzing, indeed for conceptualizing, these social groups is the 'social network'. This concept is used by Elias and Scotson in the final paper of this section, which is taken from the concluding chapter of their study of a Leicestershire community, *The Established and the Outsiders*. As they see it, the 'specific community aspects of a community' are the 'network of relationships between people organized as a residential unit'. Their delineation of the 'established' and 'outsider' groups may have a theoretical relevance beyond their own micro-sociological study. The examination of, to use more broadly-based terms, locally-oriented and nationally-oriented groups within the context of a local social system appears to be one area in which community studies will be increasingly fruitful.

Pahl, for example, sees the confrontation of the local and the national within a territorially limited setting as one of the key sets of interaction processes which the community study should analyse.[6] It is unlikely that such occurrences will take place without a certain amount of conflict, as Elias and Scotson themselves show. It seems likely therefore that analyses like theirs will lead to an increasing interest in community conflict. This is particularly welcome since, apart from James Coleman's[7] excellent attempt to synthesize existing knowledge of this aspect of community affairs, community conflict is a sadly neglected facet of most community studies.

NOTES

1 Hillery, G. A. Jnr., 'Definitions of Community: Areas of Agreement', *Rural Sociology*, 20, 1955, p. 117.
2 See, for example, McKinney, J. C., and Loomis, C. P., 'The Application of *Gemeinschaft* and *Gesellschaft* as Related to Other Typologies' in the introduction to the American edition of Tönnies' *Community and Society* (New York: Harper Torchbook, 1957), pp. 12–29.
3 Nisbet, R., *The Sociological Tradition* (London: Heinemann, 1966), p. 6.
4 Parsons, T., 'The Principle Structure of Community: A Sociological View' in *Structure and Process in Modern Societies* (Glencoe, Ill.: Free Press, 1960), p. 153.

5 Havighurst, R. J., and Jansen, A. J., 'Community Research', *Current Sociology*, XV, 1967, p. 7 (our emphasis).
6 See, Pahl, R. E., 'The Rural-Urban Continuum', *Sociologica Ruralis*, VI (3–4), 1966. Stacey, emphasizing common values rather than physical mobility as in the case of Elias and Scotson, calls the two groups traditionalists and non-traditionalists. See *Tradition and Change* (Oxford: Oxford University Press, 1960).
7 Coleman, J. S., *Community Conflict* (Glencoe, Ill.: Free Press, 1957).

CHAPTER 2

Gemeinschaft and Gesellschaft*

Ferdinand Tönnies

All intimate, private and exclusive living together, so we discover, is understood as life in Gemeinschaft (community). Gesellschaft (society) is public life—it is the world itself. In Gemeinschaft with one's family, one lives from birth on, bound to it in weal and woe. One goes into Gesellschaft as one goes into a strange country. A young man is warned against bad Gesellschaft, but the expression bad Gemeinschaft violates the meaning of the word. Lawyers may speak of domestic Gesellschaft, thinking only of the legalistic concept of social association; but the domestic Gemeinschaft, or home life with its immeasurable influence upon the human soul, has been felt by everyone who ever shared it. Likewise, a bride or groom knows that he or she goes into marriage as a complete Gemeinschaft of life. A Gesellschaft of life would be a contradiction in and of itself. One keeps or enjoys another's Gesellschaft, but not his Gemeinschaft in this sense. One becomes a part of a religious Gemeinschaft; religious Gesellschaften (associations or societies), like any other groups formed for given purposes, exist only in so far as they, viewed from without, take their places among the institutions of a political body or as they represent conceptual elements of a theory; they do not touch upon the religious Gemeinschaft as such. There exists a Gemeinschaft of language, of folkways or mores, or of beliefs; but, by way of contrast, Gesellschaft exists in the realm of business, travel, or sciences. So of special importance are the commercial Gesellschaften; whereas, even though a certain familiarity and Gemeinschaft may exist among business partners, one could indeed hardly speak of commerical Gemeinschaft. To make the word combination 'joint-stock Gemeinschaft' would be abominable. On the other hand, there exists a Gemeinschaft of ownership in fields, forest, and pasture. The Gemeinschaft of property between man and wife cannot be called Gesellschaft of property. Thus many differences become apparent.

* Reprinted by permission of The Michigan State University Press from *Community and Society* by F. Tönnies, Michigan, 1967, pp. 33–34, 35, 41–44, 76–78.

In the most general way, one could speak of a Gemeinschaft comprising the whole of mankind, such as the Church wishes to be regarded. But human Gesellschaft is conceived as mere co-existence of people independent of each other. Recently, the concept of Gesellschaft as opposed to and distinct from the state has been developed. This term will also be used in this book, but can only derive its adequate explanation from the underlying contrast to the Gemeinschaft of the people.

Gemeinschaft is old; Gesellschaft is new as a name as well as a phenomenon. All praise of rural life has pointed out that the Gemeinschaft among people is stronger there and more alive; it is the lasting and genuine form of living together. In contrast to Gemeinschaft, Gesellschaft is transitory and superficial. Accordingly, Gemeinschaft should be understood as a living organism, Gesellschaft as a mechanical aggregate and artifact.

A superior power which is exercised to the benefit of the subordinate and which, because in accordance with his will, is accepted by him, I call dignity or authority. We distinguish three kinds: authority of age, authority of force and authority of wisdom or spirit. These three are united in the authority of the father who is engaged in protecting, assisting and guiding his family. The danger inherent in such power causes fear in the weaker ones, and this by itself would mean nothing but negation and repudiation (except in so far as mingled with admiration). Beneficence and good will, however, bring forth the will to honour; and the sentiment of reverence is born in a situation where will to honour predominates. Thus, as a result of this difference in power, tenderness corresponds to reverence or, in a lesser degree of intensity, benevolence to respect; they represent the two poles of sentiment on which Gemeinschaft is based, in case there exists a definite difference of power. The existence of such motives makes possible and probable a kind of Gemeinschaft even between master and servant, and this is the rule especially if it is supported and fostered, as in the case of kinship, by an intimate, lasting and secluded common life in the home.

The Gemeinschaft by blood, denoting unity of being, is developed and differentiated into Gemeinschaft of locality, which is based on a common habitat. A further differentiation leads to the Gemeinschaft of mind, which implies only co-operation and co-ordinated action for a common goal. Gemeinschaft of locality may be conceived as a community of physical life, just as Gemeinschaft of mind expresses the community of mental life. In conjunction with the others, this last type of Gemeinschaft represents the truly human and supreme form of community. Kinship Gemeinschaft signifies a common relation to, and share in, human beings themselves, while in Gemeinschaft of locality such a common relation is established through collective ownership of land; and, in Gemeinschaft of mind, the common bond is represented by sacred places and worshipped deities. All three types of Gemeinschaft are closely interrelated in space as well as in time. They are, therefore, also related in all such single phenomena and in their development, as well as in general human culture and its history. Wherever human beings are related through their wills in an organic manner and affirm each other, we find one or another of the three types of Gemeinschaft. Either the earlier type involves the later one, or the later type has developed to relative independence from some earlier one. It is, therefore, possible to deal with (1) kinship, (2) neighbourhood and (3) friendship as definite and meaningful derivations of these original categories.

The house constitutes the realm and, as it were, the body of kinship. Here people live together under one protecting roof. Here they share their possessions and their pleasures; they feed from the same supply, they sit at the same table. The dead are venerated here as invisible spirits, as if they were still powerful and held a protecting hand over their family. Thus, common fear and common honour ensure peaceful living and co-operation with greater certainty. The will and spirit of kinship is not confined within the walls of the house nor bound up with physical proximity; but, where it is strong and alive in the closest and most intimate relationship, it can live on itself, thrive on memory alone, and overcome any distance by its feelings and its imagination of nearness and common activity. Nevertheless, it seeks all the more for physical proximity and is loath to give it up, because such nearness alone will fulfil the desire for love. The ordinary human being, therefore—in the long run and for the average of cases—feels best and most cheerful if he is surrounded by his family and relatives. He is among his own.

Neighbourhood describes the general character of living together in the rural village. The proximity of dwellings, the communal fields, and even the mere contiguity of holdings necessitate many contacts of human beings and cause inurement to and intimate knowledge of one another. They also necessitate co-operation in labour, order and management, and lead to common supplication for grace and mercy to the gods and spirits of land and water who bring blessing or menace with disaster. Although essentially based upon proximity of habitation, this neighbourhood type of Gemeinschaft can nevertheless persist during separation from the locality, but it then needs to be supported still more than ever by well-defined habits of reunion and sacred customs.

Friendship is independent of kinship and neighbourhood, being conditioned by and resulting from similarity of work and intellectual attitude. It comes most easily into existence when crafts or callings are the same or of similar nature. Such a tie, however, must be made and maintained through easy and frequent meetings, which are most likely to take place in a town. A worshipped deity created out of common mentality, has an immediate significance for the preservation of such a bond, since only, or at least mainly, this deity is able to give it living and lasting form. Such good spirit, therefore, is not bound to any place but lives in the conscience of its worshippers and accompanies them on their travels to foreign countries. Thus, those who are brethren of such a common faith feel, like members of the same craft or rank, everywhere united by a spiritual bond and the co-operation in a common task. Urban community of life may be classified as neighbourhood, as is also the case with a community of domestic life in which nonrelated members or servants participate. In contradistinction, spiritual friendship forms a kind of invisible scene or meeting which has to be kept alive by artistic intuition and creative will. The relations between human beings themselves as friends and comrades have the least organic and intrinsically necessary character. They are the least instinctive and are based less upon habit than are the relationships of neighbourhood. They are of a mental nature and seem to be founded, therefore, as compared with the earlier relationships upon chance or free choice.

*   *   *

Gesellschaft, an aggregate by convention and law of nature, is to be understood as a multitude of natural and artificial individuals, the wills, and spheres of whom are in many relations with and to one another, and remain nevertheless independent of one another and devoid of mutual familiar relationships. This gives us the general description of 'bourgeois society' or 'exchange Gesellschaft,' the nature and movements of which legislative economy attempts to understand; a condition in which, according to the expression of Adam Smith, 'Every man . . . becomes in some measure a merchant, . . .' Where merchants, companies, or firms or associations deal with one another in international or national markets and exchanges, the nature of the Gesellschaft is erected as in a concave mirror or as in an extract.

In the conception of Gesellschaft, the original or natural relations of human beings to each other must be excluded. The possibility of a relation in the Gesellschaft assumes no more than a multitude of mere persons who are capable of delivering something, and consequently of promising something. Gesellschaft as a totality to which a system of conventional rules applies is limitless; it constantly breaks

Note—a line of asterisks in the text indicates that a section of the original essay has been omitted.

through its chance and real boundaries. In Gesellschaft every person strives for that which is to his own advantage and he affirms the actions of others only in so far as and as long as they can further his interest. Before and outside of convention and also before and outside of each special contract, the relation of all to all may therefore be conceived as potential hostility or latent war. Against this condition, all agreements of the will stand out as so many treaties and peace pacts. This conception is the only one which does justice to all facts of business and trade where all rights and duties can be reduced to mere value and definitions of ability to deliver. Every theory of pure private law or law of nature understood as pertaining to the Gesellschaft has to be considered as being based upon this conception. Buyer and seller in their manifold types stand in relation one to the other in such a manner that each one, for as little of his own wealth as possible, desires and attempts to obtain as much of the wealth of others as possible. The real commercial and business people race with each other on many sprinting tracks, as it were, trying each to get the better of the other and to be the first to reach the goal: the sale of their goods and of as large a quantity as possible. Thus, they are forced to crowd each other out or to trip each other up. The loss of one is the profit of the other, and this is the case in every individual exchange, unless owners exchange goods of actually equal value. This constitutes general competition which takes place in so many other spheres, but is nowhere so evident and so much in the consciousness of people as in trade, to which, consequently, the conception is limited in its common use. Competition has been described by many pessimists as an illustration of the war of all against all, which a famous thinker has conceived as the natural state of mankind.

However, even competition carries within it, as do all forms of such war, the possibility of being ended. Even enemies like these— although among these it may be the least likely—recognize that under certain conditions it is to their advantage to agree and to spare each other. They may even unite themselves together for a common purpose (or also—and this is the most likely—against a common enemy). Thus, competition is limited and abolished by coalition.

In analogy to this situation, based upon the exchange of material goods, all conventional society life, in the narrower sense of the word, can be understood. Its supreme rule is politeness. It consists of an exchange of words and courtesies in which everyone seems to be present for the good of everyone else and everyone seems to consider everyone else as his equal, whereas in reality everyone is thinking of himself and trying to bring to the fore his importance and advantages in competition with the others. For everything pleasant which someone does for someone else, he expects, even demands, at least an equivalent. He weighs exactly his services, flatteries, presents, and so on, to determine whether they will bring about the desired result. Formless contracts are made continuously, as it were, and constantly many are pushed aside in the race by the few fortunate and powerful ones.

Since all relations in the Gesellschaft are based upon comparison of possible and offered services, it is evident that the relations with visible, material matters have preference, and that mere activities and words form the foundation for such relationships only in an unreal way. In contrast to this, Gemeinschaft as a bond of 'blood' is in the first place a physical relation, therefore expressing itself in deeds and words. Here, the common relation to the material objects is of a secondary nature, and such objects are not exchanged as often as they are used and possessed in common. Furthermore, Gesellschaft, in the sense which we may call moral, is also entirely dependent upon its relations with the state, which has not entered our theory so far because the economic Gesellschaft must be considered prior to it.

CHAPTER 3

The Myth of Community Studies*

Margaret Stacey

If community studies are to be undertaken they must be justified as one would justify any piece of sociological research, i.e. they must make it possible either (i) to test already existing propositions or (ii) to explore for hypotheses within a given conceptual framework. In particular one must expect of such studies that they should provide data in answer to questions about *how* particular aspects of society work, which may be drawn together to develop an understanding of the larger 'how' of social systems in general. Such can also provide the data upon which those theoreticians who wish to answer the question 'why society?' can develop their ideas. No distinction is here made between so-called 'pure' and 'applied' research, for whether the immediate object is to solve a practical problem or an academic one, the canons of sociological research are the same.

In relation to so-called community studies we must therefore ask: (*a*) Are there propositions which can be tested in this context? (*b*) Is it a context in which one can explore for hypotheses and, if so, of what kind? (*c*) Is this a particular aspect of society the workings of which it is reasonable or even possible to isolate in order to examine the 'how' questions?

In complex societies the critics of 'community studies' answer 'no' to this last question. If they are right, questions (*a*) and (*b*) become irrelevant. Question (*c*) must therefore be the starting point.

It is doubtful whether the concept 'community' refers to a useful abstraction. Certainly confusion continues to reign over the uses of the term community, a confusion which has been added to rather than resolved by König's recently translated work.[1] The logic of König's argument supports the view that as a concept 'community' is

* This paper has developed from earlier versions read to postgraduate seminars in Sussex, Swansea and Kent during 1966–1967 and was re-written for presentation to a day conference of the B.S.A. Western Region. I am grateful to members of these seminars and of the region and to my colleagues at Swansea for their helpful criticisms and encouragement. Reprinted by permission of Routledge and Kegan Paul Ltd from the *British Journal of Sociology*, vol. XX, 2 June 1969, pp. 134–147.

not useful for serious sociological analysis. Yet in his conclusion König retains the obstinate, but still mythical, remnants of the romantic model, which he had so cogently criticized earlier. In one place (p. 180) his definition of community is nothing more nor less than that of a social group. In another he puts forward the view that 'community' is 'the framework within which the human being is first introduced to social relations beyond the confines of the family' (p. 195). This is so vague as to be nonsense: there is no such thing as 'community' which does this, at least not in complex societies. Various agencies are involved in this process of introduction, perhaps neighbours, almost certainly parents' kin and friends (who may live next door or miles away), inevitably teachers and peers at school, perhaps the church, and so on These institutions may, or may not, be locality-based. They may, or may not, be inter-related. If they are locality-based *and* inter-related then there may well be a local social system worth studying, but one would hesitate to call this a community. If the relevant institutions were not locality-based, or were not inter-related, as might very well be the case, there would be no social system present in the locality at all.

Nor is there any less lack of confusion in earlier usages of the term. There are, broadly, those who use 'community' for social relations in a defined geographic area, and those who stress the sense of belonging to a group which 'community' is said to entail. In the ideal typical community the sense of belonging was said to be associated with the social relations within the particular geographic area. Nevertheless, definitionally it is possible to distinguish those who use 'community' in a geographic sense and those who use it in some feeling sense.

MacIver[2] defined community as a territory in which the whole of one's life may be passed. Martindale[3] has recently redefined it more sociologically as a collectivity which forms a total system of social life capable of bringing its members through the ordinary problems of a single year or a single life. Martindale has removed the geography from the concept community and has equated it with a total social system and with a total way of life. Stein,[4] on the other hand, has defined community as 'an organized system standing in a determinate relation to its environment which has a local basis but not necessarily a rigid boundary' and he is aware that large parts of the social system lie outside the community so defined. Thus, for some people a community has a relation to a relatively small local area. For others, including Martindale[5] and Zentner[6] the community is as large as the nation state and the small local area is not to be considered, at least in Zentner's view, as a community but as a local society. Martindale, although he removed 'territory' from the definition, appears to make the community co-terminus with the nation state in western society, although his arguments show that not all parts of the social system are cut off by the frontiers of nations, for social relationships continue beyond these.

Here is the difficulty of any territorially based definition: what system of social relations can one say has any geographic boundary except a global one? (Even such bounds may not for long be meaningful: in measurable time it seems likely that some kin group will have a relative on the moon, with whom, one would hope, social relations could be maintained.)

Those who stress the 'sense of belonging' may not even be concerned with a territorially defined group. Community is used by Stein, for example, in the community of two of psychiatrist and patient.[7] One also speaks of a community of interest, for example of academics, a community of interest which in this case is said to extend beyond national frontiers. Community also has been used to describe prisons and other more or less total institutions.[8]

Recently, a tendency has developed to use 'community' as a shorthand for all those social groups, institutions and relationships which fall outside the author's immediate concern, for example, the use of community by Lockwood to cover non-work relationships[9] and of Grove and Proctor to describe the social relations of the citizens of a planning authority.[10] In both cases there is a geographic element of some kind in the relationships which the term community seeks to describe. Parsons' use of 'societal community' seems more complicated and no clearer than earlier terms.[11]

The disagreement is thus not only about terms, but is about the concept the term is supposed to describe, a much more serious matter.[12] For all these reasons one shares Hillery's refusal to use the word community because it 'embraces a motley assortment of concepts and qualitatively different phenomena'.[13] As Pahl makes clear in his recent article on the rural-urban continuum[14] and as Martindale and Neuwirth point out in the introduction to the recent edition of Weber's *City*,[15] our concern as sociologists is with social relationships. A consideration of the social attributes of individuals living in a particular geographic area is therefore not sociology, although it may well be an essential preliminary to sociological analysis.

Sociological terms, however complicated, should be derived from primitive terms which should, as Zetterberg has pointed out, relate to 'actors and types of actions'.[16] It is possible that we may also be concerned with the connections between social relationships and nonsocial phenomena, geographic, for example, but, given our sociological concern, 'any attempt to tie particular patterns of social relationships to specific geographic milieu is a singularly fruitless exercise' as Pahl has said.[17] This conclusion echoes Gans who says that 'ways of life do not coincide with settlement types'.[18]

What then is the point of studying social relations in a particular locality? Would it not be better to concentrate upon an analysis of particular social institutions, e.g. the sociology of industry, religion, politics, family?

It should be noted, first of all, that there are two kinds of locality studies. One is concerned with particular institutions as they are manifested in a locality, e.g. the family as studied by Rosser and Harris or Young and Willmott. The other is concerned with the inter-relations of institutions in a locality, e.g. Gosforth, Pentrediwaith, Banbury.[19] It is the utility of the second kind of study that is being examined here, although it should be made plain that distinctions between the two types are not hard and fast. Furthermore, a study apparently falling firmly within a category such as the sociology of industry or the sociology of religion may be undertaken within a geographically confined area. Thus aspects of industrial sociology may be studied in a particular works in a particular locality.

If one postulates, then, that one is not concerned to study 'community' because this is a non-concept, but is concerned to study institutions in a locality, and particularly to examine whether there are any connections between them, is it possible to argue that this is an aspect of society which one can isolate and which it is worth studying?

Arguments against locality studies derive from a number of sources and are qualitatively different. It is said (i) that they are mere description; (ii) that they are works of art, idiosyncratic and non-replicable; therefore, (iii) it is argued that they are of no use to a science which must be based on the comparative method; (iv) that they are committed to a holistic approach to sociological theory; and (v) that they abstract from empirical social reality at a point where such abstraction is neither feasible nor useful.

There is, of course, no 'mere' description. Description is always based upon some conceptions: the vaguer these are, the vaguer are the descriptions likely to be and the less useful for hypothesis formation. On the other hand, without observation and description there could be no hypotheses and no theory. There is no doubt, however, that as a body of knowledge, and perhaps particularly a science, develops one calls for empirical data marshalled in such a way as to make an immediate addition to the accumulated store. Dilettante description will not fit these requirements, but while we may have today description that some of us feel is misguided, there is no dilettante description masquerading as *professional* sociology.

The methodological charge (ii) is a large one and relates to the whole nature of the social sciences. Three propositions are here taken as axiomatic in the study of society: (i) society is outside any one man (in the Durkheimian sense of exteriority), (ii) each man has a particular position in society and (iii) each man has internalized a particular collection of norms and values from society, involving attitudes and emotions. These statements apply to the sociologist as well as to his subjects, affecting what he works on and how he goes about it. Sociology, therefore, like the other social sciences, in this author's view is neither an art in the classic sense of the humanistic disciplines, nor a science in the sense of the physical sciences, but stands in its own right, with its own theories and methods. The utterly objective, value-free science is therefore a chimera which it is a waste of time to pursue.

Therefore those who argue that there is an element of the work of art in any locality study, and particularly in one-man studies, have undoubtedly some truth on their side. But this element of the work of art enters into *any* sociological research. It is an element which can be more or less well controlled in any study. A highly idiosyncratic non-replicable study may be seminal, but cannot be used comparatively. While imaginative insights are important for the development of any science, the most valuable researches in any field of sociology are those which can be used comparatively. This is *par excellence* the case in the study of social systems, which, if one accepts their existence *sui generis*, are larger and last longer than any team of researchers. It therefore behoves the student of social relations in localities to use commonly accepted definitions for commonly accepted concepts, to collect and analyse his data in ways which are comparable with those of other scholars. To encourage such activity the BSA are shortly to publish the deliberations of their working party on the comparability of data.

One must be clear, however, what it is one wants to compare and how. Cohen has commented on the *reductio ad absurdum* of the holistic approach. Discussing the logical criticism of the holistic approach that it inhibits comparison and generalizations he adds 'imagine the difficulty of trying to compare the family structures of English and French society by examining not only every other known feature of the two societies but the way in which these inter-relate with one another to form a whole'.[20]

In so far as so-called community studies have been based on an uncritical structural-functional approach they are not defensible (i) because there is no good reason to suppose that *everything* is connected with everything else and (ii) because there is even less reason to suppose that this should be the case in any particular small locality of a nation-state. There is no doubt, however, that some institutions are related to others: one would like to know which ones and in what ways. Studies of social relations in localities provide a unique opportunity for answering part at least of this question.

Thus the answer to the question (*b*) posed at the outset of this paper is that in addition to providing a milieu for the detailed study of any one institution or process, the locality is a context in which one can explore for hypotheses about the inter-relations of institutions. Nor does it appear to matter much for this purpose whether a locality is isolated or not. The consequences for the social relations within a locality of changes introduced from outside have after all produced some interesting studies (e.g. Westrigg, Pentrediwaith, Barton Hill, Banbury).[21]

Social relations must be seen not only in combination with each other but in the two dimensions of time and space. For it would seem that these two dimensions are not unimportant in determining the nature of social institutions. Thus, where marked local social systems have been identified they have developed in a relatively confined locality over a considerable period of time, fifty to eighty years at least, and in a locality in which all the components of social life are to be found. While Bales was not specifically concerned with space in dealing with the problem-solving process, he was concerned with time and saw the process to be distributed in time and distributed between persons. In Bales' view the distinction cannot be disposed of even in the most abstract formulations which, as he says ,'is very inconvenient theoretically', the two resultant modes of conceptualization not ever being entirely resolvable into each other.[22]

Arensberg and Kimball stress particularly the temporal element.[23] While their use of 'community' and the way they conceive it falls among those conceptualizations which are here being avoided, their stress on time is important, as Martindale also recognizes.[24]

The main justification for the study of social relations in localities must rest upon the answer to the first sub-question posed at the outset: are there propositions which can be tested in this context? Associated with this is, of course, the question 'can a series of inter-related propositions about social relations in localities be derived from existing empirical data seen in the light of general sociological theory?' An attempt to demonstrate that this question can be answered in the affirmative follows.

Some specific aspects about which it seems possible to speak at the moment are (i) the establishment and maintenance of a local social system; (ii) local conditions where no such system could be expected; (iii) some circumstances under which an existing system might be modified or destroyed; (iv) certain inter-relations between systems and their parts; (v) the interaction of local and national systems.

The concern here is with what has been called system integration or functional interdependence, especially with how such comes about. This is of course also closely involved with questions to do with 'why society'. Here I agree with Cohen when he says that the 'only theory which is in any way satisfactory is that which explains functional integration as the largely unintended product of social interaction occurring over time.'[25]

A *social system* is here used for a set of inter-related social institutions* covering all aspects of social life, familial, religious, juridical, etc., and the associated belief systems of each. This is what many sociologists have called 'social organization' and bears some resemblance to what Parsons calls the 'societal community' mentioned above. Each of the aspects mentioned, familial, political, etc., can be considered as systems themselves and are parts of any social system. A *local social system* occurs when such a set of inter-relations exists in a geographically defined locality. If there are *no* connections between the major social institutions in the locality, that is connections which are specific to that locality, there is *no* local social system. The set of inter-relations which compose the social system may be *more or less complete*. A complete social system in which all institutions are present and inter-related is an ideal type. In practice all social systems are partial in the sense that not all sub-systems are present, or not all are interconnected if present, or both. Empirically, in any one geographically defined locality, the likelihood is that there will either be no local social system, or some kind of partial local social system.

The theoretical position of a complete local social system might well be thought to be open to the objections raised earlier against the concept 'community'. This is not intended. The aim rather is to define a state, known not to exist, and to indicate the factors of which it is composed. Any one system may theoretically, or in practice, lack one or more of these factors and thus be a partial social system. The sub-systems of any local social system may be part of, or connected with, systems outside the locality. A social system of a kind may exist with a sub-system missing, for example, there might be no family or kin connections. A prison might be one such. While it is unlikely that there could be a social system without a belief system, there could be a social system without formally organized religion. Similarly a social system may not have a political system based on formal political organizations. Theoretically, it should be possible

---

* Where a social institution is defined, following Ginsberg, as 'recognized and established usages governing the relations between individuals or groups',[26] a definition which is largely consonant with that of Parsons 'Normative patterns which define what are felt to be . . . proper, legitimate, or expected modes of action or of social relationship.'[27]

to list systematically the institutions which might be present and all the interconnections. Against this model the presence or absence of institutions and connections could then be plotted. Cohen's concluding description of a Yemeni community would seem to be a good empirical example of one type of partial local social system exhibiting both partial internal and external connections.[28] The development of such a model should make systematic comparison between studies more rigorous.

The concept of a local social system in mind here involves *structure and process*. It involves not only what institutions are present, but the processes of their operation; not only which institutions are connected to which others, but the processes involved, Merton's social mechanisms. Process involves movement and it follows that no social system is static. This I take as axiomatic. Processes take *time* and the dimension of time is therefore, as was shown above, essential to the conceptualization of any social system. In this discussion time will be treated as an empirical condition relevant to the state of any local social system. That is to say the state of a system at a given moment of time will be considered and the temporal conditions which have led to that state and what may follow will be indicated. This may lend some of the states referred to in the propositions a static appearance, but it should be understood that such states are to be perceived as part of a dynamic process. The statements which refer to the conditions of probable change should make this clear.

With these concepts in mind and on the basis of existing research it seems to be possible to suggest the following tentative propositions about local social systems. The works used for illustration are principally British, but other studies have been taken into account in considering what propositions to make.

1. Certain conditions are necessary for the initial development of a local social system:

(*a*) The minimum condition is that the majority of the local population should have been present together in the locality for some period of time.

(*b*) The longer is this period the more likely is there to be a local social system present.

(*c*) Where the majority of the population have been born and bred in the locality it is highly likely that there will be some sort of local social system present. E.g. Old Banbury, Winston Parva, Zones I and II.[29]

But unless this condition 1(c) applies,

2. It does not necessarily follow that because a majority of the local population have been present in a locality for some period of time

that a local social system will develop. E.g. Winston Parva, Zone III (see propositions 21 and 22 below).

(The empirical relationship between the development of a local social system and the passing of time is not at all clearly known.)

3. Following from proposition 1, in a situation where there has been a local social system in existence one may deduce that:

(a) When the number of migrants into a locality increases, there must be a critical point at which the increase will place such a strain upon the system as to prevent its previous operation. In this case if the system continues to exist it will be in an altered state. The critical point will be determined by the number and/or type of migrants in relation to the host population.

(The empirical conditions under which this may occur are not known at all accurately.)

(b) There must be a further critical point when such an influx would destroy the system altogether, that is to say social relationships in the locality would become dominated by institutions other than those of the erstwhile local social system. In view of the inter-penetration of systems considered in propositions 16–18 and 20 below, it seems more likely that change of the kind indicated in 3(a) above will occur, except in extreme conditions such as conquest.

4. It is characteristic of a local social system that some or all of the actors in the population to which the system relates play multiplex roles to each other.

5. The more institutions are present in the locality, the more likely is a local social system to develop because the chances of multiplex role playing are increased (since the number of statuses and therefore the number of roles is increased).

6. Where there is a local social system there will be a structure of overlapping groups, as well as a structure of overlapping roles.

7. The presence or absence of certain institutions produce critical differences in the type of local social system which may be found. Thus, in a locality which is entirely residential, only sub-systems connected with neighbouring and with familial and kin relations can develop. The addition of workplaces to the locality not only increases the number of available roles, but may alter the characteristics of the relations between people and make possible, through the development of new institutions, a different type of local social system.

8. Where any substantial institutions are removed the system is modified. E.g. in Pentrediwaith where the local social system was modified by the removal of work from the locality.

9. Where any substantial institutions are greatly changed the system cannot work as it did previously, as in Banbury where new economic relations were introduced.

10. Critical differences are exhibited by social system in localities where points of power in organizations associated with the economic, political and other major sub-systems are present in the locality. E.g. the continued presence of a local social system in Banbury in 1950, despite a large influx of migrants, was connected with the continued presence of some power points of the economic, political and legal organizations in the locality.

11. Where local power points are removed the local social system is modified. E.g. the change in Westrigg, between 1900 and 1950, and the associated changes in the local social system, were closely connected with the removal of points of political power from the locality and the shift in the loci of industrial (agricultural) power.

12. Absence from the locality of power points or organizations associated with major sub-systems may result in the destruction of the local social system and even also physical destruction, as in Old Barton Hill where the local social system included institutions concerning most relationships but *not* political power. Voting (and not legislation or administration) was the only political institution present. The area was razed and redeveloped, the residents being re-housed.

13. If the size of the area which is controlled by the power point of any one major organization is increased, it follows that the locality within which a local social system containing the relevant institution can develop must increase in size. E.g. the area covered by local social systems which *include* local political power has already increased in the last 100 years. One may speculate on the consequences for such systems of the introduction of city regions.

14. As with any social system, a local social system will have a system of beliefs associated with it. In a locality where there is a local social system these beliefs will be shared by many members of the populations to which the system relates. The mechanism of this sharing operates through the multiplex role-playing and the overlapping group memberships of the local population.

15. Where a majority of the population of a locality do not share to any considerable extent common groups, institutions, beliefs and expectations, there can be no *one* local social system for that locality. E.g. Mrs. Patterson's Brixton[30] and Banbury 1950. Also Sparkbrook, where the consequences of the operation of the larger social system for social relations in a particular locality are examined.[31]

(The empirical meaning of 'majority' and 'considerable extent' are at present not at all clearly known.)

16. In any locality in Britain, not all the residents of a locality will be involved in the institutions which are components of the local social system, e.g. some may work, worship or play outside the locality, these being governed by institutions which may or may not be the same as specifically local institutions.

17. Nor will the residents who are involved in institutions associated with the local social system be totally encompassed by that system, because in no locality in Britain are all the points of power of organizations associated with the major sub-systems to be found in the locality. Much political power is centred in the national government, and the economic and religious systems extend beyond the locality and to some extent beyond the nation.

18. In localities where there is a local social system, there will also be elements of other social systems present in the locality, i.e. the local social system will not totally encompass all institutions and relationships present. E.g. migrants bring with them *nationally legitimated* rights to vote for *local* political bodies.

19. Where there is no local social system, these elements of other social systems may show no systematic connections *within* the locality, or partial connection only, e.g. commuter villages.

20. Where there is a local social system elements of it will be connected with systems outside the locality, that is, not that the local system as a whole is part of a wider system, but that its parts are parts of wider systems. Thus, while a local social system will have its own associated beliefs and cultural systems, the local system of beliefs and of culture will share elements of the beliefs and cultural systems of the wider society.

21. Some structural and cultural features of a local social system may render some individuals socially invisible to each other. E.g. as Williams reports for Gosforth (p. 105) of two in-coming families 'their existence was, and probably would remain, unrecognized.' Therefore,

22. Physical proximity does not always lead to the establishment of social relations. Thus proposition 1(a) is a necessary, but not a sufficient, condition for the development of a local social system. Therefore,

23. Physical proximity does not always lead to the establishment of social relations.

24. Multiplex social roles develop where there is a small closed population because the members are obliged to play many roles to each other.

25. In a large population, simplex role relations *can* exist. But

26. If many members of this large population are rendered socially invisible then a small group within the large population may well

establish multiplex relations. (This is true of the 'urban villages' and also of élites.)

27. An increase in the number of migrants from an area reduces the number of actors available, increases the probability of multiplex role playing, and may also lead to the modification and possible destruction of a previously existing social system.

(Empirical evidence is lacking here.)

28. Where a local social system is present there tends to be a convergence of the élites within the system, that is, a tendency to the development of a total social status in the locality.

29. The social relationships of people in the population to which the local social system relates includes those of conflict as well as co-operation. E.g. Pentrediwaith, Banbury.

30. Indifference to each other among people in a population, i.e. a lack of concern about relationships or an absence of relationships indicates a weak local social system or that no such social system is present.

31. Given that in any one locality there are persons not involved in the local social system (proposition 16) and that elements of other systems will be present (proposition 18) the local social system will be sensitive to any changes which take place in these social systems outside itself. This sensitivity is increased because of the connection of parts of the local social system with parts of wider social systems (proposition 20).

Undoubtedly there are other propositions of a similar kind which could be extracted from the considerable and increasing number of empirical studies of localities. The propositions of course attempt to generalize particular social relations in such a way that they can be related to generalizations derived from other types of studies, thus giving wider scope than can be achieved by any one study. This set is connected with the concept of the local social system and with system integration. Other specific sets could also be developed. One of the advantages of setting out the propositions in this sort of way is that it shows how, by development of particular propositions, role theory and structural theory and also cultural theory can be inter-related. Indeed one of the advantages of studying social relations in a locality is that it forces upon one considerations of this kind.

The propositions also show how irrelevant is the argument that because a totality of social relations are not to be found within a locality, the future of locality studies is in doubt. They make it plain that in any locality study some of the social processes we shall want to consider will take us outside the locality. It may well be that the division of labour should be that while some sociologists learn to deal with the horizontal patterns, to use Warren's phrase, others learn how to deal with the vertical patterns.[32] In any case it is certain that locality studies cannot stand on their own. They must be compared not only with each other, but with data gathered in other ways in other fields. Statistical generalizations about the whole country are important to place the locality in a national pattern. A local study equally shows some of the limitations of such overall generalizations. Non-statistical national studies on particular topics are also needed to illuminate the local incidence. These methods of data collection and analysis are not alternatives. All are needed to inform each other. It is only possible to move towards propositions of the kind that I have tried to make here with a knowledge of empirical studies and sociological theory derived from many fields of enquiry.

NOTES

1 René König, *The Community*, trans. Edward Fitzgerald, Routledge and Kegan Paul, 1968.
2 R. M. MacIver, *Society: A Textbook of Sociology*, Farrar and Reinhart, 1945, p. 9.
3 Don Martindale, 'The Formation and the Destruction of Community', ch. 3 of *Explorations in Social Change*, ed. Geo. K. Zollschan and Walter Hirsch, Routledge and Kegan Paul, 1964.
4 Maurice Stein, *The Eclipse of Community*, Princeton University Press, 1960 (Harper Torchbooks, 1964), pp. 100, 101.
5 Martindale, op. cit.
6 Henry Zentner, 'The State and Community: A Conceptual Clarification', *Sociol. and Soc. Res.*, vol. 48, no. 4 (July 1964), pp. 414–427.
7 Stein, op. cit.
8 For example, Hayner and Ash, 'The Prison as a Community', *Amer. Sociol. Rev.*, vol. 5, no. 4 (August 1940), pp. 577–583.
9 D. Lockwood, 'Sources of Variation in Working Class Images of Society', *Sociol. Rev.*, vol. 14, no. 3, N.S. (November 1966), p. 249.
10 J. L. Grove and S. C. Proctor, 'Citizen Participation in Planning', *J. Town Planning Inst.* (December 1966).
11 Talcott Parsons, *Societies: Evolutionary and Comparative Perspectives*, Prentice Hall Foundations of Modern Sociology Series, 1961, pp. 10 et seq.
12 For a useful and interesting summary of earlier classical uses see M. Ginsberg, *Reason and Unreason in Society*, Longmans Green, 1947, pp. 8–14.
13 Geo. A. Hillery, 'Villages, Cities and Total Institutions', *Amer. Sociol. Rev.*, vol. 28, 1963, pp. 779 et seq.
14 R. E. Pahl, 'The Rural-Urban Continuum', *Sociologia Ruralis*, vol. 6, nos. 3–4 (1966).
15 Max Weber, *The City*, trans. and ed. by Don Martindale and Gertrude Neuwirth, The Free Press, New York, 1958.
16 Hans L. Zetterberg, *On Theory and Verification in Sociology*, Bedminster Press, 1965, p. 54.
17 Op. cit., p. 322.

18 H. J. Gans, 'Urbanism and suburbanism as Ways of Life' in Arnold M. Rose
   (ed.), *Human Behaviour and Social Process*, Houghton Mifflin, 1962; quoted
   M. Banton, 'Social Alignment and Identity in a West African City', paper for
   Burg Wartenstein Symposium no. 26, 1964.
19 W. M. Williams, *The Sociology of an English Village: Gosforth*, Routledge and
   Kegan Paul, 1964; R. Frankenberg, *Village on the Border*, Cohen and West,
   1957; M. Stacey, *Tradition and Change*, O.U.P., 1960.
20 Percy S. Cohen, *Modern Social Theory*, Heinemann, 1968, pp. 53–55.
21 James Littlejohn, *Westrigg: The Sociology of a Cheviot Parish*, Routledge and
   Kegan Paul, 1963; Frankenberg, op. cit.; Hilda Jennings, *Societies in the
   Making: A Study of Development and Redevelopment within a County Borough*,
   1962; Stacey, op. cit.
22 R. F. Bales, *Interaction Process Analysis*, Addison-Wesley, 1951, pp. 57 and
   126.
23 C. M. Arensberg and S. T. Kimball, *Culture and Community*, Harcourt, Brace
   and World, 1965.
24 D. Martindale, *Institutions, Organizations and Mass Society*, Houghton
   Mifflin, 1966, pp. 198–199.
25 Cohen, op. cit., p. 151.
26 M. Ginsberg, *Sociology*, Butterworth, 1934, p. 42.
27 Talcott Parsons, *Essays in Sociological Theory, Pure and Applied*, Glencoe, Ill.,
   The Free Press, 1949, p. 203.
28 Percy S. Cohen, 'Alignments and Allegiances in the Community of Shaarayim
   in Israel', *Jewish J. Sociol.*, vol. 4, no. 1, June 1962, p. 37.
29 Stacey, op. cit.; N. Elias and J. L. Scotson, *The Established and the Outsiders*,
   Cass, 1965.
30 Sheila Patterson, *Dark Strangers: a study of West Indians in London*, Pelican,
   1965.
31 John Rex and Robert Moore, *Race, Community and Conflict: a Study of
   Sparbrook*, O.U.P., 1967.
32 Roland E. Warren, *The Community in America*, Rand McNally, Chicago,
   1963.

CHAPTER 4

Cohesion, Conflict and Community Character*

N. Elias and J. L. Scotson

In studying a community, one is faced with a great variety of problems. The question is whether they are all equally central for the understanding of what gives to a grouping of people this specific character—the character of a community.

It is quite possible to divide the problems of a community into a number of classes and to go over them one by one. One might distinguish between economic, historical, political, religious, administrative and other aspects of a community, might study each by itself and in the conclusion indicate as best one can how these aspects are connected with each other.

But one can also reverse the approach and ask what it is that binds economic, historical, political and other classes of data together as aspects of a community. What, in other words, are the specific community aspects of a community? The answer to this kind of question, at first glance, is fairly simple and perhaps rather obvious. One evidently refers to the network of relationships between people organized as a residential unit—in accordance with the place where they normally live. People establish relations if they do business, if they work, worship or play with each other and these relations may or may not be highly specialized and highly organized. But people also establish relations when they 'live together at the same place', when they make their homes in the same locality. The interdependencies which establish themselves between them as makers of homes, where they sleep and eat and rear their families, are the specific community interdependencies. Communities are essentially organizations of home-makers, residential units such as urban neighbourhoods, villages, hamlets, compounds or groups of tents. It is difficult to imagine communities without women and children, though one can imagine communities almost without men. Prisoner-of-war camps may be regarded as substitute communities.

In our times homes are often separated from the places where

---

* Reprinted from *The Established and the Outsider*, by N. Elias and J. L. Scotson, published by Frank Cass, London 1965, pp. 146–160.

people make their living, in former days they were often not. But whether specialized or unspecialized, social units with a core of home-making families raise specific sociological problems. They are what one usually calls 'community problems'. Business quarters where no-one lives, which are full of people without families on weekdays and empty on Sundays, raise different problems. So do families in a different configuration, for instance groups of families-on-holiday. If one thinks it appropriate one could call these groupings too 'communities'. The word itself does not matter much. What matters is the recognition that the types of inter-dependencies, of structures and functions, to be found in residential groups of home-making families with a degree of permanence raise certain problems of their own and that the clarification of these problems is central for the understanding of the specific character of a *community qua community*—if one may continue to use the term in a specialized sense.

Among the central problems is that which concerns the distinctions in the value attributed within such a communal network of families to the individual family. Invariably some families or perhaps some groups of families in a community, as soon as they are linked to others by the invisible threads of a neighbourhood, come to regard themselves and to be regarded by others as 'better' and, alternatively, as 'less nice', 'less good', 'less worthy' or whatever word one may use. Academically we speak in such cases of the 'order of ranking' of families or of the 'status order' of a community, and as an approximation this conceptualization is useful. But it does not indicate too clearly the central part played by such distinctions in the life of every community; it does not indicate their wide functional ramifications, the wealth of personal associations of the people concerned and the tensions inherent in these distinctions.

Some of these ramifications have been indicated here. The 'ranking of families' in Winston Parva, as one saw, played a central part in every department of the community life. It had an influence on the membership of religious and political associations. It played a part in the grouping of people in pubs and clubs. It affected the grouping of adolescents and penetrated the schools. In fact, 'ranking of families' and 'status order' are perhaps rather too narrow expressions for what one actually observed. They can easily make us forget that higher status requires for its maintenance higher resources of power as well as distinction of conduct and belief which can be handed on, and that it has often to be fought for; they make us forget that lower status, to put it bluntly, can go hand in hand with degradation and suffering. Differences in status and ranking are often demonstrated as facts but rarely explained. One could see a little more clearly in

Winston Parva how they came about, and what part they played in the lives of people.

What has been presented in this study is, seen from close range, an episode in the development of an industrial, urban area. Such a development entailed frictions and disturbances. Those who had already settled in the area and, under favourable conditions, had had time to evolve from the main stream of their national tradition a fairly set communal life, a parochial tradition of their own, were faced with the fact that more people arrived to settle near and among them who to some extent differed in their outlook, manners and beliefs from those customary and valued in their own circle. One cannot exclude the possibility that at first when new houses were built in their neighbourhood the established workers also felt that the newcomers might be potential competitors for employment and disliked them for that reason. If so, all tangible traces of this type of feeling had disappeared at the time of the research. During the war the largest group of the new workers arrived together with the factory where they were employed and, by and large, industry and chances of employment in the area were expanding.

The tensions between the old and the new residents were of a peculiar kind. The core of the old residents valued highly the standards, the norms, the way of life that had evolved among them. They all were closely associated with their self-respect and with the respect they felt was due to them from others. Over the years a few of their numbers were prospering and socially rising. Roughly speaking, England's population can be divided into those who live in terraced houses—without a 'hall' in the lower, with a small 'hall' in the upper ranges—those who live in semi-detached and those who live in detached houses with a variety of sub-divisions. In Winston Parva, a small but steady trickle of people passed from the working-class level of terraced houses into a middle-class level of modest dimensions symbolized by semi-detached houses and still far from the world of large-scale industrial management or ownership of large enterprises and of the major professions whose representatives live in houses fully detached on both sides. The rise of this minority, some of whom exercised considerable power in the old community, was in terms of the public communal values a matter of pride for a majority of the older settlers.

The newcomers who settled on the Estate were felt as a threat to this order, not because of any intention they had of upsetting it, but because their behaviour made the old residents feel that any close contact with them would lower their own standing, that it would drag them down to a lower status level in their own estimation as well as in that of the world at large, that it would impair the prestige of their neighbourhood with all the chances of pride and satisfaction that went with it. In that sense the newcomers were experienced as a threat by the old residents. With the extreme sensitivity for anything that may endanger their own standing which people usually develop in a mobile social order full of status anxieties, they immediately noticed much in the behaviour of the newcomers that offended their sensibilities and appeared to them as a mark of a lower order. Gossip fastened quickly on anything that could show up the newcomers in a bad light and could confirm their own superiority in morals and manners, symbols of their own respectability, of their claim to a higher social status, of the existing social order.

That 'oldness' is regarded as a great social asset, as a matter of pride and satisfaction can be observed in many different social settings. The study of the relationships between 'old' and 'new' families in Winston Parva may go some way towards the solution of the problem why 'length of residence' and 'age of families' can affect deeply the relationship between people. It may help particularly because here for once 'oldness' was not associated with wealth past or present. The fact that in many other respects which are usually combined with 'oldness' and 'newness' the two groups of Winston Parva were almost equals made it possible to bring out certain chances of power available to 'old' groups of people which are easily overlooked if others such as those derived from superior wealth, superior military strength or superior knowledge are also present.

The term 'old' in this context, as one could see, was not simply a reference to the greater number of years during which the one neighbourhood had existed compared to the other. It referred to a specific social configuration which one can present without leaving much scope for uncertainty. In fact, one can set it out as a general model, a template of configurations of this kind. Summed up in this form one may hold it against other similar configurations. It may help to illuminate the new evidence and in turn be illuminated by it, or, if necessary, corrected or scrapped and replaced by a better model.

If the term 'old' is used with reference to a number of families who have been residents of a certain locality for at least two or three generations, it has not the same meaning which it has if one refers to individual people as 'old'. It has no biological meaning, though people occasionally give it a pseudo-biological connotation by implying that 'old families' are decadent or decaying like old people. In strictly scientific terms 'old' in this context is a purely sociological category, and it is a sociological, not a biological, problem to which it refers. An old group of people need not be a group of old people.

If one speaks of some families as 'old' one singles them out from others which lack this quality, and it is the reference to this contrast/

configuration with its specific status differences and tensions which gives to this use of the term 'old' its specific social flavour. In a biological sense all families on earth are equally old. They all stem from 'families' of ancestral apes or, if one prefers, from Adam and Eve. In its social context, in phrases such as 'old families' the term 'old' expresses a claim to social distinction and superiority. It has a normative connotation. The families who refer to their own circle of families as 'old', though not necessarily all their individual members, regulate their conduct so that it stands out from that of others. They fashion their behaviour in accordance with a distinguishing code which they have in common. Black sheep may occur among them. But the families as such are expected to disapprove of them, perhaps to cast them out. If not, they may indeed be regarded as decaying, not because of any biological changes, but because of their inability to keep up the higher standards and obligations expected of an 'old family' in their own social cadre and often also in others.

The development of such standards is closely linked to that of the cadre itself. It requires a setting in which families have a chance to transmit distinguishing standards continuously for a number of generations. The chance to transmit such standards on others which though quite specific in their character may vary within a fairly narrow range from society to society. The transmission of distinguishing standards usually goes hand in hand with a chance to transmit property of one kind or the other, including offices or skills within the same family from generation to generation. Whatever specific form sociological inheritance may take in such cases, all these chances to transmit have this in common that they represent inheritable chances to exercise power in relation to others which, as a group, have only limited access to, or are excluded from, them. In the last resort old family networks can only develop where groups of families get the chance to transmit from one generation to the other sources of power which they as a group can monopolize to a fairly high degree and from which those who belong to other groups are correspondingly excluded. In many cases, no-one who does not belong to the circle of the monopoly holders can enter it without their consent. And as some form of monopoly is the source and condition of their continued distinction over the generations as a group of 'old families', they can continue to exist as such only as long as they have power to preserve it.

For a very long time groups of families could only acquire the sociological quality of 'oldness' if they rose above the lower orders who had no or little property to transmit. The 'village' of Winston Parva seems to indicate that property is no longer as essential a condition of sociological 'oldness' as it used to be. Old peasant families based on the inheritance of land have of course been known in the past; so have old craftsmen families whose 'oldness' was based on the monopolized transmission of special skills. 'Old' working-class families appear to be characteristic of our own age. Whether they are a freak or an omen remains to be seen. Because sociological oldness in their case is not noticeably connected with inheritance of property certain other conditions of power which are normally to be found in other cases too, but which in other cases are less conspicuous, stand out more clearly in their case, particularly the power derived from the monopolization of key positions in local institutions, from greater cohesion and solidarity, from greater uniformity and elaboration of norms and beliefs and from the greater discipline, external and internal, which went with them. Greater cohesion, solidarity, uniformity of norms and self-discipline helped to maintain monopolization, and this in turn helped to reinforce these group characteristics. Thus the continued chance of 'old groups' to stand out; their successful claim to a higher social status than that of other interdependent social formations and the satisfactions derived from them, go hand in hand with specific differences in the personality structure which play their part, positive or negative as the case may be, in the perpetuation of an old families' network.

That, in fact, is a general feature of 'old families': they stand out from others by certain distinguishing behaviour characteristics which are bred into the individual members from childhood on in accordance with the group's distinguishing tradition. Circles of old families usually have a code of conduct which demands, either in specific or in all situations, a higher degree of self-restraint than that usual among inter-dependent groups of lesser status. They may or may not be 'civilized' in the contemporary European sense of the word, but in relation to those over whom they successfully claim status superiority they are as a rule *more* 'civilized' in the factual sense of the word[1]: their code demands a higher level of self-restraint in some or in all respects; it prescribes a more firmly regulated behaviour either all round or in specific situations, which is bound up with greater foresight, greater self-restraint, greater refinement of manners and which is studded with more elaborate taboos. The relationship between firmly-established clusters of 'old families' and those who do not 'belong' to them, like many other relationships between higher and lower status groups, is often marked by a descending gradient of self-restraint; on the ladder of a civilizing process the higher social formation usually takes up a position a few rungs above their own lower social formations. Relatively stricter morals are only one form of socially induced self-restraints among many others. Better manners are another. They all enhance the chances of a superior group to assert and to maintain their power and superiority. In an appropriate configuration civilizing differentials can be an important factor in the making and perpetuation of power differentials, although in extreme cases it may weaken 'old' powerful groups to be more civilized and may contribute to their downfall.

In a relatively stable setting a more articulate code of behaviour and a higher degree of self-restraint are usually associated with a higher degree of orderliness, circumspection, foresight and group cohesion. It offers status- and power-rewards in compensation for the frustration of restraints and the relative loss of spontaneity. Shared taboos, the distinguishing restraints, strengthen the bonds within the network of 'better families'. Adherence to the common code serves their members as a social badge. It strengthens the feeling of belonging together in relation to 'inferiors' who tend to show less restraint in situations in which the 'superiors' demand it. 'Inferior' people are apt to break taboos which the 'superior' people have been trained to observe from childhood on. Breaches of such taboos are thus signs of social inferiority. They offend, often very deeply, the 'superior' people's sense of good taste, of propriety, of morals, in short their sense of emotionally rooted values. They arouse in 'superior' groups, according to circumstances, anger, hostility, disgust or contempt and, while adherence to the same code facilitates communications, breaches create barriers.

Thus people who belong to a circle of 'old families' are provided by their common code with specific emotional bonds: underlying all their differences is a certain unity of sensibilities. In that respect they know where they stand with each other and what to expect of each other, as one often says, 'instinctively' better than they know where they stand with outsiders and what to expect of them. Moreover, in a network of 'old families' people usually know who they are socially speaking. That in the last resort is what 'old' means with reference to families; it means families who are known in their locality and who are known to each other for a number of generations; it means that those who belong to an 'old family' not only have parents, grandparents and great-grandparents like everybody else, but that parents, grandparents and great-grandparents are known in their community, in their own social cadre and that they are known, by and large, as people of good standing who adhere to the established social code of that cadre.

Thus, while on the face of it 'old' may appear as an attribute of an individual family, in fact it is an attribute of a network of families, of a social formation within which men, women and their offspring in the socially regulated order of descent to which we refer as 'family' can be known to each other for several generations as in some way distinguished, as living up to certain shared standards in contradistinction to others. 'Old families' in that sense never form singly; they always come in clusters or groups as networks of families with their own internal status hierarchy and usually with a high rate of inter-marriage, as neighbourhoods, 'Societies' with a capital S, patriciates, Royals and in many other forms. In this, as in other cases, the structure of families is dependent on that of specific social groups. Except as a remnant of a social cadre which has disappeared, an 'old family' cannot exist singly; it can only form in specific social situations as correlate of a specific social formation together with others of its kind.

That 'old families' are known to each other and have strong ties with each other, however, does not mean that they necessarily like each other. It is only in relation to outsiders that they tend to stand together. Among themselves they may, and almost invariably do, compete, mildly or wildly according to circumstances, and may, often by tradition, heartily dislike or even hate one another. Familiarity produced by close acquaintance over several generations, intimacy born from a long sequel of common group experiences, gives to their relationships specific qualities which are as compatible with liking as with disliking each other. Whichever it is, they exclude outsiders. A good deal of common family lore is floating in the air of every circle of 'old families' enriched by each generation as it comes and goes. Like other aspects of the common tradition it creates an intimacy—even between people who dislike each other—which newcomers cannot share.

'Oldness' in a sociological sense thus refers to social relationships with properties of their own. They give a peculiar flavour to enmities and to friendships. They tend to produce a marked exclusivity of sentiment, if not of attitude, a preference for people with the same sensibilities as oneself strengthening the common front against outsiders. Although individual members may turn away and may even turn against the group, the intimate familiarity of several generations gives to such 'old' groups for a while a degree of cohesion which other less 'old' groups lack. Born from a common history that is remembered it forms another strong element in the configuration of chances thay have to assert and to maintain for a while their superior power and status in relation to other groups. Without their power the claim to a higher status and a specific charisma would soon decay and sound hollow whatever the distinctiveness of their behaviour. Rejecting gossip, freezing-out techniques, 'prejudice' and 'discrimination' would soon lose their edge; and so would any other of the manifold weapons used to protect their superior status and their distinction.

Thus, concentrated in the form of a model, the configuration found at Winston Parva in miniature shows more clearly its implications for a wider field. The task is not to praise and to blame; it is rather to help towards a better understanding and a better explanation of the interdependencies which trapped two groups of people in Winston Parva in a configuration not of their own making and which produced specific tensions and conflicts between them. The tensions did not arise because one side was wicked or overbearing and the other was not. They were inherent in the pattern which they formed with each other. If one had asked the 'villagers' they would probably have said they did not want an Estate at their doorstep, and if one had asked the Estate people they would probably have said they would rather not settle near an older neighbourhood such as the 'village'. Once they were thrown together they were trapped in a conflict situation which none of them could control and which one has to understand as such if one wants to do better in other similar cases. The 'villagers' naturally behaved to the newcomers as they were used to behave to deviants in their own neighbourhood. The immigrants on their part quite innocently behaved in their new place of residence in the manner which appeared natural to them. They were not aware of the existence of an established order with its power differentials and an entrenched position of the core group of leading families in the older part. Most of them did not understand at all why the older residents treated them with contempt and kept them at a distance. But the role of a lower status group in which they were placed and the indiscriminate discrimination against all people who settled on the Estate must have early discouraged any attempt to establish closer contacts with the older groups. Both sides acted in that situation without much reflection in a manner which one might have foreseen. Simply by becoming interdependent as neighbours they were thrust into an antagonistic position without quite understanding what was happening to them and most certainly without any fault of their own.

This, as has already been said, was a small-scale conflict not untypical of processes of industrialization. If one looks at the world at large one cannot fail to notice many configurations of a similar kind though they are often classified under different headings. Broad trends in the development of contemporary societies appear to lead to situations such as this with increasing frequency. Differences between sociologically 'old' and 'new' groups can be found today in many parts of the world. They are, if one may use this word, normal differences in an age in which people can travel with their belongings from one place to another more cheaply under more comfortable conditions at greater speed over wider distances than ever before, and can earn a living in many places apart from that where they have been born. One can discover variants of the same basic configuration, encounters between groups of newcomers, immigrants, foreigners and groups of old residents all over the world. The social problems created by these migratory aspects of social mobility, though varying in details, have a certain family similarity. One may be inclined to fasten attention first on the differences. In studies of specific cases they always seem to stand out more clearly. One often hesitates to envisage the relation of specific episodes such as that which formed the subject matter of this study to the overall development of societies in modern times. One is more used to perceive the questions connected with them as a multitude of local social problems than as a sociological problem. The migratory aspects of social mobility are an example. Sometimes they are simply conceived as geographical aspects. All that happens it seems is that people move physically from one place to another. In reality, they always move from one social group to another. They always have to establish new relationships with already existing groups. They have to get used to the role of newcomers who seek entry into, or are forced into interdependence with, groups with already established traditions of their own and have to cope with the specific problems of their new role. Often enough they are cast in the role of outsiders in relation to the established and more powerful groups whose standards, beliefs, sensibilities and manners are different from theirs.

If the migrants have different skin colour and other hereditary physical characteristics different from those of the older residents, the problems created by their own neighbourhood formations and by their relations with the inhabitants of older neighbourhoods are usually discussed under the heading 'racial problems'. If the newcomers are of the same 'race' but have different language and different national traditions, the problems with which they and the older residents are confronted are classified as problems of 'ethnic minorities'. If social newcomers are neither of a different 'race', nor of a different 'ethnic group', but merely of a different 'social class', the problems of social mobility are discussed as 'class problems', and, often enough, as problems of 'social mobility' in a narrower sense of the word. There is no ready-made label which one can attach to the problems that arose in the microcosm of Winston Parva because there the newcomers and the old residents, at least in the 'village', were neither of a different 'race', nor, with one or two exceptions, of different 'ethnic descent' or of a different 'social class'. But some of the basic problems arising from the encounter of established and outsider groups in Winston Parva were not very different from those which one can observe in similar encounters elsewhere, though they are often studied and conceptualized under different headings.

In all these cases the newcomers are bent on improving their position and the established groups are bent on maintaining theirs. The newcomers resent, and often try to rise from, the inferior status attributed to them and the established try to preserve their superior status which the newcomers appear to threaten. The newcomers cast in the role of outsiders are perceived by the established as people 'who do not know their place'; they offend the sensibilities of the established by behaving in a manner which bears in their eyes clearly the stigma of social inferiority, and yet, in many cases, newcomer groups quite innocently are apt to behave, at least for a time, as if they were the equals of their new neighbours. The latter show the flag; they fight for their superiority, their status and power, their standards and beliefs, and they use in that situation almost everywhere the same weapons, among them humiliating gossip, stigmatizing beliefs about the whole group modelled on observations of its worst section, degrading code words and, as far as possible, exclusion from all chances of power—in short, the features which one usually abstracts from the configuration in which they occur under headings such as 'prejudice' and 'discrimination'. As the established are usually more highly integrated and, in general, more powerful, they are able by mutual induction and ostracism of doubters to give a very strong backing to their beliefs. They can often enough induce even the outsiders to accept an image of themselves which is modelled on a 'minority of the worst' and an image of the established which is modelled on a 'minority of the best', which is an emotional generalization from the few to the whole. They can often impose on newcomers the belief that they are not only inferior in power but inferior by 'nature' to the established group. And this internalization by the socially inferior group of the disparaging belief of the superior group as part of their own conscience and self-image powerfully reinforces the superiority and the rule of the established group.

Moreover, the members of the established group and perhaps the newcomers too have been brought up often enough, as most people have today, with specific rigidities of outlook and conduct; they have often been brought up in the belief that everyone does, or ought to, feel and behave in essentials, as they themselves feel and behave. In all likelihood they have not been prepared for the problems that arise when newcomers encounter old residents who feel and behave differently and who react negatively to their own modes of behaviour. They have not been prepared, in short, for the social problems of a world with steadily heightened social mobility, but rather for a past age in which opportunities for social mobility in the wider sense of the word were less rich. By and large, the threshold of tolerance for forms of behaviour and belief which are different from one's own, if one has to live with their representatives in close contact, is still exceedingly low. It seems to correspond to social conditions under which most people were likely to live for the whole of their lives within their native group, and were less often exposed to a shock, such as that which the 'villagers' experienced, to the shock of a lasting interdependence with people of a different cast.

The situation is to some extent reflected in current sociological approaches to such problems. They, too, are perhaps more appropriate to these previous stages of social development. They are often strongly coloured by the implied assumption that 'stable' or 'immobile' communities are the normal, the desirable types of community, and others embodying a high degree of social mobility are abnormal and undesirable. Not a few of the current sociological concepts are fashioned as if the nearest approximation to the most normal, most desirable form of social life were some imaginary pre-industrial villages: there, it seems, people lived with a high degree of cohesion and stability, were fully adjusted, well integrated and as a result enjoyed a high degree of happiness and contentment. Industrialization, urbanization and similar processes, with the heightened mobility, the heightened tempo of life they brought about, seem to have changed that happy state. Confronted with the difficulties of a highly mobile and quickly changing world one is apt to seek refuge in the image of a social order which never changes and projects it into a past that never was. The current concept of adjustment itself, with its implied postulate of an unchanging, stable, balanced, integrated and cohesive social order to which one can adjust, seems a little out of place in twentieth-century societies which are rapidly changing and are anything but stable; it appears itself as a symptom of an intellectual maladjustment. Empirical investigations such as those in 'village' and Estate, may perhaps help, in time, towards the emergence of a more realistic picture. The former represents a more, the latter a less, cohesive type of community. Both, as one can see, have their specific difficulties and drawbacks.

NOTES

[1] N. Elias, *Über den Prozess der Zivilisation*, Basle 1939, vol. II, p. 163.

PART II

The Sociology of
Rural British Communities

CHAPTER 5

The Sociology of Rural British Communities

INTRODUCTION

For Tönnies, the archetypal *Gemeinschaft* community was the rural village—'the *Gemeinschaft* is stronger there and more alive.'[1] It is this identification of a particular system of social relationships with a particular geographical locale that has been his most enduring, and some would say misleading, bequest to the sociology of the community. This is not to say, however, that Tönnies was making any radical departure from prevailing nineteenth century views on the nature of community. If community was the good life, then, in the reaction to industrialization, it was also closely identified with the rural village. To an increasingly urbanized population, the deprivations of the towns and cities were altogether more manifest than those of the rural areas and as romantic visions of the countryside flourished, the rural village was increasingly viewed as man's *natural* habitat. To an apparently endless array of nineteenth century intellectuals the spiritual needs of man could only be satisfied in a rural environment where contact could be made with *real* values.[2] Meanwhile, those who actually lived in the countryside amply showed their preference by voting with their feet and moving *to* the towns. Nevertheless, as community became identified with the good life, community was also seen as essentially rural.

The pervasiveness of this theme in sociology is illustrated by Hillery in his attempt to achieve some co-ordination of the various extant definitions of community.[3] Of the ninety-four definitions which he analyzed, he distinguished two major categories—'generic' communities and 'rural' communities—though this was somewhat illogical —the former is a conceptual category, the latter substantive—Hillery believed that this was necessary due to the prevalence of conjoining community with a specifically rural environment. Such a tendency has also continued at a more theoretical level. Derivations of Tönnies' 'linked antithesis' of *Gemeinschaft* and *Gesellschaft* have appeared in such typological schemes as the folk-urban[4] and rural-urban continuum.[5] These schemes have tended to reinforce the value judgements underlying Tönnies' characterization of rural communities. In particular, they have led to an exaggeration of the degree of continuity in most rural communities—'*Gemeinschaft is old; Gesellschaft is new* as a name as well as a phenomenon'[6]—since these schemes have not only been used as classificatory devices, but as theories of social change. Since the folk, rural or *Gemeinschaft* end of the continuum has been conceptualized as the starting-point of the change, any remaining communities with its characteristics have tended to be viewed as static, unchanging entities. Moreover, if any processes of change are seen to be at work in these communities, the only way in which they can be accommodated into such a scheme is to view them as a potentially hostile threat to a stable and unchanging way of life. Hence, a pervading theme of many rural studies is the necessity to record a dying culture before it succumbs to encroaching influences from outside.

As far as the British rural studies are concerned, these tendencies have been strengthened by the historical development of community studies as a branch of sociology in this country. The influence of social anthropology, and in particular the classical structural functionalism of Malinowski and Radcliffe-Brown, is most marked in the early rural studies. This led to the assertion that rural communities *were* static social systems, rather than merely treating them as such for the heuristic benefits of such a model. The typically holistic approach of anthropologists to the study of social systems also led to a search for well-integrated, relatively isolated 'closed' communities for the objects of their studies. Hence the rural British studies by no means include a representative sample of rural British communities: there is a marked preponderance of communities in the Highland Zone in the north and west, where relations in agriculture are those of kinship rather than class, whilst rural communities in the lowland areas of the south and east, where capitalist rather than family farming is the norm remain relatively unexplored.

These early tendencies in the study of rural communities are illustrated by two of the following selections. Arensberg and Kimball's study of County Clare has been regarded as a pioneering work,[7] but it was in fact an extension of previously worked-out anthropological techniques to a new geographical area. Both had worked under Lloyd Warner in the Yankee City studies[8] and in the early 1930's work began 'to place rural Southern Ireland on the roster'.[9] They were quite explicit about their approach: 'Experience in Yankee City in New England had led the authors to the point of view which is the central hypothesis of functional anthropology. The more they worked, the more it grew certain to them that to a certain approximation it is useful to regard society as an integrated system of mutually interrelated and functionally interdependent parts. A study in Ireland, then, should be a study to test this hypothesis.'[10] Though the study of subsistence farmers in the rural areas of Western Ireland hardly seems a suitable test of a hypothesis concerning 'society', they admirably succeed in, to use a term they employ elsewhere, 'getting to grips with the social and psychological facts in the raw'[11] and no short extract can do justice to their mass of quantitative and qualitative data. Nevertheless, their theoretical perspective undoubtedly influenced what they 'saw' and their rather arcadian view of the way of life of the Irish peasantry appears to be derived in some measure from the dictates of their 'master system'.

Rees' study of Llanfihangel yng Ngwynfa,[12] a rural parish in Northern Montgomeryshire, was much more of a pioneering community study in the sense that it started almost completely from scratch, with little or no *a priori* theoretical framework for the data. This is not to say, however, that Rees had no preconceptions at all: Rees clearly saw Llanfihangel as a stable rural (Welsh), community threatened by urban (English) influences.[13] It was one of Rees' students, W. M. Williams, who carried out a study of Gosforth in Cumberland between 1948 and 1951. The main emphasis of Williams study is his analysis of the local status system, using methods not dissimilar to Warner's in Yankee City—there is, therefore, a structural-functional perspective to the study that lends emphasis to the features of continuity in the community. In addition, as a graduate student in a geography department, Williams had used Fox's *Personality of Britain*, which on the evidence of archaeological remains had argued that there had been a continuity of cultures in the Highland Zone. Continuity and stability were therefore exaggerated in the study of Gosforth, as Williams himself was later to acknowledge. The result, as in earlier rural studies, was an essentially *Gemeinschaft* view of social relationships in the village.

Most rural community studies deal with status divisions—which typically presuppose some form of evaluative consensus in the community—rather than class relations. Hired labour is in any case the exception rather than the rule in upland farming areas, where the size of farms and the type of agriculture (mainly stock-rearing) enable the bulk of the work to be carried out by the farmer and his family. Hence, until a study of a lowland rural community appears, Littlejohn's study of Westrigg, an upland parish in the Cheviot hills, must remain unique in that it considers class relations within agriculture. For this reason, Westrigg does not fit easily into any rural-urban continuum; the degree of competition and covert conflict in Westrigg appears to approximate more closely to *Gesellschaft* than *Gemeinschaft*, despite the rural locale. It is also important to point out that the farm workers in Westrigg are for the most part highly-skilled stockmen whose above-average market situation was reinforced at the time of the study by post-war labour shortages. In lowland, arable areas, where the labour force is less skilled and where the number of farms in the local labour market is fewer, apparently harmonious class relations may be preserved by the powerlessness of the subordinate group to challenge them. Certainly the tone of emancipation that runs through Littlejohn's work has not remained unquestioned among farm workers in subsequent years.

It was when Williams came to study the Devon parish of Ashworthy that he discovered that his data could not be squeezed into a static equilibrium model. His recantation, reprinted below, coming at the same time as the publication of Westrigg, marked an important new departure in the study of rural British communities and opened the way for the breakdown of the simplistic *Gemeinschaft* approach. Unfortunately, the challenge has never really been taken up (this coinciding with a general hiatus in British community studies) and only Nalson's study of an upland parish in North Staffordshire[14] has attempted to outline some of the underlying complexities of social relationships in a predominantly agricultural locality. His study is not, for some reason, usually regarded as being in the mainstream of British community studies. Nalson is primarily concerned with continuity and the 'mobility of farm families' and this theme is taken up in the final paper of this section by Hilary Hammond, in which she reappraises the work of Arensberg and Kimball and Williams. It is a salutary warning to future fieldworkers of the variable validity of informants' information even in the apparently relatively simplified social structure of isolated rural communities.

NOTES

1 Tönnies, F., *Community and Society*, Harper Torchbook edition (New York: Harper and Row, 1963), p. 35. See also p. 8 above.

2 Brief surveys of this theme in the British literary and philosophical tradition include Peterson, W., 'The Ideological Origins of Britain's New Towns', *American Institute of Planners Journal*, XXXIV, 1968, pp. 160–170 and Williams, R., 'Literature and Rural Society', *The Listener*, November 11th, 1967. For the United States see Schmitt, P. J., *Back to Nature: The Arcadian Myth in Urban America* (New York and London: Oxford University Press, 1969).

3 Hillery, G. A., 'Definitions of Community: Areas of Agreement', *Rural Sociology*, vol. 20, 1955.

4 See Redfield, R., 'The Folk Society', *American Journal of Sociology*, vol. 52, 1947, pp. 293–308.

5 See Sorokin, P. A., and Zimmerman, C. C., *Principles of Rural-Urban Sociology* (New York: Henry Holt and Co. 1929; Kraus reprint, 1969); also Frankenberg, R., *Communities in Britain* (Harmondsworth: Penguin Books, 1966).

6 Tönnies, J., op. cit., p. 34.
7 Notably by Frankenberg, R., op. cit. and in his 'British Community Studies: Problems of Synthesis' in Banton, M. (ed.), *The Social Anthropology of Complex Societies*, A.S.A. Monograph No. 4 (London: Tavistock Publications, 1966).
8 See below pp. 259–292.
9 Arensberg, C. A., and Kimball, S. T., 'Family and Community in Ireland', Second Edition (Cambridge, Mass.: Harvard University Press, 1968), p. xxv.
10 Ibid., p. xxx.
11 Arensberg, C. A., and Kimball, S. T., *Community and Culture* (New York: Harcourt Brace and World, 1967), p. 30.
12 Rees, A. D., *Life in a Welsh Countryside* (Cardiff: University of Wales Press, 1950).
13 See ibid., p. 170.
14 Nalson, J. S., *Mobility of Farm Families* (Manchester: Manchester University Press, 1968).

CHAPTER 6

Continuity and Equilibrium in County Clare*

Conrad Arensberg and Solon Kimball

The small farmers' family groups inhabit the holdings or plots of land from which they make the livelihood. Except in a few and special cases, there is no physical separation of house plot from fields; the individual family's plot is usually a continuous one, and the other forms of settlement present in Ireland are rapidly being reshaped with that condition as the ideal. Consequently, the farmhouse is most often, though not always, a comparatively isolated house standing upon its own ground and forming an integral part of the holding. In it the farm family group spends its entire life, sleeping, eating, giving birth and dying there, and sallying forth every day for work upon the fields.

Work round and inside the house is continuous and varies very little from day to day and season to season. It involves a continuous activity by which the household group orders its life and fulfils its needs of nourishment and shelter in the midst of a carefully patterned regularity of habitual behaviours. What variation there is in the accepted pattern is itself confined to narrow range. Certain chores indispensable in the day-to-day habits of the people are divided among days of the week. One woman informant, a small farmer's wife in Inagh, gave as her weekly round a much more rigid daily division of tasks than is actually to be observed. On Monday she did the washing, on Tuesday the ironing, on Thursday she made butter, on Friday she went to market, on Saturday she got ready for Sunday, and on Sunday she went to mass and did as little as she could. Really, however, it is only on Sunday that there comes any serious alteration in the daily round.

Work in the land beyond the haggard and the house is less restricted and more varied. It has a greater range of activity over the farm and over the round of the year. Coupled with such greater variety, there is also a greater freedom of choice among necessary tasks. The necessities imposed by soil and climate permit a wider range of action

* Reprinted by permission from *Family and Community in Ireland*, second edition, Harvard University Press, Cambridge, Mass., 1968, pp. 31, 39–44, 299–304.

and a less narrowly repetitive routine than do the ordered regularities of a household.

Yet within the greater range of activity there is still a constant and nearly invariant pattern of work. The progression of the seasons brings a recurrent demand upon the farmer in the care of beasts, crops and the land itself. Each season brings a task which must be performed, begun, or ended if the farmer is to raise his produce successfully. Similarly, the custom and rivalry of the community exert a further restriction upon his activity. He works within the influence of a long established tradition of ancestral experience which has established for him the best dates for planting, for reaping, for breeding cattle, and for most of the tasks of his yearly round. The community holds that tradition in common, and the farmer is caught in the midst of a mesh of rivalries, competitions, and gossip in praise and condemnation, which binds him the more strongly to the accepted patterning of his yearly activity.

The seasonal rhythm of farm work reaches its lowest pitch in winter. Activity is confined to house and haggard. On bitter wet days little can be done beyond the haggard wall, but within it there is always a variety of necessary tasks involving care of farm machinery, implements and buildings, and the housing and feeding of the cattle who cannot be driven to graze in the open field. In the house there is much that can be done. Harness can be patched, boots fitted with new soles, plates and spikes, furniture repaired and occasionally new pieces made.

These tasks fall to the males of the household, the farmer father and his grown or adolescent sons. Any discussion of the annual round of farm work necessarily describes their labours, for all the tasks not strictly connected with the household fall in their province. We shall have occasion later to examine fully the sexual dichotomy of labour such a division of tasks represents.

For the countryman the Christmas season, from the beginning of Advent to Epiphany or 'Little Christmas' (January 6), is the dead of winter. It is a period in which all farm work is at a standstill. The farmer has completed the last of his harvest and brought in the last of his potatoes from the field. The cattle are securely housed against the winter cold. The farmer feels himself free to sit round the house during the cold wet days and devote his season to holiday. The working day is at its shortest. Outside, the weather is usually unsettled, a cold rain falling on the sodden fields. It is for him as though the course of the year had stopped and were waiting, gathering its forces for the new year.

It is a period of great social activity in the local community. The very important religious ceremonies of the season call forth an intensified activity in the parish. There are constant visits back and forth; each house is ready to offer its hospitality to its neighbours; and the community gives itself over to dances, cards, talk and calls. Not until the religious season closes with Epiphany does the countryman feel that the year begins anew.

With the beginning of the year, the cold uncertain weather with its succession of bitter wet days, leaving the fields too wet to work, does not end, but the Christmas season has marked the transition. The farmer must now make his plans for the spring planting, lay in his seed, repair machinery, and make ready for the season about to begin. On drier days he can busy himself in the field in cleaning ditches and drainages. In the evenings much of the conversation on visits and at home revolves round the coming planting, and both new and traditional experience with types, varieties, growth cycles, yields and care of seeds and cattle passes round by word of mouth.

The first of February, St. Brigid's Day, marks the beginning of spring. For the countryman the return of the 'hard' days of wind and clear weather herald the season of the land's drying off. Through February and March the gardens must be prepared, potatoes planted, and the fields made ready for the return of the cattle to them. Each hard day is a welcome opportunity, for only then can work in the fields go on. With favourable weather, the work of preparation is over in the beginning of March, and the actual planting begins. By St. Patrick's Day, with its promise of continuous hard weather, the gardens are ready for a second planting.

The potatoes demand the greatest attention. A fortnight after they are planted, they must be manured well with manure brought from the pile near the cattle cabins, and the ground must be levelled so that the plant will not go to stalk and thus fail to produce tubers. A fortnight more and the ground must be 'softened' and the earth round the plant, which now shows its first leaves, must be 'stirred.' By the time May is reached, the potatoes must be 'landed'. Earth must be taken from between the long ridges in which the potatoes are planted and heaped up over them from each side. Thereafter nothing remains until the harvest but a summer spraying against blight.

Throughout the spring the cattle have demanded attention. March and April see the birth of calves and the beginning of the milk season and intensified butter-making. The great spring cattle fairs take place. The farmer must devote himself to the all-important business of buying and selling his milch and store cattle and his calves. At home the cattle demand constant care against hunger, disease, and cold as he mixes their diet of fast diminishing hay with the slowly returning pasture grass.

The farmer's work in the gardens does not end with the 'landing of the potatoes'. Mangels and turnips and whatever grains he may grow must be planted, the soil prepared for them, and the growing crop weeded and tended. With the planting of the turnips, the last crop to be 'put down', often as late as early June, his planting season is over.

With the return of warm weather and the drying off of the land, Irish summer begins. May is the first summer month. And by early May the bogs are dry enough to allow turf cutting to begin. The farmer must ordinarily find time between plantings to cut his year's supply of fuel and stack it into 'reeks' to dry under the summer warmth. The turf cutting, though not connected with growing plants or animals, is an indispensable farm activity and takes its place among the never varying tasks of the agricultural round.

Once the turf is cut and stacked, the fruits of the farmer's labour begin to appear. His first crop is cabbage which was planted in a small garden near the house at odd free times during the early spring. Cabbage is practically the only green vegetable of the small farm diet, and the old people remember 'Hungry July' or July *an chabáiste* when a delayed potato crop might condemn them to a month or more of semistarvation in which cabbage was the only food. Today new varieties of potatoes have been introduced which mature as early as late June.

The mature potatoes mark no harvest. They are left in the ground to be turned out of the ridges with spade or plough as occasion for them demands. Not until late November will the last of them be dug up.

The first true harvest and the most important one of the year is the haymaking. The cutting of hay begins in late July or early August. It is not only the most important activity of the year, insuring a year-long supply of fodder for the farm animals and the income-producing cattle, but it is also one that calls forth the united efforts of the whole family. It is a race, too, against time and rainy weather, and every effort must be bent to mow, rake, and let dry, and stack the meadow grasses, first in small haycocks, then in a great hayrick in the haggard, before rain brings rot to the lush crop. The farmers well speak of the harvest as 'saving the hay'.

No sooner is the hay saved than the corn crops demand attention. Rye and oats are ready for the scythe or the mowing machine (only the larger farmers have reapers) by late August. The farmer and his sons must bind it, stack it, and leave it for several days drying. Later they will return to the fields and cart it back to the haggard for threshing. Not long ago the flail was still the most frequent means of threshing among the small farmers. In recent years steam-powered threshing machines make the rounds, and threshing, which under the older system seems to have taken place as need arose for the grain, takes place now more regularly in late September and early October.

With the bringing in of the corn, the agricultural year draws to a close. Through October and November turnips and mangels are ready to be 'pulled' and stored in the fields, near at hand to the haggard, in straw- and earth-covered pits. The potatoes which remain in the ridges must be turned up with spade and plough and similarly stored for the winter. All the root crops are indispensable supplies for men and animals during the months to come when there is no grass. The winter's supply of turf must be brought to the haggard from the reeks alongside of the bogs, where it has been drying for the summer. The carting is an intermittent labour, performed by the men at odd times when they are free of other duties. As winter comes with November cold and rain, the cattle must be housed and made ready for the long, dark days of no grass to come; and the farmer is busy with them acquiring and disposing of his stock, as he was in the spring, for the autumn fairs bring him an important market.

If he has been fortunate and industrious, nothing remains for him to do but to prepare his fields for the next year. The soil he has used for root crops must be turned, and the gardens which he intends for grain are ploughed. As he follows the furrows, he can look back upon a year ended, and forward to another to begin. By the time his ploughing is finished, the dead of winter and the holiday season of Christmas is upon him and the yearly round is over.

Yet it is over only to repeat itself. For within the range of the seasonal variation and the demands of growing and maturing crops and animals the pattern of farm work in haggard, garden, meadow and field is a constant one. Much the same progression of labour flows along year after year, and follows the farmer from boyhood till death. Yet there is much less restriction in choice of operation to be performed, in movement over space, in the possibility of day-to-day variation than in the case of the work of the household.

*   *   *

Enough has been said already to demonstrate the conclusion to which the study of rural behaviour and social organization in the communities of the small farmers leads. The sociological conditions of Irish rural life are those determined in a system of relationships among persons based upon the Irish form of the family, family subsistence, and familistic custom. The demographical indices of population cannot be understood except in such a context.

Each topic of local life and custom, and each statistical index, as we have examined it, has led us back into this nucleus of organization

among the small farmers. Something in the course of events prescribed there by the habitual arrangement of human lives existing in
the small farmers' homes and communities has always lain behind
the form of custom and the kind of attitude we have encountered.
Something in that course of events has always likewise lain behind the
numerical indices demographic count has yielded the census-taker.

This something is of the nature of an interdependent variable. The
Irish small farmers of the present day behave as they do in the matters
in which we have investigated them because they are members of a
social system of a certain kind. A system implies a state of equilibrium
in which elements are in mutual dependence. If change is introduced
at one point, change follows at another. If the first change is not too
great—that is, if it is not so great that destruction of the system
ensues[1]—then subsequent changes do not alter the situation out of
recognition. Far from it, since the elements are woven into a common
whole, the effect of the change is soon dissipated. The system reverts
to its former state. It may be said to have thus an equilibrium which
it regains after each disturbance.

The doctrine of mutual dependence within a system helps us far
more in understanding the events of life among the country people of
Ireland than any ascription of cause and effect. The sorts of behaviour
we have dealt with do not have a single cause. They must be referred
to a setting which must be looked at as a whole. Likewise the historical, economic, or personal events which impinge upon the country
people of our communities do not ever succeed in changing very
much either the people or what is really coterminous with them, their
pattern of life. The traditional custom of life persists and continues to
wield its power in essentially similar fashion decade after decade and
generation after generation. Change goes on, in plenty, but it is
gradual change of outlines already existing. It is no new departure.

Yet that custom operates always within a framework of relations
uniting the same persons by various paths in space and having various
histories in time. On each farm and among most of the farms of each
area one cares to describe, these relations have certain uniformities.
They turn up over and over again, and the course of events which
they follow repeats itself in essentially similar fashion over and over.
Circumstances alter cases, but not very far. Custom is not to be
separated from this framework. The followers of customary behaviour
are those related in uniform fashion through the recurrence of similar
events.

We are now ready, therefore, to make a summary and tentative
definition of the communities and families of the Irish countryside.
The definition is also an interpretation of the behaviour of the persons concerned. It is also, too, an explanation of the events of human

life in which they take part. And lastly, it is a social psychology of the country people.

In the discussion of each topic, the outlines of such a summary have become clearer and clearer. New events and new patterns of action fell into place as we drew their connection with old ones. Recapitulating this progress, let us take a step toward putting these connections in an abstract and general form. The sociology of the Irish rural life and small-farm subsistence is largely a matter of the anatomy of two institutions of characteristic form. These are the family and the rural community. The latter, in turn, cannot be described apart from the former. It is a framework of long-term customary relationships uniting persons beyond their family ties. Together these two unite essentially all the persons of the rural areas. With a few other institutions not here described (not, however, autonomous as are family and community), such as the parish (the formal, hierarchic community of religious belief and observance), they make up the entire anatomy of the small-farm class, the largest in the land.

Taking these two alone, however, what can we say of this framework of relationships upon which custom moves? It is a master system articulating five major subsidiary systems. These five comprise:

1. *The relationships of the familistic order.* These are the pattern of family life and subsistence, and its extension in kinship reckoning, obligation and cooperation. They undergo periodic re-formation at the match and effect the dispersal of emigrants and the continuity of the pattern of farm subsistence.

2. *The relationships of age grading, or generation.* These are uniform habitual relations of persons of locally subsistent families who are similar and dissimilar in age. For each person we can trace them to specific events on interaction patterned by custom and compatible with the behaviour of familism. In the large, they make up a structure of cliques or age groups, usually of persons of similar sex. Such cliques are opposed to one another, yet integrated under the headship of one of them, that of the heads of families, the so-called 'old men'. They are characterized by activities of discussion, gossip and recreation, and make for common and long-established values and opinions, and membership in them bestows certain status, limited, however, by family status.

3. *The relationships of sex organization.* These are relations among persons, similarly the growth of habitual conduct, uniting the same persons of locally subsistent families who are similar and dissimilar by sex. They make up an organization of behaviour canalizing the sexual drives in the direction of family life and forming a common attitude toward sexual behaviour and a common norm of conduct

and standard of sexual morality. This organization is compatible with that of familism and that of age grading and may be said to reinforce both. It also is capable of providing a standard for differentiating farmers from others.

4. *The relationships of local division of labour.* These are still other relations, similarly formed among the same persons, uniting those of similar and different occupation and technical skill. These involve action dealing with goods and services of practical value to the farmers and their subsistence. They fit the persons of a locality into two categories of relationship, depending upon those persons' association with other local persons on the one hand and their connections with persons beyond local ken on the other. The customary behaviour marking the relations of the first of these categories duplicates that of familism in many ways and affords status similar to that found in age organization. The behaviour marking the relations of the second of these categories does not. It is in this latter case only that class difference makes its appearance in the country districts. Those of higher class than the farmer, in his own community, are those who have connections extending beyond the range of his associates.

5. *The relationships of economic exchange and distribution in fairs and markets.* Finally there are still further relations among these persons, uniting them over space among themselves and with others from outside the local area in effecting the transfer of farm produce outward and the distribution of non-local goods and services inward. These relations are habitual, customary and in many cases ceremonial, as in the fairs. They represent a form of organization reflecting familism, age, sex and local technical organization.

These five classes of relationships summarize the incidents, biographies, and events that are here observed and described. They are a classification of them that has explanatory force. They do not themselves explain every event. But they point out to us, as does any faithful map, where we must look. All together they make up a configuration of social patterns, set off and different from others in Ireland. All together as a system, they determine events in the countryside. No event can be understood without reference to them. No sociological or demographical index can be interpreted without them.

This master system is the framework of social life in the countryside. It is the form of the social network in which the greater part of the Irish population are points. It is the system of forces in which any doing of the small farmers, or anything done to them, is a movement, a change of direction, an impact either from within or without.

If a view of the conditions which administrators or legislators of any institution, governmental or private, might wish to attack is to be realistic and adequate, it must take this master system into account. It must be wide enough to allow for its existence. It is not enough to plan an attack as a unilateral action from above. One must know and assess the place in the system into which an action might fit. It is not enough to institute an agency of reform or take an economic measure or put into effect regulatory devices on the basis of a single limited purpose or a single simple diagnosis. The equilibrium of the system must not be forgotten. If it is forgotten, disaster will not follow, in the ordinary case. The social organism is very tough and can stand a great deal of rough handling. But failure of the measure will follow. If the measure is merely a wishful effort, a sop to constituents, a gesture of good will, or an act of ritual or propaganda, its failure is no matter. But, if it is a sincere attempt at changing conditions, for whatever purpose or desire, its failure will be all the more perplexing. Today, in all civilized countries, conscious efforts at social change are being made. Complexity is too great and problems too pressing to continue to rely as of old upon the traditional tools of politics: intuition, compromise, and a flair for practicalities. Great centralized bureaucracies have grown up in each country, even in one so small as Ireland. If they are to be effective, they must know the societies they serve. For them an understanding of local scenes and local social organisms, so remote from bureaucratic headquarters and national capitals, becomes more and more essential.

NOTES

1 For a discussion of the theory of the equilibrium of a social system, the reader is referred to *The Social Theory of Pareto*, by L. J. Henderson (Cambridge, Mass.: Harvard University Press, 1936).

CHAPTER 7

Class Relations in a Rural Parish: Westrigg*

James Littlejohn

There are no tenant farmers in Westrigg. Of the fourteen farms ten are occupied by the owner, while four are 'led', i.e. the owner resides elsewhere and the farm is in the charge of a manager. Sizes are as follows:

Farm	Acreage	Farm	Acreage
A	6,600	H	1,609
B	6,024	I	1,104
C	5,368	J	1,023
D	4,710	K	1,000
E	2,176	L	710
F	1,877	M	600
G	1,815	N	454

The number of permanent employees per farm varies from eleven to one. Most of the farmers say they could employ more than they have and at periods of heavy work or in the course of improvement projects such as large-scale drain digging it is normal to hire extra casual labour. The main income is from sheep: several farmers have a secondary income from fattening hill cattle and from time to time a farmer may sell a small surplus crop of some kind. Formerly the farmer's wife made an income from eggs, from which she was expected to buy the groceries for the family. Some of the wives still make a small income in this way though whether it is spent on family groceries is doubtful. The techniques and implements used are in general use throughout the country and present no distinctive features: all the farms in varying degrees use tractors, trucks, modern threshing machines, etc.

Each farm is a productive unit on its own, a business from which the farmer tries to make a profit. There is little co-operation in work

* Reprinted by permission of Routledge and Kegan Paul Ltd from *Westrigg: The Sociology of a Cheviot Parish* by J. Littlejohn, London 1963, pp. 27–36 and by permission of Humanities Press Inc., New York, for the same extract.

among them. The occasions which give rise to most are sheep clipping and threshing. Small farms seek help oftener than large ones. Help at threshing is required on farms which do not have a modern threshing machine and which hire one from the Department of Agriculture. As they are expensive to hire farmers like to get the job done in one day and invite help from anyone who can spare the time—anyone from any farm provided his own employer permits him. No payment is given but the farmer feeds everyone present. The larger farms in the parish no longer seek outside help for clipping but a few of them regularly have it offered from one or two of the small farms, because the latter do need outside help, and get it in this way. Two farms hire outside help from the Forestry. Two pairs cooperate at clipping. It is interesting to note that this latter instance of mutual aid which has sprung up since the disappearance of the clipping band follows class lines, one pair being of lower middle class farmers, the other of upper middle.

It is clear that there is much less mutual aid than among the farmers of Ireland described by Arensberg and those of Wales described by Rees.[1] Since in these other communities farms are very much smaller and small farms in Westrigg seek help oftener than large ones, it may seem that size of farm explains the difference This is not altogether the case, for in those other communities the farms are family farms and kinship bonds among the families are numerous. Co-operation among them is less of an economic necessity than an affirmation of kinship bonds. The Irish countryman explains his act of mutual aid 'as part of the traditional reciprocation of sentiment and duty which makes up his system of kinship'.[2] Rees shows that assistance is part of the relationship of kinsfolk and neighbours. There are no kinship ties among the farmers of Westrigg.

In addition however there is a less tangible factor accounting for the situation in Westrigg for it is held that a man, any man, should be as independent as possible from other people (as regards business and work). This was clearly expressed in many discussions I had with workmen about smallholdings. While they all thought that in general smallholdings were a 'good idea' they objected to them on the score that they were too small to be self-sufficient. As one said: 'A farm has to be big enough so that you have everything on it. It's no use if you've always to be beholden to your neighbour. It's no use if he has a horse and you haven't and you have to run to him for a loan of it. If your neighbour starts ploughing then it's time you were ploughing too'.

This spirit is not simply due to the lack of kinship ties among the farming population; it is a positive outlook reflecting the relation between farms, for farmers, and to a lesser extent their men with them, stand in a relationship of rivalry to each other. The farmers do not farm on a subsistence basis, as seems to be the case where the family farm predominates. If the farmer can get enough money from annual profits he buys a larger farm, or another one to leave in charge of a manager, or sets up his sons on farms, or sometimes he buys a town house and retires.

It seems that below a certain size (which could only be determined by specific research) farms have to be worked on a subsistence basis. Where this is the case the family farm is the basic economic unit and any community of such farms will be characterized by numerous kinship ties and by a high value placed on neighbourliness. In such a community mutual aid will be the norm. Above this size farms become business enterprises. A community of such farms is not characterized by kinship ties among farmers, who compete with each other in the market; among them mutual aid is uncommon. (I must add that though farmers in Westrigg compete with each other they are in no sense hostile to each other, and never refuse a request for assistance from a neighbour. The point is that such requests are rare.)

The farms competing with each other in selling lambs, wool and tups are of course much more numerous than the fourteen farms in Westrigg, and a study of such competition belongs to economics. More important for this analysis is that among farmers in any one locality competition takes on the aspect of rivalry for reputation.[3] Reputation as a good stocksman is valued in itself and also gives the farmer an advantage in another area of competition, viz. for good labour.

That esteem as a stocksman is highly valued by farmers is soon clear on moving amongst them. Open boasting or denigration of rivals is rarely indulged in but they are keenly interested in the quality of each other's stock, constantly talking about it and eagerly noting improvements and deterioration in relative quality. The signs of this are the prices got for lambs and tups in the market and to a lesser extent prizes won at fairs and shows. (Farmers distinguish sharply between 'a good show beast' and beasts good for work and breeding. The two may coincide.) In most farmhouses photos of costly or prize winning animals hang on the wall, sometimes along with photos of the forebears of the farmer. One farmer was quite explicit on the matter, saying in the course of a conversation on local political office that it didn't matter much as he supposed that most farmers like himself wanted most to win a reputation as a good stocksman. Another sometimes used to boast to me a little in the maudlin stage of a drinking session, e.g. '. . . the top of the tree, that's it . . . mind you, you get no thanks for being at the top of the tree, oh no . . . people are jealous . . . just a lot of abuse. But I never mind them . . . I've

been at the top of the tree for fifty years now and I've had my day . . .
The name of (my farm) has always stood for the best. The top of the
tree . . .'

In wanting to be at the top of the tree farmers are not thinking
solely of the financial returns this position brings. If farmers were
interested only in the amount of money they made, and accorded
reputation on this basis, obviously, those with bigger farms would
always have a bigger reputation than those with smaller. This is not
the case. The owner of the smallest farm in Westrigg is widely esteemed as a breeder of tups and is listened to with respect on the
subject in any company.

Interest in reputation is most clearly seen in the matter of breeding
tups. The majority breed and sell tups at the annual tup fair held in
Craigton. It lasts two days and is spoken of as 'the highlight of the
year'. On the first day the beasts are exhibited and three prizes
awarded: the following day they are sold by public auction. The
excitement and interest the fair arouses can be judged by the amount
of ceremony accompanying it.

About three weeks beforehand farmers start visiting each other
and inviting visits to 'view the tups'. This they do in the evenings
dressed in clean non-working clothes. The animals are penned and
visitors and host regard them closely sometimes for several hours
pointing out their good points and discussing tups in general. If a
visitor shows marked interest in one the host may ask the party in for
a drink.

During this period dressing the tups becomes the most important
job of the shepherd put in charge of them, or of the farmer himself.
Dressing means deftly and fastidiously clipping the fleece in such a
way (I was told) as to hide the animal's bad points and show off its
good ones to the best advantage. Several hours a day are spent thus,
sometimes a whole day at a stretch, with the farmer often standing
by watching if he is not doing it himself. The evening before the show
the tups have their faces washed then painted white; the fleece is
usually lightly sprinkled with sheep-dip to give it a yellow bloom. The
decoration is repeated the evening after the show so that they will be
looking their best at the sale the next day.

At the show, attended by thousands of farmers and shepherds the
excitement is intense, the atmosphere like that of a big football match.
The reputation to be won is no mere parish wonder: the most cele-
brated of the Westrigg stocksmen, for example, sells tups to farmers
in several of the dominions. Ribands are pinned on the prizewinning animals. The victors celebrate according to temperament.
One year the first prize was won by a Westrigg man normally a temperate fellow, but that afternoon he was seen dancing gleefully at the

smiddy with his friend the blacksmith. The children on prizewinning farms sometimes turn up at school with the ribands, to the chagrin of the others.

At the sale the next day excitement is equally high. When an animal sells for a sum in the region of £1,000 people say that there must have been a conspiracy between the seller and his friends, whereby they keep up the bidding (for each of their entries) and later exchange money to equalize gains and losses. When it is pointed out that not much money is likely to be made in this way people reply that it's not money the conspirators want but the 'name'. The names become widely known as accounts of the show and sale are broadcast and printed in the national newspapers.

Rivalry within friendship is always difficult. Sometimes a farmer buys a friend's tup at the sale 'just for friendship', then gives his shepherd instructions to keep the beast locked up in a shed to ensure that it never breeds with his own stock. It will be sold at some lesser sale next year.

The men who work in the fields are under close supervision by the farmer whether or not he works alongside them. Normally they assemble in the steading every morning to be given orders about the day's work. The shepherds are in a different position, especially those on outlying hirstles: one, for example, reckons that he sees his farmer only about four times a year. Each shepherd is entirely responsible for his hirstle and guards his independence. Several remarked that if the farmer came 'nosing' round their hirstles they would leave as that would imply lack of trust. All the shepherds speak of 'my hirstle'. Farmers rarely nose, acknowledging that a shepherd who did not know his job better than the farmer does would not be worth employing. The shepherd is left very much to himself and so important is his moral character and skill for the efficient running of a sheep farm that all farmers say that the most decisive control they have over the process is 'hiring the right herd'. On certain occasions the shepherds on one farm co-operate, particularly at clipping, dipping sortings and inoculations—about thirty days a year.

The shepherd's independence and responsibility is recognized in the higher wages he gets. It is probably also evident in membership of the Agricultural Workers Union. Though I was not able to check records, I was told that other agricultural workers are more enthusiastic supporters of the union than are the shepherds. However the union includes shepherds; like other unions it represents the interests of its occupational categories in opposition to those of their employers. Farmers openly express hostility to the union but at the same time often congratulate themselves that their relationship to their men is more harmonious than is the case in most industries. The truth in this latter view is considered below. For the moment, the existence of the workers' union and farmers' hostility to it indicates the opposition between farmer and farm worker.

Workmen often express the opposition openly, e.g. a shepherd noted for his skill and conscientiousness—'Farmers are mean you know. They're always good at finding excuses for not paying you more than the minimum wage.' Another shepherd—'There isn't a meaner lot than farmers.' An agricultural worker referring to farmers' complaints that men do not work hard enough now—'they've only themselves to blame. Before the war they made us work hard enough for them.' This latter is a common theme in workers' discussions on farmers—'. . . it's not so bad now but before the war you daren't say a word or out you'd go, and you had to take what wages they offered or they told you if you weren't satisfied there were plenty others who would be.'

All the workers agree that farmers have to be a bit more careful how they treat workers now that their own position *vis-à-vis* farmers has improved since the war. The latter correspondingly think their position has worsened. Their most frequent complaint is that workmen do not work so hard and are less amenable to control, mainly, farmers think, because there are not enough of them; some occasionally remark that the best thing that could happen to the countryside would be large scale unemployment in the towns, then there would be plenty of cheap labour, etc.

The opposition between the two became more openly expressed when the public hall was declared too dangerous for dancing in and parishioners decided to build a new one. Workmen started grumbling that farmers were rich enough to donate the necessary sum and ought to do so 'because they make it out of us' as one said. One, when his farmer remarked that he had heard that the hall was unsafe replied: 'And if there's not another built soon there'll be nobody in Westrigg to work for the farms.' Everyone knew that this was a hint that if farmers didn't provide the money their labour difficulties would be increased by men leaving the parish for more attractive places. Farmers were fully aware of workmen's attitudes and made remarks like this: 'These people want everything done for them. We don't use the hall, it's only they who do. If they want a hall they should raise the money.'

The opposition between the two is also apparent from the fact that farmers all have theories about the best techniques for getting the men to work harder. 'The great thing', says one, 'is not to give the impression you are ordering them. The great thing is to do it as if you were asking them.' 'I think if you work with the men and show an interest in what they are doing they will work too', says another. A young farmer once contrasted in mime the position of his father and himself with regard to the men. He imitated his father stepping out the door in the morning, twisting his moustache and snorting, 'then there wasn't a workman to be seen. They had all fled to the fields and were working like slaves. You and I can't do that' (turning to another farmer) 'they don't take any notice of us.'

Despite opposition between the two categories, workmen and farmers often work harmoniously together. To understand this relations between the men must be clarified.

RIVALRY AMONG THE MEN

Rivalry between the men on one farm is not much in evidence but is apparent between men of different farms and especially among shepherds. Interest in reputation is as keen among shepherds as among farmers. The standards by which they are judged are known to everyone and there is consensus both among farmers and shepherds as to the efficiency of shepherds in the parish. This was clear from judgements made in the course of conversation and also from a grading of shepherds on a three point scale which two shepherds and two farmers did for me. Their ratings agreed exactly.

A good shepherd is one who can control his dogs and so move the sheep without fuss, who can spot sickness in the flock before it becomes dangerous, who consistently does his hill round, who can shear neatly and in general who cares for his flock. One sign of a good shepherd is his being a 'good kenner', i.e. he can recognize each animal in his flock individually. Considering that a flock may be as many as 500, that every year one-sixth are sold and lambs retained to replace them, this is no mean feat. The most convincing sign is if, on taking a new job, the market price of lambs on his hirstle goes up relative to the others. As his work is thus publicly inspected and judged the shepherd becomes known and his reputation spreads. Even the way a shepherd moves his animals round the ring at the auction mart tells his peers whether or not he is a good craftsman.

Shepherds on the same farm do not allow each other to 'trespass' on each other's hirstles. This they sometimes explain on the grounds of jealousy. At any rate they are quite clear about the rivalry among them, often using sporting metaphors to talk about it as for example one who pointed to a neighbour's hirstle while doing the hill round and exclaimed, 'there's the bugger who beat me in the League Table last year'. (His neighbour's lambs got top price, his own second top.) Rivalry in efficiency in one of their main skills has become institutionalized through sheepdog trials, a popular entertainment in country towns and at agricultural shows. At these, shepherds (and those farmers who have learned the art) compete before an audience and judges in skilful handling of dogs. The trials are of varying importance culminating in an International Sheepdog Trial with competitors from Scotland, England and Wales. The best became known to shepherds in all three countries.

The other workers are less publicly acclaimed in this sheep rearing country. Even in Westrigg, however, the relative efficiency of the other workers is noted and experts whether in herding or other work get the regard of their fellows, are listened to and asked for advice and are usually popular at social gatherings. On a large farm it is one of the experts who is given the coveted job of preparing the tups for the fair. Even workmen who are politically antagonistic to bosses and interpret the esteem given a good workman as a trick that employers have somehow played on workmen still desire the respect accorded good workmen. One noted Socialist used to grumble that 'a good workman's the character of a horse', yet, as a noted craftsman, always took it upon himself energetically to direct the more difficult operations of the labour team.

Reputation as a good workman enables a man to get the best jobs (however he may define them). One year a new shepherd came to X farm and on his hirstle there was an extra good crop of lambs. He was very excited before the sale and said: 'This sale means a lot to me 'cos the lambs'll get a good price. Then the farmers'll start asking each other "who's herding at X now" and I'll get a name. Then I'll be able to pick the jobs I want.' The importance of this for relations between farmers and men is that a good job is defined as either a shepherd manager's or as a job on a farm run by a good farmer.

The preference for work with an efficient farmer is openly stated for these reasons: (i) that work is easier under a good farmer; (ii) that it is impossible to acquire a name for oneself under a poor farmer. The preference is not merely a matter of talk but is shown in the fact that men stay longer in the employ of a good farmer than a poor one. One of the most highly esteemed farmers is said by his men to be 'The meanest man in the parish'—yet they stay with him. A rival speaks of him thus: 'I can't understand these men. There's X (the highly esteemed farmer), he never pays his men a ha'penny more than the minimum yet they stay with him a lifetime.' The point is admitted by officials of the Farmers' Union: in a discussion on the present shortage of agricultural labour one remarked that it was difficult to estimate the real extent of the shortage since on the whole it was the more inefficient farmers who complained most about it.

Good workmen and good farmers tend to seek each other out; each helps to build the reputation of the other and on those farms on which the two are found each respects the other's skill. By virtue of the bond of mutual respect the efficient farmer and the efficient work-man work harmoniously together. This personal bond endures along with the opposition between the two administrative categories 'farmer' and 'agricultural worker'. It is because the latter are abstract administrative categories whose opposition is fought out on a national level that on any one farm work relations can be harmonious.

NOTES

1 C. Arensberg, *The Irish Countryman*, New York, 1950, p. 67. A. D. Rees, op. cit. chapter VIII.
2 C. Arensberg, op. cit., p. 67.
3 This characteristic of British farmers has long been noted. See, e.g. J. Caird, *The Landed Interest*, London, 1880, p. 58, where, speaking of tenant farmers he notes, 'Many of them are men of liberal education, and some of these are found in most parishes and in every county. A spirit of emulation exists among them, elicited by county, provincial and national exhibitions of agricultural stock, and by a natural desire, in a country where everything is open to comment, not to be behind their neighbour in the neatness, style, and success of their cultivation, or in the symmetry and condition of their live-stock.'

CHAPTER 8

Dynamic Equilibrium in Ashworthy*

W. M. Williams

'Ashworthy' is a pseudonym for a small rural community in the West Country. It is not, however, in any sense a *typical* rural community; such a vague entity does not exist. This study is of one small area with its own special features: the generality of the conclusions which have been reached can only be tested by similar studies elsewhere.

The initial aim of the research was to examine the effects of rural depopulation as a process on the structure of family and kinship within one small rural area. General studies had been made of rural depopulation, notably John Saville's *Rural Depopulation in England and Wales 1851–1951*,[1] but almost nothing was known of its social effects in detail. In this respect the study was intended to break new ground. However, as the field work progressed, new and clearly important problems emerged which, while related to the original theme of the investigation, made it necessary to re-examine the basic orientation and underlying assumptions of the study and this led in turn to a complete re-appraisal of existing rural community studies in Britain.

Before I went to Ashworthy my view of English rural social structure was based partly on the experience gained in studying Gosforth, a parish in Cumberland[2] and in making a survey of rural craftsmen on a regional scale,[3] and partly on the small number of published studies of rural communities in Great Britain and Western Europe. Both my own and these other studies portray rural society as conservative, traditional, resistant to outside pressures and above all slow to change. It is in short a stable social system. In Wales, for example, it is said that in the rural way of life:

> Much of what is distinctive is an inheritance from the pastoral and tribal past. . . . Viewed from without, the old social life displays a remarkable tenacity, and, in spite of the spread of machine-made goods, recreation and entertainment are still almost entirely home produced.[4]

* Reprinted by permission of Routledge and Kegan Paul Ltd. from *A West Country Village: Ashworthy* by W. M. Williams, London, 1963, pp. xiii–xx and by permission of Humanities Press Inc., New York, for the same extract.

In a more recent study of four Welsh rural communities we are told that (in a Montgomeryshire parish)

Even though the district is less isolated today than it was a generation or two ago—the railway came here in 1868—much of the peasant way of life has been retained'; while in the Llŷn peninsula the 'survival of ancient loyalties may serve as a token to express the unbroken unity of the area from very early times on to the present day. . . .'[5]

In the same way, C. M. Arensberg's classic study of County Clare stresses the conservatism of rural Eire:

When I first came to Luogh I knew only that in this remote little community of small farmers I should find something of the old tradition still alive.

We have followed the countryman a long way . . . He is part of an intricate social system which patterns his life along definite channels, which brings him rewards, gives him incentives, and deals its own punishments. The traditional patterns of old custom have a place in this system; folklore surrounds it as in the dichotomy between men's and women's work. But tradition is not all its secret; it is a living structure with a balance and a growth of its own.[6]

In the western Isles of Scotland:

The significance of Island life—not so much for the past, which cannot be changed, as for the future which can—lies in the intensity of its communal traditions, extinguished elsewhere.

Comprehension of this break-up of community brings out the value of the enduring elements of communal life still recorded, remembered and surviving in the 'Outermost' Hebrides, at the core of 'the North and West'.[7]

The same point of view can be seen in studies of rural communities in England and in continental Western Europe:

Closed This type of society is by far the most common in the area (i.e. in the west of England). There appears to be no disharmony within the society, but harmony is maintained by mechanisms which exclude external influences. Such societies present a compact impenetrable front behind which life is carried on in well-defined grooves. The mechanisms whereby it is effected vary, however, from locality to locality.[8]

It would be misleading to say that rural England has undergone no social change at all, but it is nevertheless true that over a long period of years change has been slow, and has failed to alter the essential social structure. . . . In other words, speaking generally, we may say that rural society has been characterized by a low degree of social change whilst modern urban society has undergone a high degree of social change.[9]

Side by side with, and perhaps in part due to, the oneness of the village form, there has grown up amongst village people a sense of belonging to the village and to each other as a community. This has taken many centuries to develop and has grown out of the dependence of village inhabitants on the village for the various services necessary and/or desirable in their season. The sense of community has persisted in spite of present-day forces, the majority of which are antagonistic to its creation or preservation.[10]

Hence Château-Gérard is still very really Gallia Belgica et Romana, is even yet a village under the crusading monks while it is being drawn more and more into the money market of Seraing steel.

The long continuity of Château-Gérard's culture is undoubtedly pushing it ahead, while the possibilities inherent in ancient Walloon metallurgy can be thought of as projecting into the beyond and constituting a pull from the future.[11]

These short extracts reveal a common orientation; their authors may be well aware that social and economic change does take place in the countryside, but they regard it as modifying a way of life which is tenaciously stable. Many (if not all) of them appear to accept a view of country life as fighting a stubborn rearguard action against antagonistic external forces, perhaps urban in origin. This dichotomy, first elaborated by Ferdinand Tönnies,[12] is still found in studies which are explicitly concerned with social, economic and technological change in rural areas. There is a strange reluctance to abandon the notion of the unchanging, traditional countryside:

There are still people who believe that the farmer—perhaps it would be better to say the peasant—should continue to live his quiet life on his farm in his village community, as little touched as possible by the outside 'urban' world. He should try to maintain the old social structure and organization of his neighbourhood and his village. In this way the traditional values of rural life and rural culture in general, as opposed to the urban culture, would be kept alive, and preserved for posterity. The number of those who take this point of view is diminishing, but it would be wrong to underestimate their influence in some countries.[13]

Le progrés rapide et incessant vient de pénétrer la vie des campagnes françaises qu'il est en voie de transformer radicalement. Certes, l'apparente stabilité des sociétés paysannes traditionelles n'interdisait pas toute innovation; . . . mais il s'agissait toujours d'un progrès lent; ces transformations suivaient la méthode empirique, faite d'essais et d'erreurs, d'échecs et de réussites. . . . Les différents aspects du conflit entre les exigences d'un progrès technique continu et des structures datant d'un époque de relative stabilité représentent un champ d'études nombreuses et variées pour toutes les sciences sociales.[14]

Indeed, in some Mediterranean countries the traditional peasant way of life is often attributed with virtues that are important to the well-being of the nation, and agricultural reform is designed deliberately to foster and preserve them.[15]

Seen from this point of view, an examination of the effects of rural depopulation on the life of Ashworthy would be in terms of the decline of a traditional social system. However, during the field work and in the period of analysis which followed, it became more and more evident that Ashworthy was not a stable community of the kind I had expected. Moreover, a re-examination of my own field material on Gosforth and the published studies by Rees, Arensberg and others suggested that rural life is characterized by conditions of 'dynamic equilibrium', i.e. that while the social structure *as a whole* appears relatively unchanged and unchanging in the absence of external stimuli, within it constant and irregular changes are in fact taking place. Country life, as exemplified by Ashworthy, is subject to piece-meal changes, is constantly in a state of internal adjustment between one part and another. This is a much less neat and tidy concept than the orthodox 'Gemeinschaft' view of rural social structure.

Once this general approach had been formulated and the evidence roughly assembled, the central problem was seen to be the maintenance of equilibrium. In other words, how is continuity of social life achieved within such an 'unstable' framework? This led in turn to considering the nature of this framework, which was seen to be ecological. The social and economic life of Ashworthy has always been based on the land, which families have farmed for centuries. Family farming has persisted from one generation to another, so that a balance has been maintained between people and land—but in conditions where individual families die out, split up, move from one farm to another: where people leave the parish and others enter; where the ownership and occupation of land has changed constantly; where farms are split up, amalgamated, or alter their shape.

This view of Ashworthy as a dynamic ecological system has two important consequences. First, it makes it virtually impossible to use the results of the very considerable study of urban social life, characterized by the analysis of rapid change, since—in Britain at least—it pays little or no regard to the environment.[16] Secondly, it has very largely determined the form of this study and in particular the emphasis which has been given to the land, its occupation, use and ownership. Sociological studies of rural areas in this country and elsewhere have paid far too little attention to analysing in detail the *spatial* relationships of social and economic change. The first Part of this study documents these relationships in the context of family farming; the second Part is largely devoted to the original aim of the research, i.e the effects of demographic change on the structure of family and kinship within one small community In accordance with the general orientation outlined above, rural de-population is regarded as one of the processes of change within an ecological system. It is merely one aspect of the dynamics of rural life.

This concern with the spatial and environmental aspects of the social structure of Ashworthy has also led to re-appraising existing 'community studies' from another point of view The notion of a rural community as a social isolate has become progressively abandoned in recent years as the importance of relationships with 'the outside world' has been realized.[17] However, the geography of these relationships has been very largely neglected in spite of its significance to the notion of a community and its 'social field'. In this study a preliminary analysis has been made of some aspects of this problem, which shows that it is often extremely difficult to separate the social and economic life of Ashworthy from that of the parishes which surround it.

NOTES

1 Dartington Hall Studies in Rural Sociology (London 1957).
2 *The Sociology of An English Village: Gosforth* (London 1956).
3 *The Country Craftsman*, Dartington Hall Studies in Rural Sociology (London 1958).
4 Alwyn D. Rees, *Life in a Welsh Countryside* (Cardiff 1960), pp. 162 and 168.
5 Elwyn Davies and Alwyn D. Rees (Eds.), *Welsh Rural Communities* (Cardiff 1960), pp. 176 and 187. Glan-llyn, the Montgomeryshire parish, was studied by Trefor M. Owen, and Aberdaron in the Llŷn peninsula by T. Jones Hughes.
6 *The Irish Countryman* (London 1937), pp. 22 and 69–70.
7 Arthur Geddes, *The Isle of Lewis and Harris* (Edinburgh 1955), pp. 14 and 22.
8 G. Duncan Mitchell, 'Depopulation and Rural Social Structure', *Sociological Review*, vol. XLII (1950), p. 81.
9 G. Duncan Mitchell, 'The Relevance of Group Dynamics to Rural Planning Problems', *Sociological Review*, vol. XLIII (1951), p. 5.
10 H. E. Bracey, *English Rural Life* (London 1959), p. 24.
11 H. H. Turney-High, *Château-Gérard. The Life and Times of a Walloon Village* (Columbia, South Carolina 1953), pp. 279 and 281.
12 In *Gemeinschaft und Gessellschaft* (Second Edition, Berlin 1912). This book was first published in 1887.
13 E. W. Hofstee, 'Rural Social Organization'. Presidential address to the Second Congress of the European Society for Rural Sociology, in *Changing Patterns of Rural Organization* (Oslo 1961), p. 18.
14 H. Mendras, *Les Paysans et la Modernisation de l'Agriculture* (Paris 1958), p. 7.
15 See, for example, the various publications of *Servicio de Concentracion Parcelaria, Instituto de Estudios Agro-Sociales* and *Instituto Nacional de Colonizacion* (for Spain) and of SVIMEZ (for Italy).
16 With some rare exceptions, for example, Terence Morris, *The Criminal Area* (London 1958). For ecological studies of urban societies in general, see George A. Theodorson (Ed.), *Studies in Human Ecology* (Evanston, Ill. 1961), where their status within the general field of social science is fully discussed.
17 This is clearly demonstrated in the various contributions to *Changing Patterns of Rural Organization*, which gives a conspectus of recent trends in West European rural sociology. See, for example, the paper by Dr. H. Morgen on West Germany, pp. 83–92.

CHAPTER 9

Continuity and Conscious Models in County Clare and Ashworthy: A Reappraisal*

Hilary Hammond

INTRODUCTION

In a graphic exposition Arensberg (1937) has described the pattern of inheritance of the farmstead in the communities of County Clare, Ireland. The heir to the farm inherits before his father's death. There is a lineal and exclusive pattern of inheritance whereby the old man 'makes over' the farm to his son at the time of the son's marriage. Marriage is crucial to the pattern of the replacement of the generations in the household, for the dowry, which the old man receives, enables him to dower at least one daughter and to compensate those sons who do not inherit and who must 'travel'. The old couple then retire to the 'west room' and the heir takes over the running of the farm, succeeding to a position of authority in the household. Continuity in County Clare is inseparable from 'keeping the name on the land'. In order to ensure continuity on the name of the land children are greatly desired. As one childless woman lamented: 'The man wants children just as much as the woman. He is afraid others will tell him he's no good if he hasn't any. Children are the curse of the country, especially if you haven't got any.'

If a man has no immediate lineal heir then ideally the name must be kept on the land by 'bringing in' a member of the kindred. Arensberg refers to such expediencies as 'makeshift devices'.

In 1963 Williams questioned the validity of the model of continuity which Arensberg had described for County Clare. In the course of a study of a West Country village, Ashworthy, Williams states:

> ... this relatively simple model is by no means entirely convincing. For example, Arensberg's striking and lucid exposition of the crucial importance of 'the name on the land' is not borne out by the great majority of his examples, which show the land passing out of the control of the elementary family. The devices he describes as 'makeshift' appear, indeed, to be a very common, *perhaps an essential*, means of achieving

* Reprinted by permission of The Clarendon Press from *Sociology*, vol. 2, 1, 1968, pp. 21–28.

continuity. Since County Clare is an area of small farms, most of which are unable to support a 'full' family of parents and children, and since the families are conjugal units, which we have seen to be an imperfect means of ensuring a succession, it seems very likely that the relationship between family and land is much more complex than that described by Arensberg.

(Williams 1963:56).

Is the questioning of Arensberg's 'relatively simple model' valid? On what basis may it be put to the test?

In approaching these questions I shall firstly review the conceptual and methodological problems. This necessitates some consideration of the different kinds of models, for it is my contention that Williams and Arensberg not only have to deal with differing communities, but that they are concerned with different levels of social reality. Secondly, I shall review the empirical data in order to contribute further substantive material.

CONSCIOUS MODELS AND DEMOGRAPHIC MODELS

When the people of County Clare express the ideal of 'keeping the name on the land' they are expressing a 'conscious model' of continuity. It will be instructive to review briefly the work of Lévi-Strauss who writes:

> A second distinction has to do with the conscious or unconscious character of the models. . . .
> A structural model may be conscious or unconscious without this difference affecting its nature. It can only be said that when the structure of a certain type of phenomena does not lie at a great depth, it is more likely that some kind of model, standing as a screen to hide it, will exist in the collective consciousness. For conscious models, which are usually *known as 'norms', are by definition very poor ones, since they are not intended to explain the phenomena but to perpetuate them.*

On the other hand, he writes in the following paragraph:

> From the point of view of the degree of consciousness the anthro-pologist is confronted with two kinds of situations. He may have to construct a model from phenomena the systematic character of which has evoked no awareness on the part of the culture; this is the kind of simpler situation referred to by Boas as providing the easiest ground for anthropological research. Or else the anthropologist will be dealing on the one hand with raw phenomena and on the other with models already constructed by the culture to interpret the former. Though it is likely that, for the reasons stated above, these models will be unsatisfactory, *it is by no means necessary that this should always be the case. . . . Thus one cannot dispense with studying a culture's 'home made' models for two*

reasons. First, these models might prove to be accurate or, at least, to provide some insight into the structure of the phenomena; after all, each culture has its own theoreticians whose contributions deserve the same attention as that which the anthropologist gives to colleagues.

(Lévi-Strauss, 1963:291—emphasis added)

These two quotations are rich in content. In the first Lévi-Strauss initially states that conscious models 'which are more usually known as "norms" . . . *are not intended to explain the phenomena but to perpetuate them*'. In the second quotation he states, in apparent contradiction, that 'these models might prove to be accurate . . . after all, each culture has its own theoreticians whose contributions deserve the same attention as that which the anthropologist gives to colleagues'. Thus it would appear to be necessary to differentiate between those conscious models which may be referred to as norms or ideals and which secure perpetuity, and, secondly, those which explain the phenomena under study, and which may be referred to as explanatory conscious models. The suggestion that conscious models may explain the phenomena under study raises many possibilities for further research for it shifts the ability to draw up abstract models to the actors or informants. However, it raises the question as to the *degree* of sociological self-awareness contained in the differing conscious models documented for various communities.

When statistical material is used to indicate the frequency with which norms and ideals are realized, I shall refer to this as a demographic model. There is abundant statistical material in Williams's study of Ashworthy but none in *The Irish Countryman* that is relevant to the problem of continuity. I shall elucidate the relationship between the conscious model and the demographic model in the course of this article. In particular, I shall compare and contrast the relative degree of sociological self-awareness expressed in the conscious models of continuity documented for County Clare and Ashworthy.

HABITATIONAL CONTINUITY IN COUNTY CLARE AND ASHWORTHY

The overruling 'ideological' aspect of continuity in terms of stability of the system in County Clare is that of 'keeping the name on the land'. Landholding is exclusively associated with men; a woman can only (in customary practice), hold the land in trust for a man. In order to keep 'the name on the land', certain 'makeshift devices' are resorted to. These I will list:

(1) The practice of the 'country divorce' whereby a man might send his wife back to her natal home if she proved barren; since according to Catholic law he was unable to marry again, he would

hand over the farm to his brother in return for a 'large fortune' on the understanding that the brother would marry.

(2) Nephews and nieces were 'brought in'. It is difficult to see how a niece could preserve the continuity of the name on the land, although a paternal nephew certainly could do so.

(3) Grandchildren were 'brought in'. A male grandchild could preserve 'the name'.

(4) In the event of widowhood a woman could remain on the farm only if her children were growing up. If she were very young she returned to her father's farm and her husband's brother took over. If she remained on the land and remarried then she, and her new husband, only held the land 'in trust'. The second husband and his children were 'strangers to the land'. We are told the rightful heir by blood, whose 'name is on the land', might turn them out.

In certain cases we hear of a man 'marrying in' to a family with no sons in which case he had to pay a large sum to compensate for the loss of the name on the land. The quintessential point to keep clearly in mind about the total pattern of 'continuity of the name on the land' is that it approximates to the definition Lévi-Strauss gives of the *conscious model*. That is to say, it is a model which serves to perpetuate the social structure. For present purposes it is important to qualify the concept of the conscious model. In the context of County Clare we find that this conscious model serves to secure continuity or perpetuity in two ways. (i) By commitment to the ideal itself, which is buttressed; and (ii) by actual devices which serve to facilitate continuity of the name on the land in a community where *it is not customary to alienate land by sale*. In cases in which we are not presented with these 'devices' (to follow Arensberg's terminology), and where the demographic model contradicts the actors' ideal, then we are dealing with a different category of conscious model.

Having maintained that Arensberg's 'relatively simple' model is by no means entirely convincing', Williams goes on to say Arensberg's 'striking and lucid exposition of the crucial importance of "the name on the land" is not borne out by the great majority of his examples, which show the land passing out of the control of the elementary family'. To assess the validity of this point—which I gather is an 'impression'—I collected together the cases of inheritance recorded in chapters Six and Seven of *Family and Community in Ireland*. It is important to recognize that these cases are recorded to exemplify specific points relating to the conscious model. They cannot be used to deduce the statistical frequency of these 'devices'. However, the cases, in my opinion, do bear out Arensberg's points and substantiate the view that in County Clare 'keeping the name on the land' may be a relatively accurate 'home-made' model.

There are five cases of lineal inheritance—father to son (pp. 116, 139, 142, 143). One case of Country divorce with the farm being handed over to the brother. There is one case of a deceased man's brother taking most of the land of the farm, although the farm had in fact been left to the deceased's wife. 'He paid her nothing for it. He took bits of it here and there until it was all gone. What-ever protest there is, must come from the growing nephews. Inagh makes none' (p. 139). In one case an American emigrant, the male heir, returned and evicted his stepfather (p. 139). There is one case of land passing to a cousin and one case to a nephew (pp. 142, 143). We are not told whether these were maternal or paternal relations. However, it is quite clear from the above cases that the conscious model and the 'devices' which support it do serve to perpetuate the social system, for only one case is given of land being sold.

In Ashworthy the relationship between man and the land is much more complex. Farms are continually changing hands; sale of farms and acquisition through marriage are found side by side with a pattern of acquisition by inheritance. There is an 'agricultural ladder', whereby individuals move to progressively better and larger farms. 'Men have moved steadily from small holding to poor farm until they acquire a good place' (Williams, 1963). The farming community both within the parish and in the area of neighbouring parishes is fairly mobile. Indeed in Ashworthy the sentiments surrounding landholding and farming are very different, and Williams states that continuity is seen to be the handing on of '*a way of life, not a particular tract of land*' (emphasis added). He states: 'In the simplest terms . . . continuity is achieved by each farmer attempting to set up *all his sons* as farmers in their own right'. He goes on to say:

'The average farmer is relatively satisfied with his occupational station, and deserves no better future for his children than that they too should become farmers or farmers wives.' *Now this situation is clearly inconsistent with a social structure based on the principle of keeping land in the hands of the same family from generation to generation, since—if it operates efficiently—there can never be more than a handful of farms available for non-inheriting sons in the course of one generation . . .*

This is in sharp contrast to the peasant societies such as Ireland, where—we are told—the maintenance of the name on the land presupposes that the farm family does not die out and where 'marrying in' or the resort to collateral kindred are 'makeshift' devices used to ensure continuity in exceptional circumstances. In Ashworthy they are not exceptional but rather essential parts of the structure. (Williams, 1963.)

As I indicated in my list of so-called makeshift devices—'marrying in' in County Clare does not ensure 'the continuity of the name on the land', nor do all the devices given to describe resort to collateral kindred. Only males in the patriline can ensure the continuity of the name on the land. Arensberg's use of the term 'makeshift' is unfortunate in the light of my suggestion that these devices reinforce and verify the assumption that 'the continuity of the name on the land' is an accurate conscious model. For far from being 'makeshift' they are integral to the working of the model. For we know that conscious models exist in order to perpetuate the social structure. This aspect of the argument in no way invalidates 'Arensberg's model'. It merely highlights the difference between the type of model Williams and Arensberg, respectively, have documented for two widely different communities. For the quotation cited above—"'The average farmer and etc. . . . '"—clearly expresses that the model that a man should set up all his sons is in Ashworthy an ideal. Continuity within the frame of this ideal pattern is achieved in Ashworthy through 'exploiting the failure of some families to reproduce, or to produce sons', i.e. through denuded families and secondly families dying out. What then is the relationship between the conscious model and the demographic model in the case of Ashworthy?

The number of denuded families has risen sharply since 1851 according to the statistical tables found on pages 218 and 220, 1963. In the light of the small number of denuded families it is difficult to see how the model 'worked' in 1851 and the period preceding this date. Williams has documented 96 cases of direct transmission in the period 1841–1960. In only 4 cases did the farm pass to a person outside the family. At first sight these figures might suggest that keeping the name on the land had some importance in Ashworthy. However, we must recall the other means of acquiring a farm, through sale and purchase, and marriage, and the total pattern of the agricultural ladder. Habitational continuity in Ashworthy, that is to say the change in the personnel in the farmstead, is regulated by two factors; (i) inheritance, and (ii) acquisition of farms by purchase etc. In the same period, between 1841–1960 Williams states that 'many of the farmers of the parish placed their sons on holdings'. He cites 20 cases with the possibility of more. Says Williams 'in contrast evidence of families which have died out or have left farming is relatively abundant'. *Here* we surely need some quantitative evidence? This is crucial to the whole argument for Williams' own model, the observer's model, rests on the assumption that the ideal of handing over a farm to one son and placing the others on farms of their own can only be achieved in a situation where the amount of cultivated land remains more or less fixed, by (a) some families dying out or leaving the land, and (b), by some sons 'marrying in' to farm families where there are only daughters. Since in the period between 1841–1960, a period covering 4 generations, only 20 cases of sons being set up have been recorded, it would appear that the actors 'ideal' itself, as distinct from Williams' model, is not 'entirely convincing' for there is a certain disparity between the 'ideal' and the demographic model. However, in the light of the decreasing number of children per family I do not doubt that in the present generation the conjugal family is an imperfect instrument for ensuring continuity (see Table Four: 1963:221).

I have attempted to expose the conceptual error in Williams' critique of the model Arensberg has recorded, in terms of differing types of conscious model. I would maintain that the 'conscious model' which Arensberg describes could 'work'. Plainly, we are on the threshold of conceptual ambiguity. For I would argue that it is, ideally, the function of the observer's model to bridge the gap between the conscious model and the empirical reality, as represented in the demographic model. This assumes that there is a disparity between the conscious model and the demographic model. In the case of the conscious model described for County Clare there is no need for an observer's model since the conscious model and empirical reality merge. The conscious model, in this case, not only secures perpetuity, it also explains the nature of this continuity.

Some sociologists might question the application of the term 'model' to the ideal of 'keeping the name on the land'. This raises a theoretical problem which requires brief discussion. Earlier, after quoting Lévi-Strauss on conscious models, I drew attention to the possibility that the informants and actors themselves may have a high degree of sociological self-awareness such that they construct abstract models of their own society. Statistical and demographic models must be elaborated to assess the accuracy on conscious models. This raises questions about *the degree* of sociological insight informants have into the working of their own community. In the course of my own fieldwork in which I studied patterns of inheritance in a Hebridean community, it became quite clear that my informants, while expressing the ideal patterns of inheritance, had at the same time an awareness of deviation from the ideals. This awareness derived from the islanders' impression of what I have described as the demographic model. It would appear that while the demographic model as a systematized collection of statistics is exclusive to the research investigator, an impressionistic awareness of the demographic model is present in the minds of the actors. An interesting point is that in certain spheres the informants have 'blind spots' where they seem to be unaware of the deviation from the ideal as expressed in the demographic model.

In the foregoing pages I have suggested that the models of continuity which Arensberg and Williams have elaborated for County Clare and Ashworthy describe different levels of social reality. What do I mean by this statement? Simply that the two 'models' of continuity imply different degrees of sociological insight or self-awareness. The pattern of replacement of personnel in the household in County Clare is coincidental with the pattern of inheritance and the inescapable factor of death. This is not the case in Ashworthy for farms regularly change hands and the pattern of habitational continuity is complicated by the pattern of acquisition brought about by the sale and purchase of farms, and acquisition through marriage. Now this dual aspect of the pattern of habitational continuity in Ashworthy is highly complex and it is to my mind doubtful whether the informants can have an impression of the demographic factors which underly the highly complex pattern of continuity. I believe it may be desirable to distinguish between the conscious model of 'keeping the name on the land' in County Clare and what I shall refer to as a 'goal'. The goal of setting up all the sons of the family in farms of their own in Ashworthy. This goal or ideal does not warrant the usage of the term model, for a sociological awareness *of all the factors* which are necessary to facilitate the pattern of continuity cannot be perceived by the informants. More significantly this goal *does not* and *could not of itself explain* the elaborate pattern of continuity in Ashworthy. It would seem desirable to refer to this as a goal or ideal of continuity in contradistinction to the explanatory conscious model of 'keeping the name on the land' in County Clare.

CONCLUSION

The ideal of 'keeping the name on the land' in County Clare may be considered to be an explanatory conscious model for two reasons: (i) because it secures perpetuity, and (ii) it explains the nature of this continuity. However, I have not been able to demonstrate that it achieves continuity for there is inadequate statistical material in the two monographs devoted to the communities of County Clare.

What are the limiting factors to the degree of sociological self-awareness? Lévi-Strauss has distinguished between two types of conscious model: ideals, and explanatory models. Both secure perpetuity. The models we are presented with in the case of County Clare and Ashworthy recapitulate this distinction. It would seem that the demographic factors affecting social patterns in Ashworthy are so complex that they prevent the actors' elaborating any explanatory model. Moreover, the preoccupation in Ashworthy with social mobility creates a 'blind spot' in the search for sociological self-awareness.

REFERENCES

Arensberg, Conrad M. 1937. *The Irish Countryman*, London: Macmillan.
Arensberg, Conrad M., and Kimball, S. T. 1940. *Family and Community in Ireland*,
    Cambridge, Mass.: Harvard University Press.
Levi-Strauss, Claude. 1963. *Structural Anthropology*, New York: Basic Books Inc.
Williams, W. M. 1963. *A West Country Village: Ashworthy*, London: Routledge
    and Kegan Paul.

PART III

Peasants and Peasant Society in Southern Italy

CHAPTER 10

Peasants and Peasant Society in Southern Italy

INTRODUCTION

The focus of attention in this section is not only a specific geographical area, but also a particular socio-political problem. Many social scientists have been attracted to southern Italy, not (or not only) by the climate and the beauty of the area, but because they have been, in Galtung's words, 'struck, amazed, almost awed by the resistance to change in that pocket of European underdevelopment'.[1] The *Mezzogiorno* has, therefore, been used as a laboratory for the study of a problem whose implications extend far beyond the boundaries of this particular geographical area. In Italy, however, the problem contains an added piquancy due to the juxtaposition within a single state of a thriving industrial economy in the north and an undeveloped, poverty-stricken agricultural economy in the south. Because these studies have centred around a problem rather than an area, there is much less emphasis than in the previous section on British rural community studies on the descriptive ethnography of the locality. Indeed the key social facts are not in dispute—rather, disagreement lies over the interpretation of these facts, differing interpretations having sprung from differing theoretical perspectives.

The extent to which studies of Southern Italy have proliferated is attributable in no small degree to Banfield's provocative study of the community of Montegrano in *The Moral Basis of a Backward Society*. Banfield was clearly attracted to the study of Montegrano by the motives outlined above—in particular, he perceived a paradox in the backwardness of the community and the political apathy of the inhabitants. Because Montegrano was so backward, Banfield also viewed it as an essentially *stable* community. It is this perspective which ermerges most clearly in his monograph and which seems likely to have led to the oversights which have been pointed out by subsequent commentators. Although Banfield's analysis may appear to have suffered at their hands, however, it is important to point out that without Banfield's stimulating arguments some of these investigations may not have been carried out. It has enabled the discussion of some of the theoretical problems concerning the underdevelopment of southern Italy to be advanced to a level not always generated by the study of communities elsewhere.

Banfield's view of the southern Italian peasantry is thrown into relief by Lopreato's study of the village of Franza in *Peasants No More*. Lopreato's approach is more dynamic than Banfield's rather static 'snap-shot' of Montegrano. In particular, Lopreato gives much more consideration to the 'southern question' in Italian history.[2] He argues that a complete understanding of the problems of the southern Italian peasantry can only be achieved by a greater depth of historical analysis than Banfield undertook—in the light of this he argues that Banfield's dismissal of some of the 'usual' explanations of underdevelopment in the *Mezzogiorno* are altogether too cavalier. Of particular importance is the degree of economic exploitation of the peasantry, which over the centuries has eliminated any of the necessary leverage which they might require in order to change the situation from within. Lopreato's study is also dynamic in the sense that he pays greater consideration to changes wrought in the community by the movement of individuals away from it over time. Emigration has, in Lopreato's view, served the function of improving the life-chances of the individual southern Italian peasant while leaving the socio-economic system of the *Mezzogiorno* relatively unchanged.

The function of emigration in maintaining social stability in Southern Italy is also an important theme of Galtung's study of three Sicilian villages in *Members of Two Worlds*. Galtung's study of 'Montagna', 'Collina' and 'Marina' is in many ways a model use of the community study as a method of social investigation. It is, however, an involved analysis, the very complexity of which makes it difficult to appreciate the context of extracts taken from it. A brief outline of Galtung's theoretical framework therefore seems necessary.

Galtung utilizes three concepts in order to understand the social mechanisms underlying the backwardness of Southern Italy. First, he adopts Sorokin's notion of cultural mentality,[3] which is interpreted as a dichotomy of 'ideational' and 'sensate' characteristics. These characteristics determine attitudes towards change—ideational individuals view stability as essential and change as accidental; sensates view change as essential and stability as accidental. Galtung notes that sensates are by no means randomly distributed throughout the population—'. . . the sensates are particularly frequent among the discontented in the periphery and the centre. And these people in the centre should, in principle, have some power; if they would dedicate all their energy to the transformation of their societies according to their own blueprints, then one would expect this to be consequential.'[4] But they do not dedicate themselves to this transformation and this leads Galtung to consider emigration through the use of Lerner's concept of 'psychic mobility.'[5] Like Lopreato, Galtung believes that these individuals who emigrate are primarily those who, if they stayed, would be most active in attempting to change local social conditions. Emigration therefore performs the function of a safety valve in preventing social unrest. Galtung's third theoretical variable is Banfield's amoral familism—part of his critique of Banfield's study is included below. Galtung argues from his own data that familism is related to *behaviour* rather than *attitudes*—in particular that geographical mobility seems to *predispose* for familism.[6] This is the reverse point of view to Banfield who argues that familism causes a lack of community action; for Galtung familism is a *result* of geographical mobility, which also accounts for the lack of community action. Galtung's linking of these three theoretical strands into 'an almost diabolic combination of factors that explains almost too well the absence of endogenous change in the region'[7] is reprinted below.

The final paper in this section is a critique of Banfield's study by John Davis, together with Banfield's reply. The exchange is symptomatic of the extent to which theory and method become interwined in community sociology. Even here, as Davis himself readily admits, the facts which Banfield describes are not disputed—what *is* in dispute is the particular theory which is brought to the data and how it has moulded the data which has emerged. This is an underlying theme of community studies that extends beyond those considered in this section.

NOTES

1 Galtung, J., *Members of Two Worlds* (New York: Columbia University Press, 1971), preface. (Page references below are to typescript edition.)
2 Lopreato, J., *Peasants No More* (San Francisco: Chandler, 1967), ch. 1.
3 See Sorokin, P. A., *Social and Cultural Dynamics* (New York; Amenian Book Co., 1937–1941).
4 Galtung, J., op cit., p. 187.
5 See Lerner, D., *The Passing of Traditional Society*, (Glencoe, Ill., Free Press, 1958).
6 Galtung, J., op cit., p. 247.
7 Ibid, p. 254.

CHAPTER 11

Emigration and Social Change in Southern Italy*

Joseph Lopreato

Until recent decades, the peasant of southern Italy, like peasants elsewhere, had led a traditionally precarious existence within an essentially static economy. Poverty, along with an accompanying isolation from the centres of civilization, resulted in a set of circumstances whereby the peasant had occupied the lowest status in the prestige and power structures of his society, and had received little or none of the social recognition that his toils, tenacity and contributions would merit. The combination of economic poverty and social castigation, in turn, had produced in the peasant a deep sense of deprivation and despair and, in his own group, a system of interpersonal relations based on tension, conflict and rampant insecurity. Thus it has often been said of the southern Italian peasant, as of many peasants elsewhere, that he is an inveterate individualist and pessimist, hopelessly alienated from his society. Above all, he is said to be endowed with a low level of achievement motivation, at the basis of which the interest of his small family nucleus is the major driving force.

The central thesis to be established in this book is that whatever the validity of this argument for the past, it is no longer applicable to the southern Italian peasant today. When the opportunities for achievement recently came in his direction, the peasant was quick to avail himself of them. As a result, though remnants of a forbidding past still linger on, the peasant now shows pronounced signs of a willingness and capacity to enjoy with his fellow citizens the conditions and the promise of an achieving society.

Until now, the major source of achievement for the southern Italian peasant has been emigration. By leaving his peasant society and then returning with the earnings from his labour abroad and with new cultural standards, or merely by remitting these from abroad, many a peasant has achieved in his society a degree of economic well-being and independence unimaginable a few decades ago. Through

* Reprinted by permission of Intext Educational Publishers from *Peasant No More* by J. Lopreato, Pennsylvania, 1967, pp. 3–5, 80, 83–89, 196, 197, 245–246, 252–257.

emigration, he has rapidly achieved a degree of social recognition that until recent times seemed to be the monopoly of the signorial class. He has achieved the social and psychological vitality with which to challenge the old social order and to demand the recognition that his achievements deserve. Finally, and more important, through emigration the southern Italian peasant has achieved a warm and invigorating sense of security in relation to the present and the future as well. In short, through emigration, the peasant has broken the formidable bonds of his secular poverty, and actively entered the current of a larger civilization. More important still, by releasing shares of previously very scarce goods through his departure from the village, he has also helped spread the new advantages to a considerable portion of those who have not themselves been directly involved in the phenomenon of emigration.

Until a few decades ago, southern peasants, like peasants everywhere, saw themselves as subject to the working of history but scarcely as makers of it. One of the chief characteristics of peasant culture was that for them history, as well as the environment, belonged to the realm of the given.[1] The cultural evolution of recent years has altered this view in the southern Italian peasant. He has now taken a step into the stream of history, and has started to manipulate, though still feebly, the processes that go into making it. Channels of communication, linking his society to the larger national society and to the world at large, have opened up to an extent previously inconceivable, and have become crucial factors in fostering a new perspective in the peasant.

Perhaps the most important factor underlying the peasant's new awareness has been emigration itself, particularly the first wave of it at the turn of the present century. Emigration begets emigration. Whatever the original causes of departure, after some profitable years abroad, some of the old emigrants returned to their old communities to enjoy at leisure the fruits of their labour. And here they have, by their improved style of life, displayed to the less fortunate previously unimagined possibilities of economic and social betterment. The impulse to throw away the hoe becomes progressively stronger and more general. Indeed the perception of even a small improvement in former peers increases the level of aspirations and accentuates the awareness that they cannot be realized at home.

Despite the innumerable hardships often suffered abroad—whether in New York, Milan, or Toronto—the peasant has experiences that reinforce his disaffection with his old society and his position in it. Or at home he hears about them. Particularly critical has been the migration to English-speaking countries, where the former peasant has earned amounts of money which by his old standards are extraordinary, and has discovered a form of social relations which, despite the well-documented handicaps of the immigrant, he has found to be greatly more 'democratic' and 'humane' than those from which he escaped. The difference has been so impressive that the peasant very often idealizes the new well beyond recognizable proportions. In comparison, the old becomes altogether despicable. A few years ago an emigrant wrote from Canada:

> The beauty of it is that here, when five o'clock comes around, I clean my fingernails, dress like a king, and I am a king, like everyone else. I am not the son of So-and-So; I am not a hodman; I am just Mr. [name deleted], and I feel a hundred times better than those *vagabondi* [lazy do-nothings—persons of leisure in his old community].

A returnee from Australia said in the anteroom of a radiologist in Messina, Sicily:

> In Australia you never have to wait very long in the office of a doctor. You have an appointment with him, and when it's time for you to go in, you go in. If you don't have an appointment, it's first-come-first-served. Here it is first-come-last-served, unless you come accompanied by a *commendatore* [honorific title].

He then proceeded to relate an experience he had had with a notary public in a town near his village. It was the sort of story which in southern Italy has been heard many times before. One day, shortly after temporarily returning from Australia, the enterprising fellow had left his village very early in the morning to arrange a transfer of property with the notary. He had waited six or seven hours in the notary's waiting room while many other clients had gone in and out of the office. On those few occasions in which he had the courage to inquire about his own status in the obviously arbitrary procession of services, he was told in brisk terms by the notary's maid that when his turn came he would be informed of it. And he waited. Finally, late that afternoon the maid approached and lashed him with the information that there was no reason to wait any longer, for the '*professore*' had gone out two hours previously. 'What are you waiting for? Can't you see he is not here? Return tomorrow.' And so it was for several additional days.

The working of foreign bureaucracies has very favourably impressed many peasant emigrants. One of them expressed his admiration for the Canadian officialdom as follows:

> In Canada you can often settle the most difficult official business with a single telephone call. In Italy you must take your hat off to hundreds of good-for-nothings throughout the country in order to solve the simplest problem. After many months or years, after having filled scores of officially stamped and expensive sheets of paper, and after having wasted

large sums of money which end up in the pockets of thieves, you are told that you may not have the document because the law has changed.

Aside from the fact that emigrants send remittances or bring back sums of money that by local standards are quite large and permit the recipients to buy many cultural symbols of social importance and superiority, they are also important agents in the diffusion of customs and beliefs that feed the most cherished of the peasants' newly developing values. This point will be discussed in more detail in a later chapter. For the present, it may suffice to note that, upon returning to his old village—permanently or temporarily—after a few years abroad, the previously deprived magnifies the better reality of foreign cultures and titillates the imagination of those who have not yet left. Stories are told of 'the complete equality of Americans'; of houses luxuriously equipped in which one can go about in shirt sleeves when the streets outside are covered with snow; of stores where one can buy most of his necessities in a few minutes and for little money; of beefsteaks and milk that are fed to the pigs; of public officials who serve with kindness and loyalty; of public notaries who notarize a document for an insignificant fee from behind a drug counter; of doctors who correct an old-standing disturbance with a single pill; of beautiful women who pursue 'the passionate Italian'.

Three important clarifications are necessary at this point of the discussion. First, the peasant's rising social resoluteness must be viewed as a process that is at least a half-century old. The considerations discussed so far would suggest only that the process has become more intensive recently.

Second, the recent wave of emigration from southern Italy is *qualitatively* different from that which reached its peak around 1913. A large number of the peasants who went to the United States five and more decades ago had to tolerate conditions which were not much better (if indeed they were not worse) than those they had left at home. Many lived in unheated shanties, isolated and lonely. Nor was their economic avail very high. The lucky ones earned $1.50 for ten hours of work, while a pair of work shoes cost $1.75, and eggs sold for ten cents a dozen. These facts may explain the large percentage of migrants who returned home after only a year or two abroad. Only those who persevered for many years profited from the building of America. Of these, some never went back to their community of origin; others returned and spread the word about 'the land of opportunities and equality'.

The situation today is radically different. Until the end of World War II, life conditions in southern Italian villages had changed but little; the world that peasants now see in Milan, in other parts of Europe, or in one of the English-speaking countries overseas often verges on the phantasmagoric. The migrant earns more money in real value; on the whole he finds a better reception by the native population; he lives a fuller cultural life; and, partly as a result of the first wave of emigration, present-day emigrants have fairly clear ideas as to what they can expect and accomplish abroad.

Third, no suggestion is here being made that currently conditions are about to bring peasant life to an end in southern Italy. The historical circumstances to which the peasant is anchored are very complex and deep-rooted. Furthermore, human values often change less than appearances would lead us to believe. What is happening in southern Italy at the present merely indicates that peasants desire a change, that they wish to help in bringing it about, and that in any case, barring a major setback, they will keep departing until the remaining few will be literally compelled to farm rationally whatever land will prove itself tillable. As a result, clear evidence already shows that the ancient poverty, fatalism, and hopelessness are for many today becoming mere memories that render the present all the more enjoyable.

A general theoretical statement may now be hazarded for a better understanding of the recent massive movement of southern peasants from their land as well as of the nature of their general situation. Because of various historical, demographic and geographic factors, the peasant lived for a long time in a world of abject poverty and precarious life conditions. Concomitant with his dire economic position has been a low social position that has inspired contempt and derision from those more fortunate than he. But for various reasons his peasant society has gradually been increasing its contact with the surrounding world. In displaying before his eyes the conditions and possibility of a more commodious, secure, and just life, this new world has also intensified his sense of poverty and strengthened his wish to escape it. As Banfield remarks:

> Unlike the primitive, the peasant feels himself part of a large society which he is 'in' but not altogether 'of'. He lives in a culture in which it is very important to be admired, and he sees that by its standards he cannot be admired in the least; by these standards he and everything about him are contemptible or ridiculous. Knowing this, he is filled with loathing for his lot and with anger for the fates which assigned him to it.[2]

It would seem that the peasant's enduring poverty, the afflicting interpersonal relations that ensue therefrom, and the subservient, handicapped social status, which also follows from his poverty and from his work conditions, constitute the objective preconditions of his decision to escape his traditional situation. Once, for whatever reason, the communication channels linking his peasant world to national and extranational societies have opened up and become objects of his awareness, the peasant sees in the outside world a model of life and standards of conduct that intensify the discomfort and discontent inherent in the objective preconditions. In his observation of this new world an intense feeling of relative deprivation emerges, and the need for achievement is greatly intensified.

What has happened is that the peasant is now in a position to evaluate the social values and opportunities of 'nonmembership groups,' and to refer to these for an appraisal of the values and opportunities of his own society. Within this 'comparative frame of reference', his society receives a negative judgement, and the need to escape that society is heightened.[3] It may be said, therefore, that when an individual's self-image feeds on stimuli deriving from his own cultural milieu which tend to denigrate it, he is likely to reject his cultural milieu and to search for nonmembership groups that will provide stimuli to restore his self-respect. He is likely to refer positively to nonmembership groups for attitude formation and for the rationale that bears on the pursuit of his future life chances. The evolution of personal goals then follows an itinerary that frequently concludes with geographic mobility and usually with an improvement in economic and social position as well as in self-evaluation.

As a way of emphasizing the changes registered in recent decades by the prestige structure of Franza, in Figure 1 the representation of the structure around 1900, according to a rough calculus projecting present criteria backwards, is in juxtaposition to the structure as it is represented today.

As a glance will show, there has been no change at the very top of the structure. The changes that have occurred in the middle of the structure, however, are dramatic. Whereas in 1900 there were two middle strata, there are now four, demonstrating largely the profound structural effects of emigration. The greatest loss, as previously indicated, has been sustained in the category of common peasants, from which has sprung most of the population that now constitutes the new strata. But it would seem that today there are almost three times as many 'wretched' people as there were around 1900. This point is relative. In 1900, most peasants were greatly impoverished, and the wretched were only those few who were totally miserable, such as the scavengers and the beggars. Today, when opportunities for achievement have multiplied, the attribute of 'wretched' seems to apply to those who have been absolutely unable to take advantage of these opportunities: they are apparently still a considerable portion of the total population.

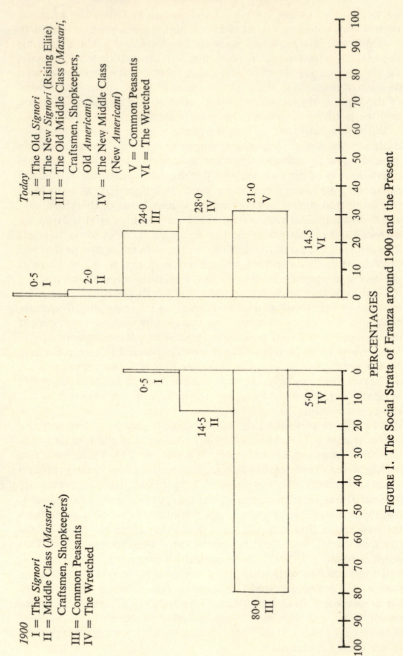

FIGURE 1. The Social Strata of Franza around 1900 and the Present

For Banfield, the state of miseria is not an inevitable by-product of natural poverty. It arises from a combination of social and psychological as well as physiological deprivations. Above all, it is a phenomenon closely linked to the southern Italian's inability to engage in co-operative undertakings outside of his narrow family circle. The peasants of Montegrano are 'amoral familists'. They lack the ability to engage in collective ventures, and their 'ethos' breeds a number of basic misfortunes, such as extreme poverty, public corruption, widespread distrust, and general pessimism.

It is not possible to agree with Banfield's explanation. On the whole, he fails to take into account what has for some time been known as 'the southern question'. His analysis is essentially ahistorical, which is to say that he is too quick to still his etiology on what are in reality the results or symptoms of a much more complex and deep-rooted set of facts. We can, however, agree essentially with Banfield's mere description of the facts, though only to the extent that it is meant to apply to the most impoverished section of the peasantry rather than to the category as a whole.[4]

The evidence shows that among the peasants of southern Italy, the hopelessness, disperazione, and miseria that have often been observed as outstanding characteristics in the psychology of the people are now on the wane. Their gradual disappearance is due to the influx of substantial sums of money, deriving from local emigrants abroad, which is invested at home to buy cultural symbols of affluence and influence, such as property and education. This and the other beneficial effects of emigration already discussed constitute an achievement of great proportions. Simultaneously, they provide distinct evidence of a strong motivation to achieve, while the ensuing style of life also provides the basis and the inducement for the sustained endeavours that are required for the continued success of the individual as well as for the social and economic development that the larger society is engaged in bringing about.

Without getting involved in a complex theoretical issue, a pervasive tendency to measure the 'need for achievement'[5] in terms of hypothetical risk-taking among school children in highly industrial societies may now be pointed out. As a result, it is no surprise that, by almost general agreement, this 'motivational structure' is weak in peasants and in underdeveloped peoples generally. This weakness is particularly apparent given the fundamental assumption—sometimes explicitly stated but more often only implicitly held—that a real need for achievement is manifested only when individuals engage in co-operative enterprises. Banfield unwittingly echoes this assumption when he argues that the miseria in Montegrano is in large measure a result of the lack of 'a spirit of co-operativeness and initiative'. By implication at least, peasants have no one to blame but themselves for their poverty and miseries.

In general, it could be argued that people will expand effort and energy in the pursuit of a given goal when there is at least some expectation of success. Given a long history of unrewarded efforts as well as a continued lack of the means for success, a people is likely to practise a pure and simple 'bread-for-today-at-all-costs' policy. Once the conditions for achievement and success have been provided, the previously 'inert' may then be expected to develop their motivation and multiply further the conditions for success. Put otherwise, after social changes have once been introduced, and the previously deprived have begun to share the opportunities of their society, attempts to partake of these opportunities can be expected to grow in vigour, and the hope of still greater future prospects will become a more general characteristic. In another part of the national survey mentioned earlier, it was found that not only were the upwardly mobile in Italy more satisfied than those who had inherited their present position from their fathers, but satisfaction and hope of future improvement also varied directly with the intensity of upward mobility. In general, the greater the intergenerational jump, the greater the present satisfaction and faith in the future.

Analogously, Tumin and Feldman argue, on the basis of their findings in Puerto Rico, that

> Depending on their past experiences and future prospects, men will hold different views of their lives and their society. Those who see an unbroken line of improvement for themselves, from past times through a projected future date, are likely to have high hopes for the future . . .[6]

In this same connection, Parsons and Weber show that economic advancement is associated with optimism and belief in the possibility of progress.[7]

In short, the chances for success and the motivation to pursue strategies that normally lead to success are not distributed equally in society. To the extent that this is true, it is likely that the lower the chances—real or imagined—of success, the lower the achievement motivation *with respect to the internal conditions of given stratification system*. This says nothing, however, with respect to the *need for achievement*, which may comprise a constant rather than a variable aspect of human personality. Motivation, moreover, may still remain high in relation to some external system.

We have seen with what readiness the peasants of southern Italy leave their home community for places many thousands of miles away. Some of them depart with their entire families, never to return to the old society. For these, despite the deplorable conditions they leave behind, and despite the hopes and dreams that they nourish for the future, emigration must constitute a risk of the greatest magnitude. Leaving behind familiar surroundings, friends, relatives, and the habits of a lifetime, and converting into a little cash all their meagre possessions in the face of a multitude of uncertainties, the emigrants undertake a grave risk. The society of destination will require new language skills, new eating habits, new work skills, and an entirely new outlook: in short, the act of emigrating entails a new process of socialization which must loom as a painful experience to even the most hopeful and optimistic. On top of this, the venture begins for many, who have never before even seen the ocean, with sea voyages that frequently involve an entire month of the most atrocious discomfort and seasickness.

Many of the emigrants leave as individuals, and for these, there is the further knowledge that they must suffer an existence of many years abroad without family, and without any of those simple but essential comforts that only family living—however destitute—makes possible.

Is this not evidence of a high motivation and a high need for achievement? These risks and sacrifices are at least as impressive as any of those hypothetical risks that students of human motivation and achievement contrive and measure within populations of school children.

The question now remains: Why do the peasants of southern Italy not address their motivation or—to put it otherwise—expend more energy in their own society in attempting to fulfil their need for achievement?

Banfield is on indefensible grounds when he argues that the people of Montegrano lack a spirit of initiative, though he is essentially correct is stating that they lack a spirit of co-operativeness and do not organize to pursue their goals at home. But why should they organize and co-operate when it appears to them that there is nothing worth co-operating about as long as they remain at home? As we have noted, their region, a country of peasants, is really not suited to agriculture. The most diligent work all too often comes to naught and does nothing to dispel the secular miseria. Moreover, in those few instances in which co-operative enterprises are undertaken, the peasants are quickly and almost invariably swindled without justice or retribution.[8] We could further remind ourselves of the particular nature of their system of inequalities, but so much will suffice.

Southern Italian peasants do not address their motivations and their initiatives more forcefully to local conditions because local conditions are correctly perceived as forbidding. In any case, the risk involved in leaving the system, entirely, by emigrating, appears less than that involved in local enterprise, and success more probable in the former than in the latter. Perhaps this flight—temporary or permanent—is the most effective mechanism of achievement for peasants everywhere and underpriviliged people in general. By going out of the system for a period of time, classes of individuals who have been trapped in the vicious cycle of self-perpetuating poverty and miseria, manage to break that cycle. They do so not only because of the economic thrust received from without, but also, and especially, because of the new outlook and self-image they gain abroad. Their absence from the old inferno affords them the opportunity to create, and eventually to project, a new self-image.

The general argument may be summarized by suggesting the over-all process by which the need for achievement among southern Italian peasants has been expressed and has become increasingly compelling during the course of this century. Traditionally, southern Italian peasants were faced with a common set of personal problems arising from the severity of the physical, economic, and social environment. The very severity of this environment, however, prevented individuals from coming together and *collectively* seeking melioration of their problems. The first serious attempts to solve them were, therefore, individual, as represented by the first wave of emigration.

The early emigration, coupled with the development of new channels of communication and the two World Wars, has served to make the problems clearer; but the individualistic tradition has been strengthened by the already obvious example of an individually effective solution by emigration. The structural characteristics of social disorganization, therefore, remain, as is evidenced by the continuing social tension and conflict.

However, as it became evident to the people that their problems were in fact soluble, individual motivations were increasingly aroused, and they, in turn, reinforced the immediate, tangible pressures for solutions. Put otherwise, the motivation was aroused in many by the initial perception that change in one's status was possible by engaging in actions that bypassed the local system. In turn, change functioned to sustain and increase efforts toward fulfilling that possibility.

In conclusion, emigration is recognized by southern Italian peasants as the most rational, perhaps the only feasible, way in which they can guide their destiny. It is the major avenue through which they strive and achieve. Through it, many have achieved in their home society a degree of economic well-being and independence unimaginable until a few decades ago. By emigrating, they have rapidly gained a degree of social recognition that until recent times seemed to be the monopoly of the signorial class. Through it, they have achieved the social and psychological vitality with which to challenge the old social order and to demand the recognition that their achievements deserve. Finally, and more important still, the southern Italian peasant has won a sense of security in relation to the present and the future as well. In short, through emigration, the peasant has broken the formidable bonds of his secular *miseria* and *disperazione*.

NOTES

1 Friedmann, F. G., 'The World of "La Misca"', *Community Development Review*, vol. VII, June 1962, p. 91.
2 Banfield, E. C., *The Moral Basis of a Backward Society* (Glencoe Ill., Free Press, 1958), p. 65.
3 Alberoni, too, recognizes that the peasants' desire to emigrate is not exclusively of an economic nature, but 'is founded on a rejection of their own community and of the social world in which they have lived and live.' He errs, however, in asserting that extranational, in contrast to internal, migration offers 'a phenomenon of this sort only in a very small measure' Alberoni, F., 'Caratteristiche e Tendenze delle Migrazioni Interne in Italia', *Studi di Sociologia*, Anno 1, January–March, 1963, p. 25.
4 Although Banfield claims to have interviewed seventy persons, 'most of them peasants,' nowhere in the book are these seventy persons treated as a sample. The burden of his argument falls on the evidence provided by several individuals from the particularly impoverished class of labourers and farmhands. This serious problem arises because Banfield felt that 'It was not practical to employ sophisticated sampling techniques. (To have done so would have left no time for interviewing)' Banfield, E. C., op. cit., p. 10. I find it difficult to appreciate this argument. Personal experience in communities analogous to Montegrano indicates that the application of sampling techniques does not impose an intolerable burden on the research enterprise. On the contrary, it contributes to the efficient use of research time.
5 McClelland defines this phenomenon as 'a desire to do well, not so much for the sake of social recognition or prestige, but to attain an inner feeling of personal accomplishment.' See McClelland, D. C., 'The Achievement Motive in Economic Growth', in Hoselitz, B. F., and Moore, W. E. (eds.), *Industrialization and Society*, (New York UNESCO—Mouton, 1963).
6 Tumin, M. M. with Feldman, A. S., *Social Class and Social Change in Puerto Rico* (Princeton, N.J.: Princeton University Press, 1961), p. 202.
7 Parsons, T., *The Social System* (Glencoe, Ill.: Free Press, 1951) and 'Some Principal Characteristics of Industrial Societies' in *The Challenge of Development* (Jerusalem: Hebrew University, 1858); Weber, M., *The Protestant Ethic and the Spirit of Capitalism* (New York: Charles Scribner and Sons, 1958).
8 A case in point is reported by an Italian sociologist, familiar with the South in the process of discussing Banfield's book. It seems that some years ago in one of the villages mentioned by Banfield, a group of peasants were tempted to sell their horses and donkeys in order to purchase together a truck and thus

facilitate the marketing of their produce. In this enterprise, they were represented by a business-minded accountant from the North. One fine day, however, the accountant went to the city and did not return. And with him disappeared the truck and the peasants' life savings. 'Can we,' the writer concludes, 'really blame those poor peasants if the "co-operation" argument is now taboo ...?' See Marselli, G. A., 'Sociologi nordoamericani e società contadina italiana: a proposito del libro di Banfield,' in Società Italiana di Sociologia Rurale, *Archivio* (Milan: Feltrinelli Editore, 1962), p. 125.

CHAPTER 12

The Role of Amoral Familism in the Structure of Traditionalism*

Johan Galtung

To move from Lerner to Banfield[1] is to move considerably closer to the field of the empirical investigation to be presented here. Although Banfield does not deal with data from Sicily he gets the empirical stimulus for his thinking about development almost from the neighbour—at least in a global perspective. The 'backward society' the book deals with is a village—called Montegrano, located in the province of Potenza in southern Italy and observed during a stay in 1954–1955. It is on the mainland, but economic conditions are not too different from the Sicilian villages in our study—it is the same arid *Mezzogiorno*. This does not mean that his findings have immediate empirical tenability outside that village itself: if anything should be the moral of his study (and of ours) it is precisely the danger of believing that there is no significant variation between villages even when economic conditions look similar to the outsider, and perhaps also to the insider. As a matter of fact, we are not even very concerned about whether the findings are tenable inside that particular village: it is the basic variable, and its use in developing a theory is our concern.

Banfield is concerned with the same problem as we are: Why this ultra-stability, this tenacious persistence in the pattern of the past—'past' relative to what the author is used to and that he knows has permeated many other sectors of Italy, to a certain point? He starts by giving a vivid description of Montegrano, based on his field notes and some statistics, and then proceeds by the method of contrast to what he calls 'some usual explanations of the phenomenon'. As the title indicates, these are the explanations with 'a strong appeal to common sense' that he is not going to accept. At the risk of presenting these six alternative hypotheses in an even flatter and more easily rejectable form than Banfield himself does, we shall summarize them as follows:[2] (1) *poverty* is so pervasive that the struggle for existence

* Reprinted by permission of Universitets Forlaget from *Members of Two Worlds* by J. Galtung, Oslo, 1969, pp. 56–66, 249–261, 263.

permits no time for political life in the time budget; (2) *ignorance* is
so pervasive that people 'can have no notion of what is possible to
accomplish politically'; (3) the *class struggle theory*, that the upper
classes exploit and organize to suppress the lower classes; (4)
differences in political behaviour are due to the circumstances of *land
tenure*; (5) the theme of *distrust* is everpresent because of centuries of
negative experiences; and (6) *fatalism* as a basic creed and style
of life makes it improbable and unnatural for the peasant to expect
or hope for much more than he has.[2] Obviously, these theories
cannot be used to explain exactly the same things, but they can be
used and have been used as levers for analyses. All of them have
a certain *prima facie* validity, and it is interesting to see how
Banfield proceeds in his efforts to discard them so that his own theory
can shine even more brightly when contrasted with all this darkness.

First, he concentrates the problem of stability (in the first page of
his book) down into one of explaining why there is almost no
concerted action—comparing Montegrano with a small United
States town of the same size in Utah. The book is permeated
by the idea that *organization at the grass-roots level* is among
the most important vehicles of progress. In repudiating these
six competing absence-of-collective-action theories, which he feels
he must because 'one could not on the basis of any of them . . . or
all of them together . . . predict how the people of Montegrano
would behave in a concrete situation'[3], he obviously has to show that
even though these theories may explain other elements in backwardness, they do not explain adequately the absence of collective
action.

He observes that 'there is hardly a man in Montegrano who could
not contribute a third of his time to some community project without
a loss of income'[4] and uses this observation to discard the *poverty*
hypothesis.[5] Objectively this may be a correct observation, but there
is an element of misplaced concreteness about time in it. In a highly
organized society it makes sense to divide the day into two parts,
work and non-work, and to divide the latter into all kinds of time
segments with a certain portion reserved for 'community projects'—
improving a road, building a sports field, etc. But in a society of this
kind there is never a clear-cut borderline between work and non-
work—the peasant cannot afford that. He can perform the well-
defined part of his job quickly, in fact he will often have to stretch
the job in order to give to his time-budget any kind of work structure.
But in his situation the remainder is not leisure, *but non-work that
may become work:* it is waiting for something to happen, to turn up.
Says a Sicilian peasant,

Why do I sit here? Because if I do not sit here you can be sure something turns up, suddenly there is a job to be done, a car breaks down and somebody needs a hand. Last week when I was not here somebody else got the chance. . . .[6]

While the problem in organized societies may often be to protect oneself against claims on one's capacity to perform a job, the problem here is to protect oneself both against not being claimed and, particularly, against others being claimed instead of oneself. The villager has to be visible, or at least that is what he believes. Two protective measures in other societies are *competence* and *entitlement*: if these are scarce, visibility is of less avail and waiting less necessary. Where there is a garage and a certified mechanic he will be called upon; where there is a caste system supported by a system of belief in pollution there will be a similar constraint on the relation between jobs and job-seekers—although in the first case the course of the constraint is mainly in the employer, in the second case in the employee. The impoverished *industrioso* in Southern Italy is only partly protected by these mechanisms: there are jobs not everybody would take, partly because they feel others are more able, partly because they do not want to. But there is a vast range of unregulated competitiveness. This does not mean that it may not be more rational to engage in collective action, as Banfield implies; but waiting is neither necessarily irrational, a rationalization of laziness or an expression of *dolce far niente*.

The *ignorance* argument is dispensed with by referring to how much the villagers know about politics, and Banfield found that 'Most of the opinions were reasonable, . . . Some were very thoughtful.'[7] It turns out that the two 'opinions' he quotes to illustrate this also illustrate that 'they are not so simple-minded, however, as to suppose that Communist claims can be taken at face value'—so the value bias in Banfield's criterion of 'thoughtfulness' seems clear. This is no essential objection against his argument that formal schooling is neither a necessary nor a sufficient condition for participation on the political opinion market, but it is impossible to dispense that easily with the importance of formal education for active political *participation*. A political leader may draw on the support of un-educated masses if some sociological conditions are fulfilled, but he may not himself easily compete with institutionalized power wielders already on the power market if he cannot legitimize his claim to power by reference to other factors than sheer force and mass size. Nor is Banfield's comparison with St. George in Mormon Utah[8] so convincing: even though 'poverty and ignorance were as great or greater than that of the Montegranesi', the Mormons had the distinct advantage of being given a fresh start. St. George had no prior history when they started; possibilities were unexplored; there would by necessity be new situations to deal with, with no age-old patterns setting precedents for distributions of value, etc., whereas Montegranesi and Silciani can look back at centuries and millennia of consistency, except that the standard of living was higher (but of course also lower) in some parts of Sicily some centuries ago than it is today. Nothing seems to breed stability as much as stability, precisely because it gives a pattern to everything and no necessity for social innovation. Still, if Banfield's Montegranesi, as he has pictured them, migrated *en bloc* to places with unexplored possibilities they would probably to a large extent fall back on the pattern Banfield mentions as his factor. To change their cultural pattern they would probably have to be substantially diluted by others.

Banfield dispenses with the other arguments, much in the same manner without giving them too much of a chance to assert themselves.

For instance, the *class struggle argument* is dealt with rather summarily:

> Like poverty and ignorance, they (class and status relations) are general conditions which, so to speak, form the causal background.[9]

But later on he is more explicit:

> In general the peasant is correct in imputing his motivations to the gentry. But he errs in attributing to them an energy and an ability to act in concert, which they do not possess.[10]

Two such examples of peasant thinking are given; the first was the idea that the upper classes systematically prevented improvement of the schools to keep them illiterate, the second that they had co-operated to prevent circulation of information about emigration. It is quite possible that Banfield is correct when he says that 'if any such circulars existed, the reason they were not distributed was almost certainly ordinary indifference and incompetence'. But a distinction should probably be made between co-operating *for* something to be done and co-operation for something *not* to be done. Given the general reason the upper classes in traditional societies have for resisting almost any change, and given the general asymmetry between preservation and innovation, the upper classes have a tremendous advantage. The innovators can rarely command so high a consensus because innovation implies a choice between alternative *kinds* of innovation, whereas preservation involves only an answer to the much more fundamental question, shall we have any innovations at all? The broad and consensual *no* is at the root of much of the organized activity by the Sicilian mafia, and it would be strange if Montegrano upper classes should not also be favoured by the differential in organizational capacity, dependent on whether it is activity in favour of or against something new.

Banfield discards the theory of *fatalism* in a different way, by pointing out that it does not account for the rationality and perseverance so often exhibited in individual action, upper or lower class; and there is nothing in the fatalism argument *per se* that explains why it should apply to collective action only. Hence, whereas the other factors in Banfield's view explain too little, the difficulty with fatalism is that it explains too much.

At this point Banfield encounters a difficulty: the high Communist vote which certainly would be seen by many as a sign of some capacity for collective action—presumably even in the non-privileged strata of society. For his argument Banfield needs some general refutation of the idea of *structural* causes for the high Communist vote, because he is most interested in the idea that there is a 'tendency of voters to shift erratically between right and left from election to election'.[11] To do this he displays a table which gives percentages of the left-wing vote, illiteracy among men, density of population and proportion of labourers for eleven villages in the Montegrano district. And then he proceeds to some of his frequently encountered reasoning of doubtful validity.

First of all he sets up an hypothesis (which 'is often said')

... that the Communist vote is heaviest where the pressure of population on resources is greatest (i.e. where chronic poverty is most severe and widespread), where lack of education—and specifically illiteracy—is greatest, and where the proportion of landless labourers to proprietors is greatest.[12]

It is true that this 'is often said' and for that reason worth testing. But Banfield's way of disproving it is by case inspection of the table:

... these factors do not seem to have any relation to the strength of the Communist vote. As Table 2 shows, illiteracy is highest in the town where the Communist vote was lightest in 1953, population density is not significantly greater where the Communist vote was heavy, and the proportion of labourers is greatest in some of the most conservative towns.[13]

However, if we calculate all possible rank correlations,[14] we get Table 1.

The Table is actually quite interesting as a basis for speculations that sound much more reasonable in view of other studies of Communist vote: it is precisely the combination of *low* illiteracy with a *high* density of population that may be conductive to left-wing

TABLE 1

Rank Correlations Between Some Structural Variables (eleven villages in the Montegrano election district, 1953 and 1956)

	Left-wing vote 1953	Left-wing vote 1956	Illiteracy among men	Density of population	Proportion of labourers
Left-wing vote 1953	1·00	(0·44)	−0·26	+0·57*	+0·01
Left-wing vote 1956	—	(1·00)	(−0·81)*	(−0·25)	(−0·28)
Illiteracy among men	—		1·0	—	+0·65*
Density of population	—		—	1·00	+0·45
Proportion of labourers	—		—	—	1·00

* Significant at the 0·05 level. This is not really a statistical sample, however, so significance levels do not express much.

radicalism.[15] A high proportion of labourers might perhaps also be conductive to a radical vote if it were not so highly correlated with illiteracy. Density of population is not correlated with illiteracy and, consequently, may yield a significant correlation with Communist vote (when Banfield says 'population density is not significantly greater where the Communist vote was heavy', this is simply not the case, even if 'significant' is taken in its statistical sense).

But the interesting factor is the negative correlation with illiteracy. Although it is not statistically significant for 1953 the findings call for a study with similar data for a great many Italian voting districts, which could also include a detailed study of the exceptions to the general trend, the exceptions that have led Banfield astray.[16] For Banfield uses his data to discard the hypothesis that illiteracy is positively linked to Communist voting—a conclusion which Table 1 would certainly warrant too—but does not explore the much more interesting finding that it is negatively related. Again, this seems to be attributable to the value bias mentioned above: if Communism is regarded as a threat or at least as negative it is better to have it as a concomitant of an undesirable condition such as illiteracy than of a desirable one such as education.

However, much more important for our purposes is the logic involved: Banfield seems to feel that a scientific hypothesis can be refuted by the single case method—but every social scientist with some experience with this type of data will safeguard himself by phrasing his pet hypotheses in terms of 'tendencies', 'correlations', etc. As a matter of fact, by Banfield's implicit criterion it would be very easy to refute his entire book—if he had presented data of a kind similar to the data he uses to refute the theories of others. Besides, Banfield would actually need a complete set of zero correlations in Table 1, because it looks as if he feels a need to discard structural hypotheses in both directions. In short, he fails to satisfy the criteria he uses to judge others.

What we have said so far may be interpreted as rather strong criticism, but we nevertheless agree with Banfield in his conclusion concerning structural explanations:

> These theories, it should also be noted, do not explain—and may even be inconsistent with—the tendency of voters to shift erratically between right and left from election to election.[17]

More needs to be explained, but here there are some indications that Banfield may have committed an ecological fallacy: structural analyses of villages never do explain individual votes. What we have shown does not mean that the *people* with high education vote Communist, only that there is something in *villages* with lower illiteracy rates that may foster a higher left-wing vote. Of course, over and above such structural factors *there may be other factors* that account for the 'erratic' variations in space and time, but the structural factors should be known. In short, Banfield should have calculated the rank correlations. But if he had done so he might have rested content with these findings and never developed his own provoking ideas. For Banfield seems to be a victim of the frequently held belief that for his own theory to be valid other theories must be shown to be invalid first—the ideas of co-existence and interaction are rarely found; theories are seen as competitive.

But even though his efforts to refute other theories are unconvincing, Banfield's positive contribution is nonetheless interesting: the Montegranesi act as if they were following the rule: *Maximize the material, short-run advantage of the nuclear family; assume that others will do likewise.*

One whose behaviour is consistent with this rule will be called an 'amoral familist'.[18] The rest of Banfield's book is an elaboration of this principle with speculations, mainly based on TAT stories, concerning the genesis and operation of this principle. This, then, is the *moral basis* of the *backward society*, according to Banfield.

But we shall put this hypothesis into a more general perspective, cutting the specific link to the family. Man is equipped with *loyalties* of different strengths that attach him to anything from the smallest micro-unit (a human being) to the largest macro-unit (the world, the human race). In most cases it is reasonable to assume that loyalties are stronger to units of which the individual himself is a number (e.g. to himself, his nuclear family, his extended family, his clan, his village, his class, his region, his nation, his power bloc, etc.). Imagine that the latter is the case; substitute 'power bloc' for 'nuclear family' in the Banfield axiom above, and a rule that can be used to account for much in contemporary international relations, especially when the system is in a polarized phase, will ensue.[19] Correspondingly, substitute 'himself' or 'his class' to get simplified versions of well-known bases for explaining economic and political behaviour.

For instance, Banfield's first 'logical implication' of this principle is that 'no one will further the interest of the group or community except as it is to his private advantage to do so'[20]—a relatively trite statement on human motivation—which is sharpened considerably in his thirteenth 'implication':

> In fact, he will vote against measures which will help the community without helping him, because, even though his position is unchanged in absolute terms, he considers himself worse off if his neighbours' position changes for the better.[21]

All this can be taken as interesting propositions about behaviour on level $n + 1$ if loyalties are firmly attached to lower levels—probably especially to the level immediately below since that is usually the strongest competitor as a source of the kind of satisfaction offered at level $n + 1$. Thus: strong national loyalties will impede international co-operation; strong village loyalties or class loyalties will impede co-operation on the national level; strong family loyalties will be detrimental to collective efforts on the village level. Nationalism, familism, egotism are structurally similar in their consequences, all depending upon the level one has in focus. In general, strong loyalties at level n are highly instrumental for concerted action at that level, detrimental for concerted action at level $n + 1$ and either or neither for action at lower levels.

We shall not examine in detail the consequences Banfield draws from his principle of 'amoral familism', where the term 'amoral' (though not the same as 'immoral') seems to indicate that Banfield considers the family level of attachment to be short of what is ethically desirable—the village level is 'better'. But from the national point of view the latter might well be called 'amoral village-ism', and the terms 'amoral egotism' and 'amoral nationalism' bring to mind other criteria of moral evaluation. We would actually prefer the neutral term 'familism', although Banfield only wants to point out that they act 'without morality only in relation to persons outside the family'. Banfield analyses, very ingeniously, how this principle prevents and disturbs collective action, and his analysis is certainly a contribution to the understanding of whimsical political behaviour: the interests of one's own family will have priority to the interests of the village, both in terms of salience and importance—hence the villager will vote for the person who can secure his short-run family advantages, not for the person who can give advantages to the village as a whole according to some ideological pattern. To raise the standard in the village, even proportionately to all families involved so that internal rankings remain undisturbed, does not in any real sense help one's own family—what a villager who is an 'amoral familist' really wants is a change in his standing relative to other families. No welfare politician, with no streak of favouritism, can bring this about. Hence, politics becomes highly particularistic and even 'corrupt'— *from the village point of view*. From the familism point of view, politics takes on the most logical form; ballots are used as punishment or reward according to what politicians have done to secure relative advancement of each family, not that of the total collectivity.

Of course, this is schematic and should be seen in our minds only as an erratic 'familistic' component, on top of the structural components alluded to already. Actually, *the essence of the reasoning is that the target of loyalty is maladapted to the level on which new institutions can emerge today*. Banfield seems to think that this is the village level, although there are reasons to believe that even in the *Mezzogiorno* the days of the village as the level of modernized economic activity and basic socio-political change are past, and that some sense of at least regional loyalty is needed to create and maintain patterns of exchange on a level better adjusted to the complexities of the socio-economic realities of modern, not to mention neo-modern society.

So far, so good. It remains only to be seen whether there is any truth to this theory. Banfield makes the theory highly acceptable by means of his many stories and quotes, and he also has some very imaginative and interesting applications of TAT stories and dilemma questions of the 'which is better: (1) he is a miser who works hard, (2) he is generous but a loafer' type.[22] The results all point in the same direction: loyalty to the family, a deep sense of immanent tragedy and catastrophe (especially premature death) and a feeling that the family is the only source of protection. A basic point here is the word 'nuclear' in the basic axiom—the extended family is not seen as sufficiently cohesive to fall back on.[23] Evidence of all this is piled upon evidence, of many different types, none quite satisfactory singly, but quite commanding when combined in Banfield's brilliant manner.

Banfield actually protects himself against efforts to falsify his hypothesis in two ways of which the first is valid but not satisfactory and the second seems invalid. He says:

> The value of the hypothesis . . . does not depend upon the possibility of showing that all, or even any, of the people of Montegrano consciously follow the rule of action set forth here. For the hypothesis to be useful, it need only be shown that they act *as if* they follow the rule.[24]

Nobody would deny the usefulness of the planetary system model of the atoms for, for instance, the chemistry of the first half of this century—regardless of whether there were a more direct sense in which the atoms 'looked' like a planetary system or not. But to *account for* empirical regularities by means of a formula, a principle, is one thing, to *explain* them another. To explain the behaviour of the Montegranesi more is needed: one has to develop indicators of familism, demonstrate its presence, show how it works both in theory and with empirical data. It is clear that Banfield also feels this, otherwise he would not have felt the necessity for including all the data, particularly data showing differences among TAT stories told by the Montegranesi, by some Northern Italians from the province of Rovigo and by 'some' (not all) of the rural Kansans to whom the test was administered—the latter 'included here only to provide a contrast which will highlight what is characteristically Italian in the others'.[25]

This last point leads to Banfield's argument about selectivity, sampling and more systematic techniques, about which he is completely frank:

> It was not practical to employ sophisticated sampling techniques. (To have done so would have left no time for interviewing.) Therefore we do not know how representative our interviews were; our impression is, however, that they were highly representative of that part of the population which lives in the town and reasonably representative of the nearby country dwellers. . . . Since our intention is not to 'prove' anything . . . we think our data . . . are sufficient. There are enough data, at least, to justify systematic inquiry along these lines. Until such inquiry has been made, the argument made here must be regarded as highly tentative.[26]

However, no 'sophisticated sampling techniques' would have been necessary. But the difficulty is not so much with being representative as with applying ideal type reasoning: everything fits too well in the book. Certainly, there must have been nuances and differentials which Banfield does not bring into the limelight: *some* heads of households, for instance, are no doubt *more familistic* than others; and *some* heads of households are no doubt less consistent in their *neglect of collective action* than others. *We would say that Banfield's thesis hinges on the correlation between these two factors, or related factors, on the individual level*, but this is never shown in the book. As the data are presented we have reason to believe that Banfield might have used data about one person to show how familistic he is and about another person to show how he neglects collective action, and then might have done what anthropologists often seem to do added together some bits of information at the individual level to produce a thesis at the level of collectivity.

THE STRUCTURE OF ULTRASTABILITY

In our effort to unravel the structure of these villages in Western Sicily we have tried to present a tapestry, using three main types of yarn, three major colours so to speak: the themes of cultural mentality, psychic mobility and amoral familism. In addition there are subsidiary colours, such as the perspectives on society, space and time. And there is the background: the basic structure, with its threads of social and economic position, with social participation, age, education, place of birth and all the familiar variables of sociological study. We now want to do what the art historian would do: focus less on detail, on the patterns formed by one colour only, on minute description, and focus more on the total picture, on general structure, on the *ideas*, the basic themes, that can be extracted. And this we shall try to do knowing well that with other colours and other materials our picture might have been somewhat different, if not in the final conclusion, at least in emphasis.

The first problem to be solved has to do with the three principal components of our analysis: What are the relations among being sensate, being a mover and being a familist? We know that they correlate differently with many other variables, but could it not be that they are, nevertheless, relatively heavily related so that we have, essentially, been saying the same things over and over again, but under different headings? Obviously, if the correlations are very high, then much of our work would have been wasted, we would have been explaining the same variance over and over again. On the other hand, if the correlations are low or nonexistent, then we would have the advantage of working with independent factors (except for common relations to third variables), and this would make the three approaches much more valuable, since they would complement each other.

And this is, in fact, the situation: with one exception the correlations are surprisingly low (Table 2). We have presented not only three, but five Tables, since we have used both indices of cultural mentality. And the conclusions are as follows:

sensates vs. movers:	no correlation for either index
sensates vs. familists:	no correlation for occupation index correlation for allegiance index: familists are more ideational
movers vs. familists:	correlation: familists tend to be movers

Some comments are now in order.

TABLE 2

Relations Among Cultural Mentality, Psychic Mobility and Amoral Familism

	Occupation items			Allegiance items		
	Ideationals	Medium	Sensate	Ideationals	Medium	Sensate
Stayers	48	42	44	44	38	46
In betweens	25	29	28	27	31	27
Movers	27	29	28	29	31	27
Total	100	100	100	100	100	100
(N)	(98)	(159)	(151)	(132)	(108)	(168)

	Occupation items			Allegiance items		
	Ideationals	Medium	Sensate	Ideationals	Medium	Sensate
Non-familists	28	28	22	17	37	26
Medium	24	24	28	34	16	35
Familists	48	48	50	49	47	39
Total	100	100	100	100	100	100
(N)	(98)	(119)	(151)	(132)	(108)	(168)

	Stayers	In betweens	Movers
Non-familists	28	30	19
Medium	32	30	26
Familists	40	40	55
Total	100	100	100
(N)	(177)	(115)	(116)

First, there is no correlation between efforts to move and cultural mentality.

Second, the correlation between cultural mentality and familism, using the allegiance items, should not be taken seriously, especially since it does not hold for the other index. The index of familism is to a large extent based on the same items, so there are intricate patterns of auto-correlation present in the data. At the same time, the direction of the correlation is not unexpected. But what this combined Table tells us is rather that there are two kinds of familists: sensate familists and ideational familists, and further analysis of the data indicate clearly that the former are what we have called the neo-familists, whereas the latter are the classical familists. We shall not develop that theme further, however; we are now heading in another direction.

Third, the correlation between efforts to move and familism is real enough, but is not very pronounced. There are many familists who want to stay and many non-familists who want to move. But this can also be said about most of the Tables we have presented: correlations are generally low, partly because our indicators are not very high on validity, which again is related to our effort to measure relatively volatile dimensions.[27]

But in this connection the conclusion is clear enough: by and large we are dealing with three themes, three approaches, which can be treated as if they were separate, although they are certainly linked to each other indirectly, and in one case directly. *This means that we cannot apply any simple reductionism to our data.* If we disregard the mediums and in betweens, then all eight possible combinations are found empirically: from sensates who are also movers and familists, to ideationals who are at the same time stayers and non-familists. All eight types have their stories to tell, not all of them equally interesting, though. It would be very simple if the whole system were polarized into two types, two camps—for instance the two groups mentioned above. In that case the sensates would probably pick up their families and move away, leaving the scene, the villages, to less family oriented ideationals who just want to stay. This is certainly a part of the story, but only a part, for the social structure and its impact are left completely out of this type of picture. And this may also serve as a warning: if one had used only these three variables essentially expressing value orientations, then one might easily have ended with this or a similar conclusion as has been done so many times in development studies focusing on values alone.

There is also another conclusion that emerges from these Tables: the sense in which these people are really members of two worlds. We have pointed out before that when index distributions tend to be peaked this is not merely due to weak indicators but is also a reflection of the lack of crystallization of attitudes, the amorphous character of attitude formation in societies in transition. Based on the present data we can now pursue this theme further: the low or even zero-correlations between basic dimensions are further signs of lack of crystallization. Many people not only feel and talk in the direction of both/and when presented with a choice between modern and traditional orientation, they also tend to defy any clear rules as to 'appropriate' combinations of basic value orientations.[28] This may be interpreted as a factor preventing or impeding basic conflict because of the potential for contact, because of the many bridges between the extreme categories. But it may also be interpreted as a factor preventing or impeding real change. For change is possible even when there is little polarization and crystallization, but only under the conditions of strong and efficient institutions—conditions that are not fulfilled in these villages. Hence, polarization and cleavage with clear cuts and divisions, would probably provide a better basis for creative conflict. But these people are *members of two worlds*, set not only against each other but against themselves.

VALUE ORIENTATION AND SOCIAL STRUCTURE: A CONSPIRACY AGAINST DEVELOPMENT

We now turn to the basic task: to place all these value orientations in the social structure in order to study the joint effect. Apart from some references to age and education and some geographical variables, we have essentially used two conceptions of *social structure* in this analysis: the *combination of rank and sector*, and the *combination of social rank and economic rank*. Both perspectives show individuals in cross-pressure, exposed to forces deriving from two social dimensions at the same time—rank with sector, and social rank with economic rank. At the same time the two perspectives give us occasion to draw some conclusions both as to causes and consequences of the value orientations. Let us summarize the basic findings with regard to both perspectives on social structure, starting with the *first structural perspective*, social position (Table 3).

Comparing all these figures, it should be remembered that, except for the effort to move, they are based on indices that have been divided into 'high', 'medium' and 'low' according to a simple grouping used in order to assist analysis, so the absolute figures in and by themselves do not convey much information. The trends read horizontally are important, not the absolute values, and the most important percentages are in heavy type in the Table.

The basic finding is in the distribution of the major value orienta-

TABLE 3

Basic Value orientations as a Function of Social Position, Percentage

	Primary high	Primary low	Tertiary high	Tertiary low
Sensates	28	44	46	23
Movers	30	24	35	27
Familists	46	50	42	36
High on social perspective	71	51	67	71
High on space perspective	22	23	49	35
High on time perspective	31	29	42	40
High on standard of living	26	9	50	28

tion, showing a clear diagonal pattern. The percentage differences for rank alone, or for sector alone, were found to be negligible, and the tertiary high and the primary low combinations distinguish themselves as the two carriers of modern values—relatively speaking. This means that reasoning based on polarization in terms of classes, or in terms of sectors, becomes too simplistic: the diagonal pattern impedes group formation along these classic cut lines. More complex analysis is needed.

This is the background. *The task now is to show that this particular distribution of value orientations provides these societies with an almost remarkably efficient protection against change, an almost diabolic combination of factors that explains almost too well the absence of endogenous change in the region* (as opposed to exogenous change, coming from the outside). This shall be done in three ways: by pointing to a factor that reduces the efficiency of the tertiary high category as an agent of change, by pointing to a factor that reduces the efficiency of the primary low category and by pointing to three factors that reduce the possibilities of co-operation between the two categories. Correspondingly, it shall be demonstrated how all these factors do not impede the two more tradition-oriented categories from being effective agents of traditional values, or from multiplying their efficiency by working in concert.

Leaving aside social perspective for a moment, the five remaining percentage rows should be inspected with a special view to a comparison of the two categories now being focused upon: the tertiary high and the primary low. It is remarkable how the tertiary high category ranks highest on three variables that all have to do with psychic mobility, with empathy in one form or the other: efforts to move, space perspective and time perspective. But if we focus on familism, then primary low ranks highest. And there seems to be some kind of complementarity at work here: where one ranks high there is a tendency for the other one to rank low, although this is only perfect for time perspective and efforts to move. (Tertiary low is lower than tertiary high on familism, and primary high a little bit lower than primary low on space perspective.) If social perspective is included, based on the percentage of respondents who wish their sons to become tertiary high, the conclusion is almost the same: the primary low down at one end and the tertiary high almost at the top. But this is a very special case. For them to want their sons to become tertiary high involves no desired mobility, thus the measure does not function so well for them. As we have said repeatedly: it is the effort to move *out*, not only *up*, that is the functional equivalent for the tertiary high category.

The conclusion is simple. *The tertiary high are, above all, oriented away from the here and now; they have empathy with other places, with the past and particularly with the future; they not only want to move but have actually tried to do so. In short, for them the village is a prison.* They have reached the top. If they want to reach higher, they have to move, which is reflected in these measures that indicate the ability of their souls, their minds, their thoughts to engage in anticipatory migration even though their bodies are still constrained to remain behind. *On the other hand are the primary low. They are certainly not the victims of excessive empathy but victims of something else, excessive familism.* Mentally they are still in the village, as witnessed by the lower empathy rates, and only half of them want their sons to come to the top. The rest are more inhibited in their desires, more restrained, which means that they still see the village, and even the lower ranks, as a possible stage for social climbing. But this does not mean that they can unleash their modernism at the village level, for precisely at this point does familism interfere and command identification with a collectivity at a lower level, the family. Or better: their experience with the village level has been of such a kind as to make them fall back on the family. Whereas the moderns in the tertiary high are embracing the whole nation in their minds, the moderns in the primary low are thinking in terms of how to advance their own families, if necessary at the expense of other families.

Between the nation and the family stands the village. *Between the excessive openness provided by the Lerner factor and the excessive closure provided by the Banfield factor is an interval that should provide ample identification with the village itself.* Typically, this would be true of categories in Table 3 that are not extreme on either empathy or familism. These categories are precisely the tertiary low and the primary high, the carriers of the traditional values. They are in a sense combining their traditionalism with the adequate focus of identification, thus *defining themselves as the legitimate owners of the villages, where the tertiary high have grown out of them and the primary low still have to grow into them.*

So much for the differences in value patterns and perspectives using the first structural perspective: *social position.* Let us then turn to the second structural perspective: *interaction.* The basic factor is the *possibility of co-operation* within the pairs of groups with similar orientation. This is divided into three parts: first, the possible differences in the nature of the value orientations held by the two groups; second, the social distance factor between them; and third, the general strength of the interaction links in the total system of interaction in this traditional society.

We have developed the idea that *the tertiary high have acquired modern values less because of protest than for the simple reason of easy access, whereas the converse probably is true for the primary low.* To some extent this is reflected in Table 3. For the tertiary high, modernism is part of a general syndrome of modern attitudes and perspectives; for the primary low it stands out as a desire for change but without the rich resonance provided by other cognitive and evaluative dimensions. Thus the tertiary high modern can compare; he can use examples from the outside: he can project into the future. These are all factors that will contribute to a more gradualist frame of mind and to a politically more 'constructive' way of thinking—in other words, to *reformism*, to evolution from the status quo, that is. The primary low will have an image of the present and an image of a better existence. But this is a mental construct to be compared with the present, not a state of affairs they can see emerging before the inner eye and map on a time scale. Social pessimism, alienation and absolutism will probably result from this and lead to such well-known patterns as the *waiting for the revolution*, which will have to come from Rome and not from themselves, for they have no experience for projecting themselves as active agents on the local scene. Contrast this with the modernism of the tertiary high: he could possibly have done it; he could have provoked change, but he is now heading for other hunting grounds.

The second factor, in terms of *social distance*, is implied by the bottom row of Table 3. It becomes even more pronounced if the category of tertiary high is divided into some of its components. Thus the professionals, tradesmen and clerical workers show a distribution on the standard of living index of 74% (high), 13% (medium) and 13% (low) as against 9%, 18% and 73% for the primary low. In a few numbers this expresses a gulf almost impossible for humans to bridge and particularly difficult in a traditional society of limited size that provides few neutral meeting grounds where status symbols are put aside. Thus, of the villages, the biggest one had only three voluntary associations at the time the data were collected.

But the third factor is perhaps the most fundamental of them all. Looking at the four cells, one may ask: Where is the *institutionalized interaction* located? Where are the *roles* in this social system? If this were painted with a rather crude brush, catching just the essentials, the interaction structure would be as follows—according to consensus of a high number of informants asked about the subject.

Of the six possible interaction lines, only four have been drawn, indicating that the other two are weak or missing. One of the two missing links is precisely the link between the tertiary high and the primary low, which would indicate that there is little experience in the structure with this kind of interaction. There are several reasons for this. The structure in Diagram 1 is in one sense only a reflection

DIAGRAM 1. The Interaction Structure of the Villages

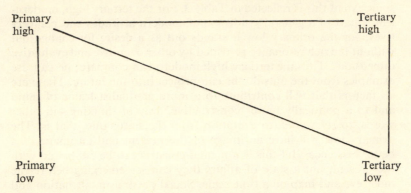

of what is customary in social affairs. The topdogs interact with each other and with underdogs (but to a lesser extent) but not (or much, much less) the underdogs with the underdogs.[29] The primary low and tertiary low do not need each other; they do not have complementary goods or services to offer. As usual, societies are organized in such a way that interaction is above all vertical, and to the advantage of the topdogs. Underdogs have only labour to offer, but cannot buy it from each other in institutionalized economic life.

But why the lack of interaction between tertiary high and primary low? It is not because the primary low do not need the tertiary high, for anyone in the village could use the services of the professionals, the tradesmen, the clerks, the artisans, etc. It is rather because the tertiary high do not need the services of the primary low, because their services (those of the tertiary high) are of a kind that are mainly demanded by other tertiary high and by the primary high, with whom they certainly interact. Thus there is no basis for symbiotic inter-action. If the primary low want the values offered by the tertiary high they must be prepared to give something different than their labour in return (whereas the tertiary low can do this, the lawyer can help his servant in a difficult situation). They can give allegiance but will run against competition from the tertiary low who, by nature of their status, have institutionalized interaction with the tertiary high. Since the tertiary low cannot coerce the tertiary high by means of money from their low social position, practically speaking, the only re-maining possibility would be to buy interaction with the tertiary high by means of money. And this is precisely what they were not able to do in the past (although this is changing very quickly and they will be able to do so increasingly more in the future).

There are two reasons for this. The first reason is simple—lack of money.[30] It is difficult to restrain oneself in efforts to describe the misery of the farm-hands in some villages of this region, but it has been so well documented by others that another attempt will not be made here. The second reason is just as important—the institution of the *companatico*. The institution is probably known in most corners of the world. The farmer pays in kind rather than in cash and may also eat bread together with the workers. The net result may be a highly familistic, warm and meaningful relationship within the primary sector. But it breaks down the possible direct link to the tertiary high position, for this interaction will be via the primary high, as seen from the figures. Thus the primary low is not only deprived of his chance to use institutionalized interaction in political co-operation with the tertiary high (which would be difficult anyway because of the social distance) *but is also deprived of the chance to establish a cyclical pattern of interaction so as to possess two channels of communication and two channels of influence, both direct and indirect, to his boss, the primary high.* He is left at the end of the interaction structure, as an appendix, unlike all the others who are tied to the system by more than one link.

Compare this with the link between the primary high and the tertiary low. It is across a much shorter span in social distance, as seen from Table 3, and is meaningful even if no ideological similarity existed, because it is institutionalized. The farmer needs not only the service of the farm-hand in the field but also somebody to see to other things, possibly servants, if he can afford them, etc. And the tertiary low with work of that kind can stay close to the sources of food. Along the lines of institutionalized interaction, values will flow more easily; people will tend to become more like each other, probably also tend to like each other more—and the net result is a far better basis for co-operation. This theme will not be developed further here but only indicated with one word loaded with the meaning of what this pattern may be in practice—the mafia, the alliance of the land-owners (but bigger ones than we have in the villages of the sample) and a tertiary, more urban proletariat,[31] often of the *lumpenproletariat* variety. Along the interaction lines of this alliance, traditional values and anti-modern values flow abundantly and provide the society with a strong backbone that can and evidently has effectively withstood efforts to change the social order. To summarize it all in one hopefully more suggestive figure, see Diagram 2.

In this Diagram we see the interplay of factors more clearly, and particularly clearly do we see how all these factors tend to favour the traditionals and disfavour the people with a more modern orientation (Table 4).

DIAGRAM 2. Value Orientation, Social Position and Interaction Structure
Combined

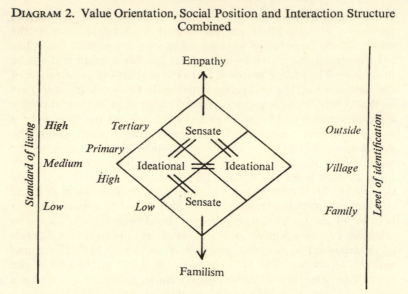

This is the 'diabolic conspiracy' of circumstances, and even if some
of the individual differences on which these assertions are based are
relatively small, the total picture nevertheless is rather clear. The
forces favouring change are *divided* by a weak interaction structure,
partly capitalist and partly feudal; and differences in outlook, level

TABLE 4

The Structure of Traditionalism: Arguments Reviewed

	Tertiary high Primary low	Tertiary low Primary high
Cultural mentality	predominantly sensate	predominantly ideational
Efforts to move	directs tertiary high away from the village, toward the *outside*	not very pronounced; attention can be focused on the *villages*
Familism	directs primary low away from the village, toward the *family*	not very pronounced; attention can be focused on the *villages*
Empathy in general (social, space and time perspectives)	separates the two groups; indicates differences in basic outlook	facilitates union of these two groups; indicates similarity in basic outlook
Standard of living	separates these two groups	facilitates union of these two groups
Institutionalized inter-action structure	does not connect these two groups	connects these two groups

of identification and standard of living make it difficult to compensate for this by associations (non-institutionalized interaction). And the forces favouring status quo are *united* by all these factors.

Let us then turn briefly to the other presentation we have used several times for social structure, based on the relation between social and economic rank. Again, we have four basic categories but shall only fill in the major findings in qualitative terms, since the approaches used in the various chapters are not always completely comparable (Table 5).

TABLE 5

Basic Value Orientations as a Function of Socio-economic Position

	High social High economic	High social Low economic	Low social High economic	Low social Low economic
Sensates	low	high	high	low
Movers	low	high	low	low
Familists	low	low	high	low

The basic point here is, again, how these distributions combine in producing a structure that is particularly unfortunate from the point of view of basic social change. The assumption, then, is that there is a potential for dynamism stemming from people in the two disequilibrated combinations: people who have one foot high and one foot low in the local structure, who consequently are treated differentially and who may be presumed to want to equilibrate upward. These people are sources of ferment in general, but, as Table 5 indicates, *this ferment seems to be lost*. For, as closer analysis of the figures reveals, the disequilibrated seem to engage *a fortiori* in the type of escapism typical of their groups. We have seen that sensates high up in society have a tendency to be very high on empathy and to translate this into efforts to move away—this is *a fortiori* true for the high level sensates who are disequilibrated. And we have seen how sensates low down in society have a tendency to be very low on empathy (although, certainly, not more than the ideationals—only relative to sensates higher up) and to translate this into familism— and this is also *a fortiori* true for the low level sensates who are disequilibrated. In other words, disequilibrium dissipates—the energy does not disappear but is steered toward a level that is too *macro* for the sensates in the tertiary high category, and too *micro* for the sensates in the primary low category.

But this means that a true revolutionary alliance between the sensates, high and low, is strongly impeded. It would probably have to derive its leadership from the disequilibrated in both groups—and there are, of course, people among them who would be village oriented and would prefer to convert the motivational energy stemming from disequilibrium into changes *of* the system rather than changes for themselves *in* the system by moving up and out of the system, by migrating. But they are few, as the Tables indicate, and they do not easily find each other because of all the factors separating them. Moreover, group atmosphere matters here. If the tendency had been for the disequilibrated to be predominantly village oriented, then one of them, a particularly charismatic individual, would be able to operate in an atmosphere of support—the group ethos would favour him. But as matters stand, such individuals would have to start fighting against tendencies in their own groups, in their closest circles—before they could start tackling antagonists. And the antagonists are village oriented. They do not have any dynamism derived from disequilibrium; nor do they need it. Their task is to preserve, not to change, and their equilibrated positions probably also provide them with the intra-personal stability needed to carry out this task with sufficient efficiency.

It may be objected that this presupposes that the categories we have used in Tables 4 and 5 are not only statistically defined groups but also action groups. This would hardly be a valid assumption; as mentioned, the villages are extremely poor in associational structure. But the assumption is not really necessary either. The argument is rather that these categories define people with relatively similar interests in these societies and consequently form a structural basis for action—a basis that may be crystallized into group action if the circumstances so permit. What we have done has only been to indicate some of the many ways in which the structural circumstances do not invite such group formation.

And that concludes the picture. The themes have now been interrelated and they add up to one simple conclusion. It is not so much that each one of them is so strong, so pronounced,[32] but together they combine in an unholy alliance, in a conspiracy against progress. This conspiracy, indeed, has its concrete manifestations in terms of the actions of particular parties, particular groups, particular men. But our method has directed us to a search for the structure underlying what meets the naked eye: the structure of ultrastability. And our search has not been in vain; many factors have been found, so many that it may look as if the phenomenon is overexplained. But the point is exactly the cumulative effect of all these factors: the silent, not necessarily deliberate, conspiracy, the type of conspiracy that is so much more resistant to change than a conspiracy of

persons because it is less concrete, less evident, less manifest—
because it is truly hidden, not only clandestine; truly evasive, not
only secretive. *The conspiracy of value orientation and social structure
—against development and progress.*[33]

NOTES

1 E. C. Banfield, *The Moral Basis of a Backward Society* (Glencoe, Ill.: The Free Press, 1958).
2 Ibid., pp. 33–35.
3 Ibid., p. 35.
4 Ibid., p. 36.
5 However, Banfield seems to be ambivalent about this. He says 'In part the peasant's melancholy is caused by worry. Having no savings, he must always dread what is likely to happen' (ibid., p. 64). But he returns to his argument on p. 66 'this complaint is ridiculous. Except at the busy times of planting and harvesting, there is nothing to prevent the peasants from playing as much as they like. What is to stop them from dancing and singing?' On the importance of poverty, see also p. 168.
6 Personal interview with the author.
7 Banfield, op. cit., p. 36.
8 Ibid., p. 37.
9 Ibid., p. 39.
10 Ibid., p. 125.
11 Ibid., p. 41.
12 Ibid., p. 40.
13 Ibid.
14 These rank correlations are based on Banfield's Table 2 (ibid., p. 40), and data for the 1956 votes are from his Table 1 (ibid., p. 27). Since he does not mention when his structural data about the village were obtained, it is difficult to know which voting records should be used. If he uses the census data (which are from 1951) the 1953 records are closest; if he uses data from the period he stayed there himself, the 1965 data are closest. We have two reasons for believing that he has used the census data: 1) the extreme difficulty in getting other data and 2) the fact that he has used the 1953 election data in his Table 2. However, we have given both in our Table, with the data relating to the 1956 elections in parentheses, since there may have been some structural changes over the five-year period, however unlikely. The rank correlations have all been corrected for ties, according to the method given in Kendall *Rank Correlation Methods* (New York: Hafner, 1955) p. 38.
15 This would also be in accordance with the general theory of rank disequilibrium. See Johan Galtung, 'A Structural Theory of Aggression', *Journal of Peace Research*, 1964, pp. 95–119.
16 The correlations, based on 1956 elections (put in parentheses in Table 1) are different in absolute size, but similar in the sense that the correlation between leftist voting and proportion of labourers is between the other two on the continuum from +1 to −1. These data emphasize even further the importance of literacy for leftism.
17 Banfield, op. cit., p. 41. Actually, Banfield is arguing that there are erratic shifts both in space and time. We have seen that the differences in 'space' have

important structural bases, with two rank correlations that are both theoretically and statistically significant. But Banfield also gives data for the
differences in time (ibid., p. 27), and here we agree that changes look almost
random: rank correlations are 0·44 for leftist votes, 0·13 for centre votes and
0·19 for right-wing votes. Changes in time can only be explained by other
changes in time—but at this point Banfield offers no data.

18 Ibid., p. 85. It should be noted that Banfield's 'familist' is 'familistic' in
Sorokin's sense only within the family; outside he is 'contractual'.

19 Only that polarization is referred to as endogamy at the level of marital ties
between different human groups.

20 Banfield, op. cit., p. 85.

21 Ibid., p. 100.

22 Ibid., p. 135.

23 Ibid., pp. 119, 150ff.

24 Ibid., p. 107.

25 Ibid., introduction to Appendix B.

26 Ibid., pp. 10ff.

27 The reader may have been surprised that we have not used standard techniques
for testing the statistical significance of our findings. The major reasons for this
have been set forth in Johan Galtung. *Theory and Methods of Social Research*,
II, 4.4. In general, the methodological orientation underlying the present work
is found in that book, since the present project to a great extent stimulated
efforts to formulate methodological theory. As to statistical tests, the major
reasons why we have not used them are 1) our concern, with the total picture,
with the type of theory that can be developed by combining a number of
scattered findings, not with the single finding, and 2) the generally unfulfilled
conditions for testing.

28 The periphery of a society is probably, in general, not steered by the same
logic or psycho-logic, socio-logic when it comes to how attitudes shall be
combined as the centre. See Johan Galtung, 'Foreign Policy Opinion as a
Function of Social Position', *Journal of Peace Research*, 1964, pp. 206–231,
and Nils Halle, 'Social Position and Foreign Policy Attitudes: A Comparative
Study between France, Norway and Poland', *Journal of Peace Research*, 1966,
pp. 46–74. Since these villages can safely be classified as belonging to the
periphery of Italian society, it may well be that the low correlations are a
sign of low crystallization in the periphery in general. And the data seem,
also, to indicate that the correlations increase somewhat when one moves
closer to the centre of these local societies.

29 This theme is developed in Johan Galtung. 'International Relations and
International Conflicts: A Sociology Approach', *Transactions of the Sixth
World Congress of Sociology* (International Sociological Association, 1966),
pp. 121–161. If one looks at the idealized and schematized interaction diagram
presented in Diagram 1, one notices that the associated number (the number
of links a given status has) is two for tertiary high and for tertiary low—but
three for primary high. In other words, the primary high have a more central
position in the interaction network than the tertiary high who, are higher in
position and standard of living—on the average. The most significant aspect
of the Diagram is the relative isolation of the primary low—as an appendix
to a triangle where the three higher statuses interact, and above all as an
appendix that does not relate directly to their fellows ideologically speaking
the tertiary high, only indirectly and via the 'enemy'.

30 Among the many excellent works that give added insight into the Sicilian
economy, we would like to mention as particularly significant Renée Roche-
fort, *Le travail en Sicile* (Paris: Presses Universitaires de France, 1961),

Erling Bjøl, *Sol og Sult: Underutviklingens Problem i Italien* (Copenhagen: Institutet for Historie og Samfundsøkonomi, 1961), Danilo Dolci, *Spreco* (Torino: Einaudi, 1960) and his numerous other works and Joseph Lopreato, *Peasants No More: Social Class and Social Changes in an Underdeveloped Society* (San Francisco: Chandler Publishing Company, 1967). The works by Dolci and Lopreato have perspectives that point far outside economic analysis, but economic factors are nevertheless basic to their analyses.

31 Perhaps the best work on the mafia is still E. J. Hobsbawm, *Primitive Rebels* (Manchester: Manchester University Press, 1959). See also Renato Candida, *Questa mafia* (Roma: Sciascia editore, 1960).

32 Thus, some of the differences encountered would not have been classified as significant by standard statistical reasoning—see footnote 27. However, we would like to draw attention to another aspect of the analysis given. When differences have been encountered, we have often asked the question: How did these differences come about? In other words, which are the antecedent factors that can be said to have *caused* these differences? Many answers of that kind have been given, and we have essentially explained the same variance over and over again. But most answers have been given to a different type of question: Given these differences, what do they mean? What are the consequences of this rather than of distribution? In other words, our analysis has often been *functional* rather than *causal*, but in general may be said to be both.

33 For another approach to the problem of ultrastability in this area, see the stimulating study by Anton Blok, 'Land Reform in a West Sicilian Village: The Persistence of a Feudal Structure', *Anthropological Quarterly*, 1966, pp. 1–16. Blok, following Sjoberg, places the blame squarely on the elite, 'since it occupies a strategic position in the existing order it is able to veto any proposed change which could pose a threat to the *status quo* with which the privileged position of the elite is so closely linked' (p. 15). We agree, but hope also to have indicated that the elite has an anti-elite in the tertiary sector; but whereas the elite has a bridge-head further down in society, the anti-elite does not. Blok also mentions the mafia explicitly, but it is a very difficult analytical category to handle, since it, understandably, tries to evade empirical investigations of recruitment and leadership patterns, etc. But the mafia as an instrument of status quo is well described in Salvatore Palazzolo, *La Mafia* (Firenze: Parenti editore, 1959), pp. 29–31. Also, see N. Lewis, *The Honoured Society: Mafia Conspiracy Observed* (London: Collins, 1963) and his article on 'The Brotherhood of Violence', *The Sunday Times*, Dec. 18, 1960, p. 21.

The documentation by Danilo Dolci on the mafia is impressive, particularly because it goes much deeper than the usual concern with big crimes and big business, and down to mechanisms built into the social structure at the micro level, effectively impeding counter-action by the small and impoverished. See, for instance, Danilo Dolci and Franco Alasia, *Un fondamentale impedimento allo sviluppo democratico della Sicilia occidentale* (Partinico: Centro, 1965).

CHAPTER 13

Morals and Backwardness*

J. Davis

This paper has two aims. The first is to remark about a book: E. C. Banfield's *The Moral Basis of a Backward Society*[1]; the second is to restate, with particular reference to southern Italy, some common principles of social organization and structure. The success of Banfield's book is attributable to a number of factors. The author has a high reputation in the discipline of political science. For a long time it was the only sociological book about southern Italy in English; in default of other works it has been taken up by American and British universities as an introduction to the sociology of south Italian peasants. Finally, there is its appeal to practical men, such as social workers and community development experts, who find that the attempt to explain individual bits and pieces of behaviour sets up sympathetic harmonies in their hearts. The book is, however, subject to criticism on several grounds: first, on the basis of inadequate method; second, on the grounds of inadequacies of formal argument; finally, on the grounds of omissions and commissions in the presentation of the material itself.

The book is based on nine months' stay in Montegrano in 1953–1954. Montegrano had then a population of 3,400. Banfield's Italian-speaking wife and a student interviewed about seventy people; an unspecified number of peasants kept records of their expenditure or wrote autobiographies, or did both; some Thematic Apperception Tests were given to sixteen people; and the usual official statistical sources were used.[2] At no time was Banfield's knowledge of Italian more than rudimentary.[3] Banfield affirms that data obtained in this way do not amount to a definitive study of Montegrano; but this was not his purpose: it was rather 'to outline and illustrate a theory which may be rigorously tested' by other people.[4] His argument, he says, is highly tentative. Yet the last

* This paper is a revised version of a lecture given at the University of Bristol. The author acknowledges with gratitude the criticism and encouragement of his colleagues in Sociology at the University of Kent. Reprinted by permission of Cambridge University Press from *Comparative Studies in Society and History*, vol. 12, 3, July 1970, pp. 340–359.

chapter considers the programme that would be necessary to raise the Montegranesi out of their condition which has become, in Banfield's view, very far from hypothetical: 'That the Montegranesi are prisoners of their family-centred, ethos . . . is a fundamental impediment to their economic and other progress.'[5] And he ends on what he calls a cheerless note: even if it were certain that his suggested plan for progress would work, the national government would have to reform itself before it could ever be implemented.[6]

Banfield's book begins with a quotation from de Tocqueville: 'In democratic countries the science of association is the mother of science; the progress of all the rest depends upon the progress it has made.' Banfield takes this as the theme for his discussion concerning the absence of a high rate of growth in the economy of a south Italian town which he calls Montegrano. If there is a low rate of growth, or no growth at all, or even a rate of shrinkage in the economy this is because people do not practise the science of association: his book is an attempt to produce an explanation of why people do not associate.

Before examining this attempt, it is worthwhile to remark that Banfield has, in a modest and unassuming way, cut a knot which sociologists and economic historians, administrators and development experts have been worrying away at for decades; in effect he says that the crucial variable in the creation of a modern capitalist economy is not the expansion of economic opportunities; it is not the creation of a strictly economizing capitalistic spirit; without the 'science of association' these are of no avail, because men would not be able to take advantage of their opportunities, nor would they rationalize their economic activities. He says that the assumption that people will organize themselves as may be necessary to take advantage of economic opportunities is wrong because it overlooks the crucial importance of culture. People live and think in very different ways, and some of these ways are radically inconsistent with the requirements of formal organization.[7] Banfield gives an example: in a society in which everyone could satisfy his aspirations by reaching out his hand, one could not create a powerful organization. It is true, of course, that if I live in a society where 'The nectarine and curious peach / Themselves into my hand do reach' I am not likely to make much effort to set up a marketing organization, or any other sort of organization, to exploit peaches and nectarines. But in general our experience is that people who live at a low level of material comfort have almost infinitely elastic wants; and the traction which expands wants is generally knowledge of possibility, comparison, and a sense of deprivation. It is no counter-argument to this interpretation of experience to hypothesize a society in which every good is a free good and to give this as an example of how 'culture' can inhibit an impoverished people's desire or ability to co-ordinate effort.

The core of the book is Chapter 5, where Banfield suggests that his impressions of Chapter 1, and the behaviour described in the intervening chapters on the economy and on class relations can be made intelligible, even predictable by 'the very simple hypothesis . . . that the Montegranesi will act as if they were following this rule: Maximize the material short-run advantage of the nuclear family; assume that all others will do likewise.'[8] Banfield is careful to point out that this is an 'as if' hypothesis: it does not require that people consciously or 'really' behave in the way described. It can be judged or assessed simply in terms of its usefulness as a predictor, of its success or failure in making the facts intelligible.

In Chapter 5 Banfield puts forward evidence—facts—which he claims coincide with his independently deduced particular propositions. This coincidence, he warns us, does not prove that his assumption of amoral familism is true.[9] In the next chapter he repeats the warning:

> The value of the hypothesis . . . does not depend upon the possibility of showing that all, or even any, of the people of Montegrano consciously follow the rule of action. . . . For the hypothesis to be useful it need only be shown that they act *as if* they follow the rule.[10]

But he goes on then to say that his *assumptions are* true:

> In fact, however, in so far as it is not habitual, behaviour in Montegrano *is* based upon sentiments, values, beliefs and ideas which *are* consistent with the rule (of amoral familism) *and which can be reduced to it.*[11]

Banfield thus uses substantially the same type of evidence to support both his so-called deductions from the general rule and the general rule itself.[12] This is inadequate because in the one case he is trying to prove something about behaviour; in the other case he is trying to prove something about attitudes: the same evidence will not serve for both demonstrations. To put it another way: if the evidence will serve for both demonstrations, then the distinction Banfield makes between a moral attitude and its observable consequences will not stand up: and if that is the case, then his formal argument that there is a moral basis to economic backwardness collapses in ruins.

Yet it would be foolish to discount Banfield's book on purely formal grounds. The facts which Banfield describes are, it is generally admitted, true.[13] Nobody denies, I think, that it is hard to get south Italians to co-operate; or that civic improvement associations are rare, and then ineffectual. Middle-class exponents of the working-class interest are often self-seeking, inconsistent and haughty. Equally the frequent quotations of what Montegranesi say are so evocative of other conversations in other similar towns that one is filled with admiration for the accuracy of his reporting—a considerable achievement this, when we remember his avowed ignorance of Italian.

Honesty and accuracy, however, are scarcely a sound basis in themselves either for a study of cultural, psychological and moral conditions, or for a development programme. For example, it is clear that Banfield suffers from two distinct ethnocentrisms. The first reveals itself in the discussion of social class, in the chapters on the Economy, and on Class Relations, where he discusses 'some usual explanations' of south Italian backwardness, and in the pages at the end of the chapter 'Ethos in Practice'.

What is revealing here is Banfield's expectation of what class conflict might achieve. In his preliminary chapter he gives various examples of political backwardness, and remarks that this backwardness cannot be explained by 'class antagonism', since there is no peasant action against the ruling class.[14] Banfield appears to think class antagonism might explain political backwardness; and that political progress would be registered if there were more collaboration between the classes. That this is his assumption is shown by the first sentence of Chapter 4: '*Although the political incapacity of Montegrano cannot be accounted for by class conflict*, the peasant's status and the relations among the classes are undoubtedly important features of the situation'.[15] It takes an Englishman, with rather different prejudices, some time to realize the full import of using St. George, Utah, as a model of a politically progressive society, as Banfield does. There, where the Business and Professional Women's Club, the Red Cross, the Future Farmers of America and the Chamber of Commerce are all working together for the good of the community,[16] the appearance of anything so sectional as class-consciousness must indeed appear a retrograde tendency.

That particular ethnocentrism might be recognized and allowance made for it by anyone who reads attentively. The second one, however, is not so apparent and is rather more disturbing. For the 'explanation' of social behaviour in Montegrano which Banfield gives is substantially the indigenous explanation. To be precise, I have frequently been told, by Lucanian peasants and gentry alike, that co-operatives and similar organizations are desirable but unachievable because 'everyone pursues his own interest', 'everyone is trustworthy', or 'everyone watches out for his own family'. It is not, after all, surprising that south Italians should be aware that they have a different sort of society from north Italians: nowadays at least, many of them have been there, as some have been to other

European countries or to the Americas. Nor is it surprising that they should have some explanation for this.

But it is not sociological, nor consistent with a thorough study of 'cultural, psychological and moral conditions', to accept the indigenous explanation without question. Indeed, I would argue that the popular indigenous explanation—what people think about their own situation—could be at most coincidentally correct, and that usually it is sociologically wrong; and should be regarded as something which itself requires explanation.

To be fair, Banfield does proffer an explanation of 'ethos': if people behave as they behave this is 'because of' their ethos—'the sum of the characteristic usages, ideas, standards and codes by which a group is differentiated and individualized in character from other groups'.[17] And in Chapter 8, 'Origins of the Ethos', he suggests why this particular sum should add up as it does. 'Structural features, so to speak',[18] are poverty and the low status of manual labourers. Another may be the fear of premature death and beggary. There may be grounds for questioning the extent to which the fear of death is widespread in Montegrano: the main evidence is from the TATs which seem to have been used without a full knowledge of essential details.[19] But in any case, *timor mortis* is one of the features of ethos whose origins the chapter sets out to explain; tabulations are given on pages 105 and 106. It is a pity that when Banfield does begin to treat ethos not as explanation, but as something to be explained, he should use *petitio principii* as his logical tool.

Family organization is another factor in the explanation of ethos. Here again is a case of a begged question: if the fact that most households consist of nuclear families is a part of ethos, then it is not an origin of ethos; and that it is a part of ethos is suggested by the principle of amoral familism: 'maximize the material short-run advantage of the nuclear family'. We are, however, told little about family organization in Montegrano. The reason nuclear families in Montegrano live in separate households is 'perhaps ... principally' the circumstances of land tenure: here we have a brief historical account of the distribution of feudal and ecclesiastical estates after the Napoleonic Wars which suggests that, since peasant farms were small and became smaller as the result of 'inheritance', there was no incentive to create extended families to work them.

Following this, there is another sort of explanation—of 'their selfishness in all relations except that of parents to children, and their tendency to think of the individual as principally moved by forces outside of himself'.[20] The explanation is 'an account—albeit a sketchy one—of childhood training in Montegrano'. The account is summarized:

Perhaps it is not too much to say that the Montegranesi act like selfish children because they are brought up as selfish children. . . . Having no internalized principles to guide him, the individual will depend upon the promise of rewards and punishment to tell him how to act.[21]

I have more to say about this below, where I argue that a discussion of social control would have been appropriate at some point in the book.

Finally, it is worth raising the issues of familism. First, the term is used to suggest, in my view rightly, that the dominant role which any individual has is his family role: not Mayor, nor Teacher nor Councillor, nor Neighbour, for these will generally give way to others, such as husband, or father or mother, whenever there may be conflict. So far, so good; except that this is clearly a variable tendency from individual to individual, and from town to town. Secondly, however, I resist the implication that only the rules of behaviour within the family are 'moral' while those within the town council or the neighbourhood are in some sense 'amoral'. This is not simply to make the debating point that rules of behaviour cannot be amoral. For it is clearly the case also that this particular term derives from Banfield's St. George, Utah, ethnocentrism, and that as a consequence the Montegrano Town Council or neighbourhood are seen by him as in some way not 'real', not what they ought to be.

This brings us to a third point: the suggestion that the family is an independent variable within an anarchy kept orderly only by the police and the fear of direct reprisals.[22] The absence of any reference to any work on the family at this point is disappointing; anthropologists, for example, are quite familiar with phenomena similar to those recorded by Banfield. In societies governed by status, moral rules vary with the social distance between individuals. It has never before been necessary to suggest any principle of 'familism' to describe this; nor has it been suggested (since the 1920's) that, except in families, primitive societies are rule-less and anarchic. Alternative explanations suggest themselves which may be more conservatively related to general principles of sociological analysis. These are offered as the fruit of some eighteen months' fieldwork in Pisticci, another town in Lucania, which is larger and has always been more prosperous than Montegrano.

First, we wish to argue that it is a man's role in the larger society that determines his family relationships, rather than the other way round. Second, we need to examine the claim that adherence to a co-operative is everywhere and always a reasonable course of action. Finally, we will point to evidence which suggests that Banfield's pessimism about the possibility of economic growth in Montegrano proved unjustified within six to ten years of his field work in southern Italy.

If we are to evaluate Banfield's hypothesis regarding 'amoral familism', we must first obtain an adequate structural account of families in Montegrano. In other towns, and maybe in Montegrano too, a husband's rights over his wife are primarily sexual; a wife's rights over her husband are primarily economic. He is obliged to feed and clothe her, to maintain her property intact if she has any, and to feed and clothe the children they may have produced together. She is obliged not to have any sort of sexual relation with anybody else; and to keep his house clean, to cook his food, to keep him warm and neat and tidy. These are general expectations, rules stated variously in Church, in law courts and in ordinary gossipy conversation. The sanctions may be legal and ritual, but as Banfield implies, the most important ones are 'moral'. That is to say, sanctions are applied in everyday relations, by no special agency, but by a man's associates.

A man's honour depends in the first instance on his domestic virtue—his performance of his duties and his exaction of his rights. It is largely in his neighbourhood, where he lives, that a running assessment of his honour is made; but most of his extra-family relationships depend on it: whether he is trusted, whether he is given opportunities to increase his income, whether he attracts more powerful or less powerful men as followers or patrons, depends on his honour. But it is not only his honour, or prestige, which is determined by his performance of his family roles. As I have suggested elsewhere,[23] a man's status as an adult, able to make political alliances, depends on his being a father of growing children. The political category in Pisticci is, with a few exceptions, the category of fathers; and within that category the amount of power—and hence, in most cases, of wealth—depends on how well the individual performs his roles as father and husband.

This suggests various ways in which the family, as an institution, interlocks with other institutions. On the one hand, status within the family is related to status within the community. Again, relationships within the family are controlled and regulated by the outside agency of the neighbourhood. Again, prestige, which is family-based, determines the individual's success in the community. Obviously it is correct here to talk of family roles being dominant in the community: if a man performs his role as, say, secretary of a Civic Improvement Association at the expense of his roles as husband and father, he ceases to be a useful secretary, since he loses prestige. But, equally obviously, the family is not an isolated unit but is interdependent with other groupings: neighbourhood, political party, trade union, patron–client groupings, all affect and are affected by family relationships: in this sense, the family has no impenetrable boundaries.

On the other hand, power and prestige and wealth are the incentives for the individual to attempt the exacting roles of husband and father: without attempting these, he cannot acquire fully adult status; similarly, it is the pressures in the neighbourhood both directly, and indirectly through the parents, which constrain unmarried individuals to marry and to raise children, if they should feel so disinclined. Yet Banfield has little to say about social control. On the basis of his account, we might think that men and women marry, raise children and look after their aged parents in all the particular and precise ways in which they do do these things simply and solely because they have internalized the rules.[24] The disunity and lack of co-operation which Banfield describes, however, are not simply the result of a negative or neutral 'morality' (which, in the sense that family roles are dominant over other roles is probably more widespread than Banfield suggests): but of actually existing specific social facts.

For the point about prestige is that it defines men's relations to one another where formal institutions do not do this: where there are no formal ranks and classes, where the range of offices is limited, men tend to assess the prestige of their day-to-day associates and to behave with respect and deference or with familiarity and contempt, as the case may be. Where formal impartial rules do not define appropriate behaviour people are differentiated in terms of prestige; where there are few universalistic rules, there are particularistic ones; where social positions are few, men look to personalities; where there is little Contract, there is Status.

The complexity and elaboration of moral rules in the south Italian towns about which we have information have as their consequences the fact that many people do indeed break the rules: they may have to send their wives out to work; they may not feed or clothe them as they are expected to; they may fail to supervise their daughters, neglect their sons' material interests, and be careless of their wives' property or husband's health. The consequence is that men are ranked in terms of prestige, as relatively good and relatively bad husbands, fathers, brothers, sons. Differentiation is not formal or impersonal, but informal and personal. A man's prestige is embedded in his neighbourhood and is not transferable, since he depends for his reputation on the people who know him.

This emphasis on prestige as a differentiating factor—rather than specific roles with specific rights and duties—appears to be connected with the absence of solidarity among people who are equals in terms of economic resources or common residence or any other 'objective' impersonal factor. The typical class relation is between patrons and clients, a relationship of vertical solidarity (however transitory this solidarity may be) and the typical intraclass relation is competitive— between equals who are competing for access to scarce and necessary resources and are competing for patrons or clients, as the case may be.

Patron–clients are people concerned in an exchange of services. These are governed by values of reciprocity like those stated by Mauss, but with one additional possibility. For where Mauss saw men faced with the possibility of either restoring the gift or losing honour, the citizens of the town I studied perceive a third alternative: they can, when momentarily in the advantage, refuse to reciprocate and increase their reputations by being known as independent, above the need to have stable relations with a particular partner; they can acquire the reputation of being *furbo*, crafty and cunning men who outwit trusting and gullible inferiors.[25] Thus 'pure' patron-client relations are potentially humiliating because there are few specific sanctions on them to ensure reciprocity and stability. Therefore people try to associate with patrons and clients with whom they have some other relationship, one which is perhaps sanctioned in some way: patrons and clients may be friends, or kin, or parents and godparents of a child; they may merely have a reputation for being trustworthy. Nowadays, party politicians are ideal patrons, not only because they have power to influence the disposition of resources but because they have a recurring need for the services which clients, voters to a man, may offer. In general terms, Pisticcesi try to bring sanctions to bear on what are officially impersonal relationships, in order to stabilize them. The most heavily sanctioned relationships are those of kinship and quasi-kinship, and it is partly by manipulating his network of kin, and by making advantageous marriages, that a Pisticcese acquires power and influence. It is not more than half-truth to describe this as 'amoral familism'.

The success which a man has in manipulating the system through patron–client relations depends on his status and prestige. His status must generally be that of an adult male, head of a family. It is his status that gives some guarantee of his probity and reliability: a man with a family has certain interests and responsibilities, sanctioned by his neighbours and kin, which make his behaviour predictable and assure that he will not be wildly irresponsible. The status of head of a family is the ticket that admits a man to participation in politics. The value of the ticket varies according to a man's prestige ranking as an honourable or dishonourable man; and this is primarily a measure of how he fulfils his duties and exercises his rights as a head of a family.

The argument might be summarized by saying that political relationships are not *sui generis*, or that political institutions are not specialized. Peasant communities do not, even in a modern industrial state like Italy, have the characteristic specialized institutions of mass-societies in which there is a high degree of division of labour. The pressure of neighbours and kin on a family man forces him out of his domestic group to engage in political activity: the needs of his family are satisfied as a result, and his status and prestige as a family man are among the factors which affect his success. To put this point in a slightly different way, one of the pressures which forces a man to assume the responsibilities of family life, which make it to his advantage to assume the role of husband and father, is his need of reputation, power and wealth.

Second, let us discuss yet another problem: how to explain the admitted reluctance of southern Italian peasants to join co-operatives.

There is a common assumption that co-operatives are always advantageous: farmers combine to provide collectively those services, such as machine pools and marketing organizations, that they cannot individually afford. The argument here is that, on the one hand, they are able to achieve economies of scale which make it economic to buy a combine harvester, say, or a tractor; and on the other, that as a collectivity, they are able to resist the forces of the impersonal market by meeting them with a more equal bargaining power.

However, it is not the case that the bigger the scale the greater the economies will be: there is a cut-out point, past which it becomes uneconomic to increase the size of the unit. Also, this cut-out point comes at a different point on the scale, for different activities.[26] An extension worker, for example, can deal effectively with a smaller number of farmers than a marketing officer can. It would be difficult to work out where, for the sort of agrarian system that persists in south Italy, the cut-out points would come. For a series of scattered and subdivided smallholdings, farmed extensively to produce a bare subsistence for the most part, the direct economic advantage of joining a co-operative is fairly marginal. The possibility that it is not always economically rational to join co-operatives should be considered seriously.

It may also be argued that co-operatives are economic only in certain sorts of market condition.[27] One of the sorts of market in which co-operation does not necessarily create economies is the small particularistic type in which market relationships are not specialized and single-stranded. Ideological advocates of co-operatives may have an unrealistic view of the relationship between merchants and peasants in south Italy. It is not correct, for example, to see the merchants as a consolidated phalanx of oppressors, intent on using their superior bargaining power to grind the peasants into the dust. On the contrary, they live in the same town as the producers who supply them; they share the same values, and for their influence and prestige they depend in part on their ability to give special terms to favoured peasants, or at least to convince the peasants with whom they are dealing that their terms are special. Merchants may be involved in politics; they certainly have kin and godchildren. In short, the relationship between merchant and peasant is not a single-stranded, impersonal market relationship in which collective bargaining by the producers can yield a clear and obvious economic advantage. The relationship is many-stranded, and gives the producer the opportunity to use other sanctions than economic ones against the buyer—gives him the opportunity, that is, to infiltrate the merchant category, to subvert the merchants' rational principles. It also gives him the opportunity to maximize other things than the cash price of his product and to take payment in political favours, influence and prestige. In these circumstances the failure to join co-operatives is not an example of economic absurdity, caused by an ethos inimical to all organization and collaboration.

There are nevertheless cases in which peasant farmers clearly perceive that it is to their economic advantage to join co-operatives, but fail to do so. Is this because of ethos, or is there a simpler explanation? If the explanation is simply ethos, Montegrano, or south Italy, is absolutely unique in general sociological experience: that is to say, we know of no other society where moral ideas, on their own, withstand economic advantage. Moral ideas always give way to economic opportunity, unless they are sanctioned: unless the new activity damages the interests of people who are in a position to apply sanctions. So it may be that a would-be economic innovator in Montegrano, although he can quite well perceive the economic advantage of joining a co-operative or even of creating one, cannot persuade his wife or his neighbours that the risk is worth taking (and, as Marselli points out, the people in that area do have a discouraging experience of co-operatives). He has to create a new role, that of Honest Co-operator, before an audience which is, if not actually hostile, at least doubtful and suspicious, and which wields a very powerful sanction, that of being able to adjust his prestige-ranking.

The ramifications of innovation are not always perceived by outside observers. Debt, for instance, is seen in Pisticci as an *ad hoc* piecemeal affair: to marry a daughter, to tide over a bad harvest, to provide medicines in sickness. Debts are associated with imprudence and misfortune, and risks and interest rates are assessed accordingly: the sums involved are also generally fairly small, between 20 and 100,000 L. When the kin and neighbours of Agrarian Reform settlers heard that their debts were in the region of one million lire they commiserated as with people who had suffered a total calamity, rather than congratulating the settlers who had acquired a capital asset on extremely favourable terms. There were many other factors involved, all of which tended, broadly speaking, to lower the prestige of the settlers, to make them and their children less eligible as spouses, less useful as friends, less worthy of consideration when decisions were made that might affect their interests. One of the objections that Pisticcesi made against co-operatives was that co-operatives go into debt for buildings, machinery and equipment, and that the members are to some extent liable for these debts.

Finally, a reader of Banfield's book will remember the author's extreme pessimism about the possibility of economic growth: this would depend on a growth of the 'science of association', which in turn would depend on changes in ethos, which 'under the most favourable conditions . . . might take two or three or four generations' to have any effect.[28]

Such as the evidence is, it suggests that Banfield's pessimism— even in the depressing atmosphere of 1954—was rather too extreme.[29] For instance, in the province as a whole the unit productivity for grain per hectare has increased, while the total product has decreased by about one-quarter on the 1938 level.[30] This strongly suggests that low-yielding fields are being turned over to other crops and is a sign of increased rationality as well as of increased productivity. Even so, grain yields are notoriously variable and might be questioned on several grounds. Take an industrial crop, tobacco: the total production for tobacco increases (from an index of 100 in 1938) to 384.4 in 1953–1954, to 1213.3 in 1958–1960. There are smaller increases in some cash crops, such as fruit and vegetables; and in some cases, production decreases. Nevertheless, the implication is that agriculture in the province is becoming much more prosperous.

These figures could be countered by arguing that they are for the province as a whole; and even though Montegrano is said to be typical of the province, the argument carries weight: fruit and vegetables are grown profitably near urban centres and Montegrano is not near a big market. The focus is somewhat more precise, however, in the published figures for animal husbandry.[31] These reveal, first, an extraordinary rise in the index for dairy cows (1938 = 100) from 133 in 1952–1954, to 1,483 in 1958–1962. This increase is so large that it is difficult to credit it; but whatever the increase, it has been paralleled by a decrease in the number of goats—goats indicating poverty: here the fall was about twelve points between 1952–1954 and 1958–1962.

Thus; my argument is that as a first procedure anyone who is planning a study of cultural, psychological and moral conditions should look at the controls on actions and the consequences of actions, before assuming the paramount influence of moral ideas on actions and choices. If we want to know why people do not create or join co-operatives, then there is a set of elementary and crude questions we ought to ask before attempting an answer: Is there an economic advantage? Are the people concerned aware of it? Are the roles involved in co-operation innovatory or traditional? We must ask this since roles which are, at least in part, traditional will not have to be invented, but modified; and relevant controls on the behaviour of officers and members involved will be invoked. If the roles are innovatory, do they conflict with traditional ones? If they conflict with traditional ones, do other people have the power and the interest to apply sanctions? The 'science of association' cannot be understood unless some principles of analysis of how people control one another's behaviour are used: no book can be illuminating on this subject, unless such concepts are used. The easy adoption of indigenous explanations as one's own is no substitute. The principle of 'amoral familism' can be heard on any *passeggiata* in southern Italy once in a while, and its proper place is not as explanation but as material which ought to be explained. For it to explain anything, Banfield would have to show not only that it was generally perceived to be a norm, but that the Montegranesi consciously apply it; this he does not do. It is unknown for moral principles to stand up on their own against economic advantage, and an account which assumes this confuses actions with ideas, to the detriment of analysis and prediction.

Reply to J. Davis

Edward Banfield

Mr. Davis finds *The Moral Basis of a Backward Society* subject to criticism on three grounds: (a) inadequacies of method, (b) inadequacies of formal argument, and (c) omissions and commissions in the presentation of the material itself. Let us examine his bill of particulars on each count.

(a) *Inadequacies of Method.* I am not sure that Mr. Davis supplies any particulars on this one. Footnote 2 can be read to imply that our interviews were too few and not sufficiently formal, but since our intention, which he quotes without comment, was merely to 'outline and illustrate a theory' it is hard to see why he would think this. Surely interviews—and method generally—must be judged adequate or otherwise in relation to a purpose. Mr. Davis does not contend that our purpose would have been better served by a different procedure, and he does not question the legitimacy of the purpose itself.

Perhaps he considers it an inadequacy of method that (as he says in footnote 1) we were unclear as to how far Montegrano is typical of southern Italy. He quotes in his footnote our statement that 'we are not competent to say how representative Montegrano is of southern Italy as a whole' and that there is 'some' evidence that it is fairly typical; despite the disavowal that immediately precedes it, he takes our 'some' to mean 'sufficient'. We were, of course, unclear about its typicality. How could we not be? To say anything definite on this we would have had to study hundreds of towns. Since we did not have time or resources to 'prove' anything about even one, how can it be suggested that we should have done that?

His charge that in the last chapter we drew policy conclusions that were 'very far from hypothetical' from a theory that had been only outlined and illustrated is made to seem plausible by quoting the first sentence of that chapter out of context. In context it must be evident that the conclusions are conditional—that they are the implications of the theory. It did not occur to us that some readers would have to be told this in so many words. If it had, we would have written 'if' in the two places where 'that' occurs in the sentence that Mr. Davis quotes.

(b) *Inadequacies of Formal Argument.* We are charged with several of these.

1. To illustrate the rather obvious point that not all cultures are compatible with the requirements of formal organization we remark (p. 8) that 'for example' one could not create a powerful organization in a place where everyone could satisfy his aspirations by reaching out his hand to the nearest coconut. This troubles Mr. Davis, who tells us that 'in general our experience is' that people who live at a low level of material comfort have almost infinitely elastic wants. I do not know whether that is indeed the general experience, but suppose that it is. Telling us so is about as much in point as it would be to tell us that coconuts grow too high to be had simply by reaching out the hand. Obviously we were merely trying to say that in so far as people do not have wants and will not respond to incentives formal organization is difficult or impossible to create.

2. Mr. Davis alleges that we use the same evidence to support the assertion that the villagers act *as if* they follow a general rule that we use to support the assertion (in our next chapter) that they actually entertain sentiments, values, beliefs, and ideas that are reducible to the rule. In fact, we supported the first assertion with behavioural data (e.g. the absence of formal associations) and the second with data about how people think and feel (e.g. that a good man is perceived as one who does not have to be feared). It is as if we supported the statement, 'He acts *as if* he were hungry', by saying that he is cramming food into his mouth and 'He feels hungry', by reporting that he *says* he feels so.

3. We are said to suffer from 'two distinct ethnocentrisms' which are 'examples' of something, it is not clear what.

One of our ethnocentrisms, Mr. Davis says, consists in holding that 'political progress would be registered if there were more collaboration between the classes'. I don't see why he thinks we hold this idea. We listed something like it as one of several 'usual explanations' that we considered unsatisfactory. His claim that we regard St. George, Utah, as 'a model of a politically progressive society' is equally hard to understand. We mentioned St. George merely to show that the absence of community activity is not something that can be taken for granted—that it is something one may reasonably try to explain. Had we been writing a book about St. George, we might have mentioned Montegrano in order to make the point that the buzz of activity in the American village required explanation. Would we have been ethnocentric if we had done that?

Our other ethnocentrism, which Mr. Davis finds 'rather more disturbing', is in giving 'substantially the indigenous explanation' of social behaviour in the village. It is not clear just which 'social behaviour'—and therefore which explanation—Mr. Davis has in mind here, but his charge is that we accept the received wisdom of the village and pass it on uncritically ('without question') as if we had invented it ourselves. Mr. Davis thinks that we should not have taken the indigenous theory seriously, since indigenous theories are usually wrong; instead we should have created a truly sociological one to put in its place. The indigenous theory, he says, was itself something to be explained, not something to be elaborated and put forward for testing.

All this is very perplexing. We were certainly not aware that the theory (*which* theory?) that we advanced was so obvious and commonplace, and I am sure that we did not accept it 'without question'. But suppose for the sake of argument that we knowingly adopted a prevailing theory as our own. How would that be ethnocentric? And why should it be assumed that a theory is not worth testing just because it is indigenous? And if the indigenous theory was in our judgement wrong, why should we have tried to find an explanation for it? We were not there to explain wrong explanations.

4. Mr. Davis acknowledges ('to be fair') that we do offer an explanation of how the villagers came to have their particular ethos, but he finds it a pity in that doing so we use *petitio principii* as our logical tool. In fact, we explained the element of ethos that he mentions, namely fear of premature death, by three interacting causes: the high death rate that prevailed prior to the Second World War, extreme poverty, and the absence of the kind of family organization that would give some protection to orphans.

5. 'Another' (what was the first?) question that we are supposed to have begged has to do with the relation between ethos and family organization. The nuclear family, Mr. Davis says, cannot be at once a *feature* of ethos and a *cause* of it. I do not see why not. We did not in fact make a point of its being a feature of ethos, but I have no objection to regarding it as one. I have no doubt that sentiments, values, beliefs and ideas are one cause, although not the only one, of the continuance of a given type of family organization and I also have no doubt that family organization is a cause, although not the only one, of the continuance of a given set of beliefs and ideas. Has Mr. Davis never heard of reciprocal causation?

(c) *Omissions and Commissions in the Presentation of the Material Itself.* Mr. Davis does not indicate where the inadequacies of formal argument leave off and the omissions and commissions begin, but I assume that the dividing line comes at his paragraph beginning, 'Finally, it is worth raising the issues of familism.' At any rate, up to this point he has not mentioned any omissions or commissions. On the contrary, with respect to commissions he has given us a clean bill of health. 'The facts which Banfield describes are, it is generally admitted, true' and 'one is filled with admiration for the accuracy of his reporting.'

It turns out, however, that we are guilty of many omissions, especially ones having to do with family and social control, both of which, it seems, are subjects Mr. Davis studied in the village of Pisticci and on which he has reported in an unpublished paper. He is disappointed, he says, that we do not refer to any work on the family, and it is clear that he disapproves of our temerity in using a concept (familism) that others have not used. ('It had never before been necessary to suggest any principle of "familism" to describe this. . . .') He asserts that alternative explanations (explanations *of what*?) that fit better into the general principles of sociological analysis (*what general principles*?) have been suggested by his work in Pisticci. The account of these that follows, in so far as it has any bearing upon what we wrote, is vitiated by his failure to understand our use of the word 'moral'. We did not say that all rules governing behaviour within the family are moral and all rules governing behaviour outside of it are amoral. What we said (p. 83) is that one who acts *as if* he follows the rule: 'Maximize the material, short-run advantage of the nuclear family' etc. is without a moral sense—that is, without feelings of right and wrong—in relation to people outside the family but not in relation to ones within it. Mr. Davis is wrong—if he is intelligible at all—when he writes, 'For it is clearly the case also (*sic*) that this particular term [amoral] derives from Banfield's St. George, Utah, ethnocentrism, and that as a consequence the Montegrano Town Council or neighbourhood are in some way not "real", not what they ought to be.' Our use of the term amoral derives from the dictionary, not from our ethnocentrism (either the St. George ethnocentrism or the other one): what we said was that the Montegranesi do not apply the categories 'right' and 'wrong' to action *vis-à-vis* persons outside the nuclear family.

Our failure to discuss social control in the familiar terminology of sociology (and I daresay also to refer to some standard works on the subject) is another error of omission. What Mr. Davis says in an effort to supply the deficiencies of our treatment of this subject does not help matters, however. Whatever may be the case in Pisticci, patron–client relationships did *not* have much importance in Montegrano, the status of head of family was *no* guarantee of probity and reliability there, and people there were *not* forced by the pressure of neighbours and kin to engage in political activity.

The 'claim that adherence to a co-operative is everywhere and always a reasonable course of action' would indeed be a serious error—one that Mr. Davis would be fully justified in devoting 700 words to—if in fact we had made it. We did not, however, make any claim faintly resembling that. We mention co-operation here and there, for example on page 164 where we say that it would be well for teachers and other local leaders to assist the villagers 'to undertake simple ventures in co-operation and community action' such as the organization of village soccer teams. But we do not once mention co-operatives. Where Mr. Davis goes wrong is in supposing that co-operation implies co-operatives (could this be an ethnocentrism of his?). In our usage, and in that prescribed by the dictionary, it is any kind of working together. In the Introduction we say repeatedly that the book is about (as Mr. Davis himself puts it at the end of his third paragraph) why people do not associate and in later chapters we use a variety of expressions—'organized action', 'community action', 'concerted action', 'group action', 'local action'—to indicate the range of possibilities that we have in mind.

Unless Mr. Davis is prepared to argue that working together, as opposed to membership in co-operatives, is often unreasonable his words are beside the point.

In connection with this irrelevant discussion of why people do not join co-operatives Mr. Davis remarks that unless they are sanctioned (by which he means unless they are reinforced by some kind of material advantage) 'moral ideas *always* [italics added] give way to economic opportunity'. One wonders how he knows this, or how anyone could know it. Does he mean that moral ideas always give way immediately, say within a month or two or perhaps a year or two, or only eventually, say after decades or centuries? It is tantalizing not to be told, the proposition is so breathtaking.

Our final error of commission is a pessimism that Mr. Davis finds 'rather too extreme'. He says that official reports show that grain yields per hectare have risen sharply in the province of Potenza as has 'the index for dairy cows' (*sic*). These reports do not tally with observations that my wife and I made when we revisited Montegrano for several days in 1966. We did indeed see striking evidences of better living conditions: the children's faces were no longer pinched and wan, no one was dressed in rags, and a great many homes had been improved in one way or another. The village's relative prosperity was not in any degree the result of increased agricultural or other productivity, however. What accounted for it (here we must again fall afoul of Mr. Davis's prohibition of 'indigenous explanations') was: (1) lively demand for unskilled labour in northern Italy, Germany and Switzerland; almost all able bodied men had gone away to work, some taking their families with them and others sending money home; (2) the doubling of the local wage rate in consequence of the exodus of so many workers; (3) introduction by the national government of unemployment compensation, old age pensions, and aid to dependent children; (4) easy credit for the purchase of consumer goods; (5) construction by the national government of various public works that subsidized home improvements; and (6) more gifts from America.

The noteworthy thing is that every item on this list resulted from action taken in Rome or some other far away place. We never claimed that the government of Italy would not, or could not, relieve the villagers' poverty with gifts nor did we rule out the possibility of their emigrating. We did say (p. 156) that *planned change in the ethos* of the village was very unlikely and that without it economic and political development were not to be looked for. Nothing that Mr. Davis writes in 1966 gives us the slightest reason to revise this opinion.

I believe that Mr. Davis is mistaken in attributing the success of our book to my reputation as a political scientist (probably few who read it know that I am one, and in any case my reputation is not very big), to the absence of other books in English that could be used as introductions to the sociology of south Italian peasantries (I doubt that many people are interested in that subject), or to its appeal to social workers and community development experts (I imagine it is too pessimistic to set up 'sympathetic harmonies' in their hearts). My conjecture, for what it is worth, is that a good many readers find the book interesting for the very reasons that Mr. Davis finds it objectionable—to wit, it addresses itself to matters of great practical importance rather than to sociology as such, it tries to explain much by very little even at the risk of what Mr. Davis calls half-truths, and it is not loaded down with a lot of useless methodological chrome and social science gadgetry.

NOTES

1 Page references are to the paperback edition of 1967, New York: Free Press. The degree to which Banfield sees Montegrano as typical of Southern Italy is unclear. In fact he makes two contrasting claims. In the introduction he remarks that since his sample was not rigorously contrived, he has no statistical measure of the typicality of his interviewees, and he continues: 'Our impression is, however, that they were highly representative of that part of the population which lives in the town and reasonably representative of the nearby country-dwellers. We are not competent to say how representative Montegrano is of southern Italy as a whole; there is some evidence, however that in the respect relevant to this study, Montegrano is fairly the "typical" south, viz., the rest of Lucania, the regions of Abruzzi and Calabria, the interior of Campania, and the coasts of Catania, Messina, Palermo and Trapani' (p. 10). And in a footnote he quotes the estimable J. S. McDonald, to the effect that these are the areas where associations tend to be lacking, and where the nuclear family is the sole or chief integrator of economic aspirations. On these grounds we may take it that Banfield is claiming that his study is representative of the typical south and that the prime feature of this is amoral nuclear familism. However, later in his book, he introduces evidence in passing that in some areas—Reggio Calabria is mentioned—the nuclears family is in fact integrated into a wider association of nuclear families which has the specific purpose of aiding emigration overseas. Montegrano is not such a town, says Banfield; and the towns where the wider association exists have a 'different' ethos (p. 88, n. 3).

2 The interviews do not seem to have been formal interviews following a consistent pattern: on page 40 he reports that various questions were asked of variously fourteen, eighteen and twenty people; on pages 129–131 the 'number of respondents' to sets of attitude testing questions varies between twenty-five and twenty-eight. In Chapter 5 the seventeen propositions are illustrated with quotations from five teachers, two merchants, four landowners (one of them resident in another town), Carlo Prato, two peasant women, a

young man, the Director of the Schools, the pharmacist, the doctor, a retired official, an engineer from northern Italy, and twenty-one peasants. In Chapter 8 the autobiographies of six people are cited; Carlo and Maria Prato, Paolo and Maria Vitello and Pasquale and Pasqualina. In Appendix A, Tables 6 and 7 give the expenses and income of Carlo Prato; Table 10 gives the expenses only of 'an artisan family'.

3 P. 10.
4 P. 11.
5 P. 155.
6 P. 177.
7 P. 8.
8 P. 8.
9 P. 83.
10 P. 103.
11 P. 103. Italics mine.
12 A rapid and to some extent arbitrary count of the isolable bits of evidence used in Chapter 5 to demonstrate the predictive value of the general rule reveals eleven descriptions of 'actions' (which range from defaulting on payment of wages to talking with haughty officiousness) and eight negative evidences (of the sort: there are no civic improvement associations, etc.). There are also thirty-nine accounts of what people said when they were asked to explain what they had done in the past or what they would do in specified circumstances, or what they thought about something. In Banfield's usage this is all behaviour. In Chapter 6, devoted to demonstrating the truth of the rule of amoral familism, Banfield adduces: the Thematic Apperception Test results; some generally excellent summary descriptions of typical worldviews; and extracts from the autobiographies which some Montegranesi wrote for the Banfields. We might summarize the components of 'behaviour' and of 'ethos' as follows. Behaviour (Chapter 5) is actions (11), or inactions (8), or explanations of past or future actions (39); Ethos (Chapter 6) is TAT responses, or *Weltanschauungen*, or explanations of past actions.
13 I shall not make any specific critique of the facts which Banfield presents. My friend and colleague Nevill Colclough points out that one reason so many Montegranesi responded to the TAT picture of a boy and violin with stories of orphans and premature death (Appendix B, pp. 175–186) may be that in southern Italy a musical training is most commonly given in orphanages. More serious, from an academic point of view, is the casualness with which many facts are presented: e.g. Logical Implication 9 (p. 90), about the reluctance of Montegranesi to enter into legal agreements, requires considerable elaboration; for in general it appears to be the case that the amount of litigation varies inversely to the prosperity of the community. See: T. Ascarelli, 'Litigiosità e Ricchezzá', *Studi Economici*, Anno X, p. 181.
14 Pp. 31, 36, 39.
15 P. 69. Italics mine.
16 P. 17.
17 Sumner's definition—surely descriptive rather than explanatory?—cited by Banfield, p. 10, n. 3.
18 P. 139.
19 See above, n. 3.
20 P. 145.
21 Pp. 151–152.
22 P. 136.
23 See J. Davis, 'Town and Country', *Anthropological Quarterly*, 42 (1969); 171–185.

24 Banfield however is self-contradictory on this point. In his account of child-training (pp. 145–152) he refers to 'a characteristic failure to establish a relationship between the punishment and an antecedent wrong-doing' (p. 149). Again (pp. 151–152) 'punishment . . . is unrelated to any principle of "oughtness" . . . (and in these circumstances no general principles can be internalized as conscience)'. So who enforces the rules?

25 J. Davis, 'Passatella, An Economic Game', *British Journal of Sociology*, vol. 15, no. 3, 1964, 191–206.

26 F. Dovring, *Land and Labour in the 20th Century*, 3rd revised edition, The Hague: M. Nijhoff, 1965, pp. 202–204.

27 Louis P. F. Smith, *The Evolution of Agricultural Co-operation*, Oxford: Basil Blackwell, 1961, *passim*, but especially pp. 3ff.

28 P. 166.

29 Montegrano is in the province of Potenza, and in the 8th agricultural-statistical zone, which is called Montagna Interna: Versante Settentrionale del Pollino. The data which follow are from: *Prodotto Netto dell'Agricoltura in Provincia di Potenza*, Camera di Commercio, Industria e Agricoltura, Potenza, 1964.

30 Prodotto Netto, etc., Table 12 (after p. 65) and p. 81.

31 M. Rossi Doria argues that in some regions of Lucania the only rational agricultural policy is to attempt a renaissance of cattle farming.

PART IV

The Sociology of the Inner City

CHAPTER 14

The Sociology of the Inner City

INTRODUCTION

The classical tradition on 'community'—derived from the nineteenth century founding fathers of sociology, has frequently been used as a means of invidious comparison with contemporarily exemplified society. It was not only the political revolutions of the late eighteenth century in America and France, but also the industrial revolution that was seen as threatening or even destroying 'community'. The old bases of social solidarity were seen as being eroded and altered with increasing industrialization. Industrial society— and its ecological derivative, the city—was seen as typified by competition and conflict, utility and contractual relationships; the 'community' in contrast—and its ecological derivative, the village, or at the most the small town—was seen as the antithesis of these. Sociologists have then frequently declared 'community' be eclipsed when speculating on—rather than analysing—the city, especially its inner parts.

Take, for example that fine product of the Chicago School,[1] Harvey Zorbaugh's *The Gold Coast and the Slum*. The actual social experience of Chicago was not that of every other city—it increased in population by half a million in each of the first three decades of this century and many were immigrants from eastern and southern Europe. Like many community sociologists, those who worked in Chicago became bound by the peculiarities of their community and assumed that the rest of the world was similar if not identical. When a Chicago sociologist writes generally about the 'community' or the 'city' he means Chicago. There was little concern with comparing Chicago to any other city to see differences as well as similarities in their adaptations to population influxes.

What precisely was the urban community for the Chicago ecologist? It 'turns out, upon closer scrutiny, to be a mosaic of minor communities, many of them strikingly different one from another, but all more or less typical. *Every City* has its central business district; the focal point of the whole urban complex. *Every City*, every great city, has its more or less exclusive residential areas of suburbs; its areas of light and of heavy industry, satellite cities, and casual labour mart, where men are recruited for rough work on distant frontiers, in the mines and the forests, in the building of railways or the borings and excavations for the vast structures of our modern cities. *Every American City* has its slums; its ghettos, its immigrant colonies, regions which maintain more or less alien and exotic culture. Nearly every large city has its bohemias and bohemians, where life is freer, more adventurous and lonely than it is elsewhere. These are the so-called natural areas of the city.'[2]

Such natural areas were studies by Zorbaugh in *The Gold Coast and the Slum*. The Gold Coast and Little Sicily (the slum) have few common customs and 'there is certainly no common view which holds the cosmopolitan population of this region together in any common purpose ... the laws which prevail are not a communal product, and there is no organized public opinion which supports and contributes to their enforcement.'[3] So Zorbaugh doubts whether 'in any proper sense of the word' that the 'Lower North Side' can be called a community at all. 'It is a region ... an area of transition, the character of its populations and the problems which it presents are at once a reflection and a consequence of the conditions which this period of transition impose.'[4] The text for this book, indeed for the Chicago school might well be 'everywhere the old order passeth, but the new order hath yet to come.' Underlying this is a very Durkheimian view of society that appreciated that the old forms of mechanical solidarity had broken down and that organic solidarity is ever precarious.

Zorbaugh's field methods are indicated by the number of para-graphs that begin 'As one walks'—for example 'One has but to walk the streets of the Near North Side to sense the cultural isolation beneath these contrasts'.[5] Some of the individuals that once lived in the slum 'have succeeded in climbing' but for the rest 'the district east of State Street exists only in the newspapers.'[6] Similarly, the 'Gold Coaster' knows little except through sensational newspaper reports of what happens in the slums. A key passage that opens our extract from Zorbaugh sums up his impressions. He seems to be exhibiting here a posture of nostalgia for the rural community, ignoring the fact that integration may be possible on other bases than *gemeinschaft*. Chicago in the 1930's appears, though, to be classical *Gesellschaft*.

In Chicago there were natural areas that have been occupied by 'one alien group after another. The Irish, the Germans, the Swedish, the Sicilians have occupied it in turn. Now it is being invaded by a migration of the Negro from the south.'[7] Here the immigrant to the city 'meets with sympathy, understanding and encouragement ... (and) ... finds his fellow-countrymen who understand his habits and his standards and share his life-experience and viewpoint. In the colony he has a status, plays a role in a group. In the life of the colony's streets and cafe's, in its churches and benevolent societies, he finds response and security. In the colony he finds that he can live, be somebody, satisfy his wishes—all of which is impossible in the strange world outside.'[8] This looks extraordinarily like the usual view of the traditional community for indeed these are what Herbert Gans later was to call 'urban villages'.[9] Zorbaugh located 28 distinct nationalities in the Near North Side Slum. He wants to call the specific areas 'ghettos' and like the medieval Jewish ghettos they form a more or less independent community with their own customs and laws. It was out of 'Little Sicily' that the Mafia emerged—they had mostly come from around Palermo. It seems that in 'Little Sicily' it was possible for many Sicilians to remain *encapsulated*—to use Mayer's term,[10] in Chicago: they continued in almost every respect the mores, especially those relating to sexual relations, of the village areas from which they had migrated. And the Mafia continued the fierce and persistent feuding between families.

Our first extract, is much more recent than Zorbaugh's work and it takes us inside one of these 'urban villages', whereas Zorbaugh was always outside. Hannerz describes brilliantly the bonds and bases for social solidarity in the negro ghetto of Washington D.C. Rex's paper is the next extract and in it he builds upon the work of the Chicago School and he attempts to join their approach with that of Max Weber in writing a sociology of the inner city. His approach to stratification in the community can be fruitfully contrasted to that of Lloyd Warner in Part IV of this Reader.[11] Janet Abu-Lughod's analysis of the Egyptian experience of urbanization clearly demonstrates that 'Cairo is not one community but, rather many separate social communities'. The important point being that, 'a member of one community may pass daily through the physical site of communities other than his own, neither 'seeing' nor admitting their relevance to his own life. But within his own community, there is little if any anonymity.'[12] This is an important corrective to crude notions of 'an urban way of life'.

The final extract in the selection—on Belfast—shows that both conflict, of the most intense variety, *and* co-operation and solidarity co-exist in the inner city. It is included as a fine example of empirical analysis that is both timely and relevant. Its perception of the social situation in Belfast can be judged in the light of subsequent events, but it shows that there can be propinquity without community.

NOTES

1 See the discussion in Bell and Newby op. cit., pp. 91–101.
2 Robert Park: *Human Communities: the city and human ecology*, New York: Free Press, 1952, p. 196 (our emphasis).
3 Harvey W. Zorbaugh: *The Gold Coast and the Slum*, Chicago: University of Chicago Press, 1929, p. vii.
4 ibid., pp. vii–viii.
5 ibid., p. 12.
6 ibid., p. 13.
7 ibid., p. 127.
8 ibid., p. 144.
9 Herbert J. Gans: *The Urban Villagers*, New York: Free Press, 1962.
10 P. Mayer: 'Migrancy and the study of Africans in Towns'. *American Anthropologist 1962*.
11 This comparison is elaborated in Bell and Newby op. cit., pp. 186–208.
12 'Migrant Adjustment to City Life: The Egyptian Case', *American Journal of Sociology* 67, 1961, p. 31. See also the collection of papers in William Mangin (ed.): *Peasants in Cities: Readings in the Anthropology of Urbanization*, Houghton Mifflin, Boston 1970.

CHAPTER 15

Soulside, Washington D.C. in the 1960's: Black Ghetto Culture and Community*

Ulf Hannerz

'Soul' is black. The black people of America's inner cities (a popular contemporary euphemism for slums, but often a less appropriate term, as the areas are often more rundown than centrally located) are soul brothers and soul sisters, listen to soul music and eat soul food at least occasionally. 'Soul' is said to be the essence of their blackness, shaped by their experience and expressed in their everyday life. 'Soulside', then, may be as good a name as any for the black side of town.

'Ghetto' is commonly used as an anti-euphemism for the same area in a northern U.S. city which some prefer to call 'inner city' and others still call 'slum'. But while the former is only a term of location, sometimes wrong and sometimes right, and the latter tells us that the area is rundown and poor, 'ghetto' tells us more about the nature of the community and its relationship to the outside world. A sociological definition of 'ghetto' might say that a ghetto is resided in by people who share a social characteristic of outstanding salience which results in their living together. Getting down from the heights of sociologese, we can simply note that hardly any social characteristic is today as important in American society as pigmentation, and that consequently, we seldom hear about any other ghettos than black ones nowadays. Of course, 'ghetto' is now a term of social rhetoric, and some people for that reason prefer to stay away from it. But even if the definition suggested above is stultified, it may say as much about the fundamental nature of this community as the definition of any alternative term, or more. If it is added that another salient characteristic, shared by most ghetto dwellers and closely connected with the colour of their skin, is a low income, the term 'ghetto' says just about all that is contained in 'slum', without its perjorative connotations.

* Reprinted by permission of Columbia University Press from *Soulside: Inquiries into Ghetto Culture and Community*, by U. Hannerz, New York and London, 1969, pp. 11–13, 19–22, 34, 111–112, 139–144, 159–160, 202–207.

It should be noted that the reason why ethnic identity is important as a basis for membership is not necessarily the same in the black ghetto as in some of its American predecessors. In them, living in a ghetto was a good deal more likely to be voluntary than it is today. Those who grew away from the homogeneous way of life of the community then were often able to pack up and leave, as Louis Wirth (1928) showed in his classical study of the Jewish ghetto. With formal and informal devices of segregation, the white outside world today makes it difficult for many black people to venture outside the ghetto in search for dwellings. Thus the ghetto keeps on accumulating members who would rather not be there. Behind the signs of homogeneity which are blackness and at least relative poverty, there is much heterogeneity of a rather uneasy kind. If there is a 'ghetto way of life', it consists of a web of inter-twining but different individual and group life styles.

When we talk of ghetto culture, we imply that in the segregated ghetto environment, there are ways of thinking and acting evolved and maintained which are communicated (as well as communicated about) between ghetto dwellers. These together constitute ghetto culture. If this sounds self-evident, we may hasten to note that some observers have felt that the culture concept has little utility for understanding the black ghetto. Thus one major problem turns out to be exactly what kind of culture the ghetto has, what makes it or does not make it a culture. We will deal with this question at length.

On to 'community': it is convenient to refer to the ghetto as a community, but it is obvious to anyone accustomed to thinking in social anthropological terms that it is a community in some ways but less so in others. Like other communities the ghetto has a territory and a rather clearly defined population, the low-income black people who reside in the territory and a minority of somewhat better-off but equally black people who also live there. In social-structural terms, however, the definition of the community meets with more problems. The economic and political self-sufficiency of the ghetto is severely limited. Ghetto people support themselves through relationships with outsiders and are dominated by them. Every morning brings white non-residents into ghetto territory and black people out of it, for a day's work. Considering the impact of the wider environment, the ghetto is only a part-community, as most overarching social institutions are not its own. Considering how their working lives put many ghetto dwellers in touch with outsiders away from home rather than with each other, the ghetto, with its territory and its population, is a part-time community for many of its members.

What, then, beside shared external characteristics which outsiders regard as important, makes the ghetto a community? To start with, its own consciousness of kind which, among blacks as well as among whites, allows for little confusion about who belongs and who has 'outsider' written all over his face. This categorization is an almost perfect guide to who can do what with whom. On the one hand there are the white people with whom the ghetto dweller has only impersonal relationships—the shopkeeper, the supervisor, the policeman, the social worker, the customer at the lunch counter downtown; on the other hand, there are the black people of the ghetto, the pool from which his partner in marriage, his intimate friends and enemies, his nextdoor neighbour are all drawn. Ghetto dwellers do not only share a position with regard to the outside and experiences with it, they are also actual or potential participants in close personal relationships with one another.

So if the outside society has, in its own way, integrated the ghetto with itself politically and economically, then family life, leisure life, and just plain neighbourship remain largely separated. These are the spheres in which a community social structure peopled only by ghetto dwellers is built up. It is serviced also by a few professions so attuned to ghetto life that an outsider hardly could or would take them on, at least not in that layer of the professional hierarchy which deals directly with the ghetto dweller: the preacher, the gospel singer, the rock-and-roll group, the disc jockey on the black radio station, the numbers runner, the bootlegger, the prostitute, the dope pusher. Not all ghetto dwellers approve of all of them, but that is beside the point. The incumbents can make some kind of living, and they are in the only service occupations to which recruitment is almost as exclusively along ghetto lines as it is for the more personal relationships. The reasons for this exclusiveness may vary. In some cases, *esprit de corps* and shared perspectives are fundamental; in others, inconspicuousness and accessibility at odd hours are requirements that call for a black incumbent, a ghetto resident.

* * *

Winston Street, Washington, D.C., is a narrow, one-way ghetto street, one block long and lined by brick row houses, two or three stories high and in varying states of repair. In the windows of some of them are flower pots, bright curtains or even venetian blinds. Others have broken blinds, dirty plastic sheets, or nothing at all. Sometimes a house is condemned as unfit to live in, and its doors and windows are covered with boards. It is largely a residential street, and since it is not really a thoroughfare, its pedestrian and auto traffic is largely confined to the street's own residents and their visitors. At the corners of Winston Street and the surrounding streets are small business establishments: groceries, liquor stores, carry-out food shops, variety stores, laundromats, shoeshine shops, barber shops, beauty salons; all very modest in appearance. These are the establishments which cater to the day-to-day needs, and supply the few luxuries, of ghetto living. The consumption of liquor is considerable. The carry-outs find most of their customers among the many single men who cannot prepare food in their rented rooms, as well as among the children and adolescents who spend much of whatever money they can get on extra food and goodies. Variety stores sell candy, school equipment, cheap toys, and a variety of other inexpensive odds and ends. The carry-outs, the barber shops, and the shoeshine shops serve not only their manifest function but are also the hangouts, the centres of sociability, of teenagers and adult men. To serve as locales of leisure, they add some more items to their furnishings: newspapers, vending machines for cigarettes and soft drinks, a pinball machine, a juke box, a public telephone. No one establishment would have them all, some would have none of this, but many have some of it. So this becomes the place of small talk, perhaps sweet talk with the girl behind the carry-out counter.

Much of this leisurely interaction takes place on the street itself, however, where people stand at the corner or sit on the high stair-cases in front of the houses. During the cold months there are few people out, although there are usually some men at the corners. But in March and April when the early spring sun shines through from the south end of Winston Street, there will already be people sitting on the front steps and children playing in the street, and through the hot and humid summer months the street scene is a lively one until late at night. Many men and some women stand or sit around talking, children throw balls, hula-hoop, ride bikes, push each other in carts, or skip rope. Sometimes, the fire hydrant at the end of the street is switched on, and the children shower in the water spray and bathe in the gutter. People go back and forth to the laundromat or to Mr. Rubin's grocery store at the corner, doing the shopping for the day or just picking up a soda or an onion. A young man in sunglasses comes up the street carrying a transistor radio and listening to the soul music of station WOL. Two teenage girls, walking elbow to elbow, exchange news about boys. 'And then I told him, "Child, I couldn't care less if you come or not"!' The old man who goes from door to door on his mission for the Jehovah's Witnesses walks by, eyes fixed on the ground and with a brown briefcase in his hand. Since the people on the staircases know most of the passers-by, they greet them and sometimes stop them for a chat. Some, of course, avoid greeting each other, for there is animosity between them. And there are also the people who have not lived very long on the block and who are thus not very well known. On the other hand, some of the long-time watchers of the Winston Street scene actually reside somewhere else, on some neighbouring street, just coming down regularly to the street to spend their free time there. And of course, in the same way some of the people of Winston Street have their regular hangouts on other streets.

The street has its regular events. In the evening, the word is spread about what is the winning number in the numbers game, one of the ghetto's illegal but nonetheless central institutions. Now and then a fortunate player may collect some money from a nearby agent, but most of the time there is no luck. '758? I was two off again. I had 742.' During the warmer months of the year, the ice cream vendor's car also comes around in the evening, drawing the children's attention with its jingling bell.

The adult streetcorner men want other refreshments. Just talking, playing a game of cards, or shooting dice, they usually get around to pooling their money for something to drink, and one of them goes to the liquor store—or to a bootlegger, if it is Sunday, or too late on a weekday evening—to get some gin, of the kind which is $1·10 a half-pint at the cheapest store, or wine, of the kind that is 35 cents a half-pint (a higher price from the bootlegger). When he comes back, they try to share the drink somewhere out of the public view, as it is illegal to drink in public places. They go into a house or into the back alley, where they may not be seen, although of course it is no more lawful to drink there. The alley has a few trees, a rose bush, overflowing garbage cans, and lots of trash on the ground, including empty and broken bottles. Here and there is a clothesline. Some children play there, dogs guard the back yards, and there are heavy-weight rats running around. Some of the men also go there to 'take a leak' if there is no toilet within reach.

There are slums which are more like villages and others which are more like jungles.[1] At times one would look down Winston Street, see only the neighbourliness and tranquillity, and place this neigh-bourhood close to the village end of the spectrum. But the people who live there know that it also has some attributes of the urban jungle. Some people and places mean trouble, and there is danger in the dark and the unknown. There is the mentally disturbed woman who shouts at the men loafing below her window: 'Get away from down there or I'll pour lye over you all.' There is the young man who is shunned by the girls and the younger women because of his reputation:

That boy Chuck is crazy about sex. He goes to a bar and picks up a girl and brings her home and then he locks her up and screws her, and when he has to go out to work he locks her up and won't leave food or

cigarettes or anything for her, and then he comes home and goes right
on screwing her again. And that nice old mother of his don't say a word,
I guess she don't care, so she just acts as if she knows nothing about it.
I've seen girls come out of there, and he keeps them in there for weeks
locked up, and they look pretty near dead when they get out. Everybody
is afraid of him and the girls around won't go near him.

There is also Winston Street's own major trouble spot, the corner
where the rougher streetcorner men hang out. Fights are rather
common there, and the men occasionally show up with fresh knife
wounds. True, most of the fights are within the group, and most
of the people who have lived in the neighbourhood for some time
know the men well and are reasonably friendly with them; even so
they warn newcomers and visitors about this corner. Yet, it is not so
bad there, Winston Street people feel, as on the neighbouring street
where tough teenage boys hang out and are a menace to everybody
who passes by. And the nearby playground is also worse. Some
young men go there only to play basketball and table tennis, of
course, but there is also a rougher clique which is held responsible
for the fact that some people who have passed by have been 'yoked'
—robbed. Thus the playground is a place to stay away from, particularly after dark, according to neighbourhood consensus. And if some
young man whom one should happen to know begins to be seen
with this clique, one points out the dangers of such company. As
one young man was given a jail sentence for his participation in a
holdup, an older acquaintance of his commented:

> It had to happen sooner or later, you know. He used to work as some
> kind of an instructor for the kids up there on the playground, and then
> when he lost that job he should have stayed away from there from then
> on, but no, he kept on hanging out there with those no-good fellows,
> gorillas, that's what they are, all of them. So he got mixed up in this
> holdup in this liquor store, and they ain't going to let him out for a while.
> I guess he thinks about what we all told him now.

Potential trouble spots such as those just described can, of course,
be reasonably well avoided. But sometimes it is quite difficult. The
people who could cause trouble may have their recurrent gatherings
on the front staircase of a house which for some reason is well
placed for the purpose while they are not necessarily on terms of
personal friendship with the occupants of the house—or at least
not with all the occupants. Sometimes the friends of one household
occupy the whole front stairs leading to several apartments, thus
making entry difficult. At times their conversation gets loud and
boisterous, disturbing the people inside the house, and it may erupt
into a fight. The empty bottles, paper bags, cigarette packets and

other things which assemble during the gatherings are often left behind littering the sidewalk, the gutter, or the little patch of grass—or bare earth—which is in front of some buildings. Some residents who want to avoid trouble do not give any expression of their resentment to the people on the staircase, only occasionally voicing it in private to others—'They should have more sense.' If they are on better terms with the loiterers, and in particular if the latter are not 'gorillas' but more peaceful streetcorner men, they may occasionally reprimand them for the intrusion into other people's rights, or make a gesture of mild annoyance now and then.

Thus the people of the ghetto maintain a working knowledge of the potential for trouble in their environment.

*   *   *

Ghetto dwellers are not much involved with one another in relationships of power and livelihood, the social structure of the ghetto community is made up primarily of a multitude of connecting personal networks of kinsmen, peers, and neighbours. Overarching institutions under community control are lacking. The networks, of course, cannot provide the ghetto with a particularly 'tight' structure. Neighbourship, mutual acquaintances, place of work, and other unpredictable contingencies influence which ghetto dwellers gain access to each other. Functional differentiation in stable social relationships is limited to age and sex roles, peer roles and kinship roles. However, there is another important kind of differentiation which we may refer to as a diversity of life styles. 'Life style' is admittedly a vague term; this may be one of its advantages, at least for a while, in that it does not commit us to some well-established form of analysis which may be less suitable for this particular case. Preliminarily, we may view a life style as the involvement of an individual with a particular set of modes of action, social relationships, and contexts. It goes beyond any more formal definition of a single role, although as we shall see later, ghetto life styles as understood here are not wholly independent of the basic roles of age and sex.

*   *   *

What is the place of narratives and mini-memories in ghetto life? One might characterize them, of course, as the recounting of unique individual experiences, but in doing so, one may miss an important point. They are experiences of common interest, variations on themes relating to the typical traits of the ghetto-specific model of masculinity—hunting women, drinking, getting into trouble or somehow getting out of it. Since the men favour such topics over others, it obviously matters to them what is the content of sociability. We must go beyond Simmel's concern only with its form, in order to determine why the men draw on these specific conversational resources from the world outside the gathering, and why these topics can be handled to such particular satisfaction in this forum. This also means that we see street-corner sociability as a phenomenon which cannot be discussed in isolation from a wider social context.

In looking for a better path to follow in the interpretation of sociable interaction we may begin with the notion of leisure as 'free time'. 'Free', of course, in this case means free from work tasks. But as Bennett Berger points out in an essay on the sociology of leisure (1963), there is no really unconstrained time: the constraints which determine an individual's activities during his leisure hours are those which affect him as a moral and intellectual being and which make these activities rewarding enough in themselves, without material consequences. And the moral and intellectual problems to be acted upon in leisure may themselves be socially structured. Sociability, as social relationships in leisure, can thus be assumed to involve such moral and intellectual concerns which the individual can most satisfactorily deal with in interaction with others.

This reasoning ties up well with the work of some more recent students of sociability. These have directed their interest particularly to the analysis of American middle-class and upper-class gatherings (cf. Watson 1958; Riesman et al. 1960; Watson and Potter 1962). However, we may find it both pleasurable and useful to assume that there is little functional difference between the small talk at these parties, luncheons, and kaffee klatsches and that which goes on at the ghetto street corner.

According to these scholars, sociability is a kind of interaction in which definitions and evaluations of self, others, and the external world are developed, maintained, and displayed with greater intensity than in other interaction. Successful sociability is that where participants find satisfying understandings of the world and support for some reasonably high degree of self-esteem. An individual's vision of reality is often a precarious thing; we can find comfort in the knowledge that it is shared by others, thus acquiring social anchoring as an objective truth. And it is an old tenet of interactionist theory in sociology that a human being is particularly dependent on what he finds to be the view of significant others as he forms his conception of himself.[2] Yet it is not necessarily laborious, exhaustive, and literal statements of the truth as one sees it that constitute the best expression of shared understandings in sociability. In Erving Goffman's terms (1961:26–34), the sociable gathering has transformation rules which determine what experiences from the outside world are to be utilized as resources for conversation as well as what form they will be given. First of all, there may be a strain toward definitions of reality which in some way support the participants' self-esteem. Conversations are also often more rewarding when understandings are only alluded to in examples, exaggerations, half-truths, jokes and other indirectly or inexact forms of reference whose relation to the consensually established reality can be taken for granted. Furthermore, it is important in sociability to avoid boredom. Thus it is better to bring new materials to bear on shared understandings and values than just to state these repeatedly in their pure form. Sociability is at best a dramatic experience for the participant.

Can these ideas about the nature of sociable interaction lead the way toward an interpretation of the ghetto conversations we have exemplified above? It appears that they can. The men seem preoccupied with creating and maintaining a definition of natural masculinity which they can all share. By seizing on individual experiences of kinds which they have all had, they 'talk through' and thereby construct the social reality of the typical Ghetto Man, a fact of life larger than any one of them. This Ghetto Man is a bit of a hero, a bit of a villain, and a bit of a fool, yet none of them all the way. He is in fact a kind of a trickster—uncertainty personified, a creature fluctuating between competence and incompetence, success and failure, good and evil. He applies his mother wit or is plainly lucky some times, as Big Bill in front of the judge, and this helps him come out victorious or at least unscathed. But not all the time for native wit and luck have their limits, for instance when David left his bottle behind and the police were watching, or when Brenda came home and prevented Charlie from sneaking out with the gorgeous chicks from North Carolina. Anyway, when Ghetto Man succeeds, he is a hero, considering his limited skills and powers in an environment full of adversaries; if he fails, it is natural because he was up to no good.

Why is it that this Ghetto Man so consistently is made the topic of street-corner sociability, out of all qualities of self and social reality which need to be defined? Of course, one part of the answer may be that he has become normatively established as an appropriate subject for discussion in the social context of the men's gathering; he is a conversational resource which it is always acceptable to draw on. But we may go beyond this understanding and ask what makes men involve themselves personally and find satisfaction in these story-telling sessions. We have said that leisure is the time for taking care of moral and intellectual business. The construction materials of the Ghetto Man certainly seem to derive from problems of this

kind. We noted in the preceding chapter that there are two definitions of masculinity which co-exist, not altogether peacefully, in
the ghetto community. Many men are prevented by macrostructural
conditions from performing satisfactorily in the mainstream male
role and therefore take on the ghetto-specific alternative; as we shall
attempt to make clear in the next chapter, they are also socialized in
some degree to the ghetto-specific role from childhood on. But they
can never ignore the mainstream model of masculinity, for it is
actively promulgated by the wider society in many of its contacts
with the people of the ghetto, and many ghetto dwellers also voice
the opinion that there is no other morality appropriate way of being
a man. Those who are men in a more ghetto-specific way, then,
are constantly morally and intellectually besieged; they have a
common baggage of role ambivalence to deal with.[3] If they are to
find support for the kind of masculinity they have achieved, they had
better look for it among other men in the same situation.

*   *   *

All communities are in some ways differentiated and in others
undifferentiated. In preceding chapters we have seen how the people
of the ghetto are ordered along the lines of age and sex, in terms of
peer group and family alignments, according to their economic
relationships to the wider society, and on the basis of variations
in life styles which to some extent accompany these other variables.
On the other hand, there are things ghetto dwellers tend to have in
common—things we will look at here as a shared perspective toward
the ghetto condition.

Not all ghetto dwellers are equally involved with this perspective,
since their individual experiences and concerns differ. We have seen
that ghetto-specific circumstances and modes of behaviour are
unevenly distributed among the population of the community. Yet
it is hardly possible for anybody to remain unaware of what is
'typical' of the ghetto and how its people define their experiences.
A mainstreamer has neighbours, relatives and perhaps friends in
other ghetto life styles, and his own past may have involved him more
directly with facts of life unique to the ghetto than his current way
of life lets on; in an earlier chapter we dwelt on how ghetto dwellers
move between life styles. All members of the community will thus
in one way or another, and to one degree or another, come to witness
the same things. Furthermore, they are aware of the fact that they
have these shared experiences. They communicate about them and
thereby influence one another's views. We have already noted how
such cultural construction and maintenance goes on in the area of
sex roles. A set of conventional understandings of ghetto life is

developed, and it is generally recognized to be the property of the entire community. This alone gives the ghetto dwellers a kind of Durkheimian mechanical solidarity.[4] Since they realize that their common perspective is not shared with the world outside their community, it also marks them off from the surrounding society in their self-definition. This contributes to making the ghetto in some ways a united community. If it does not have overarching institutions of control which are its own, at least it has an overarching perspective.[5]

The ghetto institution of bootlegging provides a simple example of how the members of the community tend to arrive at a shared view which both unites them and marks the contrast to the outside world. We have seen before that bootleggers are community members who function in the neighbourhoods where they live and whose life styles vary. Potential customers thus get to know the bootleggers as neighbours and more or less as 'whole persons'—they are not as likely as people outside the community to form a stereotype of the 'typical bootlegger' as some kind of despicable character, even though their own sense of respectability may prohibit them from engaging in such illegal enterprise themselves. For a while when the major bootlegger in the Winston Street neighbourhood went out of business a lot of people started dabbling in the trade, and one streetcorner man commented that it was indeed in a sorry state when even the lesbian alcoholic hanging out with his group could be found at the corner with a half pint of gin in a paper bag, ready for a sale; but more often the bootlegger is a long-time resident of the neighbourhood who runs the business from his home. (We use masculine pronouns here to refer to the bootlegger, but there are a number of housewives in the trade as well.) Thus the bootlegger is as stable a neighbourhood institution as the streetcorner grocery.[6] Since he cannot compete pricewise with legitimate liquor dealers but is open for business only when these are closed—in Washington, D.C., weekday nights after nine, but above all on Sundays—he caters only to immediate needs. Many of the customers are streetcorner men who have taken up a collection or done some successful panhandling and who are unlikely to have liquor acquired during legal sales hours standing around for later consumption. But others, including mainstreamers, are also among the customers, for much of the sociable drinking takes place as people go on spontaneous visits to each other, and these visits quite frequently occur during hours when liquor stores are closed. Few ghetto dwellers regularly have a supply of liquor at home for such unexpected gatherings, and nobody feels that a host has an obligation to supply refreshments. Instead, the guests pool their money with his so that he can go to the neighbourhood bootlegger—it may be noted that although this brings a higher shared cost for the liquor, it is more advantageous to both host and guests than it would be for one of them to take on the entire cost alone by stocking up at a legitimate liquor store in advance. This means that ghetto dwellers are fairly united in viewing bootlegging as a convenient institution. Yet they are aware that while they find it both useful and morally acceptable, the wider society generally condemns it and tries to put an end to it. For fear of plainclothes detectives, many bootleggers refuse to deal with customers they do not know personally or have not been introduced to by a trustworthy person—such a suspiciousness, of course, is only possible in a business where relationships to the regular patrons are close. For such reasons, a neighbourhood and the community in general, is fairly protective of its bootleggers. Anybody who spends enough time in a neighbourhood would be able to spot which household does business on Sunday, as the customers' comings and goings can hardly be hidden, but if they are aware that their actions could reveal the identity of a bootlegger to outsiders, most ghetto dwellers would attempt to be loyal to him, and thus in a sense to the community. Even storefront church preachers forever railing against the evils of drinking, seem usually to prefer not to report bootleggers in their neighbourhoods, even when there can be no doubt that they are personally against the practice.

In a minor way, then, the common perspective toward bootlegging may make ghetto dwellers aware of their unity by setting them off against the official view of the practice held by the outside world.[7] Another illegal ghetto institution, the numbers game, promotes such unity even more intensively; there is the same suspiciousness and protectiveness (although numbers agents seem to suffer less from interventions from the agents of law than bootleggers do), the same feeling that nothing very objectionable is really involved, but also an additional factor in that it provides a topic for talk which readily brings members of different segments of the community into interaction. When the winning number of the day is spread informally by word of mouth along the streets throughout the ghetto, the mainstreamer housewife who is irritated at the wineheads lounging on her front steps may still find out the number from them and exchange a few comments on it. The game is a concern above segmental conflicts.

The origin of the numbers game is obscure; it has been claimed that it was brought to the United States and introduced into the black community by Cuban immigrants at the beginning of the century, but there actually seem to have been several games of a similar kind from the late nineteenth century and on.[8] The traditions surrounding the game in any particular black ghetto today are

likely to draw on a number of these games as they have existed at
different times and in different places. The current version in
Washington, D.C., derives 'the number', a three-digit figure, in a
rather complex manner (with which ghetto dwellers are usually
no more than faintly familiar) from the payoff figures of certain
daily horse races. 'Numbers' is thus a game of chance. As the
digits become known one by one, the last one becomes known in
the ghetto late in the afternoon. One may bet one's money on one,
two, or all three of them. It is easier to get a hit with a single digit,
of course, but one cannot expect to get a big one. The three-digit
hit can involve a large sum of money, but the conditions are rather
unfavourable. One's chance of hitting is one in a thousand, but the
pay-off is only six hundred to one or less, minus handling charge,
thus leaving a handsome profit to those who run the game. 'Numbers'
has a rather complex business hierarchy; in Washington, D.C., its
higher echelons are reputedly dominated by whites, as in most other
large cities. The customers in the ghetto have no personal contact
with these numbers bankers. The agents who deal directly with them
are usually ghetto dwellers themselves. Many of these numbers
runners are known to be available at certain hours at given places,
such as certain street corners or bars. However, there are also many
agents, often women, who take up bets at home, so that the players
in the neighbourhood can seek them out there. Thus numbers, at
least on the lowest level of the organization, may be a neighbourhood
institution much like the bootlegger.

The bets can be very small. Ten-cent bets are fairly common, but
many are considerably larger. However, the agent may be reluctant
to accept too large a bet. It also happens that a certain number
becomes very popular, so that a hit on that number would cause the
bankers a serious loss. To prevent this, the agent may declare that
the number has to be 'cut'—this would bring down the payoff on
a hit yet further.

To explain why any one number would be more popular than
another, one must note the ways in which ghetto dwellers decide
what number to play. Sometimes it is a question of idiosyncratic
attachments. Somebody born on March 3 may play 303, others try
the street number of the building they are in or their apartment
number. One young man says that for the last week he has played
the apartment number of a girl he has been dreaming about. But
there are also other ways of finding a number which could make
many people choose the same. Many stores in the ghetto sell 'dream
books', in which authorities on the occult science of numerology
give advice on lucky numbers; many of the 'readers', 'spiritualists',
and 'psychic advisors' who offer ghetto dwellers their services on such

problems as love, sickness and magic also serve as experts on numbers.[9] Furthermore, there is some oral tradition on the meaning of numbers derived from numerology. Paul Oliver, in *Screening the Blues* (1968:128–147), has shown that many old blues text contain references to such numbers. However, it does not seem that today's numbers players, in Washington, D.C., at least, are usually very strongly influenced by such traditions or even very knowledgeable about them. Rather, if factors outside their personal lives influence what numbers they choose to play, they may involve considerations of what numbers had hits on the same day in previous years, or significant current events. According to a story circulating in the Washington ghetto, a lot of people in Harlem had noted the birth weight when President Johnson's daughter Luci gave birth to a son, and the number they derived from it had a hit. This caused severe strain on the numbers bankers who apparently had not had the number cut so as to bring down the payoff sufficiently.

Such lore provides a topic of conversation in which ghetto dwellers have a shared interest—everybody is familiar with the game, and most adults are either playing it or have done so in the past. There are also stories about spectacular hits, such as this one:

> I heard about a man in Baltimore, he was a hustler, so he already had a Fleetwood (Cadillac) and a ring with a stone as big as this bottle-cap here. And then he hit it for $100.00! And he got it all, too, 'cause the banker didn't take the whole thing himself, it was too much, you know, so he had other bankers share the risk, and that way they could pay.

In addition, one can exchange reminiscences about one's own hits—at least if one plays 'single action', that is, one digit, one can get small hits easily enough—and those of acquaintances, about what one did with the money, about near misses, as when one was only one digit off or when one did not play a winning number one had thought of or had been playing before, and so forth. And when in a neighbourhood such as that around Winston Street somebody has a big hit, a lot of people take an intensive interest in it, both because of a sense of excitement in general and because it may touch on their lives too, as these notes show:

> There were an unusual number of people standing around on Winston Street for a late dusky winter afternoon, but anyone who had been in the neighbourhood the previous evening would know what it was all about. Elijah Williamson had had a big hit—it was estimated that he should get about fourteen hundred dollars. There was a complication in this case, however: Elijah, drifting around from household to household and between different women, had been living lately with the woman who took numbers around the corner, and since he had no job but

ate and drank on her money, he had been rather expensive for her. Thus she felt part of his big hit rightly belonged to her, and there had been repeated arguments about this throughout the day. This had delayed the payment which is otherwise usually made around noon. Thus as darkness arrived, Elijah Williamson still had not appeared with his money.

Bee Jay and Annie Patterson were standing outside the Patterson house. 'He'd better be around soon', Bee Jay said. 'I need a drink so bad.'

A little further down the street, Annie Patterson's husband Richard sat with a couple of friends in a removal truck, watching the street and swapping numbers stories as well as other anecdotes. A few younger men passed them by and asked, 'You ain't seen him yet?'

In Carl Jones' house, Carl, Sylvester, Sonny, and Randy had been playing cards all day, pinochles most of the time, watching the street through the window and waiting for Elijah Williamson to emerge. Although they were not usually very close to him, they were very interested in his hit. When he finally passed by, they stopped playing and left the house to catch up with him. In the meantime, Elijah reached Annie Patterson and Bee Jay and dug into his pocket for some money so that they could get a drink. He brought out a handful of assorted bills but refused to tell them how much he had finally received. Later, as people started talking about how much he seemed to have, most estimates were between five hundred and seven hundred dollars, although some felt there was more. Annie Patterson got a few one dollar bills, handed out with a nonchalant gesture. A boy passed by slowly on his bike and called out, 'Mr. Williamson, could I have some?'

Elijah Williamson continued his walk, now accompanied by Sonny and Carl. They talked excitedly for a while outside the grocery at the street corner, then turned back to go to the house of the numbers agent. She had agreed to give him some of the money, but at the same time she had told Elijah to get out of her house, so he had left his belongings in a suitcase outside the door. The three men now went to get it. Then they walked up the street again, but Carl had to return home as he had promised his wife to babysit. Sylvester joined him, while Sonny went with Elijah Williamson, saying that he would help him to the bus station. Elijah was going to a sister in Philadelphia whom he had not seen for a long time. This was obviously the time for a trip; it would also let things calm down in the neighbourhood, so everybody would not be asking him for money.

As the two passed by the grocery again, they met two other men who were hanging out there as usual. After a quick conversation they got two dollars. One of them shook his head as Elijah and Sonny walked on. 'Someone gonna follow him and pick up all that money.' One of the younger mainstreamer men in the neighbourhood came out of the store and said to the two, 'You all still figuring on how to spend Elijah's money?' They all laughed, and the two men remaining outside the store wondered whether Elijah would really get to Philadelphia. After a while they got started on a medley of Supremes hits, tapping the sidewalk with their feet and shuddering a little in the cold air.

I went back to Carl's house where Sylvester and Carl were also talking about what Elijah and Sonny might be doing. Since they recognized that Sonny could really be a very persuasive person, they figured that he was probably helping Elijah to spend some money on drinks before moving on to the bus station. So they thought they could as well enjoy a little more of the action. Hoping that Carl's wife would not return before we were back, we took off for the Price-rite liquor store where they expected to find the lucky winner and his escort. This was a miscalculation, however. Sylvester got some gin anyway, and we returned to Carl's house, where his brother Harry joined us. Everybody sat down at the kitchen table, but since Carl did not touch liquor after his ailment, the others did the drinking. Carl's children were dancing upstairs to the music of a black radio station. Carl himself urged his visitors to finish the gin as quickly as possible, before his wife would come back; she disliked drinking sessions in her home. He then took the bottle outside to the trash can at the end of the street.

Sonny returned before Carl's wife. He said he had finally left Elijah at the bus station, but only after he had taken him to a trustworthy woman who had agreed to keep some of the money until Elijah returned. When the other men smiled and Sylvester wondered out aloud whether it was to Elijah or Sonny the woman was trustworthy, Sonny realized that while he was absent the image of disinterested intellectual observer of ghetto life which he had been cultivating toward me had probably suffered from the others' comments. He told them indignantly that he was willing to bet that Elijah would get all his money back from her; Sylvester asked where he got the money for the bet. Sonny then observed to me that as I could see this was a very interesting kind of life, like a novel in a way.

In the next couple of days people mentioned Elijah Williamson and his hit now and then, wondering whether he was squandering his money in Philadelphia. As he returned there did not seem to be much left of it, nor was it talked about so often very much longer. But the people of the neighbourhood added the case of Elijah Williamson and the circumstances surrounding his hit to their repertoire of anecdotes, and when the topic of numbers came up in conversations from then on, his name was occasionally mentioned.

Bootlegging and numbers contribute to a common perspective for ghetto dwellers on two levels. In a neighbourhood like that around Winston Street, at least, they provide localized foci of attention, in that the neighbourhood is more or less the territory of particular bootleggers and numbers agents who are known personally to the people in the area and recognized as providing services shared by them. Furthermore, as Elijah Williamson's case shows, a hit also tends to give a neighbourhood some sense of cohesion, and it may also be added to a common body of neighbourhood tradition.

But beyond their impact in giving a neighbourhood things in common, these institutions are known to exist and function in the same way all over the ghetto community, so ghetto dwellers can assume that a general knowledge of such things is among their shared understandings. It is particularly in this sense that numbers and bootlegging are paradigms of the common ghetto perspective. But the perspective encompasses a lot more, and phenomena which are much more pervasive in their influence on black life than are these two institutions. Since they are of many kinds, the perspective may seem rather fragmentary. Yet this also means that what is held in common seems next to all-encompassing, in a sociological sense diffuse, to the ghetto dwellers.

*   *   *

Ghetto dwellers have much to resent about the way the outside world treats them: poor jobs, unemployment, unfair practices on the part of many employers, high rents for unsatisfactory housing, inadequate schools and health and welfare services, arbitrary, inefficient, and sometimes brutal police work, the poor performance and sharp practices of many businesses aiming at ghetto customers, as well as a host of major and minor expressions of prejudice and discrimination which may confront a member of the black minority as he goes about his everyday social traffic in American society.[10] Although such circumstances do not hit every member of the community with equal force, they provide each ghetto dweller with some basis for discontent, and probably they all play some role in the accumulation of grievances which may finally result in a rising. However, they do not seem to be equally prominent in the collective articulation of resentment which occurs spontaneously in the ghetto, and some of them are obviously of greater significance than others for the understanding of the form of ghetto rebellion. Some of the grievances are discontinuous and more private in their character, and one may perhaps only diffusely conceive of who is responsible for them. Thus complaints may be aired now and then about the insufficiency of garbage collection, about hours spent in waiting rooms, about a job a no better qualified white person got, or about a landlord who refuses to make repairs. But there are fewer of these, and they tend to be assimilated to the general body of knowledge about the hostile, distant white world. In the Winston Street neighbourhood, at least, many more conversations about grievances dwell on white-owned businesses and the police, probably this is so because these are continuously present, represented by 'real people', on ghetto territory. This may make it easier for ghetto dwellers to share experiences directly and to see the relevance of one's own experience to that of others. Since merchants and policemen are also those outsiders who become most directly involved in the insurrection itself, we will pay particular attention to how ghetto dwellers define their discontent with respect to these. This obviously does not mean that they are the only objects of 'real' grievances; rather, they seem to become the foci of concern toward which discontent is channelled also from other sources.[11] Thus they are particularly important in interpreting the insurrectionary mood of the ghetto in terms of social processes within the community.

IN THE FIELD

My own introduction to neighbourhood life was a very unstructured one. Since I had found that there were no suitable living quarters in the neighbourhood when I arrived, I took an apartment which was approximately a five-minute walk from Winston Street. The neighbourhood was thus conveniently within reach at any time of day or night, and it was possible to take neighbourhood people to the apartment for occasional conversations in greater privacy than was sometimes possible in the crowded neighbourhood homes. From this base, I began to take walks in the neighbourhood where I did not yet have any personal contacts; I preferred not to be sponsored there by the direct involvement of any other outsider. To begin with, this was an odd experience of being 'not wanted'. Perhaps I was less conspicuous than I felt. In any case, I felt that a great many pairs of eyes were looking at me, and since I later came to know how people follow what happens on the neighbourhood scene, I do not doubt that a lot of people really took note of my presence. However, as soon as I tried to meet someone's eyes and establish some kind of contact, I seemed to turn invisible, as at that precise moment nobody would give me any direct attention. After a few fruitless walks of this kind during which I was not yet ready to take any more abrupt steps toward contact, I came upon a gathering of streetcorner men, one of whom called out to ask if I had a match. I did not, but I stopped to ask for the time, then went on to ask if they knew much about the neighbourhood. This may have been an odd question; anyway, for one reason or other, they were ready to engage in conversation, and I explained that I lived only a few blocks away, that I was Swedish, and that I was interested in the neighbourhood. We sat down to talk at the street corner where a few old crates served as chairs, and as it began to get dark we shared a couple of family-size bottles of beer. I asked the men various questions about

themselves and about the neighbourhood—questions which I tried
to keep as harmless as possible. Nevertheless, I discovered that later
a great many of their answers had been misleading, and a couple
of them had given me false names. On the other hand they probably
found out more about me, and from my point of view this was just
as important, as I got a chance to define my identity to someone in
the neighbourhood.

After a couple of hours of unevenly flowing conversation another
man appeared and got into an argument with my new acquaintances.
He was obviously quite intoxicated, and the exchange was loud.
I was about to go home as he said to me, 'Don't sit here with those
hoodlums, I'll let you meet some friends of mine'. This was Bee Jay.
As we walked down Winston Street he introduced me to a few other
men who were sitting on the front stairsteps we passed by. One of
them said that he had seen me around before. 'He's OK', Bee Jay
told him. We then went into the house where he was staying as a
boarder at the time. His landlord, whom we encountered in chapter 3
as Leroy, a swinger with mainstreamer learnings, was there with a
number of younger men including two brothers who were also
staying in the house at the time. (Later the composition of the household changed so that by the end of field work it included only Leroy,
his younger sister, and her baby son.) 'Guess where I found this
fellow', Bee Jay said. 'At the corner with Arthur and Ribs! They were
getting ready to yoke him.' Most of those who were in the room
laughed, and Bee Jay told them what he had found out about me
at the corner. Some of it was mistaken, so I gave a fuller account of
myself and my purposes in the neighbourhood in response to their
questions. Leroy inquired into my academic background and talked
a little about the problems I was likely to encounter; his major
point was that to start with, I had better not ask too many questions but keep my eyes open. He made a very strong impression
on me this evening and continued to do so throughout my field
work. Although he does not appear much on the preceding pages,
he gave me access to wide social circles and took much of his time
to talk about life in the ghetto community as it appeared to him. At
the same time, since he probably read more widely than most people
either in or outside the ghetto, he was very concerned about the
preservation of anonymity in works like this study, and clearly he
was worried that some neighbours should regard him as an informer
if he gave me any personal information about them which was to
be published. Thus he never discussed neighbourhood life except in
general terms unless he was sure that I already had all the personal
data involved.

This first evening, however, the conversation of the gathering soon turned to Swedish topics, particularly to the heavyweight championship fights of Ingemar Johansson. Thus my emergent identity soon seemed to be Swedish first, some-kind-of-fellow-who-wants-to-know-about-the-neighbourhood-and-maybe-write-a-book-about-it second. Relatively few knew exactly what an anthropologist is or does, of course, and 'finding out how people live here' seemed a quite satisfactory definition of my purpose. Already this evening a mispronunciation of my first name became stabilized, and this was the name by which I became known in the following period. When the mistake was later discovered, I identified the mispronunciation as my nickname. Possibly this was a useful accident, as white people in the ghetto are not usually familiar enough to have nicknames.

That evening Leroy, Bee Jay and one of Leroy's brothers walked me home, pointing out that I was not particularly safe. In the following days I returned to their household every day to meet them and more of their friends and neighbours. (Generally I was in the neighbourhood afternoons, evenings, and weekends, as these were the times when most people were there.) As I got to know more people, I gradually became less dependent on my first acquaintances, although they remained among my closest friends. Bee Jay never let me forget that he had probably saved me from yoking the first evening, and possibly he was right. Of the two men he said he had met me with at the corner, Ribs was described at length in the story about a knife fight by another streetcorner man in chapter 4, and Arthur decided to go to a mental hospital a couple of months later because he felt he was 'going crazy'. Both turned out to be 'gorillas' with lengthy crime records.

From the start at the street corner, I thus followed the natural links of social networks as I was introduced to more people. In this way I became rather readily acquainted with a great number of neighbourhood people, as neighbours in daily interaction do not remain unaware of each others' friends, particularly not when these are as consistently present as I was. Of course, such introductions may have been helped considerably by the village-like atmosphere of Winston Street to which we referred at the beginning of chapter 1—it seemed to be literally a neighbourhood to a greater extent than most ghetto areas.[12] In the introductions, it was particularly pointed out that I was Swedish, which apparently created a special position for me, clearly separated from that of other whites; this seemed quite useful in that I was not quite so readily assimilated into the perspective of black-white conflict.

At times I was a little concerned over the clarity of my anthropological identification. Often, of course, my purposes in getting to know something about the ghetto community were mentioned in introductions. When this did not happen, however, I could not always easily determine what to do. Perhaps some of the burden in such a situation could be seen as falling on the person who makes the introduction, as he sponsors the researcher in relationships where he can expect him to carry on with his observations. But if one is uncomfortable with a concealed status, this hardly seems good enough. Here I tried to be reasonable. I would rather not interrupt the situation immediately to make an alternative presentation of myself but tried instead to make my reasons for being there clear as soon as a convenient opportunity appeared. In some cases, this opportunity never came, as I met a lot of people only very superficially once or twice—this is what happens in an urban situation where there is a large turnover of acquaintances and where one sees some of one's friends quite rarely. Generally, however, I felt that I had made the point of being a student of community life clearly enough. At the same time, I must confess to being rather pleased that Winston Street people generally seemed to interact with me much more in personal terms than on the basis of my being some kind of investigator. There seemed to be few advantages with too distinct an emphasis on the latter kind of role. Perhaps if one can build up a good case for the importance of one's research to the community where it is conducted it might be good strategy to give emphasis to the role and convince people to go out of their way to be co-operative, for their own sake. However, knowing that black people's situation is what it is despite decades of social findings which could have been helpful, I did not feel that I could honestly claim that what I did would make much difference to the future of the community. To those relatively few who took a direct interest in the research angle of my presence, such as Leroy and some of his friends, I tried to be absolutely frank on this question; they would have to accept or reject my interest in the community on a personal basis, since I could not promise that my research would benefit their community much. I could only try to make life in the community more understandable to other outsiders and not to cause the neighbourhood people any inconvenience by identifying them in writing. We had a few intensive debates about this and related matters, but apparently those who raised the issue were reasonably satisfied with my views and my behaviour since we continued to be good friends.

If ghetto dwellers thus often tend to reap little advantage by interacting with researchers, it could easily be uncomfortable to them. With a more formalized researcher role I suspect that I would have been ranged more easily among the white persons of authority who dominate ghetto dwellers and, in their view, disrupt their lives: social workers, police investigators and others. These are not usually the kind of people one talks to spontaneously or in front of whom one behaves normally, nor are they people one cares to have around much. At the beginning of my presence in the neighbourhood some people asked me if I had anything to do with such categories and made it quite clear that they disliked their kind of prying. This could easily make much information either unrepresentative or unaccessible. It turned out, too, that although most of the information collected through the interviews conducted before my arrival was rather uncontroversial, there were points where Winston Street interviewees had given information which was not quite correct—for instance, fewer people actually had set meal hours and home work hours for the children, much fewer went to church regularly, and some households included members, usually men, who were not present according to the interview census data. Obviously, when people are not living up to ideals which they may hold themselves or at least impute to a researcher, they are apt to want to present themselves in a favourable light, and in some cases men prefer to avoid any kind of contact with officialdom.

In attempting to avoid such problems, I was particularly interested in observing everday life in situations where attention did not focus on me, especially ordinary interaction sequences between ghetto dwellers, most often conversations where their interests, interpretations, and evaluations were freely expressed. Of course, these are the natural processes of cultural sharing which we have taken note of repeatedly in the preceding chapters. In such situations, particularly when the participants were people who had gotten to know me well, I had a feeling that my presence did not serve as a significant constraint on them. There were some occasions when I was apparently conspicuously quiet while everybody else was talking, but I felt I could truthfully answer any comments about this by explaining that I had always been a rather quiet person. Occasionally I tried to get natural conversations started on topics which interested me particularly. Sometimes these attempts were quite fruitful; at other times they were painfully obvious failures, in which cases one could only let conversations proceed to find more spontaneous courses. Of course, I also engaged in direct conversations with people which were consequently somewhat more like interviews, but I tried to give these the form of small talk, and they usually took place in decidedly informal settings, such as on the front staircase of a house, in a carry-out, or over a kitchen table. The results at least usually had 'the ring of truth', that is, they did not seem to constitute an interaction idiom developed specifically for me, and they were generally congruent with what I could observe in other situations.

I never took notes in the presence of others in the neighbourhood, and tape recording was used only in relatively few cases with children as informants. This means that the quotations from neighbourhood people which appear in this volume are not likely to be quite exact; they should certainly not be made a basis of a precise linguistic analysis. However, I do not think they are very far from the original, for with a reasonably good memory which one is consciously straining to capacity I believe it is possible to reproduce even rather complex statements and exchanges with a fair degree of accuracy. Naturally, I hurried to take notes on observations of this kind as soon as I got home in order not to risk losing data or interfering too much with them.

While this kind of informality of data gathering may ensure that the information one gets is really from ordinary life and that it is not isolated from its context, it certainly has drawbacks from the point of view of hard science. All one's data on a certain topic are not strictly comparable, and if they are one is still likely to have the quantity of data which could be collected, on certain topics and in certain communities, by door-to-door interviewing. In this kind of situation one must simply make a decision about priorities. Since I did not feel I could combine participant observation with such a line of action, I had to choose, and my interest in the realities of household and peer group life, modes of interaction processes of culture building and the like were not of the kind which can be contained in questionnaires. Besides, of course, some of the important bases of my field work had already been established by the earlier Urban Language Study survey, so I did not have to compromise my participant observer role for example by eliciting data on household composition.[13] In general, however, I could not aim at acquiring precise quantitative data amenable to statistical analysis. The generalizations in the preceding chapters thus tend to be based on rather uncontrollable impressions of observable behaviour in combination with the statements of ghetto dwellers who gave their views on the topics in question. This, of course, is not very satisfactory. However, it may represent a typical anthropological preference in a field work situation of this kind, with its alternative constraints on the researcher role.

Clearly an anthropologist engaged in participant observation is often to some extent undercommunicating, although not usually concealing those facets of his identity which tend to separate him from other people in the community. In my case there was certainly a great deal to undercommunicate about; that is, there was little likelihood that I would ever manage not to be conspicuous wherever I was. Bee Jay suggested jokingly that I might be the real 'blue-eyed blond devil' the Muslims were talking about. But at least I could try not to make my behaviour seem equally out of place. I dressed informally in order not to look like those whites who are only in the ghetto 'on business', and although Fats once asked if he could exchange his thirty-dollar hat for mine, my clothes were not generally anything out of the ordinary—the hat in question was from a dime store. I also tried to change my speech in the direction of the ghetto dialect, although I knew I would not be able to master its complexity very easily. Of course, I could not become like a ghetto dweller. I would not have been comfortable trying too hard to be someone else than my ordinary self, and certainly there is almost nothing as contemptible as an outsider who tries to affect the style of an in-group but who is constantly falling out of it. But at least I could hope to intimate my personal acceptance of ghetto dwellers' behaviour by coming relatively close to it.

NOTES

1 Gans (1962b: 4) uses these terms to describe the quality of social life in the areas concerned. The urban village is a stable, homogeneous home of immigrants to the city; the typical example is the working-class neighbourhood of some European immigrant group, in Gans' case the Italian-Americans. The urban village is hardly a slum to anybody but outsiders ignorant of its way of life. The typical urban jungle is the skid row; it is the home of isolated individuals, families in disorder, criminals, and illegal services provided to the rest of the city. Whyte (1943) discusses two types of slums in similar terms. It seems that sociologists, following the pioneering work of the Chicago school of sociology, have been a little too prone to find only jungles in working-class and lower-class urban areas—there has been more imagery of disorganization than of organization. For an influential example see Zorbaugh (1929); also note the rubric 'in the City of Destruction' in Frazier's (1939) book on the black family.
2 For an analysis of the maintenance and transformation of reality see Berger and Luckman (1966: 135ff.). The development of the self in social process has long engaged the interest of sociologists who have had an ancestral figure in this field in Charles Horton Cooley (1902); for a recent systematization of interaction theory drawing partially on this perspective see McCall and Simmons (1966).
3 This is apparently what Merton and Barber (1963) would call sociological-ambivalence in the restricted sense, as it refers to more or less incompatible expectation incorporated into a single role, namely the male sex role.
4 Scheff (1967: 36) suggests that it is this higher order of co-orientation—a recognition of shared recognition—which is at the basis of Durkheim's conception of the 'collective consciousness', by ordering individual consciousness into a social structure. While the point is often left implicit in anthropological culture theory, it is made quite clearly in Goodenough's (1963: 257–265) analysis of interaction and public culture. This notion of shared understandings is probably of greater than ordinary interest in this case as the sharing is given prominence in community self-definition.

5 One might say that the ghetto dwellers have a clear understanding that their shared perspective is to a great extent a reference group phenomenon rather than something to be taken for granted as a universal in the society; see the very relevant paper by Shibutani (1955).

6 An extreme case of such normalization of an illegal business enterprise is that cited by Short and Strodtbeck (1965: 109) from a black area in Chicago: a marijuana pusher who was moving away included a note with each bag sold, explaining that she was leaving the area. She thanked patrons for past purchases, gave her new address, and asked them to stay with her as customers at the new place of business. Short and Strodtbeck also note that illegal businesses tend to be more strongly integrated into the black ghetto community than into white lower-class areas.

7 The point made is similar to that made by Frankenberg (1966: 78, 265) on illegal cock fighting in Cumberland. However, Frankenberg goes so far as to say that cock fights are held partially *in order to* express defiance against authority vested outside the community. I believe the intrinsic value of the numbers game and of bootlegging is quite enough to keep them alive in the ghetto, but a heightened awareness of conflict with the wider society is undoubtedly a *consequence* of involvement with the illegal institutions.

8 For more detailed, relatively early studies of the numbers game (also known as 'policy') in Harlem and the black ghetto of Chicago, see McKay (1940: 101–116) and Drake and Cayton (1962: 470–494) respectively.

9 McCall (1963) has analysed the symbiosis of occultism and the numbers game, with an emphasis on the profits derived by occult advisors and suppliers from applied numerology.

10 The Report of the National Advisory Commission on Civil Disorders (1968) may be consulted for a more general survey of ghetto dwellers' grievances. Mainstream institutional contacts with the ghetto are discussed by Jacobs (1966).

11 Goldberg (1968: 125) notes that only certain kinds of grievances seem to call forth risings directly. While this may be true—and the police would then certainly have to be seen as an object of discontent particularly often involved—it seems questionable, as Rainwater (1967: 31) points out, if unrest would be prevented by dealing with factors which may be of a largely symptomatic nature. See also the comments at the end of this chapter.

12 The Winston Street neighbourhood, as seen by the people of the street and in this volume, is an 'egocentric' territory—it refers to this street and its immediate environs beyond which it fades out. Although Winston Street people include neighbouring streets as the periphery of their neighbourhood, people on these streets certainly do not count themselves as residents of a Winston Street neighbourhood. Since each street is the centre of its world, neighbourhoods overlap.

13 Curiously enough, no neighbourhood resident mentioned these earlier interviews to me. Possibly they were connected only to the previous involvements of white outsiders rather than to me.

REFERENCES

Berger, Bennett M., 1963. The Sociology of Leisure: Some Suggestions. In *Work and Leisure*. Erwin O. Smigel (ed.). New Haven Conn.: College and University Press.

Berger, Bennett M., 1963. Soul Searching. *Trans-action*, 4:7, 54–57.

Berger, Peter L., and Thomas Luckmann, 1966. *The Social Construction of Reality.* Garden City, N.Y.: Doubleday.

Cooley, Charles H., 1902. *Human Nature and the Social Order.* New York: Scribner's.

Drake, St. Clair, and Horace R. Cayton, 1962. *Black Metropolis.* New York: Harper Torchbooks. (First edition 1954, Harcourt, Brace.)

Frankenberg, Ronald, 1966. *Communities in Britain.* Harmondsworth: Penguin.

Frazier, E. Franklin, 1939. *The Negro Family in the United States.* Chicago: University of Chicago Press.

Gans, Herbert J., 1962b. *The Urban Villagers.* New York: Free Press.

Goffman, Erving, 1961. *Encounters.* Indianapolis: Bobbs-Merrill.

Goldberg, Louis C., 1968. Ghetto Riots and Others: The Faces of Civil Disorder in 1967. *Journal of Peace Research,* 5: 116–131.

Goodenough, Ward H., 1963. *Cooperation in Change.* New York: Russell Sage Foundation.

Jacobs, Paul, 1966. *Prelude to Riot.* New York: Random House.

McCall, George J., 1963. Symbiosis: The Case of Hoodoo and the Numbers Racket. *Social Problems,* 10: 361–371.

McCall, George J., and J. L. Simmons, 1966. *Identities and Interactions.* New York: Free Press.

McKay, Claude, 1940. *Harlem: Negro Metropolis.* New York: Dutton.

Merton, Robert K., and Elinor Barber, 1963. Sociological Ambivalence. In *Sociological Theory, Values, and Sociocultural Change.* Edward A. Tityakian (ed.). New York: Free Press.

National Advisory Commission on Civil Disorders, 1968. *Report of the National Advisory Commission on Civil Disorders.* New York: Bantom Books.

Oliver, Paul, 1968. *Screening the Blues.* London: Cassell.

Rainwater, Lee, 1967. Open Letter on White Justice and the Riots. *Trans-action,* 4:9:22–32.

Riesman, David, Robert J. Potter, and Jeanne Watson, 1960. Sociability, Permissiveness, and Equality: A Preliminary Formulation. *Psychiatry,* 23: 323–340.

Scheff, Thomas J., 1967. Toward a Sociological Model of Consensus. *American Sociological Review.*

Shitbtani, Tamotsu, 1955. Reference Groups as Perspectives. *American Journal of Sociology,* 60: 562–569.

Short, James F., and Fred L. Strodtbeck, 1965. *Group Process and Gang Delinquency.* Chicago: University of Chicago Press.

Watson, Jeanne, 1958. A Formal Analysis of Sociable Interaction. *Sociometry,* 21: 269–280.

Watson, Jeanne, and Robert J. Potter, 1962. An Analytic Unit for the Study of Interaction. *Human Relations,* 15: 245–263.

Whyte, William F., 1943. Social Organization in the Slums. *American Sociological Review,* 8: 34–39.

Wirth, Louis, 1928. *The Ghetto.* Chicago: University of Chicago Press.

Zorbaugh, Harvey F., 1929. *The Gold Coast and the Slum.* Chicago: University of Chicago Press.

CHAPTER 16

The Sociology of a Zone of Transition*

J. A. Rex

It is often said nowadays that there is no special urban sociology. What goes on in the city, it is claimed, is merely an expression of general processes at work in a national industrial society. An adequate theory of this society would therefore comprehend within itself the sociology of the city. I believe there is some truth in this view, but I also believe that there are particular processes at work in the concrete urban situation. I propose to illustrate this by outlining a theoretical model which explains something at least of the community structure of what Burgess called 'the zone of transition'. This model includes three elements: (1) a general theory of housing classes in the city, (2) a theory of ethnic group relations and rural-urban culture change and (3) a theory of conflict and conflict resolution as between associations in the urban zone of transition.

The theory of housing classes is one which emerges from an attempt to make sense of the processes underlying Burgess's theory of urban zones. Burgess's broad differentiation of the city into four social and cultural zones outside the city centre (a zone of transition, a zone of working men's homes, a middle-class residential zone and a commuters' zone) may be accepted as a starting point for the analysis of European and North American cities in the inter-war period. The actual physical position of these areas is to a large extent immaterial. What his account of the city principally lacks, however, is a sufficient explanatory theory of why the social and cultural life of these areas is as it is. The general notion of 'competition for land use' and the outline of the principal ecological processes such as domination, invasion and succession is too lacking in theoretical bite to give us this. What is needed is an account in terms of the action frame of reference which explains particular kinds of land-use and building use in terms of the action-orientation of typical residents. What follows is an attempt to do this on the basis of research experience in Birmingham.

* This paper arises out of the study by John Rex and Robert Moore, *Race, Community and Conflict: A Study of Sparkbrook*, published by the Oxford University Press in 1967. Reprinted by permission of the author from *Readings in Urban Sociology*, edited by R. E. Pahl, Pergamon Press, Oxford, 1968, pp. 211–231.

The theory which emerges may in part be generalizable but clearly where important variables in the historical situation differ in other cities other models may have to be developed.

Our starting point then is the sort of industrial settlement with its civic facilities which grew up in England in the nineteenth century. At this stage one sees the first segregation of residential areas determined by position in relation to factories, civic buildings and the prevailing winds. On the one hand one has the homes of the upper middle classes—the captains of industry with good access to central facilities and yet avoiding contact with industrial dirt. On the other one has the grid iron rows of working-class cottages built in the left-over space and segregated by railway-lines, canals and natural features and in each of these a separate social sub-system with its own way of life develops amongst the residents.

The upper-middle-class way of life is based upon the independence of the family, secure in the possession of its property and not dependent upon neighbourhood and extended kinship. It is expressed in the gracious architecture of large family houses, which although they have long ago been incorporated in the central business district are still structurally sound and help to give style to parts of the city centre.

The rows of red-brick working-class cottages on the other hand were built for rent-paying hands. No concept of family or community life was built into their architecture. Yet perhaps for this reason, though much more because of shared poverty and adversity, these areas came to support a strong extra-familial communal culture which was reflected in the corner shops, the pubs and the chapels, in extended kin groups, neighbourhoods, trade unions, friendly societies and religious congregations. Mutual aid rather than property gave security to the inhabitants of this area and when that mutual aid was expressed in political terms in the socialism of the city hall it was greatly to enhance the power of the established working-classes in their struggle for housing and living space.

Gradually, however, and particularly during the period between 1880 and 1914, a third way of life began to emerge between these two. It was the way of life of growing numbers of white-collar people. In aspiration it was oriented to that of the upper middle classes. True, these people—shopkeepers, minor professionals and privileged employees in industry—paid rent and their quarters were far meaner than those of the gracious upper middle classes. But they were a cut above the small red-brick cottages, and surviving servants' bells in their attics and cellars still testify to the social position of their first tenants. Abandoned by these tenants in the suburban migration of the inter-war period, these houses form a third characteristic type within the city's inner ring.

In the twentieth century, however, the great urban game of leap-frog begins. The types of housing we have mentioned pass to other residential and commercial uses and support new differentiated styles of life while their original inhabitants open up new desirable housing options further from the centre.

The 'captains of industry' together with the most successful professionals settle in larger houses, detached and in their own grounds in the classy inner suburbs. The white-collar people, aided by mortgages, leap still further where the land is cheaper and tend their gardens around one side of their semi-detached houses. And, finally, the working classes, having attained a measure of power in the city hall, have their own suburbs built for them. They are modelled on those of the white-collar people, but are distinguished by the fact that once a week a man from the Council calls for the rent.

These three ways of life and of housing are considered desirable and normal in the city. Less desirable or less normal is the way of life of those who now inhabit the inner zone. They will include some who have bought their own houses, some who occupy houses bought by the Council pending demolition, some who have bought larger old houses but must take tenants to pay their way and some who aspire to nothing more than the tenancy of a room or two.

There will, of course, be some deviants, romantics and intellectuals who actually prefer living in the inner zone, but the persistent outward movement which takes place justifies us in saying and positing as central to our model that suburban housing is a scarce and desired resource. Given that this is so, I suggest that the basic process underlying urban social interaction is competition for scarce and desired types of housing. In this process people are distinguished from one another by their strength in the housing market, or more generally, in the system of housing allocations.

Max Weber, it will be remembered, relativized Marx's view of the nature of social classes by suggesting that any market situation and not only the labour market led to the emergence of groups with a common market position and common market interests which could be called classes. We need only qualify this slightly to include groups differentially placed with regard to a system of bureaucratic allocation to arrive at a notion of 'housing classes' which is extremely useful in analysing urban structure and processes.

Some Marxists may argue that such housing classes do nothing more than reflect the class struggle in industry and clearly they are partly right in that there is some correlation between the two. But it is also the case that among those who share the same relation to the means of production there may be considerable differences in ease of access to housing. This is part of the 'super-structure' which manifestly takes on a life of its own. A class struggle between groups differentially placed with regard to the means of housing develops, which may at local level be as acute as the class struggle in industry. Moreover, the independence of this process is emphasized the more home and industry become separated.

The following housing-classes may, then, be distinguished in a large British provincial city:

1. The outright owners of large houses in desirable areas.
2. Mortgage payers who 'own' whole houses in desirable areas.
3. Council tenants in Council built houses.
4. Council tenants in slum houses awaiting demolition.
5. Tenants of private house-owners, usually in the inner ring.
6. House owners who must take lodgers to meet loan repayments.
7. Lodgers in rooms.

In the class struggle over housing, qualification either for a mortgage or a council tenancy are crucial. They are, of course, awarded on the basis of different criteria. In the first case size and security of income are vital. In the second 'housing need', length of residence and degree of affiliation to politically powerful groups are the crucial criteria. But neither mortgages nor council tenancies are available to all so that either position is a privileged one as compared with that of the disqualified. It is likely, moreover, that those who have council houses or may get them soon will seek to defend the system of allocation which secures their privileges against all categories of potential competitors. Thus local politics usually involves a conflict between two kinds of vested interest and between those who have these interests and outsiders.

As with classes generated by industrial conflict, however, there is always some possibility of an individual moving from one class to another. To the extent that individuals feel that such a move is credible, disadvantaged groups come to see the position of the privileged as legitimate and the system of class conflict tends to be transformed into a status system. Potentially class conscious attitudes amongst the housing classes may therefore be blurred.

Before we pass to a discussion of the complications which are introduced into this model by ethnicity and urban-rural culture change, it should be noted that considerable variations in this pattern of housing-class conflict would follow from differences in the economic, political and cultural situation in different industrial countries. The model we have posited assumes the existence of a socialist movement in relation to housing amongst the native working classes, an inability to exercise political power on their own behalf by disadvantaged groups and an aspiration to relatively detached family

life in suburban conditions amongst all groups. Where these assumptions do not hold, other conflict and status patterns may emerge.
Thus in the American situation 'Council housing' does not appear
to be an important factor and low-cost public housing is likely to be
thought of as part of the destiny of the underprivileged. On the other
hand, militancy amongst the disadvantaged in the absence of privileged working-class political power may upset the prevailing pattern.
And in many countries the suburban trend may not have the same
cultural importance which it has in England so that both middle-class
and working-class citizens may prefer flatted accommodation near
the city centre.

Such differences as these, however, call for the modification of the
basic model which we have elaborated, not for its rejection. What is
common to all urban situations is that housing, and especially certain
kinds of desirable housing, is a scarce resource and that different
groups are differentially placed with regard to access to the available
housing stock.

The theory of housing classes, which we have outlined, is a theory
which tells us something of the potential bases of conflict. We cannot
immediately assume, however, that this will lead automatically to the
formation of organized and class-conscious groups. Any theory of
class conflict must further specify the ways in which those with a
common 'market situation' organize or fail to organize to take action
in pursuit of their interests. The business of organization, however,
may in any particular case lead to a blurring of the lines of conflict
and this is particularly true of the 'zone of transition' where the fact
that many of the residents are drawn from external cultures introduces another cross-cutting variable into the situation.

The zone of transition is, of course, differentiated from other zones
by a particular type of housing-class situation and to that extent its
ethnic diversity arises out of the class model we have described. If we
define it as the lodging-house area we should note that whatever the
ethnic origin of its inhabitants they will be drawn from classes 6 and
7 above. But if, in fact, the native-born population are able to discriminate against the newcomer, then it is certain that these disadvantaged classes will be affected by ethnic differences which divide
them amongst themselves.

In point of fact it is desirable, if the ideal type of the lodging-house
zone is to have empirical application, to include within it more than
just the lodging-houses. In the particular piece of empirical research
from which these theoretical conclusions were drawn, the lodging-
houses were adjacent to Council slum property and structurally
sound privately rented houses. Since the three types of housing were
united by common shopping and other facilities, the community

structure of the area could only be thought of as the result of inter-action between all the housing classes involved.

There were, in fact, four such classes:

1. The lodging-house proprietors.
2. The lodging-house tenants.
3. The slum dwellers.
4. The 'respectable' tenants of private houses.

All of these were disadvantaged groups as compared with private and council suburbanites, but there were also important and more complicated conflicts between them.

The first of these and much the most important was the conflict between the lodging-house landlords and tenants on the one hand and their ward neighbours and the City Authorities on the other. The conflict here arose from the fact that their accommodation was accommodation of the last resort and was seen by their neighbours and the authorities to be illegitimate. The landlords, having to pay short-term loans quickly, found it necessary to overcrowd their houses in order to gain as much rent as possible and the tenants, being glad to accept any alternative which gave them a roof over their heads, supported them in this. But the local authorities saw this over-crowding as undesirable from a public health and planning point of view, the slum dwellers resented the wasteful use of houses larger and structurally more sound than their own and the private tenants resented the deterioration of the neighbourhood which overcrowding produced.

Against the background of this conflict, that between lodging-house tenants and landlords and that between private tenants and slum dwellers (the latter conflict like that between private tenants and the lodging-house population being based upon the private tenants' fear of deterioration) seemed less important. But these conflicts were there nonetheless and in certain circumstances might prevent the sorts of alliance which the major conflict implied.

But the housing classes which we have mentioned were, in any case, composed in such a way that allies from the point of view of our model were divided amongst themselves and potential enemies were united. The most important reason for this was that there was diver-sity within the classes, both with regard to ethnic origin and with regard to the degree to which any individual had been fully socialized into the urban value system.

In order to understand the significance of the immigrant situation as an independent variable, it is useful to elaborate another ideal type. This ideal type assumes that the immigrant is not discriminated against and that his behaviour is affected solely by the degree to which he has adjusted himself to the life of the city. It is, of course, a highly unreal construction since it is of the essence of the competitive urban situation that discrimination does exist. But its value lies in the fact that it explains the deviation in the zone of transition from the pure conflict situation which our class model suggests.

The immigrant newly arrived in the city has necessarily broken or at least attenuated many of his community and kinship ties with his homeland. If he stays in the city and becomes assimilated to its culture and social order he will eventually achieve or at least aspire to the independent conjugal family life of the Council estates and suburbs. The various stages of immigrant adjustment therefore may be conceived as falling between the two points of full integration in his home community and full integration in the city.

The first stage for an individual immigrant is a state of almost complete anomy. Ties with home have been seriously weakened and his sole tie with the host society is the contractual tie of employment. This stage does not usually last for long and leads to the second stage where he looks for those in like condition to himself in order to form an intimate primary sub-community within which he can enjoy relaxed social interaction.

It is, of course, theoretically possible that the immigrant might find this new primary sub-community amongst his native-born hosts. But the barriers of linguistic and cultural differences are usually too great. If the choice is open to him he will turn naturally to those with whom he has the shared linguistic and cultural meanings which are essential to social interaction. He then finds himself a member of a small group which performs important functions for him.

Firstly, it overcomes his social isolation and prevents personal demoralization. Without such a group he would have to satisfy all his needs in the market place. He would have his food in the cafe, his sex in the brothel and he would live in a doss-house. Individuals in the city do sometimes live this way and may survive for a time, particularly with the aid of alcohol and other stimulants, but any attempt to sustain a life of this kind for a long time would lead to mental breakdown or to suicide. It seems to be the case that all men require some kind of intimate primary community to keep them alive and sane.

Secondly, however, the group will do more than this for him. It will not merely use those shared cultural meanings which are already available to facilitate social interaction. It will create new ones. For the individual who talks out his problems with his kin and intimate friends, constructs a social world for himself in so doing. And the rituals of the group will serve to give expression to and reinforce the meanings thus created. Life in the immigrant colony is always remarkable by comparison with other groupings in the city for the emphasis which is placed upon this ritualistic reaffirmation and reinforcement of meanings.

Thirdly, the social network which the group creates will provide the means for solving the individual's personal problems. If he is short of money, if he is unemployed, if he is seeking a house, if he is in trouble with the police, if he has a moral problem or if he needs help in caring for his dependants he will turn in the first place to this group. The aid he needs may ultimately come from some bureaucratic agency but even if it does it may come to him through the mediation of some group member who is skilled in these matters.

In the third stage of his adjustment the individual becomes much less dependent upon this small group. He has friends outside the group with whom he shares new meanings and he becomes less punctilious about adhering to the group's activities and rituals. He begins to solve his own problems and exercises his rights as a citizen going direct to the various civic agencies which can help him without the need for any mediator. Eventually, having created a stable family life of his own and having a secure income and employment he might be able to dispense entirely with any primary community or colony.

The important stage in this adjustment, however, is the second one. It is not, as is often thought, an alternative to becoming fully urbanized. It is a stage on the way. It is not surprising, therefore, that as Oscar Lewis has pointed out, communal social relations become more extensive and intensive during the early stages of the individual's migration. It is inevitable that they should, for the colony is the springboard from which the individual launches himself into the city. It may, of course, be the case that amongst short-term immigrants there will be no progress beyond the colony and that it will simply provide a home from home until his eventual return. But even amongst these groups, if the colony gives sufficient personal security for the individual in the city it may enable him to venture forth into a wider world and establish new contacts.

One thing which is certain, however, is that colony and primary community ties are too important to be broken simply because of economic interests. The landlord and tenant who belong to the same ethnic group cannot see their relationship as based solely on the cash nexus. In fact, the relationship is likely to be greatly modified with the landlord charging far less than the market rent, and the balance of power between the two parties being quite different from what is normal in such circumstances. Hence it is certainly to be expected that as far as the housing-class conflict is concerned, there will be alliances across class lines.

It should now be noted, however, that the zone of transition includes others apart from immigrants who are undergoing a process of urbanization. In a sense all its inhabitants are, for though they are at the back of the queue for housing facilities, the more successful they are the more they will aspire to something like the suburban ideal. And just as the immigrant first uses the ladder of his colony and then kicks it away, so also for the native-born, kinship and neighbourhood are useful supports in the time of adversity, but may be dispensed with as a man becomes successful.

One sub-group amongst the native-born, however, presents special problems. This is the group who have become isolated from their own society through deviance or through personal or family breakdown. They have no colony to turn to and their problems are not easily shared with one another. For the individual in this group very often the most important relationships are those with a social worker. But this alone is not sufficient for the interpretation of their situation and they must look elsewhere for an adequate set of social meanings. Almost certainly they find it in the residue of meanings left over from their former social experience and far from being driven into the community of immigrants, they will be inclined in the presence of immigrants to assert their native culture as strongly as possible. Thus, even though this down-and-out group may share the condition of the immigrants, its affiliation will be to the host society. One cannot expect united action by native and immigrant tenants in such circumstances.

It may now be asked whether, if what we have said about ethnic ties, colonies and sub-communities is true, interaction in the zone of transition is at all affected by the housing classes which we have discussed previously. On this two things may be said. In the first place, the whole process of selection which brings these groups together results from the competition for housing in the city. And, secondly, colonies and similar groupings may take on quite different meanings as a result of the competitive process.

In order to explain the first of these points it is necessary to say something about the way in which the lodging-house area develops. What happens is that some individuals who are denied access to legitimate and desired forms of housing obtain short-term and costly loans in order to buy houses. To make such ventures financially viable they must buy large houses and they must take as many tenants as possible. Since this form of landlordism is regarded as morally illegitimate by the city, it will most frequently be an outsider who undertakes such an enterprise. He will, it is true, make special provision for tenancies for his own kinsmen and fellow-countrymen, but in the nature of the case he must have tenants from other groups whom he can exploit. These will include both immigrants from other countries than his own and disadvantaged groups from the host society. The lodging-house then will be a multi-racial unit run by foreigners.

Any immigrant group which is prominent amongst the lodging-house landlords will have a peculiar relationship to the host society. The task which it is performing is socially a vital one for it provides housing for larger numbers who are provided for in no other way. But it is also one which is inconsistent with the ideal values of the society. The group concerned, therefore, becomes a pariah group in the technical sense in which the Jews in Medieval Europe were said to be a pariah group because they performed the socially necessary function of usury.

Inevitably, then, inter-ethnic group attitudes are affected by the housing situation. The native residents' attitude to the immigrants does not depend solely upon the fact that they are ethnically different or upon psychologically determined racial prejudice. The immigrant is identified as a man who overcrowds and destroys good houses and it is his position in the housing market which defines his situation for the native.

In these circumstances, immigrant groups must be more than merely a haven of retreat and a cultural home for their members. The immigrants have interests to defend and these interests must be protected by something like a trade union. Hence the system of colonies tends to become structured as a system of conflict groups. Very often, it is true, what set out to be interest-group organizations become colony centres and cultural groups. But equally cultural groups find themselves involved in 'trade union' activity on behalf of an economic interest group.

We still have to consider, however, the question of the associational means through which these conflicts are played out. We have indicated that these are a variety of ethnic groups engaged in conflict about housing, but we have still to show how this happens. We have spoken of colonies and conflict and interest groups, but the concrete associations which exist may not set out to be either of these. They are churches, political parties, clubs, immigrant welfare associations, sports clubs and pub clienteles. Our problem is to show the relationship between these and the natural tendency to form 'colonies' and economic interest groups which we have described.

What is suggested here is that nearly all associations in the zone of transition, whatever their particular charters may declare their aims to be, do fulfil one or more of the main functions which we have outlined for colonies and conflict groups. These may now be listed as:

1. Overcoming social isolation.
2. The affirmation of meanings, values and beliefs.
3. Administering 'pastoral' care to members.
4. The attainment of group goals.

These four functions cannot be sharply separated from one another. Overcoming social isolation depends upon the affirmation and establishment of social meanings and values. The affirmation of values may impose on the individual certain duties whose performance are functional to the attainment of group goals. Participation in goal-attainment activity may assume a ritualistic character whose prime effect is to reinforce values and beliefs. And pastoral care may be concerned with winning the adherence of the individual to a goal-attainment and belief-affirming organization as much as with solving his personal problems. That this overlapping of functions exists follows from the fact that the same organizations are at once colonies and conflict groups. This may be illustrated in the case of the churches and the political parties.

Membership of a religious congregation is one of the main forms of group life available to the inhabitants. It provides a home for those who belong. But the reason why it provides a home is that the assertion of common beliefs and an interpretation of the world is at the centre of its activity. Those who share these beliefs are better able to understand and to interact with one another. The beliefs, however, do more than merely interpret the world. Their point is to change it. Christianity especially provides a rich range of possible beliefs about the relationship between the holy community and the world, and those who affiliate to one of its belief systems thereby come to adopt attitudes of co-operation or conflict towards the various out-groups with whom they are confronted. Finally, in the process of carrying out their pastoral function the churches exercise surveillance over the belief systems of their members and incorporate them more fully into their goal-attainment systems.

The political parties on the other hand appear at first to be concerned with obtaining and using legitimate political power on behalf of interest groups. But as one participates in the life of the party one finds the other functions equally in evidence. For many the party and its social clubs provide a home much in the way the churches do. The enunciation of the party's programme requires a diagnosis of the ills of the world not unlike that offered by the churches. And the councillors or M.P.s surgery performs functions very similar to those of the pastor on his rounds.

What is true of these highly structured organizations is also to a large extent true of more diffuse groupings, such as sports organizations, social clubs and pub clienteles. All of these are marked by a flight of their members from loneliness and isolation, by the affirmation of shared meanings and beliefs, by co-operative group activity and by a concern for their members' welfare. Some may emphasize one function more than another but potentially these organizations may fulfil any of them. Thus we should not be surprised if an immigrant sports and welfare organization becomes a crucially important conflict group any more than we should if a political party becomes primarily a social club.

This merging of functions is of the greatest importance for the conflict model in terms of which we are seeking to interpret the community of the zone of transition. It remains the case that there is considerable potential for conflict between groups and the existence of group goal attainment organizations is central to the structure of the community. But the fact that there is such a variety of organizations and that these organizations also perform other functions means that the conflict will, to some extent, be blurred and muted. Three points may be made to emphasize this.

The first of these is the cathartic function of group membership. In a conflict situation one might expect that the attempt to realize group goals would lead to open conflict and the use of force. And to some extent in the zone of transition it does. But as men organize for the achievement of their goals they are willing to postpone their attainment. They concentrate on the building up of the organization and ensuring the loyalty and doctrinal purity of their fellow members. This may then become a goal in itself and many of the discontents felt in the community may be channelled into ritualistic activity and expression. Thus we should not say that if there is no actual fighting in the streets, consensus has been achieved. The real index of conflict is to be found in the passion of belief and the energy put into organizational activity.

But secondly we have to notice that the residents come to see that there are alternative associational means open to them. If one has a problem one may find that the Catholic priest, the secretary of the immigrant welfare organization, the local doctor, the social worker and the city councillor are all available to deal with it. It remains true that a man will by and large take his problem to his own organization. But this is consistent with some recognition that the associational facilities available belong to the community as a whole. Just as a Labour voter may take a ride to the polling booth in a Conservative car, regarding the car as part of the common electoral facilities, so an individual from any one group may use the facilities which another group provides. It is here that we see the uneasy beginnings of a genuine community structure which transcends the conflict situation.

Conflict still exists and may be intense and bitter, but it has begun to take place within a larger ordered structure of organizations.

This use of one's enemy's facilities in this way is the more likely to occur because of a third factor. This is that many of the associations which operate in the area are not merely local organizations. They cannot respond solely to the needs of interests of a particular group and they cannot exclude particular individuals from membership. Thus a Nonconformist denomination whose local native members might find deep satisfaction in affirming predestinarian beliefs and rejoicing in their own election have to accept the fact that their Church also has branches in the West Indies and the West Indian immigrant has a legitimate claim to membership of their church. And the trades unionist who believes in the solidarity of the international working class cannot easily be excluded because he does not share the racial resentments of his comrades in the local party. So organizations find themselves with potentially subversive members and individuals affiliated to organizations often quite inappropriate to the attainment of their goals and interests.

To say that conflict is blurred and muted in these ways, however, is not to deny its existence. What we are trying to do is to follow through our analysis of conflict and to show how it is modified in the process of social interaction. This does not mean that we accept that the community in the zone of transition is forced to reach some sort of value consensus. It does not mean that the various groups achieve a kind of segregated and peaceful co-existence. And it does not mean that with a number of cross-cutting conflicts cancelling one another out an overall stability is realized. The essence of the situation is still that there are a number of ethnic groups engaged in conflict over the allocation of housing, and though their conflict may not be carried through to the point of violence it remains at the centre of the overall interaction system. It is always possible in such a situation that if there were a crisis organizations would become functionally and ethnically specialized and that the lines of the conflict would be more sharply drawn.

There remains, however, one further problem to consider. This is the development of a relatively community-wide organization incorporating all groups. Nearly all community organizations in the zone of transition develop some organization of this kind and it is important that we should understand something of their structure and functioning, of their bases and potential stability.

The kind of community which we are discussing is thought by residents of the city as a whole, as well as by those who live within it, to be a problem community. It is inevitable, therefore, that at some point in its history leading citizens will come together on the basis that 'something must be done'. Differential developments then occur, depending upon who comes together and what it is they propose to do.

In some cases those who come together simply represent one interest group. If this happens the community organization which is formed may be expected to promote punitive policies against groups other than those to which the organization's members belong. But it is unlikely that such an organization would ever become clearly differentiated from other special interest organizations and make its claim to being a community-wide organization effective. What is perhaps more significant is the possibility that a particular group might come to play a predominant role within the context of a more widely based organization.

One group of individuals, however, is usually in a strategic position to exercise influence in the formation of such organizations. This is the group of professional and semi-professional social workers. They command recognition because they already enjoy some measure of confidence among those who do pastoral work in the various associations and because they have a quasi-official role within the governmental structure of the city. We have seen that colony structures produce leaders who do pastoral work amongst their members and mediate between their members and the bureaucratic agencies. We now see that there is a further group of mediators. The social workers are sufficiently close to the problems of the individuals in the area to have their confidence, but they also bring to these problems a relatively universalistic approach derived from their professional training.

It has, of course, to be recognized that the group of social workers to which we refer here may fall short of achieving these standards of behaviour or of occupying this role. There are a variety of motivations and approaches to social work and the fact that community organizations are likely to be subject to pressures from the various conflict groups makes it less likely that their behaviour will be completely governed by some conception of their professional role. But the fact that such professionalism enters into the situation at all is an important factor and in so far as it does it may help the association to perform two important functions for the local community and for the city as a whole.

The first of these is that of conflict resolution in the zone of transition. In so far as the association co-opts the officials of the various associations to its committees and councils, it confronts them with one another in circumstances where common interests are paramount and this could mean that bargains and contracts will be struck between them. This, we must stress again, does not mean that the basis of conflict will disappear. But it does create the circumstances in which men will at least ask whether there are not less costly ways of pursuing them. And if it were possible for the community organizations to achieve a degree of permanence there might emerge some degree of consensus at least about the legitimate ways in which conflict should be pursued.

The other important function is that of socializing the organization's clients into the wider social system of the city. The organization may be inhibited about doing this by the fact that its charter is to save the local community itself. Nonetheless, its own roots are in the town hall and in various city offices and the mere process of casework involves facilitating the mobility of some individuals to other parts of the city. Thus, the main role of the association becomes that of maintaining some degree of peace between the various groups while they are still resident in the area, but at the same time facilitating the process of mobility and urbanization which will lead some at least of their clients to move from transit camp conditions to full urban acceptance.

It is not to be supposed, however, from this ideal-type analysis of the role of community organizations that such organizations will automatically arise out of some inherent tendency of the urban social system towards equilibrium. Whether they arise at all will depend upon the availability of individuals motivated to perform this function and, in any case, they constitute a very imperfect mechanism for resolving the built-in tensions which exist. A city is conceivable in which the reasons for these tensions were dealt with at source in a restructuring of the system of housing allocation. But given that there is privilege and discrimination and exploitation of one group by another, and given that the level of life at which many inhabitants of the zone of transition live is nearly intolerable, community organization of this kind is a fall-back social mechanism of potentially considerable importance. It is not surprising, therefore, that it recurs in very different circumstances in European and American cities.

Life in the zone of transition has a very recognizable quality and those who have ever known it recognize it when they see it again. It is a life of squalor, of under-privilege and of conflict and for those who work there professionally it means sitting with clients in dreary church halls, offices and club rooms trying to solve their personal problems and trying to reconcile the attainment of their ends with those of others. It is a world far from the functionally integrated social systems which sociologists are too fond of discussing. Only as sociologists begin to understand it will they begin to understand what the city is like on its underside.

In conclusion, then, we may summarize the central propositions of this essay as follows:

1. Urban development in advanced industrial societies divides men into classes differentially placed with regard to housing.

2. The zone of transition is that area of the city where the least privileged housing classes live, especially the landlords and tenants of lodging-houses.

3. The community life of the zone of transition is shaped by conflicts between these housing classes.

4. Since many of the under-privileged are newcomers to the city their organizations will also perform functions in the re-orientation of men from foreign, traditional and rural societies to urban life.

5. The actual associations such as churches, political parties and clubs will perform important functions in regard to both 3 and 4 above.

6. They will perform these functions relatively imperfectly both because of their functional diversity and because of their responsiveness to outside pressures from parent organizations.

7. Community-wide organizations may arise which have the function for the local community of peaceful conflict resolution and for the city as a whole of mediating and facilitating mobility between its problem areas and the larger urban society.

8. The situation in the zone of transition is a highly unstable one and in any sudden crisis ethnic and class conflicts which are temporarily contained may crystallize and be pursued by more violent means.

These are propositions which relate the study of the urban zone of transition dynamically to a wider concept of the city as a social system.

CHAPTER 17

Territoriality[1] in Belfast*

F. W. Boal

For myself, earthbound and fettered to the scene of my activities,
I confess that I do feel the differences of mankind, national and
individual. . . . I am, in plainer words, a bundle of prejudices—
made of likings and dislikings—the veriest thrall to sympathies,
apathies, antipathies.

> Charles Lamb, quoted
> by Gordon W. Allport,
> *The Nature of Prejudice.*

Segregation, on the basis of both economic and ethnic characteristics,
is a feature of most cities. Segregation is usually measured on the basis
of the spatial distribution of individuals or households belonging to a
particular economic or ethnic group. Most commonly, the actual
distribution of group members is compared to the pattern that would
exist if the group members were distributed evenly throughout the
area under study—the deviation between the actual and even distributions forming a measure of the degree of segregation.

This type of segregation is frequently referred to as residential
segregation. Associated with residential segregation, there is a second
form—activity segregation. That is, different groups not only do not
live in the same area, they also do not interact with each other. While
residential segregation has received a great deal of attention, the concomitant activity segregation is a relatively neglected field. It is the
aim of this paper to examine both types of segregation in a small area
of working-class Belfast.

The data used in the present study is a byproduct of a larger study
of spatial activity patterns in the Belfast urban area. The latter study
is attempting to specify the nature of activity patterns for a variety of
sample groups. This larger study may be designated an output study,
following the conceptual scheme for activity systems analysis, outlined by F. S. Chapin.[2] The elements of Chapin's scheme are: (1) a
value system component that operates on (2) the choice mechanism
which in turn produces (3) an activity component. Essentially his

* Reprinted by permission of the Editorial Committee from *Irish Geography*,
VI, 1969, pp. 30–50.

scheme utilizes choice theory to convert human motivations (input) into human activity in the city (output) with the social system mediating men's choices. Thus we can envisage a cycle moving from motivation through choice to activity, with feedback affecting the next round.

When one examines activities, then, one is examining *output*. Until recently human geography has been heavily output-oriented with motivational aspects receiving scant attention. In fact not only have we ignored, by and large, motivational studies, we have also ignored the study of activities themselves. Instead, in urban geography, we have examined the results of activity as displayed in the townscape. The present study examines activity patterns as features of geographic interest in their own right. Explanation, at a fundamental behavioural level, must await further work, probably of an interdisciplinary nature.

STUDY AREA

The fact of religious segregation in Belfast and elsewhere in Northern Ireland is well known. The deep historical roots of the segregation have been discussed in detail elsewhere and do not directly concern us here.[3] According to Boserup and Iversen,[4] Northern Irish society is both polarized and ranked. Polarized communities have little or no interaction between their distinctive component groups, 'except that the presence of the other ethnic group functions as an external enemy, increasing group consciousness and enhancing ideological conformity within the groups and ideological distance between them.'[5] A community which is polarized along an ethnic dimension, is, according to Boserup and Iversen, also 'ranked in the sense that the dimension of division is not merely an ethnic label, it is also in some respects a rank dimension.'[6] In the Northern Ireland context the ranking is one that places Protestants at the top and Catholics at the bottom. Polarity and rankedness combine to reduce the likelihood of group interaction to low levels, particularly when, as in this paper, we are examining the lower socio-economic portions of the respective groups.

Most of the previous work on religious residential segregation in Belfast has been done by Evans[7] and Jones.[8] However neither explored the extent of activity segregation. In this present paper the aim is to examine the activity patterns in a small area of the city where the Protestant and Roman Catholic groups are residentially segregated from each other, but where the two groups are in close spatial proximity. At the same time socio-economic characteristics of the two groups are held approximately constant by investigating a working-class area. The type of study area required was one that lay astride two major segregated residential concentrations, one Roman

Catholic and the other Protestant, and where there was continuity of residential land use. Where these conditions might be found is suggested by Evans in his 1944 paper where he notes, when writing about the distribution of Roman Catholics in Belfast, that:

> The outstanding feature is the 90 per cent concentration in two wards Smithfield and Falls, and the high proportion of Catholics in the centre of the city. The sharpest junction between districts where the Catholics are respectively in proportion of 90 per cent and 5 per cent, runs in a line of cleavage due west from the city centre.[9]

Evans had to use ward boundaries to delimit his zones. Emrys Jones was able to produce a more spatially refined delimitation by using the census enumeration districts employed in the 1951 census (Fig. 1).[10] The 'line of cleavage' or what we will call the 'divide',

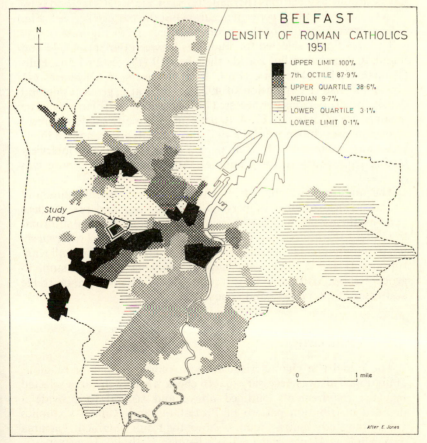

FIGURE 1

running west from the centre is striking, with overwhelmingly Protestant areas to the north of the line and Roman Catholic to the south. Other cartographic techniques can also be utilized to locate the Divide. For instance, Figure 2 shows the pattern of street decorations in the area running west from the city centre, erected for the Orange (Protestant) July the Twelfth celebrations. The complete absence of decorations in the Falls Road area and their concentration in the Shankill Road area are notable features. A further, somewhat more subjective technique was also utilized. This involved scanning the Electoral Register for the relevant part of the city and indicating all households where at least one member had a surname or first name that could be classified as 'Roman Catholic.' A large number of surnames are anglicized from the Irish, while a range of first names also have Catholic associations (Bernadette, Sean, etc.). This method is by no means one hundred per cent accurate but the pattern derived (Fig. 3) is a striking inverse of the decorations pattern in Figure 2.

The area finally selected for study lies between the Springfield and Shankill Roads and lies astride the Shankill (Protestant) and Falls (Roman Catholic) sectors. (Figs. 1–3). It covers 16·6 hectares (41 acres) and had a population of 4922 persons at a gross residential density of 297 persons per hectare (120 persons per acre) in 1966. The mean house valuation is £9. A 10 per cent systematic random sample of persons was drawn from the 1967 Electoral Register, and an interview was obtained with each person thus selected, the interview lasting from thirty to forty minutes. An 89 per cent response was achieved.

The questionnaire elicited information about general household characteristics (number of persons in house, age and sex of these persons, their work or school location, if any) and personal information about the interviewee which falls into two groups—*site characteristics* (religion, newspapers read, name given to area, football team supported) and *activity characteristics* (movement to bus stop, to grocery shop, visits and visitor connections, and the pre-marriage addresses of interviewee and spouse).

SITE CHARACTERISTICS

The initial site characteristic to be explored is that of religious affiliation. This was necessary first to check whether the area selected met the requirements outlined above and second to provide a detailed distribution pattern of Protestants and Roman Catholics within the study limits. Figure 4 shows the result obtained. The area as a whole is 44 per cent ($\pm 5\cdot5$)[11] Roman Catholic. However it is

BELFAST
SHANKILL—FALLS AREA
JULY TWELTH DECORATIONS
1967

Flags •
Bunting and Kerb Painting
Non Residential Areas

¼ Mile

FIGURE 2

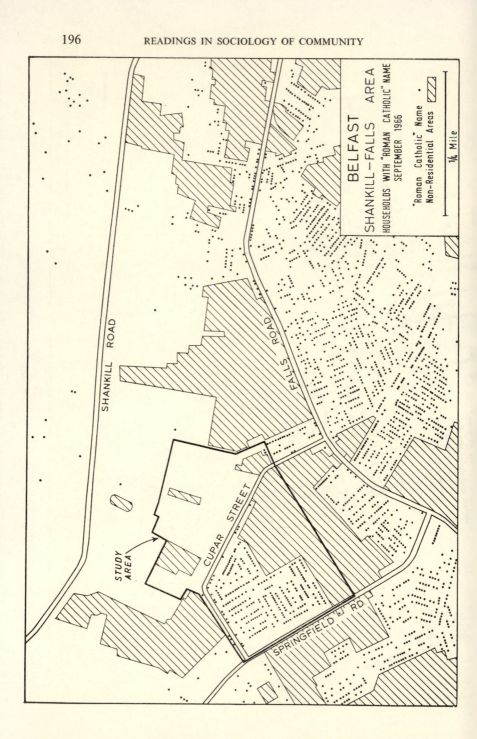

BELFAST
SHANKILL–FALLS AREA
HOUSEHOLDS WITH "ROMAN CATHOLIC" NAME
SEPTEMBER 1966

"Roman Catholic" Name   .
Non-Residential Areas

¼ Mile

SHANKILL ROAD

FALLS ROAD

CUPAR STREET

STUDY AREA

SPRINGFIELD RD

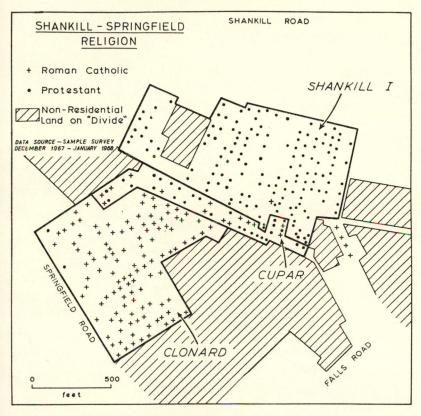

SHANKILL - SPRINGFIELD
RELIGION

SHANKILL   ROAD

+ Roman Catholic

• Protestant

Non-Residential
Land on "Divide"

DATA SOURCE—SAMPLE SURVEY
DECEMBER 1967 – JANUARY 1968

SHANKILL I

CUPAR

SPRINGFIELD ROAD

CLONARD

FALLS ROAD

0   500
feet

FIGURE 4

obvious that we are dealing, in fact, with two quite distinct areas, the
one (Clonard) overwhelmingly Catholic, the other (Shankill I) overwhelmingly Protestant. The two areas meet in a very narrow band
which is almost entirely restricted to one street (Cupar Street). On
this basis three areas were finally distinguished—Clonard, Shankill I
and the transitional Cupar. Clonard is 98 per cent Catholic, Shankill
I 99 per cent Protestant while Cupar has a two to one Protestant
predominance.

Newspaper readership was examined to see whether there were
significant differences between the Roman Catholic and Protestant
territories. The readership amongst the sample of the three local
dailies was plotted. The most interesting distribution to emerge is the
readership of the morning *Irish News* which was read by 83 per cent of

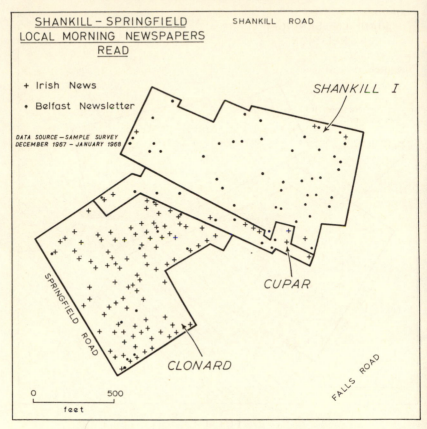

FIGURE 5

the sample in Clonard, but only 3 per cent in Shankill I (Fig. 5). The alternative local morning paper, the *Belfast Newsletter* is not widely taken in either area. Evidence from elsewhere suggests that the *Newsletter* is more of a middle class paper in appeal. Morning newspaper readership in Shankill I concentrated on the English-based popular dailies. *Irish News* readership is a very distinguishing feature of the two religious subdivisions of the study area. The strong Roman Catholic loyalty to the paper is not surprising in that it takes an anti-Unionist line in politics and gives substantial cover to Gaelic games and Roman Catholic church news. The third local daily, the evening *Belfast Telegraph* has, spatially, a much more uniform readership, in that it was read by 58 per cent ($\pm$9·2) in Clonard and 68 per cent ($\pm$7·4) in Shankill I. This common readership gives to the *Telegraph* an important role as a potential integrator operating across the religious community boundary. This role is reflected in its treatment of local issues.

Many areas of Belfast are widely known by their local names. It was therefore of potential value to find out what the interviewees called the area they lived in (if they thought it had a name). In terms of area name 94 per cent of those in Clonard named the area as Clonard, Springfield or Falls while none used the term Shankill. In Shankill I, on the other hand, no one used the Clonard-Springfield-Falls label and 77 per cent used the term Shankill. In the transitional Cupar 37 per cent used the Clonard-Springfield-Falls designation, 26 per cent the Shankill term while 23 per cent said the area they lived in had no name at all (Fig. 6). Local nomenclature clearly differentiates the various parts of the study area.

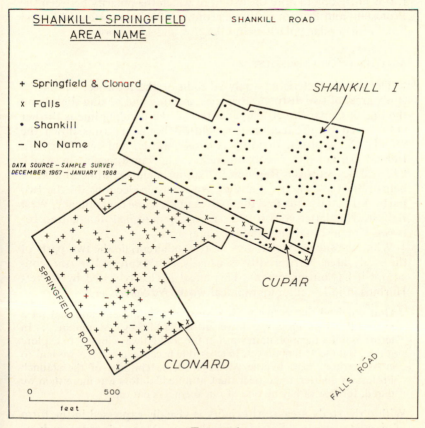

FIGURE 6

Local group loyalties are frequently linked with support for a particular association football team. In the past, in west Belfast, support was given to either Linfield or Belfast Celtic. With the demise of the latter club, loyalties are now allotted mainly to Linfield or to Glasgow Celtic. Which team one supports depends on one's religion and, in the area under consideration, one's religion indicates which area one lives in. Consequently it is not surprising to find that in Clonard 73 per cent of football team supporters favoured Glasgow Celtic while none mentioned Linfield. In Shankill I, on the other hand, 74 per cent of football team supporters favoured Linfield, with no support whatsoever for Celtic. The balance of support in both areas was divided amongst a large number of clubs, but again with very little overlap, Everton (Liverpool) and Distillery (Belfast) being notable in Clonard, and Glasgow Rangers, Liverpool and Manchester United in Shankill I. It is intriguing to note the extent to which the polarity between the Protestant and Roman Catholic groups in Belfast is extended to and links with similar polarities in Glasgow and Liverpool.

ACTIVITY CHARACTERISTICS

The site characteristics analysed indicate the presence, within the study area, of two distinct territories, meeting and mixing slightly on the line of Cupar Street. Cupar Street as the dividing line is further emphasized by the fact that a political boundary runs down the middle of the street, dividing two city wards, and two Northern Ireland parliamentary constituencies. The constituency in which Clonard lies returns a Republican Labour member, while Shankill I helps return a Unionist. Only at Westminster elections do the two parts of the study area find themselves in the same constituency, West Belfast. This latter constituency is highly marginal, fluctuating between Unionist and anti-Unionist majorities.

While the site characteristics sharply differentiate the two parts of the study area, territoriality is usually best expressed by the constraint it has on movement. This effect is clearly stated by Robert Harbinson in his autobiographical work, *No Surrender*.

> God ordained that even the Bog Meadows should end and had set a great hill at their limit, which we called the Mickey's Mountain. . . . In terms of miles the mountain was not far, and I always longed to explore it . . . . But the Mountain was inaccessible because to reach it we had to cross territory held by the Mickeys. Being children of the staunch Protestant quarter, to go near the Catholic idolators was more than we dared, for fear of having one of our members cut off.[12]

Within the study area, territoriality is visually expressed in the form of a great variety of gable-end slogans. Many slogans, such as

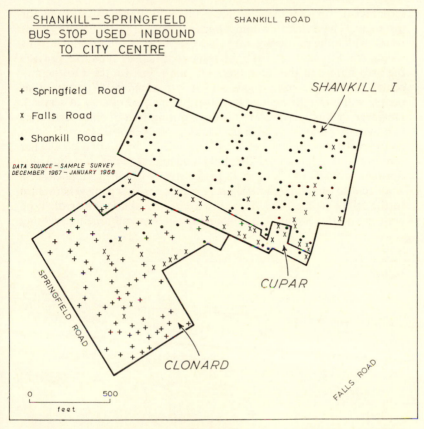

FIGURE 7

'Linfield' and 'Celtic' indicate local loyalties, but are not explicitly territorial. Other slogans, however, have obvious territorial as well as loyalty connotations—'Taigues [Catholics] Keep Out', 'Prods [Protestants] Keep Out', 'No Pope Here', 'No Queen Here' are good examples.

We can now turn to examine some activity characteristics, to see whether the activities are as distinctive, spatially, as the site characteristics. For the purposes of this paper four sets of movements are examined briefly—movement to bus stop to get bus to city centre, movement to buy groceries, movements associated with visits to or from relations or friends and linkages suggested by pre-marriage addresses of interviewee and spouse.

The inner segregated districts of Belfast have almost all dominant radial roads running through them (Shankill, Falls, Sandy Row, for instance). These roads would appear, intuitively, to be the spines round which the residential areas have developed and on which focus a significant level of activity. The spine roads, also, of course, provide the area names in the inner city. The main bus routes into the city centre run on the spine roads and it is reasonable to assume that people will go to the nearest bus stop (with equal quality of service). However in this case we are also examining two distinct territories and therefore one might also assume that people would be inclined to go to get the bus on their 'own' spine road. In fact we find that 89 per cent in Shankill I go to the Shankill Road and 11 per cent to the Falls/Springfield while in Clonard 93 per cent go to Falls/Springfield and 7 per cent go to Shankill (Fig. 7). There is therefore a strong general bias to the 'right' spine road. However a considerable number of those who go to the Shankill road are in fact not minimizing walking

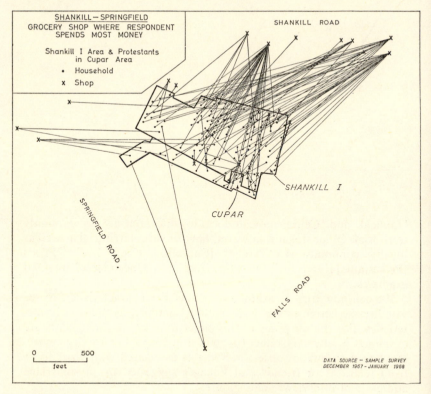

FIGURE 8

distance—they are going to a more distant bus stop. Out of 33 interviewees in Shankill I who live nearer the Falls/Springfield stops 79
per cent go to the Shankill (all Protestants), while in Cupar, out of 31
interviewees, 13 go to the more distant stop (Shankill) and 12 of the
13 who do this are Protestants. Thus with the bus data we can see
what seems to be two basic influences at work—minimizing trip
distance and territoriality.

The second type of activity where distance minimization can be
assumed (with equal facilities available) is the trip to the grocery shop
where the bulk of the weekly groceries is purchased. Here we find that
in Shankill I 93 per cent of the trips are made to the Shankill Road or
to local shops on the Shankill side of the Divide and 4 per cent to the
Springfield Road and local shops in Clonard (Fig. 8). In Clonard, on
the other hand, 90 per cent of the trips are to the Springfield Road and
local shops in Clonard while 10 per cent of trips are to the Shankill
Road (Fig. 9). Again we observe a very strong focusing of each area

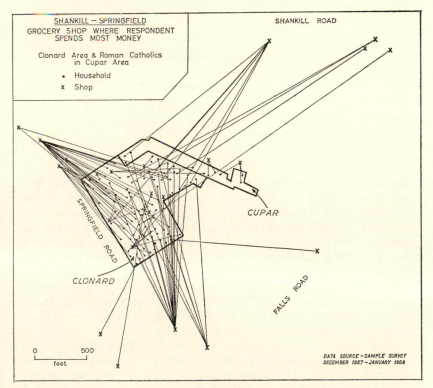

FIGURE 9

on its own spine road. If we examine the whole study area (including Cupar), we find that 6 per cent of those living nearer the Shankill stores go to the Springfield Road while 23 per cent of those living nearer the Springfield stores go to the Shankill. Again religion is important here, though 45 per cent of those making the longer trip to the Shankill Road are Roman Catholics. This confirms to some extent the locally held opinion that the Shankill Road is a more attractive shopping area than the Falls/Springfield.

The spine roads provide the basis for quite distinctive orientations for bus stop and grocery shop trips. The religious factor accentuates their role. However, as the data demonstrates, there is some movement across the Divide—about 10 per cent of trips are 'deviant' in this regard.

When we examine the third activity type, visits to and from relatives and friends in a one-week period, a much more highly segregated pattern emerges. If we examine all visit connections of interviewees within the study area only, the links are as shown in the table.

TABLE 1

Visit Connections Within Study Area

	% of connections within study area with		
UNIT	Shankill I	Clonard	Cupar
Shankill I	96	0	4
Clonard	1	99	0

Broadening the view beyond the immediate study area, we find that about half of all the Shankill I visit connections fall within the Shankill Road Protestant sector, 66 per cent of these being with relatives, while 53 per cent of the Clonard connections are within the general Falls Road Roman Catholic sector, in this case 35 per cent being with relatives. Two comments are relevant here, first that we are dealing with the standard working class community pattern described by Fried as 'an overlapping series of close-knit networks',[13] and second that we are dealing with two almost mutually exclusive sets of such networks. There are practically no visitor connections across the religious divide (Figs. 10 and 11).

The visit connections analysis can be extended out beyond the purely local level to include connections within the Belfast urban area as a whole. In this case point locations, being the addresses of persons visiting or being visited by the interviewee, were classified

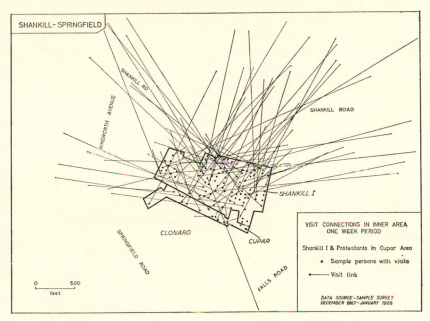

FIGURE 10

according to whether they were associated with a Protestant or a Roman Catholic in the study area. The points were then further classified as being segregated or unsegregated using a first nearest neighbour technique whereby a given point is unsegregated if the nearest other point is of a different religious classification. The result for point connections lying outside the immediate study area is shown in Figure 12. Eighty per cent of the points are segregated. These segregated connections coincide with the better known segregated residential areas of the city. Thus, with an activity where connections are socially very meaningful, there is effectively no direct linkage between the two main portions of the study area and even very little indirect linkage in the urban area in general. This high level of activity segregation in terms of visiting is further accentuated, and in part caused by the separate school systems. Not only do Catholics and Protestants attend different schools—the schools themselves are located within the relevant religious sectors and consequently movement to school, as with so many other activities, is away from the Divide, not towards or across it.

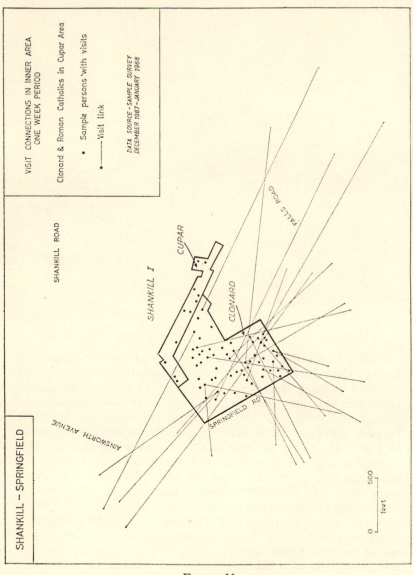

FIGURE 11

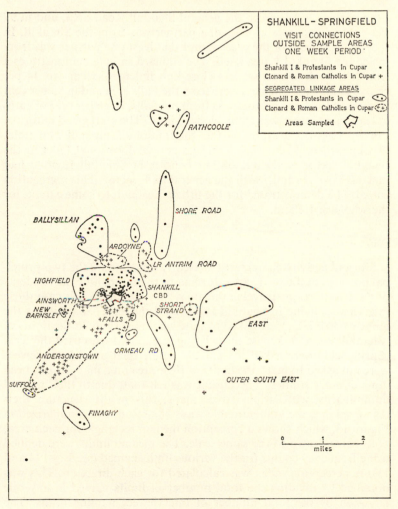

FIGURE 12

The existence of Fried's close-knit networks and of high segregation between the two basic sets of networks (Roman Catholic and Protestant) analysed in this paper are further demonstrated when one examines marriage linkages—the paired locations of the two marriage partners immediately before marriage. The close-knit network aspect is demonstrated as follows: in Shankill I, in 63 per cent of the cases both partners came from the general Shankill Road area, and in 97 per cent of the cases at least one partner was from the Shankill. In fact in 56 per cent of the cases sampled at least one partner was from inside the Shankill I area itself. The Clonard sample demonstrates a similar though somewhat less close-knit linkage system—in 44 per cent of cases both partners were from the Falls area and in 83 per cent of cases at least one partner was from the Falls. In 46 per cent of cases at least one partner was from Clonard itself. The segregated nature of the networks is shown by the fact that out of a sample of 79 couples in Clonard, only one had marriage partner locational links in the Shankill sector while out of 117 couples in Shankill I, none had marriage partner links with the general Falls sector. This segregation can also be demonstrated for the urban area and, to some extent, for the whole of Ireland.

PERCEPTION

Site and activity characteristics clearly differentiate the two principal portions of the study area. It remains to inquire how the residents of the two portions perceive the areas they live in. In this case those interviewees living in Shankill I who used the term 'Shankill' as the name of their area were asked to state what they thought the limits of 'Shankill' were. Likewise those living in Clonard who used the term 'Springfield' were asked to spatially define their area. Interviewees were not asked to mark the limits of their area on a map, as has been done in other studies,[14] because it was felt that, due to their general unfamiliarity with urban street maps, this might structure their responses in some unidentifiable way. The results are summarized in Figure 13, which shows a perception median rectangle for each area, both being drawn to the same scale. The median limits were defined using frequency counts for the various limits named (see Figs. 14 and 15). A perception index was calculated for each direction. This was obtained by dividing the total number of limits named in any one direction by the total number of interviewees naming limits. The values show a much stronger perception of limits which lie up and down the spine roads. This corresponds with the findings of Steinitz, in Boston, Massachussetts, where he noted that ' . . . the edges of congruent form—activity districts which were reinforced by busy paths were the strongest.[15] In the Belfast case, as the activity analysis suggests, there is much greater movement down the spine roads to the city centre, and also up them to outlying housing estates, than across them into 'alien' territory.

The lateral limits of 'Shankill' and 'Springfield' are less strongly perceived, but the strength of perception of these lateral limits is, in

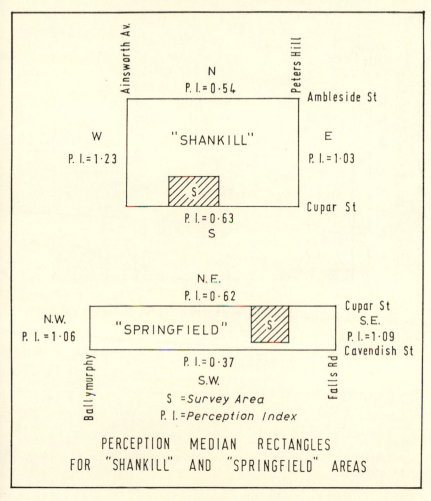

FIGURE 13

turn, asymmetrical. That is, the limit on the side towards the religious Divide is much more strongly perceived than the limit away from it. This is, in part, probably due to proximity of this limit to the study area. However the importance of the limit in the religious geography of the city undoubtedly is a further influence. In addition, not only is the Divide limit more strongly perceived—there is also a high level of agreement on both sides of the Divide as to where the limit lies. It is

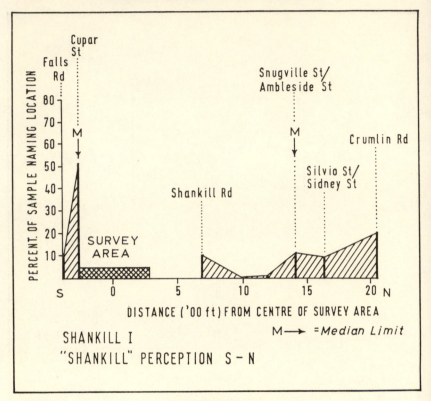

FIGURE 14

not in the least surprising that this agreed limit is Cupar Street (Figs. 14 and 15).

CONCLUSION

This paper is an attempt to define on the basis of the religious affinities of residents, distinctive areas within a working class portion of Belfast, and then to see to what extent selected site and activity characteristics correspond with the underlying religious pattern. The cumulative evidence indicates the presence of two very distinctive territories. Religion is a strong factor in group formation even where religious residential segregation does not exist, as has been shown in a recent study of white Protestants, Roman Catholics and Mormons in the United States.[16] Where the groups are also spatially segregated,

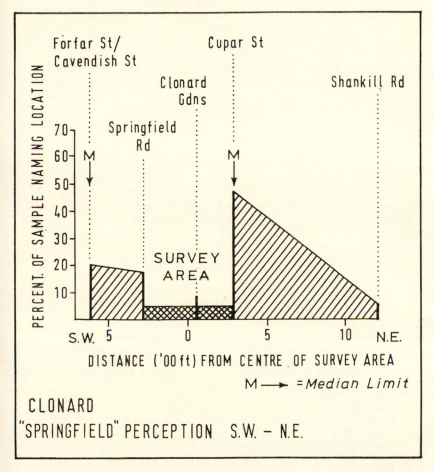

FIGURE 15

as in West Belfast, the mutual exclusiveness of the two groups becomes most marked. In the American study cited above the term 'ethnic enclosure' was coined. This could be used in a territorial sense in Belfast.

The present study is both experimental and descriptive. Fundamental explanation of the origin and maintenance of current segregation must await further motivationally based work, though possible explanations have been touched on elsewhere.[17] In addition future public policies towards religiously segregated residential areas need careful examination. Should such areas be allowed to continue in existence, even after redevelopment, or should urban renewal be used as a desegregating technique? At this stage we can only note the warning given by Herbert Gans:

> Plans and policies aimed at changing people's behaviour cannot be implemented through prescribing alterations in the physical community or by directives aimed at builders; they must be directed at the national sources and agents which bring about the present behaviour.[18]

ACKNOWLEDGMENTS

I would like to acknowledge assistance from W. J. McGaughey and Miss J. Orr, Department of Geography, Queen's University, and from the team of interviewers. Financial assistance was provided by the Frederick Soddy Trust, James Munce Partnership and Queen's University.

NOTES

1 The use of the term 'territoriality' is suggested by M. M. Webber's stimulating paper 'Culture, Territoriality and the Elastic Mile' *Papers and Proceedings, Regional Science Association*, 13, 1964, 59–69.
2 Chapin, F. S., 'Activity Systems and Urban Structure: A Working Scheme,' *Journal of the American Institute of Planners*, January 1968, 11–18.
3 Barritt, D. P. and Carter, C. F., *The Northern Ireland Problem*, 1962.
4 Boserup, A. and Iversen, C. 'Rank Analysis of a Polarized Community: A case Study from Northern Ireland,' *Peace Research Society (International) Papers*, 7, 1967, 59–76.
5 Ibid., 60.
6 Ibid., 60.
7 Evans, E. E. 'Belfast: The Site and the City,' *Ulster Jour. Arch.* Third Series, 7, 1944, 25–9.
8 Jones, E., *A Social Geography of Belfast*, 1960, 172–206.
9 Evans, op. cit., 25.
10 Jones, op. cit., 196.
11 Where confidence limits are quoted they are for 95 per cent probability.
12 Harbinson, R., *No Surrender*, 1960, 16.
13 Fried, M., 'Functions of the Working Class Community in Modern Urban Society—Implications for Forced Relocation,' *Journal of the American Institute of Planners*, 33, March 1967, 92.
14 Lee, T., 'Psychology and Living Space,' *Transactions of the Bartlett Society*, 2, 1963–4, 11–36; Willmott, P., 'Social Research and New Communities,' *Journal of the American Institute of Planners*, 33, November 1967, 393–4.
15 Steinitz, C., 'Meaning and Congruence of Urban Form and Activity,' *Journal of the American Institute of Planners*, 34, July 1968, 244.
16 Anderson, C. H., 'Religious Communality among White Protestants, Catholics and Mormons,' *Social Forces*, 46, June 1968, 501–508.
17 Barritt and Carter, op. cit., 52–76; Boal, F. W., and Buchanan, R. H., 'Conflict in Northern Ireland,' *Geographical Magazine*, 41, February 1969, 331–336.
18 Gans, H. J., *The Levittowners*, 1967, 289–290.

PART V

The Sociology Study
of Suburban Communities

CHAPTER 18

The Sociological Study of Suburban Communities

INTRODUCTION

Suburbs replaced the inner city as the purported location of 'non-community'. This, like the earlier judgements on the inner city was more an ideological response than one based on sociological analysis. There are now several community studies that have taken suburbia as their locale and so there can be no excuse for the crudities of the 'suburban myth'.

The first extract is from one of the most perceptive accounts of suburban culture, that of Seeley, Sim and Loosley, of *Crestwood Heights*. The authors of this community study appreciate that their locale will be familiar to most of their readers 'for some community like it is to be seen in and around almost any great city of this continent'.[1] They are prepared to call Crestwood Heights a community, because of the relationships that exist between people '—relationships revealed in the functioning of the institutions which they have created: family school, church, community centre, club, association, summer-camp'.[2] Not all these groups to which the inhabitants belong are actually to be found within the geographical boundaries of Crestwood Heights. However, there is clearly a local social system: institutions are interrelated locally and what is more this complex net of human relationships which is the community exists from the view point of the participants for a definite purpose (i.e. the community is viewed by the authors of this particular monograph as a purposive organization). This purpose is child rearing.

The exaggeration and extension of findings on middle-class suburbs such as Crestwood Heights and Park Forest, the notorious habitat of *Organisation Man*[3] has led to the 'suburban myth'. This myth is firmly criticized in the next extract, Berger's analysis based on a working class suburb in California.

'Suburbia' in the sociological and quasi-sociological literature has confused ecology ('the growth of the suburbs'), with a 'way of life'. It has been a short step from noting the ecological shift in location of residence or urban populations to saying that the facts of suburban residence *caused* what has become viewed as a 'suburban way of life'. What is worse, as Berger shows, much of what was the received wisdom on suburbs was largely mythical. The elements of this myth may be arrived at by taking certain facts from studies such as that of Crestwood Heights, exaggerating them and claiming they apply to all suburbs. If this were true, there would be little alternative but to suggest that suburban residence engendered a particular style of life, for suburbs in fact have little else in common when examined closely. The elements of the myth are as follows: there is a common physical prospect (Pete Seeger's 'Little Boxes') of similar houses in which temporarily reside, a 'new middle class' of upwardly mobile executives who are, together with their wives, college educated. There is a hyper-active social life both at the neighbouring and organizational level, encouraged by the absence of older people who would normally be leaders. This rich social life is fostered by the homogeneity of the suburbanities. As Berger says 'they have a maximum of similar interests and preoccupations which promote their solidarity.' In the familiar pattern of community studies there is a rapid shift from his empirically variable proposition to claiming that this caused 'conformity': this is the shift form community as empirical description to community as normative prescription.

Gans shows in his study[4] that Levittowners do not want to be transients, they are not organization men. Yet they do not have one characteristic beloved of traditional writers on the community: 'intergeneration rootedness'. This will be increasingly rare in industrial society for it requires the kind of economic stability (or stagnancy) characteristic of only the most backward areas. The romanticizing of this type of rootedness, at the core of prescriptive notions of community ignores the fact that for many people it blocked progress, especially for those at the bottom of the social heap who were permanently labelled in their home community in which they were 'known' as 'shiftless' and 'good for nothing'. Levittown, like many suburban communities was planned for families with young children, for breeding. These young children, for whom it was home will move away to work, to marry and have children of their own. Any satisfactory theory of community must take account of the mobility (without over stressing it) of modern society. Gans provided a model for the analysis of one emerging community and it is through sociological analysis of this kind that our knowledge and understanding of society will grow, not through the armchair-bound condemnations of suburban living by sensitive intellectuals. Few changes could be traced to the suburban qualities of Levittown. The crucial differences between communities is that they are home for different kinds of people. Such concepts as 'rural', 'urban' and 'suburban' add little by themselves to our knowledge.

The last extract from one of the editors own field work on a middle class housing estate shows through an analysis of a 'dramatic incident'[5] the emergence of new bases of solidarity in the suburbs. This is included because it partially describes community study as a method of investigation in suburbia.

NOTES

1 J. R. Seeley, R. A. Sim and E. W. Loosley, *Crestwood Heights*, Wiley, New York 1963 (originally Basic Books, New York, 1956), p. 3.
2 Ibid., p. 4.
3 *The Organisation Man* by William H. Whyte, originally published in 1956.
4 Herbert J. Gans, *The Levittowners: Anatomy of Suburbia*, Allen Lane, the Penguin Press, London, 1967.
5 See R. Frankenburg, *British Community Studies: Problems of Synthesis*, pp. 123–154, in Banton (ed.) Tavistock, 1966.

CHAPTER 19

Crestwood Heights:
A Canadian Middle Class Suburb*

J. R. Seeley, R. A. Sim and E. W. Loosley

This book attempts to depict, in part, the life of a community. North Americans may know its external features well, for some community like it is to be seen in and around almost any great city on this continent, from New York to San Francisco, from Halifax to Vancouver. In infinite variety, yet with an eternal sameness, it flashes on the movie screen, in one of those neat comedies about the upper middle class family which Hollywood delights to repeat again and again as nurture for the American Dream. It fills the pages of glossy magazines devoted to the current best in architecture, house decoration, food, dress and social behaviour. The innumerable service occupations bred of an urban culture will think anxiously about people in such a community in terms of what 'they' will buy or use this year. Any authority in the field of art, literature, or science probably at some time has had, or will have, its name on a lecture itinerary. A teacher will consider it a privilege to serve in its schools. For those thousands of North Americans who struggle to translate the promise of America into a concrete reality for themselves, and, even more important, for their children, it is in some sense a Mecca.

The book attempts to pin down in time and space this thing of dreams for the many, and actual experience for the very few. One such community from among the many of its kind has been chosen. It will be called 'Crestwood Heights.'[1] It is 'somewhere in central Canada'; the time falls in the years immediately following World War II.

Since the word 'community' will be used throughout this study in reference to Crestwood Heights, it is important that the sense in which the term is apt be established in the very beginning. Although Crestwood Heights is officially a separate municipality within a greater metropolitan area, it is also something else. It exists *as a*

* Reprinted by permission of Basic Books Inc. from *Crestwood Heights: A Study of the Culture of Suburban Life* by J. R. Seeley, R. A. Sim and E. W. Loosley, New York 1956, pp. 3–11 and by permission of University of Toronto Press for the same extract.

community because of the relationships that exist between people—relationships revealed in the functioning of the institutions which they have created: family, school, church, community centre, club, association, summer camp and other more peripheral institutions and services. (Some of the many groups to which Crestwooders belong are to be found within the geographic boundaries of Crestwood Heights, though some are outside the area altogether.) These relationships develop within a material setting of brick, stone, wood, concrete and steel—and of flowering gardens, shaded in several sections by trees which once arched over an earlier and a very different enterprise, the clearing of the forest by a more simple type of pioneer. Yet the Crestwood resident of the present day is also, in his way, a pioneer.

This complex network of human relationships which *is* the community exists from the viewpoint of the participants for a definite purpose. In Crestwood Heights the major institutional focus is upon child-rearing. How is a Crestwood Heights adult to be made? How will he grow and mature into manhood and womanhood? What ideals are to be placed before him? What are the pressures to be laid upon him for conformity? What are the obstacles to orderly, predictable growth? What are to be the stages of maturation? What is to be understood by 'maturity' itself, and how is it finally to be achieved? Here are eminent local preoccupations.

These questions, which once primarily concerned poet, novelist, dramatist and philosopher, now also supply data for scientific scrutiny. In this study, we as social scientists have attempted to look at some facts about child growth as it takes place in a comparatively homogeneous, prosperous, modern, urban and suburban environment.

Crestwood Heights exists both as a physical entity and as a psychological fact.

As the name suggests, it is built on a choice brow of land, overlooking a wide sweep of the metropolitan area. Yet, although it is literally a city built upon a hill, the closest investigation of the terrain from the air would fail to reveal definite boundaries. Should an intruder from outside wander through its streets, he would find little, except a slight difference in sign-posts, to distinguish Crestwood Heights from Big City—or from other suburbs near it.

There is, however, a subtle but decided line drawn between Crestwood Heights and Big City. The very name 'Crestwood Heights' expresses to perfection the 'total personality' of the community, particularly in its relation to the metropolis of which it is a part. That name suggests, as it is clearly meant to do, the sylvan, the natural, and the romantic, the lofty and serene, the distant but not withdrawn; the suburb that looks out upon, and over the city, not in it or of it, but at its border and on its crest. The name is a source of pride, a guide for differential conduct (to some degree at least), but first and foremost a symbol evoking deference. Crestwood Heights is bound inescapably to Big City by many ties, but the proximity of the heterogeneous metropolitan area provides chiefly a foil against which Crestwood Heights can measure its own superiority and exclusiveness, core of its communal identity. The psychological climate of Crestwood Heights is, otherwise, no easier to assess than are its physical contours.

Certain basic problems have always concerned all human groups. And upon the answers given, depend the particular flavour of a culture, the subtle qualities which differentiate it from all others. One anthropologist, Dr. C. Kluckhohn, lists as the fundamental questions, these:

What are assumed to be the *innate predispositions* of man?
What is the relation of man to *nature*?
What is the significant *time* dimension?
What is the dominant relationship of man to *other men*?

To these might be added:

What is man's relationship to *space*?

One might attempt a general answer to these questions for Crestwood Heights. First, human nature is seen as a mixture of good and evil, which may rather readily be modified in the direction of greater good. This orientation is both like and unlike the traditional Christian belief that man is conceived in sin, but may be redeemed through God's grace. Under the growing influence of a newer, expert-mediated ideology, however, the child is seen rather as being endowed at birth with all the potentialities for good, potentialities which may be thwarted later by the environment (especially if it fails to provide maternal warmth and paternal support). Here, then, the shared view of human nature inclines towards 'positive neutral'.

The fundamental attitude towards nature and super-nature is definitely that of mastery: man is *over* nature. The Crestwooder tends to assume that little or nothing is beyond his control. Although he may cherish a somewhat sentimental reverence for nature, he is carefully screened by technology from its power. In the psychological and religious realms, he subscribes almost whole-heartedly to the proposition that he and he alone is the master of his fate—or ought to be.

As for time, Crestwooders live almost entirely *in* the present but *for* the near future (with the past largely obliterated). Its people fall almost entirely into two generations: parents who have moved into

Crestwood Heights when adult, and their children who have been born or brought up there. Closely associated with the Crestwood orientation towards time, is the attitude to personality and human activity. Here, as in their concept of human nature, Crestwooders are divided, but in this instance, by sex. Men incline almost invariably towards 'doing' in the present with a definite future reference; women tend more towards 'being-in-becoming' (as Dr. Kluckhohn calls it) though it is doubtful if their active lives really allow for the joy of unfolding to be felt.

In their relationships with other human beings, Crestwooders are highly individualistic.

Finally, in their orientation towards space, Crestwooders again experience a sense of mastery and fluidity. They are in a position to buy privacy and sunlight, in spacious homes and gardens; and by their possession of cars, in their freedom to travel, by plane, boat, train or automobile, they have the sense of conquering both time and space.

Intertwined with these orientations is a deep allegiance to the great North American dream, a dream of a material heaven in the here and now, to be entered by the successful elect. The dream is, of course, not confined to North America alone; it is perhaps as old as the world itself. In other ages and in other lands it has occurred and recurred. It led thousands of men and women from warring Europe to North America. It was dreamed by starving Irish peasants in the peat bogs, and by deposed Highland clans amid the northern heather. Without it the waste lands of the North American continent would not today be filled. The dreamers of Crestwood Heights are, in this sense, both innovators and heirs of a long and strong tradition.

The dream has a specific content. Nothing in it suggests an age of innocence and peace in the future, when 'the wolf shall dwell with the lamb' and 'a little child shall lead them'; nor is the goal a 'land flowing with milk and honey', where men shall live without effort. What is envisioned is rather a material abundance to be achieved and maintained only by unremitting struggle and constant sacrifice. No citizen of Big City or its hinterland, casting a longing and covetous eye towards Crestwood Heights, could easily envisage a life of leisure there. Should he, by some stroke of fortune or through his own exertions, enter the promised land, he will fully accept continuing work and increasing anxiety as the price he must pay if he does not wish to be cast out of his paradise. His character will have been so firmly structured by the time he finally arrives in Crestwood Heights that leisure and inactivity are now his greatest threats. Once there, the grandchild of Irish peasants, propelled towards North America by the dream, could no more freely shed his cultural inheritance of thrift and industry, hoarding and frugality, than could the Jewish child of ghetto parentage cast off completely his age-old fear of segregation and persecution.

With material abundance social status is closely linked in the dream. Here, in North America, the possession of wealth confers prestige upon its holders. *Because there are few strong ties of locality or kinship, a man is judged largely by the number and the quality of the things he owns.* These objects must be seen, approved, and envied by other men—as they are in Crestwood Heights. In this sense, the community serves the psychological purpose of a super-marketplace, where status may be validated in the acquisition and exhibition of non-material 'objects': houses, cars, clothes, jewellery, gadgets, furniture, works of art, stocks, bonds, membership in exclusive clubs, attendance at private schools.[3]

The accumulation of the latest and the best materially is paralleled by an urge to acquire the latest and the best in ideas, values, and 'experiences'. These are diligently 'collected', often with little apparent reference to the person's own tastes or interests. A cult, a political party, a traditional religious denomination, or a university education may be 'collected' and cherished in much the same fashion as a new car or a television set—and with much of the same desire to impress others.

Material abundance and social status are not, however, pursued openly and cynically for the direct and sole satisfaction of the competitors. The peculiar twist of the American dream is that the pursuit of the goal is not for oneself alone but for one's children (and, less importantly, less urgently, 'for the community'). Other peoples have used this motivation, but it is particularly emphasized in North America, where the social structure is still sufficiently flexible to hold out some promise to the great majority of at least a measure of upward social mobility. The freedom from struggle which is deleted from the traditional version of the dream, is, in Crestwood Heights, somewhat wistfully and without too much hope, transferred to the children's future. 'If there is to be a millennium of the more conventional utopian variety (which is doubtful) let it be for the children, since we, their parents, will stand forever without its gates.'

In its main themes, then, the North American dream, as it looks to material abundance and social status, is also the dream of Crestwood Heights. But because Crestwood Heights is situated in Canada and not in the United States, its dream, interwoven with English threads, cannot be wholly 'American'. The *New Yorker*, correct reading for the smart urban American, may be on the living-room table, but *Punch* is sometimes found beside it. For some Crestwooders, laughing spontaneously at a Peter Arno cartoon, also feel that there *must* be something to *Punch*, even if their enjoyment of its pages is sometimes strained or altogether absent. Although the Crestwooder may consult *Home Beautiful* or *House and Garden* as a guide to 'interior decoration', he may also deal at first hand with a firm importing textiles and furniture direct from England. He makes his uneasy choice between American modern or eighteenth- and nineteenth-century reproductions of English period furniture, never quite certain in his own mind which is 'right.' He is as likely to set his table with Spode or Minton as with Russel Wright. The astute art dealers of Big City know very well that a dim, gilt-framed oil, supposed once to have hung in some ducal gallery, will have a ready sale in Crestwood Heights. And, where education is concerned, some Crestwood residents select a private school taught by British 'masters', in a pattern borrowed directly from the British Public Schools. Even the vast majority of parents who send their children to the tax-supported schools of the Heights proudly approve the word 'Prep' which tags each elementary school name. In the absence of a strong, indigenous Canadian culture, the Crestwood Heighter, more so perhaps than his American counterpart, is inclined to waver eternally under influences from outside.

Once arrived in Crestwood Heights, the new resident finds himself in an environment exceedingly well equipped to materialize, feed, and cherish his particular version of the common dream. The real estate companies of Big City vie with each other to offer him a selection of houses, complete with garden, gadgets, space, sun and privacy. The municipality provides winding, tree-shaded streets, paved and well-kept, and excellent protective services. But the necessity of continuous work, if the dream is to be kept alive, is recognized in Crestwood's close proximity to the heart of Big City where the office buildings, the financial houses, the hospitals, the university, the big hotels are clustered. The few stores in the Heights, mostly food purveyors, also understand the dream. They provide delicacies from all parts of the world—side by side with the common necessities to be found, nation-wide, in the chain grocery stores. These fashionable accretions to the regular food outlets are skilfully geared towards guiding the uninitiated in the proper use of unfamiliar foods, as well as towards the satisfying of an already sophisticated taste. Beyond, in the outer wilderness of Big City, lies the wealth of department stores and specialty shops where one may range at will in the gratification of every imaginable material desire.

To feed the non-material aspects of the dream there are the schools. Here the parent and the child alike may 'acquire' ideas and values. These schools are more than locally famous for knowing their business exceedingly well. No longer need the newcomer feel uncertain and alone, wondering how he should conduct himself in Crestwood Heights. In the schools are men and women whose business it is to help him in this task. Here there are teachers and psychologists whose office doors are always open to the questioner. He has only to ask in order to receive. It is better, of course, if one does not have to ask too urgently, too obviously, or too often; but for the child or the adult who needs to find a way there are directions forthcoming, free and abundant. If the resources of the school prove insufficient, there are the summer camps, the private practitioners of psychology and psychiatry, the pediatricians of Big City and beyond. The churches too, on the fringes of Crestwood Heights, offer various forms of spiritual solace, from which one may make a selection. No longer need one feel compelled to attend a synagogue in the working class 'Ward', Sabbath after Sabbath, or sit in the family pew of a half-empty downtown church. One may go to a beautiful new synagogue or 'Temple', even, on occasion, with Gentile friends; one may try, if the more conventional denominations do not satisfy, the congregation of the Unitarians, where all are welcome, or enjoy a cosy 'fireside' in the home of a Bahá'í.

Big City has further attractions which encourage the dream. Into Big City, beyond the tree-protected bounds of Crestwood Heights, one can sally forth with friends to cocktails at an exclusive club, to dinner, to concerts, plays or movies. There is dancing in a variety of hotels, with the opportunity for adventures not to be had within Crestwood Heights itself. There are museums where one may pass an hour or two with wide-eyed children; art galleries, which one may attend in evening dress on opening night; a conservatory of music with its eurhythmics class for children and its ballet to help small girls towards a graceful manipulation of their bodies; a university where one may take a course or two during the serious winter months before the trip to Florida.

And, far beyond Big City, there is the North, into which one may penetrate in the summer time, the North of camps and cottages beside small wooded lakes or open sheets of rockbound water. It is as necessary to Crestwood Heights as is the South. Alternate retreats from a too strenuous pursuit of the dream, they mark the slowing phase in the rhythmically beating pulse: work and relaxation, leisure and renewed effort. In the South adults may escape from the children; or they may send them to the North to camp, secure in the knowledge that the dream will not let them go, while they forget it for a little while themselves. Indeed in the North child and adult can briefly pretend the dream does not exist, for here no elaborate technological screen divides one from the earth and rock, water, sun and rain. It is good to live by these alone—not too long, of course, for it is equally good to come back to the metered hot water in the coloured tub, to the efficient sanitary toilet, to the oil-generated heat that comes at the flick of an automatic switch, to electric light, to all the amenities of the material and psychological environment which is Crestwood Heights.

Here then, is the raw material from which the dream may take on a form and shape. But, selecting and rejecting elements, each family or person builds a special version, a particular cultural pattern, like and yet unlike the neighbour's. The process is never fixed and final, for one learns to make few choices and new combinations endlessly. But although everyone, in some measure, has the power of choice, it is the adults, ultimately the controllers of the money which alone makes a choice a possibility, who have the greatest power. The sum total of all these choices creates the matrix in which the Crestwood Heights child is reared and in which his character is formed.

Crestwood Heights, at the local level, maintains a symbiotic relationship with the sprawling, variegated metropolitan area. As a separate municipality with a population of roughly 17,000[4] it does maintain some services: a council, municipal police and fire departments, schools. It has a voluntary community council, a community centre, a very active Home and School Association, as well as some minor organizations. But, on the other hand, Crestwood Heights has no industry, no hospital, no large stores, no sewage disposal plant, no Community Chest or other social agencies; and virtually no slums, no service clubs, and only one church. Thus Crestwood Heights, together with other comparable upper middle class neighbourhoods, is highly interdependent with the metropolitan area, however much it tries to hold itself aloof, for each offers services which make it attractive and necessary to the other. The institutional meshing between Crestwood Heights and Big City is well illustrated in the occupational pattern. Few of those employed in the institutions of Crestwood Heights live in the community. They commute there to work, leaving their families behind in some other, less expensive, section of the metropolis. Conversely, the institutions of Big City provide the incomes which maintain the homes of Crestwood Heights.[5]

In the highly organized industrial and commercial civilization into which this urban complex fits, there is a growing need for highly trained, highly specialized persons in management and professional positions. Their importance to that civilization is reflected in the favourable incomes which they receive, and by the relatively high standard of consumption enjoyed by them because of their status. These are the people who can afford the exclusive environment of Crestwood Heights, who, in very truth, *must* be able to afford it as part of their careers. The Crestwood resident proudly feels that he is outside the city—but by no means beyond the reach of urban amenities and conveniences. Although to the casual observer this distinction might seem tenuous, the Crestwooder jealously guards his privileged suburban status. Harder work, struggle, anxiety, and sacrifice are not considered too high a price to pay for a Crestwood Heights address, an address which symbolizes the screening out of the unpleasant features of urban existence, leaving only the rewards and joys.

It is not that Crestwood is merely a dormitory within the metropolis, though sleep is one common bond which brings family members with otherwise diverse interests together. The sharing of food and of many other forms of familial and communal activity and association, also play their part in making Crestwood the locus of a common life. While the Crestwood Heights father, and any other wage-earning members of the family, do carry on their occupations beyond the physical limits of Crestwood Heights, their removal is much less complete than it would be from a more distant commuting centre. Frequent interchanges by telephone between downtown and Crestwood Heights, a member of the family picking up the car at the office, a luncheon rendezvous with friends or family at a Big City restaurant—all are easily arranged. Conversely, a series of services enters the back door as the wage-earning member takes his leave through the front. Cleaning women, deliveries of all kinds, repair services, stream into the community from the city. These are the men and women who help in multitudinous ways to sustain the prosperous but servantless[6] modern household of Crestwood Heights.

The fact that employment, golf clubs, symphonies, and like activities are almost all extra-communal tends to specialize, if not to deepen, those relations which are left exclusively local. These ties are institutionalized primarily in the family, secondarily in the school and its affiliated activities, and less powerfully, in the municipal services. The institutions of Crestwood Heights tend therefore to converge upon the family, existing as they do to regulate the life of a purely residential community devoted to child-rearing.

NOTES

1 The authors and their associates had great difficulty in creating a pseudonym that would suitably denote the psychological and social overtones of the original name. The one selected very nearly catches these subtle nuances. Among the pseudonyms thought of were: Hillgrove, Interwalden, Uppertown, Maple Heights, Montsylvania, Hillbrow Heights, Richview Heights, Hilltop Heights, Woodmount, Newmount and Urban Heights.

2 See F. R. Kluckhohn, 'Dominant and Variant Value Orientations,' in *Personality in Nature, Society, and Culture*, ed. C. Kluckhohn and H. A. Murray (2nd ed.; New York: Alfred A. Knopf, 1953), p. 346. These concepts are further elaborated by C. Kluckhohn in 'Universal Categories of Culture,' *Anthropology Today: An Encyclopedic Inventory* (Chicago: University of Chicago Press, 1953), pp. 507–523.

Dr. Kluckhohn gives three range-points covering the variability in each dimension:

Innate disposition: Good—neither good nor bad—bad
Relation to nature: Man subjugated to—in—over nature
Significant time: Past—present—future
Valued personality: Being—being-in-becoming—doing
Relation to others: Lineal—Collateral—Individualistic

To the possibilities offered by these range-points, she adds methods of further specification that permit a more subtle analysis than has been employed in the text.

3 This infinite variety of subtle transactions dwarfs in mass and scope the essentially similar, if more primitive, practices of peoples like the Kwakiuti. See R. F. Benedict, *Patterns of Culture* (Boston: Houghton Mifflin Company, 1934), pp. 173–222; D. Riesman (in collaboration with R. Denney and N. Glazer), *The Lonely Crowd: A Study of the Changing American Character* (New Haven: Yale University Press, 1950), pp. 271–282.

4 The official population in 1951 was 15,305 which is the figure used in demographic analysis. At the time of writing, the municipal office gave 17,000 as the estimated population of Crestwood Heights. The population of Big City in 1951 was 676,000; that of the total metropolitan area 1,117,000. SOURCE: Canada, Bureau of Statistics, *Ninth Census of Canada 1951* (Ottawa: Queen's Printer, 1953), vol. I, Tables 1, 9, 17, 18.

5 Of the male labour force of Crestwood Heights 14 years of age and over (1951), 50·4 per cent were engaged in proprietary and managerial occupations and 18·3 per cent in professions, as against 10·4 per cent and 8·0 per cent respectively for Big City. Of the professional people of Crestwood Heights (1951), 18·1 per cent were lawyers and notaries, 16 per cent accountants and auditors, 14·8 per cent physicians and surgeons, 6·3 per cent teachers; all others, 44·8 per cent. SOURCE: Canada, Bureau of Statistics, *Ninth Census of Canada, 1951* vol. IV, Table 6.

6 Crestwood Heights is not completely servantless. The proportion of wage-earning females 14 years of age and over listed as domestic workers diminished from 58·53 per cent in 1941 to 40·32 per cent in 1951. In 1941, female domestic workers made up 8·55 per cent of the total population of the Heights; in 1951, 5·07 per cent.

CHAPTER 20

Myths of American Suburbia

B. Berger

In recent years a myth of suburbia has developed in the United States. In saying this, I refer not to the physical facts of the movement to the suburbs; this is an ecological tendency to which all recent statistics on population mobility bear eloquent testimony.[1] I refer instead to the social and cultural ramifications that are perceived to have been inherent in the suburban exodus. Brunner and Hallenbeck, for example, call the rise of suburbia, 'one of the major social changes of the twentieth century',[2] and the popular literature especially is full of characterizations of suburbia as 'a new way of life'.

The significance of the past decade cannot be overestimated since it is only in this period that suburbia has become a *mass* phenomenon and hence prone to the manufacture of modern myth. Suburbanization, however, goes back as far as the latter part of the nineteenth century, when the very wealthy began to build country estates along the way of suburban railroad stations. Improvements in the automobile and the development of good highways after World War I brought greater numbers of wealthy people to suburban areas in the 1920's. The depression of the 1930's slowed the process of suburbanization, but the late 1930's saw the development of some new residential construction at the peripheries of city limits. The big boom in suburban development, of course, came after World War II with the proliferation of 'the mass produced suburbs' all over the country, and well within the reach of middle- and lower-middle-income people. And in the last few years, suburbanization of secondary and tertiary industry has followed closely upon residential suburbanization. Carl Bridenbaugh has noted that suburbanization began as far back as the early part of the eighteenth century. 'One ordinarily thinks of the suburban movement of the present century as being of recent origin, and it will come as a surprise to many that the flight from the city began in the first half of the eighteenth century—and for the same reasons as today. The differences were in degree only. Just as Londoners moved westward from the City in search of quiet, air, com-

* Reprinted by permission of the University of California Press from *Working Class Suburb* by B. Berger, California 1960, pp. 1–13.

fort, lower rents, and more room for display, so did Philadelphians cross the northern and southern bounds of the metropolis in a perennial search for the "green".... That greatest of townsmen, Benjamin Franklin, even moved from High Street to Second and Sassafras, grumbling that "the din of the Market increases upon me; and that, with frequent interruptions, has, I find, made me say some things twice over.''[3]

The literature on suburbanization seems to fall roughly into two categories. Studies of suburbanization by sociologists have been going on for a long time; with few exceptions, however, these have been primarily ecological or demographic in character.[4] On the other hand, studies of and comment on the culture and social psychology of suburban life have, again with a few exceptions, been left largely to popular writers, journalists, and intellectuals.[5] To urban sociologists in general, 'suburbs' is a term of ecological reference; ecologists and demographers may often dispute the most useful way of conceiving 'suburbs' for the purposes of their work, but the dispute is largely a technical one. 'Suburbia', on the other hand, is a term of cultural reference; it is intended to connote a way of life, or, rather, the intent of those who use it is to connote a way of life.[6] The ubiquity of the term suburbia in current popular literature suggests that its meaning is well on its way to standardization—that what it is supposed to connote is widely enough accepted to permit free use of the term with a reasonable amount of certainty that it will convey the images it intends. In the last ten or twelve years, these images have coalesced into a full-blown myth, complete with its articles of faith, its sacred symbols, its rituals, its promise for the future, and its resolution of ultimate questions. The details of the myth are rife in many of the mass circulation magazines as well as in more intellectual periodicals and books; and although the details should be familiar to almost everyone interested in contemporary cultural trends, it may be well to summarize them briefly.

ELEMENTS OF THE MYTH

Approaching the myth of suburbia from the outside, one is immediately struck by rows of new ranch-type houses either identical in design or with minor variations in a basic plan, winding streets, neat lawns, two-car garages, infant trees, and bicycles and tricycles lining the sidewalks. Near at hand is the modern ranch-type school and the even more modern shopping centre, dominated by the giant supermarket, which is flanked by a pastel-dotted expanse of parking lot. Beneath the television aerial and behind the modestly but charmingly landscaped entrance to the tract home reside the suburbanite and his family. I should perhaps say 'temporarily reside' because the most prominent element of the myth is that residence in a tract suburb is temporary; suburbia is a 'transient centre' because its bread-winners are upward mobile, and live there only until a promotion and/or a company transfer permits or requires something somewhat more opulent in the way of a home. The suburbanites are upward mobile because they are predominantly young (most commentators seem to agree that almost all are between twenty-five and thirty-five), well educated, and have a promising place in some organizational hierarchy—promising because of a continuing expansion of the economy with no serious slowdown in sight. They are engineers, middle-management men, young lawyers, salesmen, insurance agents, teachers, civil service bureaucrats—occupational groups sometimes designated as organization men, and sometimes as 'the new middle class'. Most such occupations require some college education, so it comes as no surprise to hear and read that the suburbanites are well educated. Their wives too seem to be well educated; their reported conversation, their patois, and especially their apparently avid interest in theories of child development all suggest their exposure to higher education.

According to the myth, a new kind of hyperactive social life has apparently developed in suburbia. This is manifest not only in the informal visiting or 'neighbouring' that is said to be rife, but also in the lively organizational life that goes on. Associations, clubs, and organizations are said to exist for almost every conceivable hobby, interest or preoccupation. The hyperactive participation of suburbanites is said to extend beyond the limits of voluntary associations to include an equally active participation in local civic affairs. This active, busy participation by young families is encouraged by the absence of an older generation who, in other communities, would normally be the leaders. The absence of an older generation is said to have an especially strong effect upon the young women of the community who, thrown back upon their own resources, develop a marked independence and initiative in civic affairs. The informal social life revolves around the daytime female 'kaffeeklatsch' at which 'the girls' discuss everything from the problems of handling salesmen to the problems of handling Susie. In the evening the sociability (made possible by the baby-sitting pool) is continued with rounds of couples dropping in on each other for bridge, a drink or some conversation.

This rich social life is fostered by the homogeneity of the suburbanites; they are in the same age range and have similar jobs and incomes, their children are around the same age, their problems of housing and furnishing are similar. In short, they have a maximum of similar interests and preoccupations which promote their solidarity. This very solidarity and homogeneity (when combined with the uniformities of the physical context) are often perceived as the sources of 'conformity' in the suburbia; aloofness or detachment is frowned upon. The intenseness of the social life is sometimes interpreted as a lack of privacy, and this lack of privacy, when added to the immediate visibility of deviation from accepted norms, permits strong, if informal, sanctions to be wielded against nonconformity. The 'involvement of everyone in everyone else's life' submits one to the constant scrutiny of the community, and everything from an unclipped lawn to an unclipped head of hair may be cause for invidious comment. On the other hand, the uniformity and homogeneity make suburbia classless or one-class (variously designated as middle or upper middle class). For those interlopers who arrive in the suburbs bearing the unmistakable marks of a more deprived upbringing, suburbia is said to serve as a kind of 'second melting pot' in which those who are mobile upward out of the lower orders learn to take on the appropriate folkways of the milieu to which they aspire.

During the daylight hours, suburbia, in the imagery of the myth, is a place almost wholly given over to child rearing. Manless during the day, suburbia is a female society in which the young mothers, well educated and without the interference of tradition (represented by doting grandparents), can rear their children according to the best modern methods. 'In the absence of older people, the top authorities on child guidance [in suburbia] are two books: Spock's *Infant Care*, and Gesell's *The First Five Years of Life*. You hear frequent references to them.'[8]

The widely commented upon 'return to religion' is said to be most visible in suburbia. Clergymen are swamped, not only with their spiritual duties but with marriage counselling and other family problems as well. The revivified religious life in suburbia is not merely a matter of the increasing size of Sunday congregations; the church is not only a house of worship but a local civic institution also, and as such it benefits from the generally active civic life of the suburbanites.

Part of the myth of suburbia is the image of suburbanites as commuters: they work in the city. For cartoonists and other mythmakers, this mass morning exodus to the city has provided opportunity for the creation of images such as 'the race to make the 7:12,' getting the station wagon started on a cold morning, or the army of wives waiting at the Scarsdale station for the 5:05 from the city. A good deal has been deduced about the way of life in the suburbs from the fact of commuting. For father, commuting means an extra hour or two away from the family, for example, with its debilitating effects upon the relation between father and children. Sometimes this means that Dad leaves for work before the children are up and comes home after they are put to bed. Naturally, these extra hours put a greater burden upon the mother, and have implications for the relation between husband and wife.

In commuting, the commuter returns in the morning to the place where he was bred, for the residents of suburbia are apparently former city people who 'escaped' to the suburbs. By moving to the suburbs, however, the erstwhile Democrat from the 'urban ward'[9] becomes the suburban Republican. The voting shift has been commented on or worried about at great length; there seems to be something about suburbia that makes Republicans out of people who were Democrats while they lived in the city. But the political life in the suburbs is said to be characterized not only by the voting shift, but by the vigour with which it is carried on. Political activity takes its place beside other civic and organizational activity, intense and spirited.

SOURCES OF THE MYTH

The foregoing characterization is intended neither as ethnography nor as caricature. Brief and sketchy as it is, it does not, I think, misrepresent the typical image of suburbia that, by way of highbrow as well as middlebrow periodicals (as well as some recent books), has come to dominate the minds of most Americans, including intellectuals. It takes scarcely more than a moment's reflection, however, for the perplexing question to arise: why should a group of tract houses, mass produced and quickly thrown up on the outskirts of a large city, apparently generate so uniform a way of life? What is the logic that links tract living with 'suburbanism as a way of life'?

If the homes characteristic of suburbia were all within a narrow price range, we might expect them to be occupied by families of similar income, and this might account for some of the homogeneity of the neighbourhood ethos. But suburban developments are themselves a heterogeneous phenomenon. The term 'suburbia' has not only been used to refer to tract-housing developments as low as $7,000 per unit and as high as $65,000 per unit,[10] but also to rental developments whose occupants do not think of themselves as homeowners. The same term has been used to cover old rural towns (such as those in the Westchester-Fairfield county complex around New York City) which, because of the expansion of the city and improvements in transportation, have only gradually become suburban in character;[11] it has been applied also to gradually developing residential neighbourhoods near the peripheries of city limits. Clearly, then, the ecological nature of suburbs cannot justify so monolithic an image as that of 'suburbia.'

If the image of suburbia is limited to the mass-produced tract developments, perhaps it is the fact of commuting that links suburban residence with 'suburbanism as a way of life.' Clearly, the demands of daily commuting create certain common conditions which might go far to explain some of the ostensible uniformities of suburban living. But certainly commuting is not inherent in suburban living despite the many students of suburbia who have made commuting an essential part of their definitions of suburbs. *Fortune*, for example, says that, 'The basic characteristic of suburbia is that it is inhabited by people who work in a city, but prefer to live where there is more open space, and are willing to suffer both inconvenience and expense to live there.' Von Rhode says, 'The distinguishing aspect of the suburb is, of course, the commuter.' And Walter Martin says, '. . . the characteristics essential to suburban status . . . are a unique ecological position in relation to a larger city and a high rate of commuting to that city.' These definitions would exclude the community reported on in this study from the category 'suburb,' but more than twenty-five years ago, Lundberg noted, '. . . perhaps too much has been made of commuting as a phenomenon unique to the suburb. As a matter of fact, comparatively few people in a large city live within walking distance of their work. From this point of view a great number of people living in the city are also commuters . . . commuting can certainly not be stressed as a unique feature or a fundamental distinction of suburban life as contrasted with urban.'[12]

It may have been true that the occupations of most suburbanites required a daily trip to and from the central business district of the city; it may still be true, but it is likely to be decreasingly true with the passage of time. The pioneers to the suburban residential frontier have been followed not only by masses of retail trade outlets, but by industry also. Modern mass production technology has made obsolete many two- and three-story plants in urban areas,[13] and today's modern factories are vast one-story operations which require wide expanses of land, which are either unavailable or too expensive in the city itself. Thus with the passage of time, 'industrial parks' will increasingly dot suburban areas, and the proportions of suburbanites commuting to the city each day will decrease.[11]

If the occupations of most suburbanites were similar in their demands, this might help account for the development of a generic way of life in the suburbs. Or indeed, if suburbs were populated largely by organization men and their families, then we could understand more readily the style of life that is said to go on. Or, lacking this, if organization men, as Whyte puts it, give the prevailing *tone* to life in the suburbs, then we could more readily understand the prevalence of his model in the literature. But there is no ready hypothesis to explain why the occupations of suburbanites should be so homogeneous. It may be true that the typical organization man is a suburbanite. But it is one thing to assert this and quite another thing to assert that the typical tract suburb is populated by organization men and their families and/or dominated by an 'organization' way of life.

Clearly then (and with all due respect for the selective aspects of suburban migration), one suburb is apt to differ from another not only in price range of its homes, the income characteristics of its residents, their occupational make-up, and the home-to-work traveling patterns of its breadwinners, but also in its educational levels, the character of the region, the size of the suburb, the social-geographical origin of its residents, and countless more indices—all of which, presumably, may be expected to lead to differences in 'way of life'.

But we not only have good reason to expect suburbs to *differ* markedly from one another; we have reason to expect striking *similarities* between life in urban residential neighbourhoods and tract suburbs of a similar socioeconomic make-up. Most residential neighbourhoods are 'manless' during the day; why not? Husbands are at work, and the only men around are likely to be salesmen and local tradespeople. Even in large cities many men 'commute' to work, that is, take subways, buses or other forms of public transportation to their jobs which may be on the other side of town.[15] Also there are thousands of blocks in American cities with rows of identical or similar houses within a narrow rental or price range, and presumably occupied by families in a similar income bracket.[16] Certainly, urban neighbourhoods have always had a class character and a 'way of life' associated with them. Certainly the whole image of 'conformity' in suburbia closely parallels the older image of the tyranny of gossip in the American small town.

There is, then, apparently no reason to believe, no ready and viable hypotheses to explain why 'suburbia' should be the new and homogeneous phenomenon it is usually conceived to be. What are the sources of the alleged new way of life? Why should the occupations of suburbanites be so homogeneous? Why should there be more conformity? Why should the 'social life' be so intense? Why should organizational participation be so widespread? Why should the churches be so much busier than elsewhere? Why should educational levels be so much higher than average? Why should the residents vote Republican? In short, why does 'suburbia' set off this chain reaction of images, associations, and ideas that have coalesced into a single myth?

WORKING-CLASS SUBURBS

This is, of course, a large question, and it would be premature to attempt an answer at this point. It is enough for the present to observe that the myth of suburbia flourishes in spite of an apparent lack of logic in its formulation. In continually referring to 'the myth of suburbia' I do not mean to imply that the reports on the culture of suburban life have been falsified, and it would be a mistake to interpret the tone of my remarks as a debunking one. I mean only to say that the reports we have had so far are extremely selective; they are based, for the most part, upon life in Levittown, New York; Park Forest, Illinois; Lakewood, near Los Angeles; and, most recently (the best study so far), a fashionable suburb of Toronto, Canada. The studies that have given rise to the myth of suburbia have been studies of *middle-class suburbs*, that is, suburbs of very large cities [17] populated primarily by people in the occupational groups often thought of as making up the 'new middle class'—the engineers, teachers and organization men mentioned earlier.[18] If the phrase 'middle class suburb' strikes the eye as redundant, it is testimony to the efficacy of the myth, for as I have suggested, there is certainly no reason to believe that residence in a new tract suburb in and of itself immediately (or even within a few years) generates a uniquely new middle-class style of life. Nor is there any reason to believe that the self-selective processes of suburban migration are such that suburbs attract an overwhelming majority of white-collar people to them.

These remarks are intended to suggest that the extant image of suburbia may be a distorted one; that its accuracy may be limited to the suburbs of great metropolises which are populated by former residents of the central city who work in its white-collar hierarchies. Thus whereas in most minds, Westchester and Nassau counties in New York, and Park Forest, Illinois, are ideal typical representatives of 'suburbia', they may, in fact, be representative only of suburbs of great cities and of a way of life lived by metropolis-bred, well-educated people of white-collar status. If this or something like this is, in fact, the case, then it is clearly a mistake to identify 'suburbanism' exclusively with the kind of life that is said to go on in places like these. Large tracts of suburban housing, in many respects indistinguishable from those on Long Island and in Park Forest, have gone up and are continuing to go up all over the country, not only near large cities, but near middle-sized and small ones as well. And if, as is not unlikely, many of the residents of these are rural-bred, with relatively little education, and innocent of white-collar status or aspirations, then we may expect sharp differences between their social and cultural life and that of their more sophisticated counterparts in white-collar suburbs.

This is hardly a revolutionary supposition; indeed, the fact that it should have to be asserted at all is still further testimony to the vitality of the myth I have been describing. This study, then, is based upon the most conventional of sociological assumptions: that a 'way of life' is a function of such variables as age, income, occupation, education, rural-urban background and so forth, and that this is as true for suburbs as it is for any other kind of modern community. To be more specific, a mass-produced tract suburb, rapidly occupied, has little chance to develop gradually a neighbourhood 'character' of its own. It is thus quite likely that a mass-produced suburb of, say, Chicago or New York, which attracts a large group of relatively well-educated, white-collar New Yorkers or Chicagoans, is apt to take on the 'social character' (in Fromm's phrase) which was incipient while the young suburbanites were still resident in the urban apartments of their parents; the 'other directedness' they learned in the city may, in the physical context of the tract suburb, be permitted its full development. On the other hand, as I have repeatedly emphasized, there is no reason to suppose that most suburbs have this character of sophisticated 'urbanism transplanted'. There *is* good reason to suppose that increasing numbers of unquestionably working-class people will be migrating to new tract suburbs; *not*, it should be emphasized, to new suburbs immediately and visibly characterizable as 'working class,' but to suburbs which to all intents and purposes look from the *outside* like the fulfilment of the promise of America symbolized in the myth. Large numbers of semiskilled as well as skilled factory workers in strongly unionized heavy industry are clearly able to afford to buy new tract homes in the $12,000 to $16,000 price range;[19] many are doing so, and presumably even more will be doing so as increasing numbers of factories move out of the city to the hinterlands.

BIBLIOGRAPHY

Allen, Frederick Lewis (1954) The Big Change in Suburbia, Part I. *Harper's* June 1954, pp. 21–28.

Allen, Frederick Lewis (1954) The Big Change in Suburbia, Part II, Crisis in the Suburbs. *Harper's*, July 1954, pp. 47–53.

Beegle, J. Allen (1947) Characteristics of Michigan's Fringe Population. *Rural Sociology*, September 1947, pp. 254–263.

Bogue, Donald (1953) *Population Growth in Standard Metropolitan Areas, 1900–1950*. Washington, D.C.: U.S. Government Printing Office.

Bridenbaugh, Carl (1955) *Cities in Revolt: Urban Life in America, 1743–1776*. New York: Alfred A. Knopf.

Bridgman, H. A. (1902) The Suburbanite. *Independent*, April 10, 1902, pp. 862–864.

Brunner, Edmund deS. and Wilbur C. Hallenbeck (1955) *American Society: Urban and Rural Patterns*. New York: Harper & Brothers.

Cuzzort, Raymond (1955) *Suburbanization of Service Industries Within Standard Metropolitan Areas*. Miami, Ohio: The Scripps Foundation.

Dobriner, William (ed.) (1958) *The Suburban Community*. New York: G. P. Putnam's Sons.

Douglass, Harlan P. (1925) *The Suburban Trend*. New York: D. Appleton Century Co.

Durkheim, Emile (1947) *The Elementary Forms of the Religious Life*. Glencoe, Illinois: The Free Press.

Fava, Sylvia (1956) Suburbanism as a Way of Life. *American Sociological Review*, February 1956, pp. 34–37.

Gist, Noel P. (1952) Developing Patterns of Urban Decentralization. *Social Forces*, March 1952, pp. 257–267.

Greeley, Andrew M. (1958) Suburbia, A New Way of Life. *The Sign*, January 1958.

Greeley, Andrew M. (1958) The Catholic Suburbanite. *The Sign*, February 1958.

Harris, Chauncey (1943) Suburbs. *American Journal of Sociology*, July 1943, pp. 1–13.

Henderson, Harry (1953) The Mass-Produced Suburbs, Part I. *Harper's*, November 1953, pp. 25–32.

Henderson, Harry (1953) Rugged American Collectivism, The Mass-Produced Suburbs, Part II. *Harper's*, December 1953, pp. 80–86.

Jones, Lewis W. (1955) The Hinterland Reconsidered. *American Sociological Review*, February 1955, pp. 40–44.

Keats, John (1957) *The Crack in the Picture Window*. New York: Ballantine Books.

Kitagawa, Evelyn and Donald Bogue (1953) *Suburbanization of Manufacturing Activities Within Standard Metropolitan Areas*. Miami, Ohio: The Scripps Foundation.

Lowry, Ritchie (1955) Toward a Sociology of Suburbia. *Berkeley Publications in Society and Institutions*, Spring 1955, pp. 12–24.

Lundberg, George, Mirra Komarovsky and Mary A. McInerny (1934) *Leisure: A Suburban Study*. New York: Columbia University Press.

Martin, Walter T. (1953) *The Rural-Urban Fringe*. Eugene: University of Oregon Press.

Martin, Walter T. (1956) The Structuring of Social Relationships Engendered by Suburban Residence. *American Sociological Review*, August 1956, pp. 446–453.

McGinley, Phyllis (1949) Suburbia. Of Thee I Sing. *Harper's* December 1949, pp. 78–82.

Mumford, Lewis. The Wilderness of Suburbia. *New Republic*, pp. 44–45. The New America: Living Atop a Civic Mushroom. *Newsweek*, April 1, 1957.

Newman, William (1957) Americans in Subtopia. *Dissent*, Summer 1957, pp. 256–266.

Phillips, H. I. (1925) The 7:58 Loses a Passenger. *Collier's*, April 11, 1925, pp. 11, 44.

Reissman, Leonard (1953) Levels of Aspiration and Social Class. *American Sociological Review*, June 1953, pp. 233–242.

Reissman, Leonard (1954) Class, Leisure, and Social Participation. *American Sociological Review*, February 1954, pp. 76–84.

Riesman, David (1957) The Suburban Dislocation. *Annals of the American Academy of Political and Social Science*, November 1957, pp. 123–146.

Rhode, Carl von (1946) The Suburban Mind. *Harper's*, April 1946, pp. 289–299.

Schnore, Leo F. (1956) The Functions of Metropolitan Suburbs. *American Journal of Sociology*, March 1956, pp. 453–458.

Schnore, Leo F. (1957) The Growth of Metropolitan Suburbs. *American Sociological Review*, April 1957, pp. 165–173.

Schnore, Leo F. (1957) Satellites and Suburbs. *Social Forces*, December 1957, pp. 121–127.

Seeley, John R., Alexander Sim and Elizabeth Loosley (1956) *Crestwood Heights: A Study of the Culture of Suburban Life*. New York: Basic Books.

Spectorsky, A. C. (1957) *The Exurbanites*. Philadelphia: Lippincott.

Stein, Maurice (1957) Suburbia, A Walk on the Mild Side. *Dissent*, Autumn 1957, pp. 267–275.

Swift, Ethel (1928) In Defense of Suburbia. *Outlook*, April 4, 1928, pp. 543–544, 558.

Tarver, James D. (1957) Suburbanization of Retail Trade in the Standard Metropolitan Areas of the U.S., 1948–1954. *American Sociological Review*, August 1957, pp. 427–433.

Whetten, Nathan (1951) Suburbanization as a Field for Sociological Research. *Rural Sociology*, December 1951, pp. 319–330.

Whyte, William H., Jr. (1953) The Transients. *Fortune*, May 1953, pp. 112–117, 221–226.

Whyte, William H., Jr. (1953) The Transients, II—The Future, c/o Park Forest. *Fortune*, June 1953, pp. 126–131, 186–196.

Whyte, William H., Jr. (1953) The Transients, III—The Outgoing Life. *Fortune*, July 1953, pp. 84–89, 160.

Whyte, William H., Jr. (1953) The Transients, IV—How the New Suburbia Socializes. *Fortune*, August 1953, pp. 120–122, 186–190.

Whyte, William H., Jr. (1957) *The Organization Man*. New York: Doubleday Anchor Books.

Woodbury, Coleman (1955) Suburbanization and Suburbia. *American Journal of Public Health*, January 1955, pp. 1–7.

NOTES

1 In 1953, for example, *Fortune* reported that suburban population had increased by 75 per cent over 1934, although total population was increasing by only 25 per cent; between 1947 and 1953 the increase was 43 per cent. See The New Suburban Market, *Fortune* (November 1953), p. 234. That this trend is continuing is indicated by a recent Census Bureau report showing that between 1950 and 1956 the population of suburbs increased by 29·3 per cent, although their central cities gained by only 4·7 per cent. For a full discussion of this whole tendency, see Donald Bogue, *Population Growth in Standard Metropolitan Areas, 1900–1950*, especially pp. 18–19, tables 13 and 14, p. 30, and table 19, p. 34.

2 Edmund deS. Brunner and Wilbur C. Hallenbeck, *American Society: Urban and Rural Patterns*, p. 253.

3 See Frederick Lewis Allen's classification of the five stages of suburbanization in The Big Change in Suburbia, Part I. For some pungent commentaries on the

early periods of suburbanization in this century, see H. A. Bridgman, The Suburbanite; Lewis Mumford, The Wilderness of Suburbia; H. I. Phillips, The 7:58 Loses a Passenger; Christine Frederick, Is Suburban Living a Delusion?; and Ethel Swift, In Defense of Suburbia. For the beginnings of suburbanization, see Carl Bridenbaugh, *Cities in Revolt: Urban Life in America, 1743–1776*, p. 24.

4 Some of the more recent work includes: J. Allen Beegle, Characteristic of Michigan's Fringe Population; Noel P. Gist, Developing Patterns of Urban Decentralization; Chauncey Harris, Suburbs; Lewis W. Jones, The Hinterland Reconsidered; Leo F. Schnore, The Functions of Metropolitan Suburbs; Leo F. Schnore, Satellites and Suburbs; Leo F. Schnore, The Growth of Metropolitan Suburbs. See also Walter T. Martin, *The Rural-Urban Fringe*.

5 See, for example, William H. Whyte's famous series of articles, later revised and reprinted as Part VII of his *The Organization of Man*; Harry Henderson, The Mass-Produced Suburbs, Part I, and The Mass-Produced Suburbs, Part II: Rugged American Collectivism; Frederick Lewis Allen, The Big Change in Suburbia, Part I, and The Big Change in Suburbia, Part II: Crisis in the Suburbs; John Keats, *The Crack in the Picture Window*; Carl von Rhode, The Suburban Mind; William Newman, Americans in Subtopia, and Maurice Stein, Suburbia, A Walk on the Mild Side; and Phyllis McGinley, Suburbia, Of Thee I Sing. Some of the exceptions, that is, work by sociologists, include John Seeley *et al.*, *Crestwood Heights* . . .; Sylvia Fava, Suburbanism as a Way of Life; David Riesman, The Suburban Dislocation; Nathan Whetton, Suburbanization as a Field for Sociological Research; Ritchie Lowry, Toward a Sociology of Suburbia; and the early works by Harlan P. Douglas, *The Suburban Trend*, and George Lundberg *et al.*, *Leisure: A Suburban Study*; William Dobriner (ed.), *The Suburban Community*. The following references were published too late for consideration here: Andrew M. Greeley, *The Church and the Suburbs*, New York, 1959; Albert I. Gordon, *Jews in Suburbia*, Boston, 1959; Robert C. Wood, *Suburbia, Its People and Their Politics*, Boston, 1959; Thomas Ktsanes and Leonard Reissman, Suburbia-New Homes for Old Values, *Social Problems*, Winter, 1959–1960.

6 David Riesman comments in a melancholy vein that the ecological work on suburbs and the sociopsychological work do not complement each other: '. . . the characteristic situation in sociology today [is] that research in the macrocosmic and in the microcosmic scarcely connect, scarcely inform each other.' David Riesman, op. cit., p. 125.

7 The following characterization is a distillation of the literature cited in note 5, above. Since what follows is essentially a sketch, the literature, in general, will not be cited. Detailed and specific references to this literature *will* be made, however, in appropriate places in succeeding chapters. In a sense, what follows is more than a sketch; it is really a *definition* of 'suburbia,' for though there is no standard definition of 'suburb' in any rigorous sense (see Brunner and Hallenbeck, op. cit., p. 255), 'suburbia' almost universally implies a *tract housing development* within commuting distance of a large city. We will use the terms 'suburb' to refer to tract housing developments within standard metropolitan areas and 'suburbia' to refer to the kind of life that is said to be led in them. We suggest, however, that commuting is an irrelevant aspect of the definition.

8 Harry Henderson, The Mass-Produced Suburbs, Part II: Rugged American Collectivism, p. 84.

9 William Whyte has a way of making the phrase 'urban ward' resound with connotations of poverty, deprivation, soot and brick—as if 'urban ward' were a synonym for 'slum'.

10 'In a single suburb of Chicago, for example, you can buy ranch houses that cost $10,000 or $65,000 just a few hundred yards apart.' Russell Lynes, *The Tastemakers*, p. 253. $7,000 was the original price for homes in Levittown, Long Island.

11 The articles by Carl von Rhode and Phyllis McGinley, cited earlier, clearly evoke the image of a Connecticut town on Long Island Sound. It is perhaps all to the good that this kind of suburb has recently been designated an 'exurb'. See A. C. Spectorsky's diverting book, *The Exurbanites*.

12 See The New Suburban Market, p. 129. See also Carl von Rhode, op. cit., p. 294; Walter T. Martin, The Structuring of Social Relationships Engendered by Suburban Residence; and George Lundberg *et al.*, *Leisure: A Suburban Study*, p. 47.

13 In 1954, *Time* reported, '. . . now industry is seeking the country too, looking for large tracts of open land to build efficient one-story plants. Of 2,658 plants built in the New York area from 1946 to 1951 only 593 went up in the city proper.' Flight to the Suburbs *Time* March 22, 1954, p. 102. For more detailed reports of this trend see Evelyn Kitagawa and Donald Bogue, *Suburbanization of Manufacturing Activities within Standard Metropolitan Areas*. For tertiary industry, see Raymond Cuzzort, *Suburbanization of Service Industries within Standard Metropolitan Areas*, and James D. Tarver, Suburbanization of Retail Trade in the Standard Metropolitan Areas of the U.S., 1948–1954.

14 What this means, of course, is that increasing numbers of factory workers will be living in suburbs—not necessarily satellite industrial cities, but new tract suburbs. Woodbury has noted that the decline in the proportion of production workers in cities has been matched by increases in suburban areas of the same cities. See Coleman Woodbury, Suburbanization and Suburbia, p. 7.

15 Webster still prefers to define 'commuter' as someone who travels by way of a commutation ticket.

16 The same fears for massification and conformity were felt regarding these urban neighbourhoods as are now felt for the mass-produced suburbs. See Riesman, The Suburban Dislocation, p. 123.

17 Suburbanization, of course, has not only occurred around our largest cities, but around smaller ones as well: '. . . with the exception of a general tendency for SMA's of one million inhabitants or more to grow at a slightly less rapid rate than SMA's smaller than this, there has been no pronounced or consistent trend for rates of total metropolitan growth to vary with size. . . .' Quoted by Woodbury, op. cit., from Bogue, op. cit. David Riesman has observed, 'so far as I can see we know almost nothing about the suburbs (old or new) surrounding the smaller cities.' David Riesman, op. cit., p. 124.

18 The Toronto study is frankly a study of a wealthy suburb and is, without doubt, quite reliable. The unanimity about well-studied Park Forest also lends credence to its portrayal. However, Levittown, New York, and Lakewood, California, are more ambiguous cases. One sharp resident of Levittown writes me that suburb is not *only* white collar, but contains plenty of 'blue collar, frayed collar and turned collar people also,' and that the different groups have different ways of life. The vast Lakewood development is heavily populated with southern California aircraft workers, and there is considerable doubt that *Newsweek's* report on Lakewood, so heavily laden with the mobility motif, took adequate account of them.

19 *Time* reports that 27 per cent of all new American homes fall into the price category represented by the $13,000 house shown at the U.S. exhibition in Moscow in the summer of 1959. *Time*, April 20, 1959, p. 91.

CHAPTER 21

The Use of Gossip and Event Analysis in the Study of Suburban Communities*

Colin Bell

1. GOSSIP

This is a discussion of the use of gossip in analysing the structure of social relations on two suburban estates. During the initial door-to-door census on both estates it soon became apparent that there was a great deal of gossip and I began to systematically collect as much of it as possible. I noted who said what, about whom and when. Firstly I must add a note about the field situation. Most of the time when I was both formally and informally collecting data there was no one outside the household present. This meant that my informants were free to gossip as much as they wished about other families on the estate. On the other hand they were all aware that I was interviewing all other households on the estate on which they lived and so was in unique possession of a great deal of information about the estate's inhabitants. When I had been in the field for a couple of weeks I began to find that I could gossip with my informants and failed to resist the temptation. The short-term gains were very great because I found that I could swop information and proceed very rapidly. After two such gossip sessions I did not repeat this practice for two reasons that are connected. Firstly there was the purely practical consideration that my informants began to dry up on me when they realized that I may well gossip about them to other people. Secondly there was the ethics of the situation. During these initial stages of the fieldwork I had not developed a satisfactory fieldwork role. When I realized that the most satisfactory, and the only really honest one was of 'sociological fieldworker' I had to stop gossiping about other households on the estate. In creating this role it was necessary for it to be seen that confidences were kept and that I took no part in gossip. On the larger of the two estates this

* Reprinted by permission of Routledge and Kegan Paul Ltd. from *Middle Class Families: Social and Geographical Mobility* by C. R. Bell, London, 1969, pp. 139–144, 147–158 and by permission of Humanities Press Inc. for the same extracts.

was adhered to as far as humanly possible, my two major lapses being on the small estate.

In the field I was constantly probed for information by very skilled gossipers and while some information was given away, this was kept to a minimum. My position on both estates was tenuous enough without being caught gossiping. However it was possible to turn this questioning to great advantage in an analysis of the effects of social and geographical mobility on the estates. It became apparent that some people were gossiped about more than others, and I was questioned about them more intensively, whereas other families were virtually unknown and seemed to be socially insignificant. Nobody asked me about them. After my resolve not to gossip as far as possible about estate households with other estate households I not unnaturally found that it was a far slower process in gathering the kind of information in which I was interested. I was no longer prepared to swop gossip and consequently people did not so often gossip with me. I attempted to get round this problem by developing key informants from whom I systematically collected their entire knowledge about other households on the estate. The analysis that follows is based on (a) information gathered indirectly whilst interviewing more formally and (b) information from the dozen female informants I interviewed specifically about gossip over a period of time.

The analysis of gossip is divided into two parts: (a) who gossips about whom and (b) the content of this gossip. A careful analysis of who gossips about whom goes a long way towards providing a description of the social structure of the two estates (which can be related to the facts of social and geographical mobility as presented in the earlier chapters of the book). I found this method, although very laborious, more rewarding than the previous methods used, e.g. micro-ecology. I drew up two lists of all the households, one for each estate, and systematically went through all my field material to see who had mentioned them. Theoretically this meant that a household could possibly have been mentioned by all the other households on the estate on which they lived or by no others. Most were towards the latter. Further analysis proved that the households could be divided into groups that could be related to other variables that have already been introduced into this study: stage in family cycle (which is obviously related to age) and to geographical mobility—in terms of whether the households were local or not. At this stage of the analysis, social mobility (defined occupationally and inter-generationally) did not appear as a variable, but it appeared in the second stage of the analysis, that of the content of gossip.

What appeared was that the younger households knew very little of the older households and did not mention them in talking about other households on the estate. It was also the case that the older households did not know the younger households as well as they knew other older households. This was not so well marked, because there were relatively few older households and that as a consequence they did not have as wide a choice of contacts in their own age group on the estate as did the younger households. The younger households on the other hand had no real need to know the older households because they had a wide choice of households in a similar age group.

More significant was the local/non-local distinction. (The age grouping applied to both.) It emerged that the non-local tended to gossip about other non-locals and similarly that the locals tended to gossip about other locals. Some of the key households, in terms of the number of people that knew them and gossiped about them, were almost unknown across the local/non-local division, i.e. 'gossip cells' as West (1945) called them did not often include both locals and non-locals. For example one informant gave me information about 47 other households, some of which was very detailed. She herself had been geographically mobile and had come to the estate and South Wales three years previously, but she could only give me information about two local households, one of which was a neighbour. It was unusual for the distinction between locals and non-locals to be as marked as this. A local informant gave me information about 24 non-local households out of a total of 34 but did not know anywhere near as much about them. The information was very detailed about the other local households (none of whom she had known before she came to the estate) but much more scantly and often inaccurate about the non-locals.

It was suggested earlier that the estate performed differing functions for the locals and non-locals, the estate providing neighbours for the non-locals whereas the locals were reluctant to be drawn into such reciprocal relationships. The analysis of patterns of gossip would support this. In the groups and cliques that emerged from this analysis there were very few 'cross-cutting alliances' between locals and non-locals and consequently there was very little gossip about locals by non-locals and vice versa.

The fact that the local households gossiped about each other I first thought contradicted my hypothesis that the estate performs differing functions for the locals and non-locals because I did not expect the locals to be able, or want to gossip about other families local or non-local living on the estate. But it really supports this hypothesis, because the local households, although they gossiped with and about other local households, had developed a different relationship with each other compared with that between the non-local households. One local informant, wife of a teacher told me she was very friendly with Mrs. N. and Mrs. O., both locals and she then proceeded to gossip about them to me. She said she was particularly friendly with them because 'they don't want too much from me, we call at arranged times and we are not demanding. That's how it should be.'

It would be wrong to suggest that no local was friendly with a non-local and vice versa, or that there was no gossip about locals among non-locals and vice versa, but there were very few instances of this. The most significant exception seemed to be based upon a geographical neighbouring relationship (micro-ecology), i.e., sharing a common garden fence, or on the fact that their children, no respecters of sociological categories, played together.

I now pass to the second part of the analysis of gossip on the two estates: that of its content. On both estates gossip was not only widespread, it was also catholic, there were few aspects of private or public life that were not subject to the examination and scrutiny of other households on the estate. Anyone who has lived in such an environment will know the richness of such gossip, most of which cannot be presented here because not only would it allow individuals to be identified but it would open the author to charges of libel and neighbours to slander. Just two topics of gossip will be concentrated on to give some idea of the richness of gossip as field material, both of which are particularly relevant to the major themes of this book, that of occupation and career mobility, and secondly of kinship information.

Unlike the situation described by Pahl (1965) for a commuter village where other husbands' occupations were often unknown, on both estates the occupations of all husbands seemed to be common knowledge. There was a great interest in the topic among both husbands and wives. It was not sufficient to know what a man's job was, it was necessary to know his actual position. A design engineer who had recently been promoted to being head of a large department when he moved to Swansea was accurately placed in his organization for me by three different informants (all also non-locals). Gossip flowed about applications for a new job by a man in banking; the man himself and his wife never told me about this application but five other households did (again they were all non-locals). This interest in career pattern was almost universal and as pointed out in Chapter One led me to stress the centrality of the career in the middle class life style.

Groups of husbands from the estate, when out at a pub together would talk about their jobs and try to compare their relative positions in their respective hierarchies. Very detailed information about their positions would be discussed over a pint at Sunday lunch time and later this would be passed to their wives. It then entered the estate gossip network. Because all the husbands in this case were non-locals (as were their wives) and the friends of their wives were similarly non-local this information never passed to the locals.

Closely related to gossip about careers was that about social mobility. I have no evidence of social mobility as opposed to geographical mobility having any effect on the structure of social relations on the estate. This is a major conclusion of this research. The facts of social mobility were a subject for gossip but their effects on groups and cliques or participation on the estate were negligible. Of the 31 households that had been socially mobile, I was told about 25 of these by people outside the households concerned. This gives some indication of the nature and detail of the gossip on both estates. The facts of social mobility were not hidden. A fact which is relevant to the second area of gossip to be considered, that of kinship.

Kinship information circulated in the gossip networks of both estates. There was as much interest in it as there was in occupation and career. Just as details of occupational position allowed other households to be 'placed', particularly in relation to oneself, so kinship information was similarly seized upon. For example living on one of the estates were the in-laws of a very famous (local) sportsman; this fact was repeated to me by many of the other families living on the estate. All the local households knew about them but not all of the non-locals. Similarly any kin connection that could be used to link a family living on the estate with a famous product was known, e.g. 'his father is Bloggs fish-paste'. Siblings of people living on the estate that were in some way notable were often brought up in general gossip. When I asked about a household, from a housewife who lived two doors away, after I was told the husband's job, I was told about his brother-in-law (a well-known author) of whom it was expected that I would have heard. But this kind of kinship information was often limited to gossip cells that only contained locals or only non-locals.

Across this division there was little gossip about kin and although there was gossip about occupation it was of a different kind. Instead of the detail about actual position within a hierarchy the gossip was far more in terms of national or universal occupational stereotypes. There was a local estate agent living on one of the estates and another local household told me in detail about the development of his business, how he had made his money, what his father and mother did, and what his wife's father did. The non-locals were not in possession of this kind of information and that which I was told was often highly inaccurate and inflammatory, relating to stereotypes of estate agents being 'sharks' and extremely shrewd dealers. Similarly there was a non-local senior academic about whose entire and bewildering career I was told in great detail by other informants, all non-local. Before I interviewed him I was in possession of an accurate biography picked up from the gossip network of other non-locals. To the locals he was, however, an 'absent minded professor' because of his (not very) eccentric appearance and unusual gardening techniques. (Compare the situation discussed by Gluckman where a character in a Jane Austen novel never actually appears in the book 'yet in the gossip of others we see him as an individual, influencing their dealings with one another' (1963, p. 309).)

2. AN ANALYSIS OF AN EVENT

In any given social situation individuals are faced with the possibility of alternative modes of action. Any analysis of a social situation should be concerned with the way individuals and groups are able to exercise choices within the limits of a specified social structure. A prerequisite, then, should be some outline of the social structure within which action takes place. In practice this is not always possible.

When I began interviewing on the new privately owned middle class housing estates the situation seemed at first very close to that described by Marx in *The Eighteenth Brumaire of Louis Napoleon*, when he referred to the French peasantry as being 'formed by the simple addition of equal magnitudes, much as potatoes in a sack form a sack of potatoes'. The mid-twentieth century spiralist may not bear immediate resemblance to the mid-nineteenth century French peasantry but the above quotation suggests some of the initial difficulties with which I felt I was faced when attempting to analyse the social structure of a new housing development. There is, however, an approach utilized by anthropologists working in Africa that offers a solution. (Gluckman: 1940, 1942, 1958 and Mitchell: 1956.) This chapter is an attempt to apply their techniques in an urban situation in Britain, and focuses on a 'dramatic occurrence'. It takes the form of a case history of a specific incident, or series of incidents associated with the signing of a petition on the larger of the two estates studied.

(i) *The Public Events*

The public side of the issues and events described below can be briefly summarized by an account of the public enquiry held before a change in the town's development plan could be made to provide for the erection of multi-storey halls of residence for the local university after the purchase of a site adjacent to the estate.

The case for the changes was based on three main points: the national need for university expansion, its local importance, and the preservation of this site from speculative housing development. The local Ratepayers' Association had officially come round to support the university and as counsel for the university said ,'It is not often that objectors become supporters in an enquiry of this kind.' Later it is possible to suggest how this came about, at least on the housing development adjacent to the proposed university site.

A crucial factor for the local residents was the actual number of students that would live in the new residences. 1400 was quoted at the public enquiry by the university. This figure is important because it was manipulated widely by different individuals and groups on the housing development at different times.

The local residents had been adamant against the development but had become supporters of the university: or so runs the account in the local press. In fact this was not so. They had been persuaded that the real choice was between the proposed university development and speculative housing, and not between development and no development, consequently they became reluctant supporters of the university. There had emerged among the residents a compromise position of wanting 'reasonable assurances' on three main points: on the maintenance of the natural beauty of the area, restrictions of the height of the new buildings and most strongly on the amount of traffic through the housing development. On all three points assurances were received. The spokesman for the housing development said 'we have no objections, in fact, we would welcome pedestrian access from the university site across the estate. But we object to heavy vehicles.' In conclusion the local residents were given the assurance that 'the least possible interference with the estate will take place'.

Permission was granted for a change to be made in the town's development plan.

(ii) *Dissenters, Hedgers and Ditchers, Activists*

Having briefly described the public events, attention will now be concentrated on events concerning the 89 households living on the estate. They are divided between those who signed the petition and those who did not, or dissented from doing so. Those who did not sign have been called *dissenters*. Those who signed the petition have been further divided into two groups: *hedgers* and *ditchers*. The former adopted the compromise position, with 'adequate assurances' they were supporters of the university. The ditchers continued to object and would admit no compromise. Within this inclusive classification are a small group; the *activists:* those who took round the petition. Ideologically all the activists were hedgers.

The petition was taken round by the activists on a Friday evening and the following weekend. Of the 89 households, two were away that weekend and one was overlooked by mistake. So 86 households were asked to sign: 51 did so and 35 dissented. (All the household signed or did not sign, there was no 'mixed' household. Although husbands and wives often disagreed in their emphasis about whether to sign the petition or not, it is possible to use households as units.)

For any argument based on participation of individuals in this event it is necessary to at least attempt to control for two independent variables. Firstly willingness to sign petitions at all. It was possible that some refused to sign 'on principle': all the dissenters denied this when asked but there is some further evidence which is also related to the second variable: whether dissenters did not sign because of antipathy towards the activists. Before this issue of the university development, two of the activists petitioned against a road closure. Not as many households were approached to sign: 74. All but two signed, both maintained that the closure should take place, but both signed the second petition. So there was no feeling against signing petitions 'on principle'. It is not possible to control for the fact that a third activist also took round the second petition but from a knowledge of the field it is possible to say that nobody refused to sign because of him.

The petition form was headed by the legend of the local Ratepayers' Association and stated that the university had bought the site and was seeking planning permission to build multi-storey accommodation for up to 3,000 students of both sexes: 'And we the undersigned would like to protest against the wholesale destruction of amenities of the ... estate and to object to the danger and inconvenience that the resulting increase in traffic would cause.' In the situation of latent if not manifest neighbourliness (Mann 1954) and of quasi-kin groups and in the face of activists whose belief in the rightness of their cause was Cromwellian, dissent was not to be expected. So it is very surprising that 35 households did in fact dissent in this situation.

It is necessary here to suggest the significance of the petition. It brought out into the open conflicts which are normally not apparent. It illustrates the relationships between the two groups with different reference groups and career orientation; between those whose careers will take them beyond the town and for whom the estate and the town are only relatively brief stopping places, and those who expect their careers to take place within the local community. Between those Watson called 'spiralists' and those he called 'burgesses' or what Merton had earlier called 'cosmopolitans' and 'locals'.[1] Between those who have been geographically mobile and those who have not.

This can be made clearer if the basic differences between the dissenters and the hedgers and ditchers are outlined. Only 13 of the 35 dissenting households had members who had been born or brought up within 15 miles of the town compared with 37 of the 51 hedgers and ditchers. More importantly 33 of the dissenting households expected their future careers to take them away from the town, compared with 11 out of 51 of the hedgers and ditchers (and three of these had close neighbouring relations with the activists). Another 18 of the hedgers and ditchers thought that they would move from the development within five years, but stay in the town either with increased prosperity or to make adjustments with a stage change in life cycle. This included all the activists.

Of the 35 dissenting households 29 had a member that had been to a university compared with only five out of the 51 signers of the petition. Another correlation with signing the petition is with professed voting behaviour. Of the 34 non-Conservative voting households on the housing development 29 did not sign the petition, i.e. five non-Conservative voters signed the petition: two Liberal and three Labour (one of whom was a neighbour of an activist).[2]

As a further indication of differences between dissenters and hedgers and ditchers: no dissenting household took the morning daily local paper, 17 hedgers and ditchers did, and less than a quarter of the dissenters took the evening daily local paper (seven households) compared with three-quarters (38 households) of the hedgers and ditchers. All households had been asked their opinion about the introduction of comprehensive schools. The results are tabulated below.

	For	Against	Don't know	Totals
Dissenters	21	6	8	35
Hedgers and ditchers	19	20	12	51
Total	40	26	20	86

It can be seen that more signers of the petition were against the introduction of comprehensive schools than were for, whereas the dissenters were 3:1 in favour. Too much importance must not be given to these details of professed voting behaviour, opinions on comprehensive schools and local newspaper consumption but they are indicators of broad differences in orientation, and interest in the local community (Larsen and Edelstein: 1961) of the two groups.

Merton described the locals in Rovere as 'parochial' and pre-occupied with local problems to the virtual exclusion of the national and international scene; and cosmopolitans as identifying and relating themselves to issues and events and social organizations outside the local community. Taking university expansion as an issue, the hedgers and ditchers did not think of the university as part of the local scene but as part of wider affairs. This can be shown by a content analysis of the arguments used about the university development. The dissenters tended to stress the national importance of universities and that the university was a great, some said the only asset to the community. But the ditchers in particular stressed the nuisance value of students, the destruction of local amenities by the proposed development by invading hordes, the decline in the value of their houses and the shattering of their peace and quiet. Their arguments were what Tucker (1966) has recently called the 'Lebensraum Fear': 'given the slightest opportunity innumerable predators will swoop down and swallow up all the tidy, respectable underpopulated private estates.' (Similarly Collison: 1963.) The local/cosmopolitan dimension refers to the scale of the social environment in which the individual sees himself, and the hedgers and ditchers were not prepared to include the university within their environment. Also for the dissenters, universities were part of their experience, for the hedgers and ditchers they were not.

During the initial stages of the observation of these events it was thought that the non-locals would be against the university development because of their transience and lack of ties with a locality that reputedly takes great pride in its educational institutions. Similarly I thought that the locals would support it for precisely these reasons, together with the fact that the university is one of the largest employers in the town and that as locals they would realize its economic significance. This proved not to be so. The locals although orientated towards the community economically and often in terms of their social relations and future careers tended to oppose the university development. This was particularly evident among the ditchers whose interpretation of their interest was very 'parochial' indeed, to use Merton's term. It was the cosmopolitans that welcomed the university development, people who had few ties with the community and who would move on.

The dissenters have been more mobile, have lived in a succession of communities in different parts of the country and differ markedly in their attachment to the town and in attitudes towards leaving it, compared with the hedgers and ditchers. Like Merton's locals and cosmopolitans the hedgers and ditchers and the dissenters did not differ significantly in age or family composition. But unlike the locals and cosmopolitans in Rovere they did differ in education and occupation suggesting that their differing orientation towards the community may be a reflection of educational and occupational differences which was associated with greater geographical and social mobility for the dissenters.

Here I will describe a typical dissenter and a typical signer of the petition. In these descriptions will be recognized the characteristics of the mobile and immobile with which I have been concerned in this book.

Mrs. C. was 34 with two children and dissented from signing the petition. Both she and her husband have been socially mobile, and both went to a provincial university. She has a music degree and her husband a science degree from the same university. He is a Ph.D and now is an engineer at a large metallurgical plant. She taught in a primary school before the birth of her first child. Since marriage they have lived in two towns in the Midlands, in suburban London, south Wales and expect to move to Scotland within a year. They have no local kin. At the public meeting of the local Ratepayers she was quite prepared to speak out in favour of the university, in marked contrast to the hedging and ditching wives who remained silent. She argued that it was better the university had the land than a speculative housing developer, but more strongly that the university must expand and that it was a good thing for the country that they should. All her friends on the estate dissented and three of the four came from households that had members that had been to a university. All four were non-locals. She belonged to the Labour Party and two associations that were nationwide.

Throughout these events the ditchers were the most difficult respondents. Their opposition to the university unfortunately manifested itself in opposition to the fieldworker as a visible and accessible representative of the university.

Mr. D. a ditcher, aged 40, married with no children, left school at 16. He and his wife have always lived in the town. He has always worked in the 'motor trade' and now owns a garage. He does not expect to live on the estate for ever, but will not leave the town. He does not have any friends, 'not what I would call friends', on the estate. He is a regular member of a chapel and the local Chamber of Trade. He said of the university development, 'I don't want them here, I bought this house and now they are going to ruin my privacy. Why can't they go somewhere else? We pay enough in rates not to have to put up with this sort of thing.' He was surprised that some people had not signed the petition: 'I thought they were all sensible people.' He has a very localized kin network, seeing both his and his wife's siblings regularly.

Ditchers were not activists. The activists were two households, neighbours. They were born and brought up well away from the town. Both had been socially and geographically mobile. Neither household contained a member that had been to a university. Both thought that it was unlikely that they would move from the town, both husbands being in their early 40's, but both expected to be in a financial position to move from the estate within five years. For both the activist households the petition itself was at least as important as the issues involved. They varied the number of students with the likelihood of people signing the petition (the petition itself quotes more than double the correct figure, a fact of which the activists were aware), the number being increased with resistance to signing. Several dissenters claimed that while activists were on the doorstep the supposed upheaval accompanying the university expansion became steadily more exaggerated the longer they refused to sign.

When it was clear that the choice was not between development and no development but between speculative housing development and university development, the local Ratepayers advised against a further petition. But against this advice the activists took round the petition described above.

Why were the activists so active? This is an example of *cross-mobility* (Plowman, Minchinton and Stacey: 1962) but in the opposite direction to its original usage when it was used to describe leaving the local, and by implication traditional, social system or a non-tradition, and by implication non-local, social system involving important changes in attitudes without necessarily altering the level of status. The petition for the activists was one of the mechanisms by which they were attempting to enter a local, if not a traditional social system. An examination of their associational membership pattern supports this argument. Both households were members of very local and very traditional associations important in local culture. Both were active in politics at the ward level. One household had been in the town two years, the other three. One activist, after the report of the public enquiry had been published in the local press made a very revealing remark when he saw that he was mentioned by name: 'that should do me a bit of good'. He appeared to be more pleased about this than in getting 'adequate assurances' from the university.

Having a neighbouring relationship with an activist was an important factor in signing the petition (i.e. micro-ecology). None of the 35 dissenting households were neighbours of the activists, neither in the geographical sense (the closest dissenter lived seven doors away) nor in the definitional sense of being able to call without warning. There were three households who by other characteristics alone may have been expected to dissent but were neighbours of the activists. To the fieldworker they stressed they had no objection to the university itself but did not want heavy traffic through the estate. They included a household who said they did not sign when in fact they did.

(iii) *The Consequences for Social Relationships*

The earlier quotation from Marx indicates some of the confusion felt during the initial observation when the fieldworker was faced with a bewildering tangled network of friendship ties, neighbouring ties, quasi-kin groups, ties of common geographical origin, of occupation, of common school or university. On this housing development it was possible to identify over fifty groupings varying from groups with a recognizable structure, through quasi-groups to almost casual meetings (Mayer 1966), some permanent, some ephemeral. The list was not of course exhaustive and was constantly becoming longer. But very few of these groupings cross the local/ non-local division, and as there is a close correspondence, the hedger and ditcher/dissenter division. Those that do, are based mainly on micro-ecology: the fact of geographical neighbouring. Two of these groupings will be described to show the consequences of the events described above.

Firstly there was a group of six men who went drinking together every Sunday lunch time. There were four locals and two non-locals. Two of the locals had been to school with each other and had renewed their friendship when they discovered each other on the same housing development. The third was a cousin of the first (father's, sister's son) and the fourth was a colleague of the second. The two non-locals were neighbours of the second and third locals. But the two non-locals had very little contact with the others besides Sunday drinking; neither their wives not their children being particularly friendly. All four locals signed the petition: the two non-locals dissented. The locals took up the hedging position of wanting 'adequate assurances', rather than the ditching position of absolute opposition. On the weekend of the petition they went drinking as usual and the petition was the main topic of conversation. They told each other whether they had signed or not, the locals were not very surprised that the two non-locals had not signed and they argued vigorously. Both non-locals defended their dissent strongly and called the locals 'narrow-minded' and they appealed to the wider issues of university expansion. The following Sunday one non-local was unwell and the other was away. The four locals went drinking as usual. They decided that on future Sundays they would go to a different pub because it would be less crowded and that the beer would be better. It would involve driving, the first pub was within walking distance which was its original attraction. The two non-locals were told of the change of plans indirectly through their wives. Both independently decided that they would not go to the second pub because it was too far and they did not want to drive. Two Sundays later they stopped going to the original pub because they had both started to go to a third pub on a weekday evening with two other men from the housing estate, both also non-locals. One was a colleague, the other met through the friendship of their children. When the two original non-locals were asked about this change and why they did not go with the original four locals any more on Sundays, neither mentioned the hiatus that had occurred in their attendance immediately after the petition but both mentioned the petition itself. And then said how much more they had in common with the two others they now drank with during the week.

The second group was a weekday coffee morning based on six wives who here hosts in rotation. The other five attending the sixth, together with any others that that week's hostess had invited. There were four non-locals and two locals but all had dissented. They had discussed the petition in advance and had said that they would not sign it because they thought it would be a good thing if the university developed the land. The group consisted of four wives who lived in close proximity and between whom there was intense neighbouring relationships: three non-locals plus one local; together with two others from a distance, one of whose sons was very friendly with the daughter of one of the other four, and her neighbour, a local. On the Wednesday after the petition they met as usual but before they arrived one of the activist wives called to discuss arrangements about the 'daily woman' they shared. They had no other contact. She was asked to stay for coffee, which she did, but had not realized it was *the* coffee morning. The activist wife said she felt awful when she saw 'the opposition trooping down the drive'. She left as soon as she could and until she did the atmosphere was very strained. When she left the hostess quickly told the others she had not really invited her, she was only being polite. As soon as she had gone they gossiped about her and the petition. Here face-to-face contact had if anything reinforced the division between the dissenters and the rest, gossip being confined to those who did not differ on the issues at stake.

(iv) *Conclusions*

In discussing 'The Neighbourhood Idea' Dennis, echoing Marx, has written 'people seem to find it extraordinarily difficult to realize that mere living together in the same locality can result in a con-glomeration of very little sociological importance. The difficulty is immeasurably increased when the people in the locality are sociolo-gically homogeneous' (1958, p. 191). But as Frankenberg has recently stressed 'however large scale the society we wish to study and however massive the residential unit there is always social interaction in small face-to-face groups' (1966a, p. 149) (see also Pons, 1961, who shows the value of intensive small group studies in shedding light on the system of social relations in an urban situation, in this case Stanleyville in the Congo). By close and detailed observation of this face-to-face interaction it is possible to describe social processes.

If the fieldworker is fortunate there will be some social drama that will perhaps reveal some underlying conflict of interests. The nature of a middle class private housing estate makes it very difficult to find situations in which conflicts became socially manifest.

The petition provided an opportunity for such an analysis but has the obvious weakness that it was not an observable incident in the usual anthropological sense. Compared for example with Gluckman's description of a ceremony whereby a new bridge in Zululand is opened. He isolated the important elements in the ceremony and then traces each of these elements back into the larger society, to demonstrate their significance in the ceremony he has described. Or compared with what is perhaps the finest example of event analysis: Mitchell's analysis of the Kalela Dance, where by working outwards from the specific social situation of the Dance the whole social fabric of the Copper Belt is taken in. It is only when this process has been followed to a conclusion that he returns to the dance and explains its significance.

The housing estate never acted as an entity and only rarely did any happening involve more than a relatively few households. But the petition was at least presented to most households and this crucial occasion revealed and articulated the division between locals and non-locals. It was not as circumscribed an event as the funeral described by Loudon, nor as temporarily limited as the bridge opening described by Gluckman, nor as dramatic even as the Kalela Dance described by Mitchell but it allowed in Turner's penetrating phrase 'a limited area of transparency on the otherwise opaque surface of regular, uneventful social life' (1957, p. 93), through which the relationships between spiralists and burgesses could be observed.

REFERENCES

Banton, M. (ed.), *The Social Anthropology of Complex Societies*, A.S.A. Mono-graph 4, Tavistock, 1966.

Collison, P., *The Cutteslowe Walls*, Faber, 1963.

Dennis, N., 'The Popularity of the Neighbourhood Community Idea', *Sociological Review*, Vol. 6 (N.S.), 1958.

Frankenberg, R., *British Community Studies: Problems of Synthesis*, pp. 123–154 of Banton (1966) (ed.), Tavistock, 1966a.

Gluckman, M., 'Analysis of a Social Situation in Modern Zululand', *Rhodes-Livingstone Paper No. 28*, 1940, 1942 and 1958.

Gluckman, M., 'Gossip and Scandal', *Current Anthropology*, Vol. 4, 1963.

Larsen, O. N. and Edelstein, A. S., 'Communication, Consensus and the Community Involvement of Urban Husbands and Wives', *Acta Sociologica*, Vol. 5, 1961.

Mann, P., 'The Concept of Neighborliness', *American Journal of Sociology*, Vol. 60, 1954.

Mayer, A., *The Significance of Quasi-Groups in the Study of Complex Societies*, A.S.A. 4, pp. 97–122 of Banton (1966) (ed.), 1966.

Merton, R. K., *Social Theory and Social Structure*, Free Press of Glencoe, 1957.

Mitchell, J. Clyde, 'The Kalela Dance', *Rhodes-Livingstone Paper No. 27*, 1956.

Pahl, R., 'Class and Community in English Commuter Villages, *Socialogis Ruralis*, Vol. 2, 1965.

Plowman, G., Minchinton, W. and Stacey, M., 'Local Status in England and Wales', *Sociological Review*, Vol. 10 (N.S.), 1962.

Pons, V., *Two Small Groups in Avenue 21*, in Southall (1961) (ed.), Oxford U.P., 1961.

Tucker, J., *Honourable Estates*, Gollancz, 1966.

Turner, V. W., *Schism and Continuity in an African Society*, Manchester U.P., 1957.

Watson, W., *Social Mobility and Social Class in Industrial Communities*, in Gluckman and Devons, Oliver and Boyd, 1964.

West, W., *Plainville*: U.S.A., Columbia U.P., 1945.

NOTES

1 There is a danger in too glib a use of these hyphenated neologisms, opposite sides of the equation are not necessarily transferable from neologism to neologism. Spiralists are not necessarily cosmopolitan as Merton wished to use the term and Merton's term local may not be applicable to all burgesses.

2 Ratepayers' Associations are sometimes seen as a Conservative Party 'front' organization, although in this particular ward at the last local election, Conservative, Labour and Ratepayers fought the ward and the Conservatives gained it from the Ratepayers. But from the interviews it can safely be said that nobody objected to the petition on the party political grounds that it was under the legend of the Local Ratepayers.

PART VI

Lloyd Warner's
Yankee City Studies

CHAPTER 22

Lloyd Warner's Yankee City Studies

INTRODUCTION

The Yankee City project ranks as the most intensive, exhaustive and expensive single study ever made of a small American community, or any other for that matter.[1] The first of the five volumes that reports the findings of Lloyd Warner and his colleagues lists a research staff of 30: four were writers, analysts and field workers, nine were analysts and field workers, five were just field workers and twelve were just analysts, i.e. eighteen people, at least, had done field work in Newburyport, the small New England town for which Yankee City is the pseudonym (the use of pseudonyms are a verbal manifestation of his assumptions of the broader generalization of this study). The project was conceived as part of a research programme conducted from Harvard and it was originally aimed to examine the 'non-work' aspect of the lives of the workers being studied by Elton Mayo at Western Electric (the famous Hawthorne experiments). Warner found this prospect impossible. He had just returned from three years field work among Australian aborigines and wanted to apply the same techniques used there to the study of American communities. Unfortunately 'Cicero and Hawthorne (the location of the Western Electric factory) and other industrial sub-communities in Chicago . . . seemed to be disorganized; they had a social organization which was highly dysfunctional if not in partial disintegration. If we were to compare easily the other societies of the world with one of our own civilization, and if we were readily to accommodate our techniques, developed by the study of primitive society, to modern groups, *it seemed wise to choose a community with a social organization which had developed over a long period of time under the domination of a single group with a coherent tradition.*'[2] New England and the Deep South seemed likely locations of such a community. Warner's fatal error was that his anthropological orientation and techniques misled him into believing Yankee City was in fact like that. It has been shown that he had serious misconceptions particularly about the communities history that his ahistorical functionalist conceptual framework and methods never allowed him to realize. Warner's strength was his lack of ethnocentricity that certainly allowed him to see and report phenomena long ignored in American society, for example, stratification and yet he was blind to other aspects of the community. Warner wrote that 'to be sure we were not ethnocentrically biased in our judgements, we decided to use no previous summaries of data collected by anyone else (maps, handbooks, histories, etc.) until we had formed our own opinion of the community.'[3] In the fifth volume: *The Living and the Dead: the symbolic life of a community* Warner commenting on the 'history' portrayed in Yankee City pageants said that it 'was what community leaders now *wished* it were and what they *wished* it were not. They ignored this or that difficult period of time or unpleasant occurrence and embarrassing group of men and women; they left out awkward political passions; they selected small items out of large time contexts, sizing them up to express today's values.'[4] It is unfortunately true that Warner's own words quoted above can be used as a similar indictment against his work in Yankee City as a whole. His unwillingness to consult the historical record and his complete dependence on materials susceptible to traditional anthropological analysis—i.e. the acts and opinions of living members of the community, served to obliterate the distinction between the actual past and current myths about the past. This is particularly ironic, as the determination of the Yankee City investigators to escape the ethnocentric biases of culture-bound history led them to accept uncritically the community's legends about itself. This is, as Stephen Thernstrom, Yankee City's historian, has remarked, 'surely the most ethnocentric of all possible views.'[5]

The two extracts by Lloyd Warner present firstly some of his most important substantive findings—particularly on local stratification, and secondly some of his assumptions about the 'community as a laboratory'. The Yankee City volumes are well known for their characterization of the population of Newburyport into six distinctively named classes. Warner claims to have started with a general economic interpretation of human behaviour. He does not say that it was a marxist orientation, but it would seem to have been very similar. Yet while in Yankee City he discovered that some people were ranked lower even when they had higher incomes than people ranked above them and that others with low incomes were ranked high. People with the same jobs were ranked differently, e.g. doctors and this was *not* related to how good a physician he was. The famous Warner definition of social class is 'two or more orders of people who are believed to be and are accordingly ranked by the members of the community in socially superior and inferior positions.'[6]

The extract that follows those written by Lloyd Warner himself was written by the editors of this volume and it sums up some of the key points of criticism that have been made against the Yankee City series. Warner clearly believes that a community has a social structure with 'classes' as 'real entities' (not categories) into which *all* the inhabitants can unambiguously be placed and that people use their local community as a reference group and that people agree on their criteria of ranking and can classify each other by them. This definition of class led to an extraordinary outburst from other social scientists. C. Wright Mills, for instance, wrote that, 'Warner's insistence upon merely one vertical dimension led to the consequent absorbing of three analytically separable dimensions [economic, status and power] into one "sponge" word "class".' [7] Mills adds that most of the confusions and inadequacies of Warner's study flow from this fact. Warner had threaded *all* the many coloured beads on one vertical string.

The final extract is by Yankee City's historian, Stephen Thernstrom. Thernstrom demonstrates the hazardous nature of the assumptions about a community's past that are frequently made by community sociologists. Warner, in this instance computes the 'social position' (average occupational status) for the Irish for 1850, 1864, 1883 and 1893 and goes straight on to talk about their 'moderate and slight mobility'. Thernstrom in a magnificent piece of historical research into nineteenth century Newburyport has shown though that (1) the Irish were not an 'entity' in that 'to compute overall occupational status indices for all Irish names in the community in 1864 and in 1883 was of dubious value, because in fact a majority of the Irishmen living in Newburyport in 1864 had left the community by 1883 and the bulk of the 1883 group consisted of newcomers to the city' [8] and (2) manual Irish immigrants who stayed in the community though they begat manual sons, they bought property and so certainly should have been seen as socially mobile. Warner's techniques do not allow him to differentiate different dimensions of social mobility. Thernstrom shows that paradoxically Yankee City may in fact have been a 'sample' of the main trends of American society, though Warner was wrong about what they were. A host of critics have attacked the assumption that seemingly small and static communities like Newburyport and Morris (Jonesville) [9] are adequate laboratories for observing American social life. Thernstrom has shown that Newburyport was far less deviant than Warner made it out to be. Newburyport was not the dormant, self-contained, predominantly old American *Gemeinschaft* village portrayed in the Yankee City volumes. [10]

NOTES

1 W. Lloyd Warner and Paul S. Lunt, *The Social Life of a Modern Community* (Yankee City Series, I) New Haven, Yale University Press, 1941; *The Status System of a Modern Community*, 1942; Warner and Leo Srole, *The Social Systems of American Ethnic Groups*, 1945; Warner and J. O. Low, *The Social System of a Modern Factory*, 1947; Warner, *The Living and the Dead*, 1959. These five volumes will be referred to respectively as Yankee City I (YCI), YCII, YCIII, YCIV and YCV. Students may like to know that Warner has abridged the series into one volume published in 1963. (New Haven, Yale University Press.)

2 YCI, p. 4. our emphasis.

3 Ibid., p. 40.

4 YCV, p. 110.

5 Stephen Thernstrom, *Poverty and Progress: Social Mobility in a nineteenth century city*. Cambridge, Mass. Harvard University Press, 1964, p. 230.

6 YCI, p. 82.

7 C. Wright Mills, review of YCI in *American Sociological Review*, 7, 1942, reprinted in his collected essays edited by I. L. Horowitz *People, Politics and Power*, Oxford University Press, London, 1965.

8 Thernstrom, op. cit., p. 238.

9 Studies by Warner and his colleages and reported in the community study, *Democracy in Jonesville*, Harper Row, 1949.

10 Warner decribes the Upper Uppers as having lived in Yankee City for generations but in fact a close examination of his data shows that less than 60% had been born in or near Newburyport and almost a quarter had been born outside New England (YCI, p. 209).

CHAPTER 23

Social Class in Yankee City*

W. Lloyd Warner

When the research of Yankee City began, the director wrote a description of what he believed was fundamental in our social system, in order that the assumptions he held be explicitly stated and not become unconscious biases which would distort the field work, later analysis, and ultimate conclusions. If these assumptions could be stated as hypotheses they were then subject to criticism by the collection of data which would prove, modify, or disprove them. Most of the several hypotheses so stated were subsumed under a general economic interpretation of human behaviour in our society. It was believed that the fundamental structure of our society, that which ultimately controls and dominates the thinking and actions of our people, is economic, and that the most vital and far-reaching value systems which motivate Americans are to be ultimately traced to an economic order. Our first interviews tended to sustain this hypothesis. They were filled with references to 'the big people with money' and to 'the little people who are poor'. They assigned people high status by referring to them as bankers, large property owners, people of high salary, and professional men, or they placed people in a low status by calling them labourers, ditchdiggers and low-wage earners. Other similar economic terms were used, all designating superior and inferior positions.

All our informants agreed that certain groups, of whom we shall soon speak, were at the bottom of the social order, yet many of the members of these groups were making an income which was considerably more than that made by people whom our informants placed far higher in the social scale. It seemed evident that other factors contributed to their lower positions.

Other evidences began to accumulate which made it difficult to accept a simple economic hypothesis. Several men were doctors; and while some of them enjoyed the highest social status in the community and were so evaluated in the interviews, others were ranked

* Reprinted by permission of Yale University Press from *Yankee City* by W. Lloyd Warner, J. O. Low, Paul S. Lunt, and L. Srole, New York and London, 1963, pp. 34–46.

beneath them although some of the latter were often admitted to be better physicians. Such ranking was frequently unconsciously done and for this reason was often more reliable than a conscious estimate of a man's status. We found similar inequalities of status among the ministers, lawyers, and other professional men. When we examined the business and industrial world, we discovered that bankers, large manufacturers, and corporation heads also were not ranked equally but were graded as higher or lower in status. An analysis of comparative wealth and occupational status in relation to all the other factors in the total social participation of the individuals we studied demonstrated that, while occupation and wealth could and did contribute greatly to the rank-status of an individual, they were but two of the many factors which decided a man's ranking in the whole community. For example, a banker was never at the bottom of the society, and none in fact fell below the middle class, but he was not always at the top. Great wealth did not guarantee the highest social position. Something more was necessary.

In our efforts to find out what this 'something more' was, we finally developed a social-class hypothesis which withstood the later test of a vast collection of data and of subsequent rigorous analysis. By social class is meant two or more orders of people who are believed to be, and are accordingly ranked by the members of the community, in socially superior and inferior positions. Members of a class tend to marry within their own order, but the values of the society permits marriage up and down. A class system also provides that children are born into the same status as their parents. A class society distributes rights and privileges, duties and obligations, unequally among its inferior and superior grades. A system of classes, unlike a system of castes, provides by its own values for movement up and down the social ladder. In common parlance, this is social climbing, or in technical terms, social mobility. The social system of Yankee City, we found, was dominated by a class order.

When we examined the behaviour of a person who was said by some to be 'the wealthiest man in our town' to find out why he did not have a higher position, we were told that 'he and his family do not act right'. Their moral behaviour was 'all right', but they 'did not do the right things'. Although they were Yankees by tradition and not members of any ethnic group, we were told that 'they did not belong to the right families' and that 'they did not go around with the right kind of people'. Our informants further said that the members of this family 'didn't know how to act', and that they were not and could not be members of the 'right' groups. The interviews clearly demonstrated, however, that all the members of the family were regarded as 'good people', and their name was always a lure when marriage was contemplated for a young woman 'of good breeding', even though there was some danger that she would be looked upon as 'lowering herself' by such a marriage. Similar analysis of the men in industry and business who occupied lower positions brought forth the same kind of information.

Interviews about, and with, people who were ranked socially high by our informants but had little money or occupational status brought out the opposite kind of information, supplying further confirmatory evidence for our first tentative theory of a class system. These interviews revealed that 'you don't need but a little money in Yankee City to do the right thing', or as it was sometimes said, 'you have to have a little money but it is the way one uses it which counts'. Questions about such people often brought out such statements as: 'John Smith belongs to the X group', followed by remarks to the effect that 'Henry Taylor and Frank Dixon and other prominent men who are at the top also belong to it'. These same people, we were informed, 'went around with the Fred Brown clique' or 'went with the Country Club crowd', which were small groups of close friends.

In these interviews certain facts became clear which might be summarized by saying a person needed specific characteristics associated with his 'station in life' and he needed to go with the 'right kind' of people for the informants to be certain of his ranking. If a man's education, occupation, wealth, income, family, intimate friends, clubs and fraternities, as well as his manners, speech and general outward behaviour were known, it was not difficult for his fellow citizens to give a fairly exact estimate of his status. If only his social participation in family, clique, and association were known, he could be placed to the satisfaction of all the better informants by the process of identifying his social place with that of the others who were like him.

While making these observations on the criteria of class and attempting to locate people in the class hierarchy, we made a valuable discovery. In the expressions about wealth and occupation to which higher and lower valuations were attached, we noticed that certain geographical terms were used not only to locate people in the city's geographical space but also to evaluate their comparative place in the rank order. The first generalization of this kind which we noticed people using in interviews was the identification of a small percentage of the population as 'Hill-Streeters' or people who 'live up on Hill Street', these expressions often being used as equivalent of 'Brahmin', the rarer 'aristocrat', or the less elegant 'high mucky-muck', or 'swell', or 'snoot'. The term Hill-Streeter, we soon learned, was employed by people both within and outside of this classification.

Whenever an individual was called a Hill-Streeter, all our evidence showed that he was near or at the top of the hierarchy.

Another geographical term with a strong evaluative class meaning was Riverbrook. When a man was said to be a 'Riverbrooker' or to live in Riverbrook, he was held to be at the bottom of the social hierarchy. Interviews showed this generalization to be true regardless of the informant's place in the social scale. Riverbrookers were contemptuously referred to by all, their sexual morals were considered low, and their behaviour was usually looked upon as ludicrous and uncouth. An obscene story concerning the seasonal activities of the Riverbrook fishermen was told scores of times by our male informants, usually with amusement, and one heard much about incestuous relations and homosexual behaviour among them. These depreciatory stories were told despite the fact that it was easily verifiable that they were no more true of Riverbrookers than they were of other classes. The Riverbrooker was often a good and highly skilled worker in the shoe factories. He frequently earned a good wage by clamming. Usually a good family man, he was but one of the many variants of what is called the typical Yankee. The 'low' behaviour was attributed to him (as it usually is in similar social situations) because of his low social position, and these beliefs helped subordinate him when expressed by those who felt themselves above him.

With the acquisition of the terms Hill-Streeter and Riverbrooker as designations for the two extremes of class, our next problems were (1) to find out to whom the expression did and did not refer, (2) to learn what distinctions, if any, were made to differentiate other groups than these two, and (3) to discover who used any or all of these terms.

A descriptive expression which appeared with considerable frequency in our interviews was 'the classes and the masses'. This expression was seldom used by the people referred to as 'the masses' but quite frequently by those who considered themselves 'the classes'. The lower members of the community sometimes spoke of those in the higher statuses as 'the upper classes'. and when this expression was used by them it was ordinarily synonymous with Hill-Streeter. We soon found, however, that when 'the masses' was used, not all the people who were so designated were Riverbrookers, and that most of them were believed to be higher in status. A distinction was made within the masses between Riverbrookers and people of somewhat higher status.

Another geographical expression which frequently appeared in the interviews was 'Side-Streeter', used in contradiction to Hill-Streeter. In some contexts a Side-Streeter was anyone who was not a

Hill-Streeter, but more careful interviewing indicated that to a Hill-Streeter a Side-Streeter and a Riverbrooker were different. 'People who live in Riverbrook are at the bottom' and 'Of course Side-Streeters are better than Riverbrookers' were frequently explicitly stated by the better informants. A Side-Streeter was one who was not on the social heights of Hill Street or in the social depths of Riverbrook. He was somewhere in between. Living along the streets connecting the river area with Hill Street, the Side-Streeters were socially as well as territorially intermediate.

All Side-Streeters were not the same, we discovered. Some were superior and others inferior, the former being commonly called by another geographical term—'Homevillers'. The Homevillers were 'good people', but few of them were in any way 'socially acceptable'. Certain informants placed all of them in 'the classes'. Homeville is a fairly definitely defined area in Yankee City at the northern end of the community. The Homeville people, we roughly estimated at the time, were people in the midsection of the social scale but on the whole nearer the top than the bottom. The term 'middle class' or 'upper-middle class' was often used as equivalent for Homeviller. The Homevillers and their like, it developed through our later associational analysis, were graded ordinarily into two groups (upper-middle and lower-middle classes) and separated from a lower stratum of Side-Streeters who were too much like the Riverbrookers in many of their characteristics to be classed with the Side-Streeters of high status. The distinctions between the lower group of Homevillers and this lowest group of Side-Streeters were not so clearly marked as the others.

At this point we saw that Hill Street was roughly equivalent to upper class, Homeville to at least a good section of the middle class, and Riverbrook to the lowest class. We perceived, too, that these geographical terms were generalizing expressions by which a large number of people could be given a class designation but which nevertheless did not define class position explicitly. When the people classed as Hill-Streeters were located on a spot map it soon developed that not all of them lived on Hill Street and that not all the people living on Hill Street were Hill-Streeters (upper class). Many of the people who were by class Hill-Streeters lived elsewhere in the city, and some of them were fairly well concentrated in two areas other than Hill Street. We found a similar generalization to be true of the Riverbrookers and Homevillers. This discovery further demonstrated that these designations were terms of rank employed by the members of a 'democratic' society to refer obliquely to higher and lower social statuses in the community.

Careful interviewing among people who were called Hill-Streeters showed that the members of this group divided the general upper class into a higher and a lower subdivision. Our informants made frequent references to people of 'old family' and to those of 'new families'. The former were individuals whose families, it was believed, had participated in upper-class behaviour for several generations and who could trace this behaviour through the father's or mother's line or both for three or more generations. An upper-class genealogy of this kind has been called a lineage for the purposes of this report. Long residence in Yankee City was very important, but length of residence by itself did not establish a family at the apex of the class system since in all of the six classes later established we found families with written and attested genealogies which went back two hundred and in some cases even three hundred years to the founding of the community. Some of the lower members of the upper class could also trace their genealogies well back, but their recent mobility upward if they had 'come up from below' was enough to prevent an immediate claim to such a lineage. Their recent ancestors, unlike those of the uppermost members of the upper class, had not participated for a sufficient period of time in the forms of behaviour and the social position which were ranked as upper class by the community. With the separation of the upper-upper from the lower-upper class, and the upper-middle from the lower-middle, we had distinguished five classes clearly and a sixth less definitely. We knew at this time that the sixth class fell somewhere in between the middle and the lowest class, but it was still possible that it might be not one but several classes. Eventually, however, we were able to establish the existence of six classes: an upper-lower and a lower-lower class in addition to the upper and lower subdivisions of the middle and upper classes.

The amount of membership in associations is comparatively larger than that in most of the social structures of Yankee City. Despite their size, associations tend to segment the society into separate groups, and some of them help to maintain higher and lower ranking in the community. With this knowledge, we were able to place with greater exactness than we could by the use of the geographical classification a large sample of the members of Yankee City society.

Certain clubs, our interviews showed, were ranked at such extreme heights by people highly placed in the society that most of the lower classes did not even know of their existence, while middle-class people showed that they regarded them as much too high for their expectations. A very few of them, indeed, were looked upon as so exclusive that some of the Hill-Streeters might be excluded on family grounds. Of other clubs whose members were mainly Hill-Streeters, it was felt that any Hill-Streeter was eligible for membership if he had the other necessary qualifications (such as being a male of a certain age or interested in certain kinds of hobbies). These clubs, however, were considered too high for the vast majority of the people of Yankee City to aspire to, and it was clear that many, if not most, of the lower classes did not know of their existence. It was also felt that others did aspire to them but were not chosen because 'they did not belong socially'.

Below this last level of clubs were other associations which included Hill-Streeters but also had members 'from further down' who were 'not acceptable socially'. There were still other associations

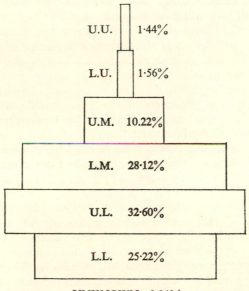

FIGURE 2. The Class Hierarchy of Yankee City

where these same individuals who were not accepted socially were members and were considered to be at the top of the membership, and all other members were felt to be below them. Some associations of this kind were sufficiently high so that there were members of the community who were too low to do more than aspire to membership. There were other associations too low for Hill-Streeters to join and still others which the two middle classes refused to enter. While interviews demonstrated that certain associations or clubs were believed to contain only the 'best people', others mostly the 'best people' but with additions, and still others only the 'lowest people', some associations did not seem to be graded in class; people 'of all kinds' were said to belong to them.

From a later understanding of associations, we discovered that members of the three higher classes belonged to associations which we named social clubs. The three lower classes did not. All three of the upper classes belonged to associations organized for charitable purposes. Certain of these clubs had only female members, others only male, and still others were mixed. Several female clubs included women of the three uppermost classes, but interviews showed that their lower members had some difficulty in entering them. Some female clubs refused to admit 'ordinary better-class people', and some members said, 'We will have only our own kind'.

Ordinarily Hill-Streeters did not belong to occupational associations, but Homevillers did. Hill-Streeters tended to avoid fraternal organizations, secret societies and insurance orders, and associations with formal age grading. Members of the upper-middle class also tended to stay out of fraternal orders and associations with auxiliaries. On the other hand, members of the lower-middle class favoured fraternal orders and semi-auxiliaries. The upper-middle people, moreover, were allowed into and favoured charitable organizations, while the lower-middle members were excluded from or refused to join them. The breaks in association behaviour of the members of the two middle classes greatly aided us in making our classification and in separating members of the two groups.

Lower-middle-class people did not participate in female and mixed social clubs, and since women were very conscious of class in Yankee City, the knowledge of this fact greatly aided us in our interviewing. If a person was a member of several charitable organizations, a social club or two, and possibly an occupational association, but not of a fraternal lodge, and he was not considered a member of the new or old families of Hill-Streeters, it was more than likely that he was upper-middle class. A small amount of interviewing soon demonstrated whether this was true or not. Ordinarily he had a family and was a member of a few cliques; usually we possessed information about their members; often some of them had been placed by earlier interviews. With this information it was not too hard to locate this individual in his exact place in the class system.

Associations were of great value in placing large groups of people in a fairly exact status within the class system. But because these people belonged to other social structures, such as the family and clique, which made much finer status discriminations, it was possible to place them with even greater exactness. Our study of family membership demonstrated that the vast majority of families had but one class represented in their membership. Although there were very minor rank differences in family membership, the members of a family ordinarily participated as a unit in their place in the social structure. Ultimately, we estimated that 95·15 per cent of the members of the upper-upper class belonged to families in which there were only upper-upper-class people; that 87·26 per cent of lower-upper persons belonged to families confined to their own class; and that the corresponding percentages for the other classes were 91·36 for upper-middle; 90·17 for lower-middle; 86·33 for upper-lower; and 95·98 for lower-lower.

Cliques tended to include two or even three classes in their membership, but on the whole they, too, drew fairly sharp class lines. Of the upper-upper class, 36·59 per cent belonged to cliques in which there were only upper-uppers; 20·74 per cent of the clique members in the lower-upper class, 20·12 per cent in upper-middle, 14·47 per cent in lower-middle, 15·68 per cent in upper-lower, and 24·64 per cent in the lower-lower class belonged to cliques confined to their own class.

All of the types of social structure and each of the thousands of families, thousands of cliques, and hundreds of associations were, member by member, interrelated in our research. With the use of all structural participation, and with the aid of such additional testimony as the area lived in, the type of house, kind of education, manners and other symbols of class, it was possible to determine very quickly the approximate place of any individual in the society. In the final analysis, however, individuals were placed by the evaluations of the members of Yankee City itself, e.g. by such explicit statements as 'she does not belong' or 'they belong to our club'. Naturally there were many borderline cases. A class system, unlike a caste or any other clearly and formally marked rank order, is one in which movement up and down is constantly taking place in the lives of many people. At the time of our study, for example, some people were moving into the lower-upper class from the upper-middle. Our interviews showed pressure on these mobile people from those above them and the development of new social behaviour and memberships among them. It was a problem in these and similar cases from other classes where such people should be placed. In order to make a complete study, it was necessary to locate all of them in one of the six classes, and this we did to the best of our ability on the basis of the entire range of phenomena covered by our data.

Distinctions between the upper-upper and lower-upper, old family and new family, groups are quite clear. Differences between the upper-middle people who were not new family but who belonged to associations like them, and who were of the 'better class' in Home-ville and similar areas, are quite easily observed. The separation of the upper-middle from the lower-middle class is clear and distinct, but that between the lower-middle and upper-lower is less clear and, in certain respects, at least distinct of all. The distinction between the lower-lower and upper-lower class is easily made by finding out to whom the expressions 'he is a Riverbrooker' or 'he is the same as a Riverbrooker' apply.

It must not be thought that all the people in Yankee City are aware of all the minute distinctions made in this book. The terms used to refer to such definitions as are made vary according to the class of the individual and his period of residence. The terms Hill-Streeter, Side-Streeter, Homeviller, and Riverbrooker would be known to all classes. Occasionally such terms are used only in their geographical sense, but far more often they are applied as terms of status and rank.

CHAPTER 24

The Modern Community as a Laboratory*

W. Lloyd Warner

In my research, the local community was made to serve as a microcosmic whole representing the total American community. When
selected by exacting criteria, including a suitable location in economic,
geographical and social regions, it meets most if not all the necessary
research specifications. Some twenty-two criteria were used to select
the community we are presently studying. Questions of size, industrial life, agricultural background marketing facilities and services,
ethnic and racial composition, as well as the presence or absence of
certain kinds of schools, churches, associations, civic enterprises and
governmental institutions were embodied in the criteria which served
as a testing screen to eliminate hundreds of towns and cities in five
large, middle-western states and to retain a very small number for
further investigation. The few remaining communities could then be
inspected by preliminary field investigations to validate the screening
process and to select one of them for intensive study.

From what has been said, several questions immediately arise: In
what sense are these communities representative? In what way are
they typical? How adequately do they serve as trial laboratories for
understanding American life? And does the microcosm of the community yield everything that a study of the whole society would
yield?

Meaningful answers to these questions may take at least two forms:
Are the cities and towns selected representative of the thousands of
communities in the United States? And are they typical of the general
culture of the United States?

To satisfy these questions, the criteria used were designed to
identify communities which are expressions of some of the central
tendencies of American society. Those which met the test possessed
social and economic characteristics which most nearly approached
the ideal-typical expression of these central tendencies. For example,
we know America is a huge industrial nation, founded on a vast
agricultural base, that it constantly assimilates and fails to assimilate

* Reprinted by permission of The University of Chicago Press from *Structure
of American Life* by W. Lloyd Warner, pp. 33–34.

large numbers of immigrants from different European cultures, that its religious life is largely Protestant but that is has a strong Catholic minority, that it has powerful political and economic hierarchies, that its associational and civic enterprises are deeply pervasive, and that there is a considerable distance from the bottom to the top levels of the socio-economic heap. These and many other known facts supplied the materials for the selective criteria.

A community chosen by such criteria represents not only certain central tendencies of American culture but conforms to a basic type of American community. Although many other types do exist—for example, the isolated, poor-white mountain hamlet, the great metropolis, or the suburban industrial mill town—we believe that, for the present, they are less likely to give significant answers about the core of American life than those chosen.

We should not continue without pointing out some of the difficulties. I have just indicated that the study of the central core of a society will not tell one what the varieties are, but such a study makes the varieties much more easily understood. However, there is still a need for a community typology composed of several types. Representative studies should be made for each type. We have only one such typology for one major region of the United States. It must be said, too, that community studies give only part of the evidence about the vast superstructure of American life. The greatly extended economic and political hierarchies, for example, whose centres of decision are in New York and Washington, can be only partly understood by these studies. However, careful examination of the evidence elicited from local studies, when related to what is known about our national economic life, gives great insight and sound knowledge about the processes at work throughout the system.

Let us conclude our discussion about the adequacy of the community study as a sampling device by saying that, although such studies do not provide all the answers, they do give us many of the most important ones and that, although they suffer from limitations, they open whole new areas for our understanding of modern man.

A number of difficulties become immediately apparent as soon as the field researcher begins his work on contemporary communities. At first these difficulties seem simple and obvious, but the implications of each become exceedingly subtle. One of the most important problems is the presence of written symbols to stand for oral words and statements.

The invention of written words to stand for oral communication and the more recent appearance of technological inventions for the mass distribution of symbols have created a great variety of media of public communication which symbolically interrelate millions of people in common reference to the same meaningful stimuli and present a very difficult and, at first, terrifying problem for the field researcher. The newspaper, the motion picture, radio, mass magazines, television, lithographs and picture magazines present entirely new methodological problems; they demand new field techniques and fresh analytical disciplines. The problems arising from the use of these mass-symbol systems take several forms. The principal ones are:

What are the meaning and significance of the symbols themselves and what do they mean to their audience? What effect do they have on the individuals who see and listen to them? What effect do they have on various groups in the society? The latter question takes two forms: the first, what effect do mass media have on the thinking of the people; the second, what is the effect of such stimuli on the relations of the community, its several institutions, and on the larger American society?

How to deal with these problems is an exceedingly difficult question. To solve them the anthropologist must depend on modifications of some of his old field procedures and borrow others from his colleagues in psychology, sociology and the other social sciences. Although he must be primarily dependent upon the use of the interview, a whole series of psychological and sociological instruments must be added to his equipment. Some of them I might mention are projective and sociometric techniques, schedules, tests and numerous other devices which examine such things as the relation of the individual to the symbols, the relations of individuals to each other because of the presence of such symbols and the functions of these symbols for the whole society.

From its earliest beginnings, anthropology has been concerned with social change; in fact, many anthropologists have defined their discipline as being no more than history or its reconstruction. Through use of the several sub-disciplines—archaeology, physical anthropology, linguistics and ethnology—anthropologists have attempted to reconstruct the prehistory of our own and other societies. More recently, social anthropologists have dealt with history when they studied the processes of acculturation and assimilation following the impact of Western civilization on native cultures. Ordinarily, these studies by their very nature have to do with historical processes and forces emanating from *outside* the cultures, whereas the study of European and American social change, for the most part, necessarily searches for explanations of the changes emanating from *within* the culture.

When the social anthropologist turns his attention to modern society, he finds that the sociologists have developed a large body of valuable knowledge and a great variety of theories about social change in Western civilization. Social change has been studied under such rubrics as social and business cycles, historical rhythms, the 'social lag', and a great variety of other concepts which attempt to examine social behaviour in terms of events that are in a time sequence.

Perhaps the most interesting thing about the study of social change is the fact that so much attention has been given to it and so little to social persistence. We largely take for granted that social groups persist. We rarely stop to ask why persistence occurs and try to determine its nature. The interdependence of personality formation and the persistence of a social system is now clearly demonstrable. They are but two aspects of the same ongoing process of socialization. The study of the effect of social class on personality at the same time can be an investigation of how social class persists in a free society.

Other problems harass the anthropologist who attempts to study contemporary social life. They are: the presence of complex number systems and their written forms, the existence of huge populations and multitudes of people and things to which the numbers are applied and the fact that the number systems and their relations to the people and things have significance and meaning to the members of the society and are factors helping control behaviour. The problems thus created are exceedingly complex. I cannot claim too much for our efforts to solve them.

In the very simple societies such as aboriginal Australia, mathematical systems are rudimentary and unimportant, but in contemporary society problems of number continually appear, usually in the several forms just mentioned. Let me analyse the significance of this contrast between very primitive tribes and our own.

In a simple undifferentiated culture, one principal informant aided by assistants can tell the researcher what the norms of the society are for such things as marriage and divorce. Further interviewing with others will demonstrate that the evidence he cites is all that is necessary and available. He can do this because the universe for which he speaks is usually restricted in population, limited territorially and simple socially.

In our own society the very opposite is true. Norms about marriage and divorce, for example, vary from group to group and within each group. How much and how often become questions of the utmost importance. The knowledge of the mere presence of divorce is insufficient. We need to know how frequent it is to answer a whole variety of important questions having to do with everything from the family, child-rearing and the status of woman to the meaning of contemporary mass media or the significance of certain fictional themes in our literature.

In primitive society such as Australia, numerical concepts are simple, limited and sufficient; 'two or three people', 'a whole lot of people', or 'lots and lots of people' satisfied any intelligent Murngin. Not so the native of Yankee City. He wants to know what per cent of the total vote Jones received and how did this percentage compare with those of Smith, Brown and the others. He and his wife guide their behaviour by numbers that stand for days of the years by price indices and by huge columns of figures on the financial page. Out of all these calculations, diverse meanings and significances are reached which everyone uses to guide and direct his activities. In Yankee City, Mid-west or Deep South, the meaning of numbers prevents and frustrates or sometimes positively stimulates the behaviour of the members of these societies.

The use of statistics helps the scientist to solve the ordinary problem of how much and how many. Symbolic analysis gives some aid and a little comfort for the problem of the meaning and significance of numbers and their use by contemporary peoples. So far the latter and most important problem has not advanced much beyond the first step of asking some of the right questions.

I must briefly touch on another problem that besets the anthropologist foolish or hardy enough to tackle the study of his own society. I refer to ethnocentrism. Simply put, this means does he see and hear what he is looking at? And, equally simple and devastating, will he look at, and give attention to, what is there to be seen and heard? Since he is a living product of his own culture and subject to its control and direction, can he look objectively at what he studies? It can be said that the processes of social science, with their constant testing and retesting, provide us with the same apparatus for indentifying and analysing social reality as physical science does for its subdisciplines. But, before accepting this persuasive argument, it must be remembered that science is one kind of symbol system recently invented by Western man. It too is an artifact of our culture, subject to the controls of our basic ideas and emotional systems. This argument holds true for the study not only of our society but of other societies as well. The same sets or ways of seeing and hearing things will prevail everywhere.

Fortunately, the comparative method of anthropology helps us out of this difficulty. The charge of ethnocentrism is difficult to combat when scientists of our society study only their own culture. Perhaps they do mirror only what is in the mirror; but, when other societies are studied and great diversities are recorded, they become capable of identifying social similarities and differences. Furthermore, when students from other cultures go to these same societies, including our own and report the same cultural occurrences and events as we do, a large measure of assurance is given us that, in so far as man is capable of dealing with reality beyond himself, it seems likely he can study himself, including not only investigations of his culture but of the private worlds of those who live in it.

I have mentioned some of the important difficulties that need overcoming; I have not told of the many advantages. I will do no more than list a few. Problems of language and meaning are partly reduced by the field worker's control of the language and the many scientific devices to check and control semantic problems. The mass media and other literate symbols are difficult to comprehend but, as permanent documents, they provide evidence about our past and present that are used to first advantage by the scientific analyst. Numbers are often a curse to the researcher, but when they accumulate a certain amount of sense can be made from them. The intimate inner knowledge one has about himself and his own world often permits the sympathetic field worker to enter the private worlds of those he studies with greater ease and assurance than when he studies an alien group. Finally, the accumulated results, techniques and skills of other social and psychological sciences are more available to the anthropologist who studies our society than to the students who do research on New Guinea, Australia or the Amazon. The latter, too often, must be jacks-of-all-trades and masters of none.

Since the community is central to our discussion, we must now take time to say what it is as a social object, what we mean by it and similar terms, and show how this concept is related to the key concepts of social anthropology.

Sociology and anthropology employ a large number of terms referring to a great variety of human territorial groups. Some of those commonly used by anthropologists are hordes, bands, villages, as well as towns and cities; those more familiar to the sociologist are metropolitan areas, rural and urban neighbourhoods, as well as cities towns, villages and hamlets. The term, community, although largely used by the sociologist to take general account of the variety of territorial groups of contemporary civilization, necessarily includes and defines all similar groupings among non-literate peoples. It, therefore, can be used safely as a term and concept that is meaningful for research which is done on the local groups of any society. Its customary usage is extended by me to fit the needs of a science of man which refuses to separate contemporary society from its kind, namely all societies of human beings.

A community so defined may be autonomous to the point that it is a separate group exercising complete sovereignty, possessing a complete economy and social system, and worshipping its own unique and ethnocentric deities; or it may be, as it often is in contemporary life, a smaller segment of a larger whole, a very tiny part of it, such as a small neighbourhood in a larger metropolitan centre, functioning only to provide living space for a group of families who earn their bread elsewhere, who have no political autonomy, belong to other social groups which meet beyond their limits, and pray to gods whose churches are elsewhere and whose secular chiefs may be thousands of miles distant.

So viewed, the several varieties of communities and local groups studied by sociologists and anthropologists—although they vary widely among themselves, socially from the very simple to the very complex, technically from the low hunters and gatherers to the technology of the machine and, in population, from a score or so to the millions of metropolises—are essentially the same in kind. They all are located in a given territory which they partly transform for purposes of maintaining the life of the group. All the individual members have social relations directly or indirectly with each other. The social relations are ordered and their totality forms the social structure of the local group. Although social change continually occurs, it is relatively small. The organization of a group continues through the changing generations of individuals who are born into it. There may or may not be great variation in the autonomy exercised by the different groups and their differentiation from other communities, yet all differ sufficiently everywhere for the individuals in them to be conscious of belonging to one group and not to another, even though the other may be but little different from their own.

All societies are essentially adaptive orders where accumulated human learning experience is organized, contained and directed in symbol systems which adjust human biological groups with varying degrees of success to their several environments. Although human adaptation *seems* largely social, there can be little doubt that its core continues to be species behaviour.

Social organization should not be understood simply as a method man invented to integrate otherwise isolated (non-social) individuals. There are no isolated human individuals. Since all of them are members of the species, they interact at a species level as well as a social level. The rules and symbols of the social structure only modify the species-system of relations and give it social form.

The problem of the social scientist is not the false one usually posed of how humans become social beings, but rather how they learn to become autonomous individuals. Later I shall consider certain aspects of this problem when I discuss the meaning of the role and status of individuals.

From the larger point of view, all human society which is not species-behaviour is symbolic. A symbol is anything which has meaning and significance for the human mind. Human society is composed of symbolic processes in the sense that what we are to ourselves, what others are to us, what we are to them and they to themselves, consist outwardly of words and acts which inwardly are evaluated beliefs. In other words, the social relations and entire social organization of any human society consist of evaluated beliefs and their application to human conduct as it occurs in the interaction of individuals within particular relational contexts. Such are the rules and the conditions in which they operate. The sanctions enforcing them are socially defined, but the testimony from primate societies teaches us that we almost certainly inherited our methods of enforcing the rules from our animal forebears, for punishment and reward are the foundation stones not only of human learning but of animal learning.

The very technology that adjusts us to the natural environment, usually not considered a symbolic system, partly consists of knowledge which directs, organizes and adjusts our control over the natural environment. But here the symbolic analysis of all human conduct can be pushed too far. The tools, weapons and instruments man invents and uses for adjusting himself to his natural environment are things in themselves. Their form and function need no more meaning and no more interpretation by those who use them than knowing what it is they are and what it is they can and cannot do. They do not necessarily stand for anything else. In this sense, they are not symbols. But, in another sense, they are, for each artifact and each of their functions are meaningful and symbols of direct reference in the same way the concepts and instruments of science are. The concepts of science represent reality; their instruments constantly test it. As such, they are a language and its related behaviour. They directly refer to, and are tested by, the realities of natural experience. The science of today's technology is no more than a development of the simpler technologies of yesterday. Just as the meaningful and evaluated acts and words composing the social organization adjust human beings to each other, so the meaningful acts and tools of the technology adjust us to nature. A nature without meaning, that is to say, without symbolic representation in man's technology, would be a nature to which there was no technological adjustment.

Finally, our society and all others adjust man to the unknown and to all those forces which his technology and social organization cannot control sufficiently to give him the safety he feels necessary. Religion and magic, composed of myth and rite, are the evaluated beliefs, the meaningful words and acts which all societies use to accomplish this fearful task. There can be no doubt about their symbolic nature. The sacred symbol systems are symbols of symbols. They relate man to sacred beings whose nature for science can be comprehended only by understanding to what they refer in human existence and what they mean for the inner world of man's emotions and his public world of social experience.

These three adaptations—technologies, the skills and tools which adjust man to nature, the rules, composed of meaningful words and acts and religion, the symbols that relate man to the sacred—provide a basic framework not only for studying contemporary communities of our society but for comparing similar studies of other societies with our own.

CHAPTER 25

Lloyd Warner and his Critics*

Colin Bell and Howard Newby

The position of Lloyd Warner, in his *Yankee City* volumes, on local social stratification, is highly provocative, and can serve as a vehicle for a full discussion of the central problems involved. Besides his community studies, Warner and two colleagues have written another book solely on the topic of stratification. One's suspicions are aroused by its title: *Social Class in America: The Evaluation of Status*.[1] This should put the reader on his guard against the conceptual confusion that this title implies, which is the more surprising as there are numerous references to both Karl Marx and to Max Weber. The book is really written on three levels; it is a political tract, a manual of procedure for the measurement of social status and a theoretical treatise.

Firstly, and this will be dealt with most briefly, it is an attack on 'The American Dream'. Whilst the book is an attempt to cool 'the bright and warm presence of the American Dream that all men are born free and equal', as will be shown below it has a markedly 'conservative' bias. Everyone in the American Dream has the right and often the duty to try to succeed and to do his best to reach the top. Warner points out that the dream's two fundamental themes and propositions, 'that all . . . are equal and that each . . . has the right to the chance of reaching the top, are mutually contradictory, for if all men are equal there can be no top level to aim for, no bottom one to get away from, there can be no superior or inferior positions, but only one common level into which all Americans are born and in which all of them will spend their lives.'[2] 'Americans though realize from their own (local community) experience that this is not so, but despite the presence of social hierarchies which places people at higher and lower levels in American communities,'[3] the 'rags to riches' saga appear to prove that enough of the Dream is true. Yet Americans 'have little scientific knowledge about the powerful presence of social status and how it works for good and evil'. And so

* Reprinted by permission of George Allen and Unwin Ltd, from *Community Studies* by Colin Bell and Howard Newby, London 1972, pp. 189–199 and by permission of Praeger Publishers Inc. for the same extract.

the (incredible) aim of the book is 'to provide a corrective instrument which will permit men and women better to evaluate their social situations and thereby better adapt themselves to social reality and fit their dreams and aspirations to what is possible.'[4] Thus it can be said that whilst he emphasizes mobility striving he also stresses the necessity of individuals adjusting to their situation in life, where mobility is not possible. He is advocating the desirability of fitting the individual into the class system rather than considering the possibility of changing the system. However, one aim of his book is to make the stratification system more visible and this is the second aspect to be discussed.

What this book does, it is claimed, is to provide a way of measuring status and particularly one's own status in a community. As an introduction to a discussion of social class in America there is a discussion of stratification in Yankee City (17,000), Jonesville (6,000), Old City (10,000), (Deep South): all are, of course, relatively small and relatively stable communities and Jonesville was a company town to boot. The kind of bias that this leads to is suggested by, for example, Warner's insistence that whilst economic factors *are* significant and important they are not sufficient 'to predict where a particular family or individual will be or to explain completely the phenomena of social class'. In Warner's view money had to be translated into *socially approved behaviour and possessions* and 'they in turn into intimate participation with and acceptance by members of a superior class.'[5]

Warner writes that, 'talking to and observing the people of [from his own and novelists' accounts] communities demonstrate that they too know how real these status levels are, and they prove it by agreeing among themselves about the status levels and who belongs to them in their particular city.'[6] The local stratification system is, then, viewed by Warner as an *inclusive mono-dimensional* system *recognized* by all the community. It would seem that very rapidly he has moved from a 'scientific objective' model of stratification to adopting a local subjective model. His emphasis on social approval and intimate participation show clearly that he is talking about an *interactional* stratification system, and his rejection of what he calls 'economic factors', that he is not dealing with an *attributional* system. If, as he claims to believe, Jonesville *is* America, it is not unreasonable for him to impute its local stratification system onto America. Yet, as will be shown below, some doubt can be thrown on the assumption that he analysed satisfactorily even that community's local stratification system. What Warner has done is to extrapolate a mistaken view of a local stratification system onto the whole of American society. All his examples are taken from some *local* context, for example, the exclusion of a man from a particular club and from interactional *status* systems. Whilst, what he describes undoubtedly occurs in many communities, this is, at best only very indirect evidence of the workings of class in American society taken as a whole. Warner recognizes inter-community variations in stratification—for example, old stable towns will differ to metropolises like Chicago—yet he claims that 'systematic studies from coast to coast in cities large and small and of many economic types indicate that, despite the variations and diversity, class levels do exist and that they conform to a particular pattern of organization.'[7] What it means to belong to what he calls a ' particular level' in the social class system *of America* is 'that a family or individual has gained acceptance as an equal by those who belong in the class. The behaviour in this class and the participation of those in it *must be related by the rest of the community* as being at a particular place in the social scale.'[8] Some of the empirical difficulties with this approach can be readily appreciated if, instead of visualizing Yankee City or Jonesville, the area described by Zorbaugh in *The Gold Coast and the Slum* is considered. Many of those living in Chicago Near North Side were unaware of each other's existence. How would the *mafiosi* of 'Little Sicily' rank those living on Lake Shore Drive and *vice versa*? Certainly not by interaction. Similarly, it will be remembered that in Levittown, analysed by Gans, there were three class cultures 'each of which will consider itself to be of most worth, if perhaps not of highest status in the community.'[9] It might be more realistic to stress the difference between communities than their similarities and certainly to be very wary of extrapolation from one sort of community to the whole of society.

Warner compares the task of the student of the social status structure[10] with that of the ecologist, whose first task in a community is to produce maps, and he says correctly that the 'map can represent nothing more about the territory than the knowledge he possesses . . . Structure and status analysts can also construct scientific representations (or maps) which represent *their* knowledge of the structure and status interrelations which compose the community's status system.'[11] The two methods that Warner uses to draw his 'maps' of the local stratification system are called Evaluated Participation (E.P.) and the Index of Status Characteristics (I.S.C.). He claims that together they provide accurate procedures for 'measuring' social class and the class positions of individuals, for validating results obtained and 'for translating social class and socio-economic status categories into terms which are *interchangeable*.'[12]

E.P. is 'posed on the propositions that those who interact in the social system of a community evaluate the participation of those around them, that the place where an individual participates is evaluated and that the members of the community are explicitly or implicitly aware of the ranking and translate their evaluation of such social participation with social class ratings that can be communicated to the investigator.'[13] The E.P. is based on six techniques for rating an individual's social class position:

1. *Rating by Matched Agreements:* informants are asked to rank named social classes and then individuals are assigned to particular classes. When there is a high amount of agreement the analyst will know that 'the class system . . . is strong and pervades the whole community.'[14]

2. *Rating by Symbolic Placements:* individuals are rated into a particular class because they are identified by informants with certain superior or inferior symbols.

3. *Rating by Status Reputation:* individuals are rated 'because (informants say) he has a reputation for engaging in activities and possessing certain traits which are considered to be superior or inferior.'[15]

4. *Rating by Comparison:* individuals are rated 'because informants assert he is equal superior or inferior to others whose social-class position has been previously determined.'[16]

5. *Rating by Simple Assignment to a Class:* individuals are rated because one or more *qualified* informant assigns the individual to that particular class. (How an informant *qualifies* we are not told.)

6. *Rating by Institutional Membership:* individuals are rated by their membership of certain institutions which are ranked as superior or inferior (but how? the student may reasonably ask).

What is clear is that Warner abdicates from having what was called earlier a 'scientific objective' position at all. The analysis of any problem in sociology cannot make people's opinions of that problem its point of departure. It is one thing to be wary of imposing categories onto reality but quite another to say that not only 'we must try to see the problem from the point of view of the informants', but also 'that they are the final authorities about the realities of American social class.'[17] Lipset and Bendix, for example, in a classic caustic remark say that all he had done is to 'systematize the gossip and rumour of the town.'[18] For surely no resident of Yankee City or Jonesville knows that much about the interaction patterns of the community. Other than the upper class, the other five classes are much too numerous to permit that degree of personal acquaintance which would alone make a system of interlocking status evaluations feasible.

I.S.C. is primarily an index of the earlier disparaged socio-economic factors. It is meant to be 'objective', cheap and simple. I.S.C. was used in both Yankee City and Jonesville 'where it correlated highly with class'.[19] It is based on occupation source of income, house type and dwelling area. But 'it is not the house, or the job, or the income, or the neighbourhood that is being measured, as much as the evaluations that are *in the backs of our heads*—evaluations placed there by our cultural tradition and our society.'[20] Each component of this index is broken down on a (only) seven point scale then summed— the scale is *nominal* for dwelling area and house type, *ordinal* for occupation and *interval* for income and so breaks just about every rule in the index construction book. The scales are weighted (it would appear somewhat arbitrarily) as the example below shows. The score for an individual is the sum of his scores on each dimension times the weight of that dimension. The range of possible scores is from 12 (very high) to 84 (very low). Warner's example is as follows:

Status Characteristic	Rating × Weight = Weighted Rating
Occupation	2 × 4 = 8
Source of Income	3 × 3 = 9
House type	2 × 3 = 6
Dwelling area	3 × 2 = 6
	Weighted total 29

The conversion table for Jonesville is as follows:

Weighted Total Ratings	Social Class Equivalents
12–17	Upper class
18–22	Upper class probably, with some possibility of upper middle class
23–24	Intermediate: either upper or upper middle class
25–33	Upper middle class
34–37	Intermediate: either upper middle or lower middle class
38–50	Lower middle class
51–53	Intermediate: either low middle or upper lower class
54–62	Upper lower class
63–66	Intermediate: either upper lower of lower lower class
67–69	Lower lower class probably, with some possibility of upper lower class
70–84	Lower lower class

Warner argues that though E.P. and I.S.C. measures two different factors E.P. is the more basic, I.S.C. was shown in Warner's community studies, though, to have quite a high predictive power on social class participation.[21]

The bulk of the remainder of Warner's *Social Class in America* consists of detailed instructions for using Evaluated Participation and the Index of Status Characteristics. He takes passages very similar to the 'profiles' discussed in Chapter Three and analyses them in great detail against these two indices. To add to the previously voiced suspicions he gives practical instructions on using the indices through the medium of an analysis of Babbit and Social Class in Zenith. It is interesting to note that when Warner correlates his two indices he finds it very high (0.97).

The third and final contribution of this book is the theoretical chapter on 'several types of rank'. It is made quite clear that Warner realizes and appreciates that there are other forms of ranking system besides that detailed above: caste, for example. The system he has described is but one *type* of stratification he argues—with this there can be little disagreement. The basis for differentiation of stratification systems which he adopts is, firstly, the amount and quality of *mobility* between positions in the system, and, secondly, the *pervasiveness* of the stratification system in 'the life of a society'.[22] The classification that he then can produce is as follows (somewhat simplified):

	Pervasive and general	Mixed	Limited
High mobility (open)	1	2	3
Neither open nor closed	4	5	6
Low mobility (closed)	7	8	9

American communities (and by implication American society) falls into mainly box number 1 except in the Deep South where there is no mobility across the 'colour caste' line and so in some senses they would fall in box 7. It must be stressed that Warner is using a very limited and specific definition of class, but what this typology provokes is the seeking of reasons for movement along the two axes. If this is considered it may be possible to provide a classification of local stratification systems. Warner's discussion of class is now being limited, as seems reasonable, to local interactional status sytems. It is possible to produce from this typology propositions that can be treated as hypotheses.

(a) The smaller and the more stable a community (meaning economically and in terms of population turnover) the lower the mobility and the more general and pervasive will be the local interactional status system (what Warner calls class) and conversely

(b) the larger and the more unstable (both meaning economically and in terms of population turnover) the more mobility and the less pervasive the local interactional status system.

However, though this approach allows for significant differences between communities, one problem that should be faced is that for many people in localities of any size the locality itself will not be a significant reference group. For example, in Springdale, it was possible to distinguish entrepreneurial and bureaucratic segments of the community, neither of which could precisely rank the other. For the former, in Springdale as for some of the called 'traditionalists' in Banbury, the local community *was* a significant reference group, but for the latter and for some of the non-traditionalists in Banbury it was not. There may well be communities where there are several status hierarchies that, while they all use the community as a reference group, would not be comparable with each other. What is clear, however, is that there can be living in quite small communities quite large segments of the population who are not members of local interactional status groups. It would not be possible for the field-worker to collect their 'local subjective' models because they do not have any. Warner himself provides, surprisingly, perhaps, some evidence on the differences felt by a newcomer to a community—and it might be added, on the differences between cities and the kind of communities studied by Warner. We are told that Mr. Donnelly came to Jonesville from a large city. 'It seems to me', he said, 'there's quite a difference in the type of relation you have in a big and a small town. In large cities people aren't closely connected with one another. In small towns the people know all their neighbours. They are more closely connected. They can see everything you do. And they follow all your goings and comings.'[23]

Pfautz and Duncan's *Critical Evaluation of Warner's Work in Community Stratification*[24] lays most of the blame for the shortcomings of his approach on his anthropological orientation. This has been discussed in some detail in Chapter Three. They comment in addition, 'More is involved here than the tendency shared with many American sociologists to confine studies to the local community level for the sake of ease of gathering data. The traditional anthropological perspective of Warner *et al.* together with their studied indifference to previous sociological literature leads them to a failure to distinguish between "community" on the one hand and "society" on the other.'[25] Their criticisms are interesting as both the authors of this paper were brought up in the Chicago School in its dying days. Warner could have benefited from a close reading of the Chicago monographs before he went into the field. The seeming sufficiency of Warner's anthropological ethnographic approach kept him isolated from a considerable body of literature on social stratification and hence he failed to discern the crucial problems that it had raised—particularly the multi-dimensional nature of stratification.

Pfautz and Duncan are particularly critical of some of Warner's technical deficiencies, for example, they point out that as the E.P. Method, necessarily depends on interview data, 'It is incumbent on the investigator to be quite specific regarding the sampling.'[26] Warner gives no information about sample size, selection or characteristics. It can rather alarmingly be gleaned from *Democracy in Jonesville* that though the 'upper class' was three per cent of the population of the community it found 13 per cent of the sample used to work out E.P. Pfautz and Duncan write strongly that 'altogether it would appear that unscientific sampling practice vitiates to a considerable extent the claims for the I.S.C. as an instrument for determining class level by the criteria of E.P.'[27] If Warner's science is suspect, so equally is his theory, as Warner's classes are not necessarily the same phenomena with which Mosca, Marx or Weber were concerned. And Warner's critics also point out that a confusion enters in when the protagonists of the prestige class define their concept on the basis of such criteria as intimate association, culture, way of life, etc. and then because they fail to find group closure and intimate participation on the national level, conclude that power classes do not exist—or as in the case of Warner, assume that the study of (local) prestige classes encompasses the whole field. Merton has argued that if Warner and his associates 'intend only to assert that *contemporary* income, wealth and occupation are insufficient to assign all members of the community to their "correct" position within the prestige hierarchy their evidence is adequate. But this is a perilously narrow conception of an "economic" interpretation. Unfortunately (there are no) case studies of families who, *over a period of generations*, have not had their claims to upper-upper status validated by "economic" criteria which must serve as means for maintaining the behavioural attributes of that status.'[28] Despite Warner's emphasis on *mobility* as being a crucial differentiating criteria for ranking systems and being a vital element in the American Dream, there are hardly any figures in the five *Yankee City* volumes on how much mobility takes place and at what points in the class system. The only data are contained in the fictionalized profiles. Anyway, it will be impossible to assess social mobility on the basis of what people believe that mobility to have been.[29]

What is more, Warner has also biased the supposed objective I.S.C. criteria—for example, by taking house type as a criteria of rank. This matter of class bias is much more serious than technical deficiencies in sampling. This point has been argued in two papers in the first volume of the *British Journal of Sociology* by Lipset and Bendix. What they argue, in effect, is that there is not an analysis of the status structure as it actually exists, but only the way in which the status structure looks through the eyes of upper middle and upper class residents. For example, the emphasis is on 'acting right' and not just having money. There is clearly evidence—for example, in *Deep South*—that the upper groups made finer distinction than the lower groups. In *Yankee City* we are told that 'the greater the social distance from the other classes, the less clearly are fine distinctions made.' Similarly it is clear from the designations used by one group about the others that the criteria for judgement vary from class to class: the lower groups making designations primarily in terms of money, the middle classes in terms of money and morality and the upper classes giving more emphasis to style of life and ancestry. So it seems that what Warner has produced is a *composite* version of the prestige hierarchy which is built from the varied perspectives of the local residents and, despite all Warner's protestations, was more *his* construction than the community's. Kornhauser asks 'why does Warner describe a large number of classes when only the upper strata recognize that many? Why are six divisions more 'real' than the three or four that are recognized by the local strata? Why has Warner adopted the view of class held by the upper and upper middle class when members of the lower middle, upper lower and lower lower classes (the vast majority of the population) are said to base *their* rankings *solely* on money.'[30] The answer seems to be that Warner himself adopted the view of class held by the upper and upper middle class so that class is not what *all* people say it is, but what *some* people say it is. Lipset and Bendix point out that nine of his ten informants in Jonesville were upper middle class and so his community study reveals 'the perspective of the social climbers just below the upper crust of small town society. To people at this level class appears as a matter of inter-personal relations, manners, family and so on. It is not polite to suggest that class is a reflection of one's economic position . . .'[31] His one working class informant said he 'saw class as purely a matter of income and power'. The claim, therefore, that Warner's classes far from being 'real entities' as he frequently stresses, are the results of his conceptual scheme and his methods.

The concepts used reflect the social reality primarily as seen from the perspective of the higher strata.

Does the 'upper-upper' of the one community equal the 'upper-upper' of another? Warner's answer would seem to be in the positive. But it is clearly difficult to demonstrate. There is, then, the problem of extrapolation from and between communities. However uniform the smaller communities that have been studied are and however universally the social classes extend, the community is still part of a wider culture. The upper and perhaps most significant strata are *not* represented at the very local level, but are to be found in large urban centres, in the American case, Boston, New York and Washington. Yankee City, Old City and Jonesville do *not* represent a microcosm or a sample of the United States: they contained no industrial leaders, no bankers, no big politicians, etc., who surely are central to a consideration of the *national* class structure. The upper classes in small communities are but pseudo-elites taking their powers and prerogatives within the narrower context of the local community.

NOTES

1 W. Lloyd Warner, Marchia Meeker and Kenneth Eells, *Social Class in America: the Evaluation of Status*, New York, Harper Torchbook (first published 1949).
2 Ibid., p. 3.
3 Ibid., p. 4.
4 Ibid., p. 5.
5 Ibid., p. 21.
6 Ibid., p. 6.
7 Ibid., p. 24.
8 Ibid., p. 23, our emphasis.
9 H. J. Gans, *The Levittowners*, 1967, p. 132.
10 We are deliberately following their usage of terms for various forms of stratification and have made no attempt to impose what we would consider to be some consistency.
11 Warner *et al.*, op. cit., p. 34
12 Ibid., p. 35, our emphasis.
13 Ibid., p. 35. It should be noted that they are in fact unproven assumptions.
14 Ibid., p. 37.
15 Ibid., p. 37.
16 Ibid., pp. 37–38.
17 Ibid., p. 38.
18 S. M. Lipset and Bendix, 'Social Status and Social Structure: A Reexamination of the data and interpretations', *British Journal of Sociology*, 1, 1951, p. 156.
19 We take this to mean the E.P. index.
20 Ibid., p. 40, our emphasis.
21 The former identifies the actual social-class group with which an individual is

found to participate in the community, whereas the latter rates certain socio-economic characteristics 'which it is thought, (i) play a part in determining what the social class participation will be and what level it will occur and (ii) are in part determined by the level of social participation'. (Ibid., p. 42.)

22 There has been an attempt to apply the I.S.C. method to an English community, by W. M. Williams, in Gosforth. Despite Warner's claim that it can be used anywhere, it was in fact a failure when Williams used it. The four dimensions of the I.S.C. were found not to correlate highly with class in Gosforth. The importance of this finding is increased as it will be remembered that Williams' usage of the term 'class' is very similar to that of Warner's and meant something like an 'interacting status group'. Williams writes that 'when applied to the housing estate (in Gosforth) every family received exactly the same rating in "housing" and "area lived in" and all but a few had the same rating in the other categories as well.' It would appear, therefore, that the people of this housing estate are of the same 'socio-economic level' and that 'in socio-economic terms' one class is exactly the equivalent of another, so that the concept is valueless to an understanding of the social class system of this very common type of community. In fact, he stresses, 'the housing estate showed every evidence of possessing a highly developed form of class distinction', p. 213.

23 *Jonesville*, p. 29.
24 *American Sociological Review*, 15, 1950.
25 Ibid., p. 231.
26 Ibid., p. 233.
27 Ibid., p. 237.
28 Quoted by Ruth Rosner Kornhauser in her 'The Warner Approach to Social Stratification', in Lipset and Bendix, *Class, Status and Power*, first edition, p. 246. It is interesting to note that this article was omitted from the second edition of *Class, Status and Power*, and one by S. Thernstrom substituted.
29 The best thing for a small town resident to do in order to improve his position to be socially mobile is to migrate. This is both well known and unmentioned as far as we can ascertain in any of Warner's voluminous writing. Social geographical mobility are just a convergence of terms, one often implies the other (see Bell, C. R., *Middle Class Families*, London, Routledge and Kegan Paul, 1969). Warner implies (wrongly as shown by Thernstrom and discussed in Chapter Three) that relatively few people moved up in Yankee City. There were many who moved in and out of Newburyport on their way up. There will always therefore be a serious limitation to what community studies, particularly if they are naïvely ahistorical, can tell us about social and geographical mobility.
30 Kornhauser, op. cit., p. 249.
31 Lipset and Bendix, op. cit., p. 162.

CHAPTER 26

'Yankee City' Revisited: The Perils of Historical Naïveté*

Stephan Thernstrom

It is easy enough to nod agreement at E. H. Carr's remark that 'the more sociological history becomes, and the more historical sociology becomes, the better for both'.[1] But in truth, unhappily, the mutually-enriching dialogue between history and sociology that Carr calls for has barely begun; so far, communication between the two disciplines has largely been in the form of a monologue, with history on the receiving end. Sociologists and social anthropologists have been eager to suggest how their brethren in the most traditional and least theoretical of the social sciences might broaden their horizons and deepen their insights into man's behaviour in the past. It is clear, from a number of recent books and articles, that this advice has not gone entirely unheard.[2] What seems to have been neglected, however, is that if historians have much to learn from their colleagues in sociology, the converse of this proposition is also true. Carr's remark cuts both ways. Sociological work based on erroneous historical assumptions can be as superficial as sociologically primitive history, and it is no less common.[3] Close scrutiny of an influential specimen of contemporary social research which is particularly vulnerable to this charge may help to clarify why an accurate sense of historical perspective is indispensable to students of modern society.

One of the richest and most inviting sources of knowledge about modern American life is the *genre* that includes such books as *Black Metropolis*, *Caste and Class in a Southern Town*, *Streetcorner Society*,

* I am indebted to the Joint Center for Urban Studies of the Massachusetts Institute of Technology and Harvard University for supporting this research, and to Oscar Handlin, P. M. G. Harris and David Riesman for constructive criticism. Some of the materials included here are drawn from Chapter 8 and the Appendix to my book, *Poverty and Progress: Social Mobility in a Nineteenth Century City*, Cambridge: Harvard University Press, 1964, and are reprinted with the permission of Harvard University Press. Detailed citations to the historical evidence alluded to below will be found in the book. Reprinted by permission of The American Sociological Association from the *American Sociological Review*, vol. 30, 1965, pp. 234–242.

Elmtown's Youth and *Middletown*. Maurice Stein has recently urged the relevance of these works to the student of twentieth-century America in his stimulating study, *The Eclipse of Community: An Interpretation of American Studies*.[4] Stein, himself a sociologist, is surely correct in urging that the community studies conducted by American sociologists and anthropologists in the past 50 years are an exceptionally rich source of knowledge about the history of American civilization. But these works must be approached with a large measure of caution and critical reserve, for too many of them have been built upon shaky historical foundations. In particular, W. Lloyd Warner's famous 'Yankee City' series well illustrates the distortions that historical ignorance and naïveté can produce.

The 'Yankee City' series, five bulky volumes reporting on field research conducted in 'an old New England community' in the 1930's made W. Lloyd Warner the most influential American student of social stratification.[5] The first Yankee City publication, *The Social Life of a Modern Community* (1941), was widely praised, and the subsequent volumes and a host of other books by Warner and his students served to establish members of 'the Warner school' as leading interpreters of American community life. In recent years, it is true, the techniques of social analysis pioneered in the Yankee City study have been severely criticized, but the abundant literature on the Warner school does not include a detailed analysis of the mistaken historical assumptions out of which so many of Warner's errors grew.[6] Future investigators of social stratification in American communities will no doubt avoid the methodological blunders tellingly exposed by Mills, Lipset and Bendix, Pfautz and Duncan and other sociological critics; that glaring misinterpretations and distortions can stem from failure to utilize relevant historical data is less widely understood.

What follows is in no sense a full and balanced appraisal of the five Yankee City volumes or of Lloyd Warner's contributions to an understanding of American society. Such an appraisal would pay Warner the tribute he deserves as a pioneer in his field—for having gathered a wealth of interesting material about a subject that had been too little studied, and for having inspired an enormous amount of further research and controversy. It would applaud certain fruitful insights and note that Warner had the gift for social portraiture of a lesser social novelist; portions of the Yankee City volumes display some of the virtues of the novels of John P. Marquand, a writer who dealt with the same New England community. Such an assessment would be more appreciative, in short, and perhaps it is overdue. That, however, is a different task than the one undertaken here, and a larger one. These critical observations focus on what Warner failed to see about the community he studied so intensively in the 1930's and particularly on what he failed to see because of his misconceptions about the community's history.

That community was Newburyport, Mass., a city whose social and economic history I have been studying for the past five years. Like many another sociological field worker, Warner made evaluation and criticism of his work more difficult by obscuring the identity of the community studied with a pseudonym. The usual justification for this step is that is protects the identity of local informants. Whatever the merits of this argument, it seems clear that a latent function of this device is to lend an aura of typicality to the community in question: 'Yankee City' is manifestly a place of more universal significance than Newburyport, Mass., 'Jonesville' is more truly American than Morris, Ill. To say this is not to endorse the familiar criticism that cities like Newburyport were 'unrepresentative' of the larger society. With respect to the problems that interested Warner, Newburyport was much more 'representative' than his critics have allowed—though it is admittedly difficult to discern this from Warner's distorted and idealized description of the city.[7] The point is rather that Warner *assumed* Newburyport's representativeness without any critical examination of the issue, and that he made it difficult for others to think critically about the question by disguising the identity of the community.

THE USES OF THE PAST

The Yankee City project was carried out on a scale that can only be described as prodigious. It still ranks as the most intensive, exhaustive and expensive survey ever made of a small American city. The five published volumes occupy more than 1700 pages, with 208 tables, charts and maps. The field work extended over a period of several years, and required the labour of some 30 research assistants. The amount of data collected was staggering. Warner at one point refers to 'the millions of social facts' recorded; the study is replete with comments like this: 'All of the types of social structures and each of the thousands of families, thousands of cliques and hundreds of associations were, member by member, interrelated in our research.' 'Social personality cards' were compiled for all 17,000 members of the community, and interviews with local citizens occupied thousands of hours. Aerial photographs were made of Newburyport and environs; detailed questionnaires were administered at gas stations and lunch stands along the highway to discover what transients had stopped in the city and why; the plots of plays performed

by students and various social organizations were collected and sub-
jected to content analysis (which yielded the illuminating conclusion
that they all 'clearly conformed to the standards of the local group').
An observer was stationed at the movie house to 'see who attended
the pictures and with whom they attended', and newstands were
closely scrutinized to see how actual purchases conformed to professed reading preferences. (One must sympathize with the haunted
'upper upper' of Warner's Newburyport seeking furtively to pick up
his monthly *Esquire* under the cool stare of a Radcliffe graduate
student in sociology.) Death itself brought the citizen no more than
partial respite from surveillance: 'All the names of those persons
buried in the several cemeteries were gathered and compilations were
made of the members of several ethnic groups.'[8]

Virtually every aspect of Newburyport life was probed by the
Yankee City team—every aspect but one. Early in the first volume of
the series the authors casually commented: 'To be sure that we were
not ethnocentrically biased in our judgment, we decided to use no
previous summaries of data collected by anyone else (maps, handbooks, histories, etc.) until we had formed our own opinion of the
city.'[9] This was a remarkable and revealing utterance. To consult the
historical record would be to fall victim to the biases and preconceptions of the historian, a man necessarily 'unscientific', 'culture-
bound', 'ethnocentric'.

How, then were Warner and his associates to form their 'own
opinion' about the Newburyport past? At times Warner was inclined
to speak as if the past was simply irrelevant. He was contemptuous of
the historical school in anthropology; the merely 'ethnological or
temporal aspects of social behaviour' were of much less interest to
him than 'the scientific problems of explanation of the facts by classification and their interpretation by the formulation of laws and
principles.'[10] 'The facts', in this context, meant the facts visible in the
present.

It was quite impossible, however, for the Yankee City researchers
to avoid making assumptions about what Newburyport has been
like prior to their arrival on the scene; the reasons they gave for
selecting Newburyport as a research site included a host of historical
assumptions. They sought a small community which was 'above all a
well-integrated community'. It was to be self-contained, as insulated
as possible from 'disruptive' influences emanating from large cities
undergoing 'rapid social change'. Its population was to be 'predominantly old American', and it was to have 'developed over a long
period of time under the domination of a single group with coherent
tradition'. Newburyport, Warner took for granted, was such a city,
one whose 'Puritan tradition' remained 'unshattered', one whose

'social superstructure remained very much what it had been at the end of the War of 1812.'[11]

How did Warner decide that Newburyport met this rather unusual set of specifications? He found out 'scientifically', by direct observation of the image of the past held by present members of the community. This seemed a plausible procedure for men determined to 'use the techniques and ideas which have been developed by social anthropologists in primitive society in order to obtain a more accurate understanding of an American community.'[12] Warner came to Newburyport after three years of observing a tribe of Australian aborigines, a people without a written history. In a community without written records, the dead exist only in the minds and deeds of the living; there history survives only as tradition, ritual, myth, 'remembered experiences . . . newly felt and understood by the living members of the collectivity.'[13]

Rarely is the student of a primitive community able to find sources that allow him to penetrate beneath this tissue of myths; much of the past is irrevocably lost. The modern social investigator, however, need not remain entirely at the mercy of such subjective data. He may ask not only 'what is remembered of things past?' but also 'what was the actual past?'[14] The historical record available to him, it need hardly be said, is not pure, disembodied Truth; even the simple factual information it contains was gathered by men whose interests and passions coloured their perceptions, men who were 'culture-bound'. The point to be underscored, though, is that this record may be read in a way that allows us to discriminate, at least to some degree between the mythic past and the actual past.

Warner eventually became aware of this crucial distinction. The last of the Yankee City volumes, published long after the others (1959), includes a lengthy and perceptive analysis of the image of the Newburyport past presented in the pageants staged during the tercentenary celebration of 1935. By utilizing historical sources Warner was able to detect and interpret some interesting discrepancies between the real past and the 'history' portrayed in the pageants, which was what community leaders 'now *wished* it . . . were and what they wished it were not. They ignored this or that difficult period of time or unpleasant occurrences or embarrassing group of men and women; they left out awkward political passions; they selected small items out of large time contexts, seizing them to express today's values.'[15]

Regrettably, however, a similar indictment must be returned against the first four volumes of Warner's own study. 'Where truth ends and idealization begins cannot be learned,' the authors of *The Social System of the Modern Factory* tell us.[16] This was not a limitation imposed by the absence of historical evidence; it was the result of Warner's own methodological commitments. In this instance and in many others his interpretations rested on assumptions about the past which were demonstrably false. Warner's unwillingness to consult the historical record and his complete dependence on materials susceptible to anthropological analysis—the acts and opinions of living members of the community—served to obliterate the distinction between the actual past and current myths about the past. Thus, the Yankee City investigators' determination to escape the ethnocentric biases of culture-bound history led them to accept uncritically the community's legends about itself—surely the most ethnocentric of all possible views.

The ahistorical predilections of Warner and his associate produced a number of glaring misconceptions about the character of the community they studied. The static old 'Yankee' city whose 'social superstructure remained very much what it had been at the end of the War of 1812' was largely a creation of Warner's imagination. Every investigator admittedly sees the community he studies from a particular, limiting perspective; a degree of subjectivity is perhaps inescapable in treating a complex social object. But, whatever the bounds of legitimate subjectivity, the Yankee City series far exceeds them. As late as the 1930's, according to Warner, the 'Puritan tradition' of Yankee City remained 'unshattered', for the community's population was happily still 'predominantly old American'. But in point of fact the population of Newburyport had ceased to be predominantly 'old American' more than half a century before the Yankee City team began its labours! The effects of mass immigration, the high birth rate of the newcomers, and the heavy migration of old residents from the community produced radical changes in the composition of the Newburyport population during the 1850–1880 period. By 1885, first- and second-generation immigrants constituted almost half of the city's population; their descendants and later immigrants together made up the overwhelming majority of the Newburyport population at the time of the Yankee City study. Furthermore, only a small minority of the 'Yankee' families remaining in the community in 1880 were actually from old Newburyport families. A comparison of local city directories for 1849 and 1879 provides a precise measure of the extent of this devastating change: little more than a *tenth* of the family names recorded in the directory of 1879 could be located in the first local directory 30 years before. The economic and social transformation the community underwent midway in the nineteenth century, when it became a bustling manufacturing city, effectively shattered the social structure of preindustrial Newburyport. The Federalist ethos lingered on in a few old families, but the dominant values in this city of mobile newcomers bore no resemblance to Warner's description. It is true that the community's economic growth slowed after the Civil War, and that its total population was little larger in 1930 than it was in 1855, but to infer from these facts that Newburyport was a static, old Yankee community sealed off from the larger society was utterly mistaken.[17]

These misconceptions about the community become more comprehensible when we realize that the key concepts of the study—class and ethnicity—were both based entirely on the opinion of Warner's local respondents, and were defined so as to render difficult any systematic study of the relations between subjective opinion and objective social reality. An 'ethnic', for example, was said to be a Newburyport resident who 'considered himself or was considered by' others to be an 'ethnic' and who 'participated in the activities' of an 'ethnic' association; any citizen who did not fulfil these two criteria, amazingly, Warner classified a 'Yankee'. Thus, a community in which immigrants, their children and grandchildren were an overwhelmingly majority could become, in Warner's mind, a city whose population was 'predominantly old American'.[18]

Not only did the Yankee City investigators accept uncritically the opinions of informants living in the community at the time; they tended to accept the opinion of informants from a particular social group with very special biases—Yankee City's 'upper uppers'. This group fascinated Warner; he devoted an inordinate amount of space to them, despite the fact that they constituted less than 2 per cent of the Newburyport population. The upper uppers were the few dozen prominent old Yankee families who presumably had enjoyed high status in the community for more than a century. In fact Warner overestimated the continuity and rootedness of even this tiny elite, as they themselves were wont to do; while each of his vivid 'composite drawings' of upper uppers depicted a family that had resided in the community for several generations, Warner's own questionnaires showed that at the time of the study fewer than 60 per cent of this group had been born in or near Newburyport, and that almost a quarter of them had been born outside of New England entirely.[19] These were the Yankee City families whose sense of subtle prestige distinctions was translated into Warner's famous theory that the community was stratified into six discrete prestige classes; this was the 'single group with a coherent tradition' whose eagerness to equate Newburyport history with their own history led Warner to believe that the community's 'social superstructure . . . remained very much what it had been at the end of the War of 1812' and to attribute the apparent stability of the Newburyport social order to the fictitious dominance of the 'Yankee'.[20]

INDUSTRIALIZATION AND THE BLOCKED MOBILITY THEORY

The American class sytem was becoming 'less open and mobility increasingly difficult for those at the bottom of the social heap,' Warner wrote in 1947. 'The evidence from Yankee City and other places in the United States,' it seemed to him, 'strongly' indicated that both manual labourers and their children enjoyed fewer opportunities to rise than was common in the nineteenth century; on the expanding frontier and in the idyllic craft structure of the nineteenth century city, social mobility had been 'certain', but the spread of the factory system had degraded the worker and had blocked the 'ladder to the stars.'[21] On the basis of his interpretation of 'the industrial history' of Newburyport in *The Social System of the Modern Factory*, Warner concluded that the 'traditional' American open class structure was becoming increasingly rigid; the 'blue print of tomorrow' drawn up in Yankee City included the growing likelihood that America would soon see 'revolutionary outbreaks expressing frustrated aspirations.'[22]

The historical event that inspired these dark forebodings was the strike which closed all the shoe factories of Newburyport in 1933 and eventually resulted in management recognition of the shoe worker's union. Warner portrayed this strike as a dramatic success, and argued that such a radical departure from the community's tradition of social peace and labour quiescence required elaborate explanation. The initial field interviews, Warner admitted, revealed that Newburyport citizens tended to think of the strike as a struggle over economic grievances provoked by the depression: 'Each man, owner and worker, and townsman, spoke his own brand of economic determinism.' But Warner found these answers superficial; there had been depressions, wage cuts and the rest in the city before, he observed, yet this was the first 'successful' strike. There had to be some 'secret' as to 'why the Yankee City workers struck and . . . why men in other cities strike.' That secret, Warner decided, lay 'beyond the words and deeds of the strike'; it could only be ferreted out by probing deeply into the evolution of the community's productive system.[23] A knowledge of history, he now seemed to concede, could supply deeper insight into an event in the present.

Warner began his excursion into the Newburyport past with a hymn to the Golden Age of the craftsman, when every youngster became an apprentice and every apprentice a master. The local youth was gradually trained in the complex skills of his calling, and eventually became 'an inextricable member of the honourable fraternity of those who made, and who knew how to make, shoes.' In this system, presumably, 'workers and managers were indissolubly interwoven into a common enterprise, with a common set of values.'[24] To strike was unthinkable. The workman held a respected place in the community, and there was little social distance between him and the men for whom he worked. Economic power was concentrated at the local level, and the age-graded skill hierarchy of the craft assured maximum so-called mobility opportunities.

One day, however, the serpent 'mechanization' entered this Eden:

> The machine took the virtue and respect from the worker, at the same time breaking the skill hierarchy which dominated his occupation. There was no longer a period for young men to learn to respect those in the age grade above them and in so doing to become self-respecting workers. The 'ladder to the stars' was gone and with it much of the structure of the 'American Dream'.[25]

The shoe industry, Warner argued, underwent a technological revolution that shattered the craft order and destroyed local economic autonomy. The Newburyport labourers' sudden decision that a union was necessary to defend their rights was an inescapable consequence of this revolution. The growth of giant factories controlled by absentee owners opened up a vast social gulf between worker and manager. The steady encroachment of the machine rendered all manual skills useless; there resulted a sharp 'break in the skill hierarchy'. The status of all labouring jobs became equally degraded, and opportunities to rise into supervisory and managerial posts were eliminated. The 'secret' behind the upsurge of union support in 1933 was thus a series of fundamental changes in the productive system, which separated the shoe workers from the community, blocked the mobility opportunities they had once enjoyed, and inspired a new sense of labour solidarity and class consciousness.

This portrait of a community in crisis, of course, represents a stunning reversal of the image of Newburyport presented in earlier volumes of the Yankee City series. The reader may well wonder if there were *two* Yankee Cities; the research for *The Social System of the Modern Factory* might almost have been conducted in another community. The placid New England town Warner selected for investigation because of its extraordinary continuity and stability suddenly became the site of a study in social disorganization and class conflict.[26]

Warner's new interest in historical change and his determination to present a dynamic analysis of the impact of larger social forces on Yankee City was commendable. Unhappily, however, his account of the evolution of Newburyport from 'the simple folk economy of the earliest community' to the 1930's grossly distorted the city's actual history; it is a classic example of the old American habit of judging

the present against a standard supplied by a romantic and sentimental view of the past. The sweeping conclusions about the American class structure he drew from this case study are not in accord with
the Newburyport evidence, nor do they square with the findings of
recent mobility studies conducted in other communities.

As an attempt to explain the shoe strike of 1933, *The Social System
of the Modern Factory* can be quickly dismissed. This strike did not in
fact represent as radical a departure from community traditions as
Warner believed. 'Everyone in management and labour agreed that
the strike could not have happened' in the good old days, Warner
reports, but strikes *had* taken place in Newburyport—in 1858, in
1875, and a good many times since.[27] The strike of 1933 was distinctive only in that it was more successful than previous strikes, and not
very much more successful at that. As Handlin pointed out, the union
asked for a closed shop and a 10 per cent wage increase, but it won
simple recognition and no raise. And within three years the union
had lost out in one of the two factories still open.[28] The events of
1933, therefore, were not unprecedented, and massive changes in the
community need not be invoked to explain them.

Even if this be doubted, Warner's explanation of the strike is wholly
unsatisfactory, because the causes to which he attributed the supposedly drastic changes of the 1930's were fully operative in Newburyport several decades before the events they presumably explain.
Once upon a time, the Newburyport economy was organized along
craft lines; labour was content, social mobility was 'certain', to strike
was unthinkable. Warner was exceedingly vague as to the actual dates
of this idyllic craft age, but he assumed that memories of it were alive
in the minds of the strikers of 1933, and one chart made it appear that
craft and apprenticeship relations prevailed in local shoe production
until 'approximately World War I.'[29] The vagueness is not accidental, for the craft order portrayed in this volume was but a Never
Never land conjured up by the author. Not a shred of evidence pertaining to Newburyport itself is cited in support of this account; none
could be. If one goes back as far as 1800, one can indeed find evidence
of a well-integrated craft order in Newburyport, but its outstanding
features were not equality and mobility but hierarchy, religiously-
sanctioned elite rule, and institutionalized deference of the lower
classes.[30] And, in any case, the craft order had virtually disappeared
in Newburyport and industrial cities like it long before the 19th
century drew to a close without producing a powerful union movement, much less 'revolutionary outbreaks expressing frustrated
aspirations.'

Well before 1880 the Newburyport economy was dominated by
large textile and shoe firms. Production was highly mechanized in

both industries; all of the textile mills and some of the shoe factories were already controlled by absentee owners.[31] Factory labourers found no inviting 'ladder to the stars' before them; in the substantial sample of workers and their sons I studied for the 1850–1880 period, there was not a single instance of mobility into the ranks of management or even into a foreman's position! Since Warner failed to present any quantitative evidence to substantiate his assertions about the supposed decline in mobility rates, no detailed comparison of mobility rates in Newburyport in the 1850–1880 period with those in the 1930's can be made.[32] Extensive comparisons between my own findings concerning the intra-generational and inter-generational occupational mobility of unskilled labourers in nineteenth century Newburyport and mobility rates in several other twentieth century American communities, however, provide no support at all for Warner's claim that to rise 'from the bottom of the social heap' has become increasingly difficult in modern America. Instead, both types of upward mobility seem to have become somewhat less difficult over the past century.[33]

Nor is Warner's stress on the importance of absentee ownership confirmed by the history of the community. Several of the Newburyport plants were controlled by outside capitalists in this early period; this was a common pattern in many American industries from the very beginning of industrialization. And, more important, labour-management relations in the firms still in local hands were not in fact characterized by the happy solidarity Warner attributes to them, local mythology to the contrary notwithstanding. Whether the Yankee Protestant mill-owner lived on High Street or in Boston could have mattered little to his Irish-Catholic employees, whose willingness or unwillingness to strike was governed by more tangible and impersonal considerations.

The clue to these errors, I believe, lay in the fact that Warner's newfound appreciation of history did not lead him to any critical awareness of what constituted historical *evidence*. Though he cited a few secondary historical accounts that were tangentially relevant to his analysis, Warner derived the main outlines of his romantic interpretation of 'the industrial history of Yankee City' from his informants in the community in the 1930's. That this set of myths flourished in the city is indeed a social datum of great interest (though one might well be sceptical about how widespread these attitudes really were, given Warner's initial admission that most local residents viewed the strike as a simple and familiar contest over wage grievances). To comprehend the function of myths like these in the social struggles of the present, however, is impossible when they are taken for an accurate description of past social reality and used as the foundation for an ambitious theory of social change in industrial society.

The distortions that pervade the Yankee City volumes suggest that the student of modern society is not free to take his history or leave it alone. Interpretations of the present requires a host of assumptions about the past. The real choice is between explicit history, based on a careful examination of the sources, and implicit history, rooted in ideological preconceptions and uncritical acceptance of local mythology.

NOTES

1 Edward Hallett Carr, *What is History?* New York: Knopf, 1962, p. 84.
2 For a useful discussion of the impact on historical writing of some recent developments in the social sciences, see two essays by H. Stuart Hughes: 'The Historian and the Social Scientist,' *American Historical Review*, 66 (October, 1960), pp. 20–46; 'History, the Humanities, and Anthropological Change,' *Current Anthropology*, 4 (April, 1963), pp. 140–145. Both of these have been reprinted in Hughes' book, *History as an Art and as a Science*, New York: Harper and Row, 1964.
3 For a historical critique of ahistorical social science, see Barrington Moore, Jr., *Political Power and Social Theory: Six Studies*, Cambridge: Harvard University Press, 1958, esp. ch. 4. For an excellent case study written from a similar point of view, see E. R. Leach, *Political Systems of Highland Burma: A Study in Kachin Social Structure*, Cambridge: Harvard University Press, 1954. Carl Degler's 'The Sociologist as Historian: A Look at Riesman, Whyte and Mills,' *American Quarterly*, 15 (Winter, 1963), pp. 483–497, raises some of the issues considered below, though I believe Degler's substantive conclusions to be mistaken.
4 Princeton: Princeton University Press, 1960; Harper Torchbook paperback edition, 1964.
5 The five Yankee City volumes were published as follows: vol. I, W. Lloyd Warner and Paul S. Lunt, *The Social Life of a Modern Community*, New Haven: Yale University Press, 1941; vol. II, W. Lloyd Warner and Paul S. Lunt, *The Status System of a Modern Community*, New Haven: Yale University Press, 1942; vol. III, W. Lloyd Warner and Leo Srole, *The Social Systems of American Ethnic Groups*, New Haven: Yale University Press, 1945; vol. IV, W. Lloyd Warner and J. O. Low, *The Social System of the Modern Factory*, New Haven: Yale University Press, 1947; vol. V, W. Lloyd Warner, *The Living and the Dead: A Study of Symbolic Life of Americans*, New Haven: Yale University Press, 1959. A one-volume abridgement of the series has recently been published by Yale University Press under the title *Yankee City* (1963). For a guide to other publications by Warner and his students, and to the critical literature as of 1953, see Ruth Rosner Kornhauser, 'The Warner Approach to Social Stratification,' in Reinhard Bendix and Seymour M. Lipset, *Class, Status and Power: A Reader in Social Stratification*, Glencoe, Ill.: The Free Press, 1953, pp. 224–254.
6 See, however, the penetrating reviews by historians Oscar Handlin and Henry F. May. Handlin reviewed vols. I and II of the Yankee City series in the *New*

England Quarterly, 15 (September, 1942), pp. 554–557; vol. III in the *New England Quarterly*, 18 (September, 1945), pp. 523–524; and vol. IV in *The Journal of Economic History*, 7 (June, 1947), pp. 275–277. May reviewed vol. IV for the *New England Quarterly*, 21 (June, 1948), pp. 276–277.

7 For a discussion of Newburyport's representativeness and the controversy provoked by Warner's claims, see Thernstrom, op. cit., pp. 192–206.

8 Warner and Lunt, *The Status System of a Modern Community*, p. 13; *Social Life of a Modern Community*, p. 90. These are but a few examples to suggest the monumental scale of the Yankee City venture. For a full account of 'The Field Techniques Used and the Materials Gathered,' see *Social Life*, pp. 38–75.

9 *Social Life*, p. 400.

10 Ibid., ch. 2.

11 Ibid., pp. 1–5, 38–39; Warner and Low, *The Social System of the Modern Factory*, p. 2.

12 *Social Life*, p. 14.

13 Warner, *The Living and the Dead*, p. 4.

14 Cf. Robert Bierstedt, 'The Limitations of Anthropological Methods in Sociology,' *American Journal of Sociology*, 54 (January, 1948), pp. 22–30; Handlin, review of vols. I and II of the Yankee City series, op. cit.

15 *The Living and the Dead*, p. 110.

16 *Social System of the Modern Factory*, p. 139.

17 See Thernstrom, op. cit., pp. 84–86, 167–168, 195–196.

18 Warner and Srole, *The Social Systems of American Ethnic Groups*, p. 28. In his excellent study of Burlington, Vt., Elin L. Anderson found a similar myth, particularly among the upper classes. Anderson was unwilling to accept their claims without investigation, and discovered that in fact the 'pure' Yankee stock made up less than a third of the population; *We Americans: A Study of Cleavage in an American City*, Cambridge: Harvard University Press, 1937, ch. 3. For a similar finding in another Vermont community, see the unpublished study by Martin and Margy Ellin Meyerson described in David Riesman, *Faces in the Crowd: Individual Studies in Character and Politics*, New Haven: Yale University Press, 1952, p. 274.

19 *Social Life*, p. 209. 'Composite drawings' of 'fictive persons' play a crucial role in the Yankee City volumes. They occupy much space, and are often referred to in support of subsequent analyses. In these narrative sketches of local residents, 'no one actual individual or family in Yankee City is depicted;' instead, 'the lives of several individuals are compressed into that of one fictive person.' Warner did not hesistate to 'exclude all material which might indentify specific persons in the community, and . . . included generalized material whenever necessary to prevent recognition. The people and situations in some of the sketches are entirely imaginary,' *Social Life*, p. 129.

These sketches often seem illuminating. But have they any value as evidence? As the example cited in the text indicates, the method gives free rein to any biases and preconceptions the social scientist brings to his subject. Warner assures us that all the liberties taken with the original evidence were checked to see that 'the essential social reality' was not impaired. This is a commendable effort, but is it an adequate substitute for the ordinary safeguards which the historian imposes upon himself by guiding the critical reader to the body of evidence on which he bases his interpretation? *Quis custodiet ipsos custodes?* Warner's desire to 'protect' his subjects and to tell his story 'economically' is understandable, but he paid a rather heavy price to satisfy these requirements. All too rarely in the Yankee City series is the ordinary reader able to check the assertions of a composite drawing against data of genuine probative weight.

20 *Social Life*, p. 5; *Modern Factory*, p. 2. John P. Marquand's savage lampooning of Warner as the 'Malcolm Bryant' of *Point of No Return* should not be allowed to obscure the fact that the two men viewed the community from a very similar perspective. Marquand appears to have felt that Warner betrayed the confidence placed in him by Marquand himself and other upper-class respondents. Whatever the merits of this accusation, Warner's image of the community seems to have been shaped by this group to a striking degree.

21 *The Social System of the Modern Factory*, pp. 182–185, 87–89.

22 Ibid., ch. 10.

23 Ibid., pp. 4–7.

24 Ibid., p. 87.

25 Ibid., pp. 88–89.

26 A possible explanation of this startling shift in Warner's image of the community would be that events in Newburyport since the publication of the early volumes had given the Yankee City researchers a different perspective. The actual chronology of the series, however, does not support this suggestion. The strike took place in 1933; the volumes stressing the harmony of social relations in what was supposedly 'above all a well-integrated community' (*Social Life*, p. 38) appeared in the early 1940's; the factory study, whose dark fears of 'revolutionary outbreaks expressing frustrated aspirations' (*Modern Factory*, p. 185) were allegedly inspired by the 1933 strike, was published in 1947. A better explanation may be that Warner, though he never replied to his critics overtly, was stung by the charge that the Yankee City he portrayed was static, 'trendless,' and thus entirely unrepresentative of changing industrial America. Certainly this criticism could never be made of *The Social System of the Modern Factory*, for here Warner pursued trends with a vengeance, elaborating not only the national but the 'world implications' of the dramatic changes he now perceived taking place in Newburyport.

27 *Modern Factory*, p. 5.

28 Handlin, op. cit.

29 *Modern Factory*, chart i, p. 65.

30 See Thernstrom, op. cit., pp. 34–42, for a discussion of the craft order of pre-industrial Newburyport. In the Middletown volumes, Robert and Helen Lynd offered a more convincing sketch of the craft order and a more sophisticated version of the blocked mobility theory. For some critical reflections on their analysis, see ibid., pp. 214–216.

31 It is ironic that Warner, in discussing the idyllic craft order in shoe manufacturing, alludes to the efforts of the Knights of Crispins to preserve stringent apprenticeship requirements and to prevent the use of 'green hands' in the post-Civil War decade. Not only had the Knights everywhere lost this crucial struggle more than half a century before the 'successful' Newburyport strike; it was precisely in Newburyport that the craft order was so weak as to permit capitalists from the great shoe centre, Lynn, to set up 'runaway shops' as a means of avoiding 'Crispin trouble.'

32 In *The Social Systems of American Ethnic Groups* Warner did attempt to supply quantitative data about social mobility in Newburyport, and his effort to analyse historically the occupational and residential mobility patterns of local ethnic groups was not completely unfruitful. But because he believed that the essence of class was *prestige*, Warner was too predisposed against objective indices to use them properly. See Thernstrom, op. cit., pp. 236–238, for a detailed critique of the mobility study reported in *The Social Systems of American Ethnic Groups*.

33 See Thernstrom, op. cit., pp. 202–203, 216–221.

PART VII

The Sociology of Community—
Appraisals of the Field

CHAPTER 27

The Sociology of Community—
Appraisals of the Field

INTRODUCTION

More than any other methodological technique, community studies typically employ that of participant observation. The fact that community sociologists have usually gone, even if only for a short time, to live in a community and have shared some of the experiences of some of the inhabitants of the locality in which they are interested accounts for the vividness of many of the resulting monographs. This sharing of experience is not, however, conducive to the supposed ideal detachment of the scientist. Thus, whilst community studies have been plundered for source materials for some of the most influential theoretical contributions in other fields of sociology, they have also attracted the derision of other sociologists, summed up by Ruth Glass, that they are 'the poor sociologist's substitute for the novel'.[1]

It is not too difficult to see the basis of her accusation. Participant observation by one or a few research workers lends itself to a degree of subjectivity, and even downright idiosyncracy and eccentricity, which many find intolerable. This is particularly unfortunate in an area such as that of community studies, since they are by definition micro-sociological studies, which to some degree must be cumulative and replicable if they are to contribute to an understanding of society as a whole. In particular, the sheer innumeracy of many community studies, a simple lack of figures, has hindered attempts at comparability. This is particularly inexcusable in view of the wealth of statistical data in some of the earlier studies. It also has certain problematical consequences for the researchers' data, not the least of which is how reliable and valid they are. An observational, rather than a statistical or experimental method, means that the usual procedures of control, verification and reliability are quite different from those of, for example, survey research or small group experiments. The best community studies, however, are eclectic, utilizing whole batteries of techniques over and above the central one of observation. These allow internal checks upon the validity and representativeness of data resulting from participant observation.[2] Nevertheless, although community studies have some clear advantages in bringing the researcher closer to the interconnections of the data, idiosyncratic and non-comparable monographs do tend to be produced as a result. Justifiable attempts to synthesize disparate studies and to elicit the underlying social processes which they seek to analyse are therefore fraught with difficulties.

For example, Plowman, Minchinton and Stacey's paper[3] is an insightful and ambitious attempt at systematic inter-community comparison which illustrates both the potential gains of the comparative approach and the ever-present difficulties. They survey twenty-one British community studies, containing data collected between 1946 and 1959. Their chief concern is with status and they conclude that there is 'evidence for the existence both of systems of local social status and of forms of local social status not constituting systems'. Local status systems tend to be 'traditional' in Weber's terms, but non-traditional status does not consist of a single system— 'it is an unorganized set of levels'. These are termed 'interactional' and 'attributional' status respectively. The derivation of these two concepts is highly suggestive for the further analysis of local social systems, particularly in localities (such as 'commuter' villages[4]) where the attributional status of newcomers impinges on a local interactional status system. Unfortunately, however, there have been few subsequent studies, due to something of a hiatus in British community studies during the 1960's, which have taken the analysis of local status any further along these lines.

This kind of exercise in surveying a wide range of community studies is not only useful in directing subsequent research efforts to areas of ignorance or controversy, but it is also helpful in structuring a rather amorphous field. Frankenburg[5], for example, has attempted this for British community studies, incorporating a number of important studies that appeared after the publication of Plowman, Minchinton and Stacey's paper. Simpson's paper, reprinted below, is mainly concerned with developments in the United States. In addition to providing a useful framework for the consideration of the sociology of the community, its wealth of footnotes add up to a serviceable bibliography.

The final paper by Arensberg and Kimball provides a critique of previous attempts at synthesization—notably by Stein and Frankenberg. It is at once an overview of the theoretical orientations which have underpinned preceding studies and a guide to the directions in which the sociological study of community might move. Certainly in Britain at least, there is room for a renewed interest in community studies. Whilst it is clear that one cannot ignore the particular configuration of social institutions that has resulted from the unique history of a particular community, there is, nevertheless, as Arensberg and Kimball point out, a great deal to be gained from using the community as a laboratory for the empirical study of a particular sociological problem. By utilizing new research techniques and, of equal importance, by a greater understanding of the limitations and possibilities of community studies, there is no reason why such studies should continue to be stultified by charges of abstracted empiricism or idiosyncracy.

NOTES

1 Glass, R., 'Conflict in Cities', in de Reuck, A. and Knight, J. (eds.), *Conflict in Society* (London: Churchill, 1966, p. 148).
2 For a more detailed consideration of these problems see Bell, C. and Newby, H., *Community Studies* (London: Allen and Unwin, 1972), especially Chapter Three.
3 Plowman, D. E. G., Minchinton, W. E. and Stacey, M.: 'Local Social Status in England & Wales', *Sociological Review*, 10, 2, 1962.
4 Such analysis has been carried out, though without consideration of the concepts of interactional and attributional status, by, for instance, R. E. Pahl in *Urbs in Rure* (L.S.E. Geographical Papers, No. 2, 1965), and M. Elias and J. L. Scotson in *The Established and the Outsiders* (London: Frank Cass, 1965).
5 See Frankenberg, R., 'British Community Studies: Problems of Synthesis' in Banton, M. (ed.), *The Social Anthropology of Complex Societies* (London: Tavistock Publications, 1966). Also *Communities in Britain* (Harmondsworth: Penguin Books, 1966).

CHAPTER 28

Sociology of the Community: Current Status and Prospects*

Richard L. Simpson

Community-centred research covers a broad range of topics. In such a large and diverse field, it is helpful to take stock occasionally. This paper is an attempt to assess the present status and prospects of community sociology by identifying and evaluating some main varieties of current efforts in the field.

In the sociological study of communities it is possible to identify three principal approaches or research foci. First, there are what might be called studies of *life in communities*. These are not really studies of communities as such, but of social life which happens to take place and be studied within community settings. Studies of social mobility, for example, often use cities as sources of their samples of workers—one thinks of Natalie Rogoff's Indianapolis mobility study[1] and of Lipset and Bendix's study of mobility in Oakland, California,[2] among others—but the object of study is not the community but its occupational structure, or its workers. Rural sociology offers similar examples, in which the behaviour under examination takes place within a specified community which provides a sample of respondents, but the community as such is not the object of inquiry.

A second kind of community-oriented research is research on *social life as affected by community settings*. A sociologist might, for example, be interested in understanding juvenile delinquency, and he might conclude that some kinds of urban neighbourhoods have characteristics which cause high rates of delinquency.[3] Or he might study race relations as influenced by residential segregation and by the interracial contacts taking place where racial enclaves meet.[4] In this second kind of research, behaviour is explicitly explained on the basis of community characteristics, but the community as such still is not the object of study.

The third kind of research can genuinely be called *sociology of the*

* Reprinted with permission of the author and publisher from *Rural Sociology*, Vol. 30, No. 2 June, 1965, pp. 127–149.

community. The community as such and its characteristics are the objects of study. It is with this kind of community sociology that this paper is concerned, not because the other two research foci are any less valuable, but to keep the topics to be covered within reasonable bounds. *Sociology of the community*, in turn, lends itself to a classification of approaches. We shall identify and discuss three such approaches which deal, respectively, with (1) communities as wholes, (2) communities as types, and (3) social processes and dimensions which are specific to the community and which distinguish it as a sociological category from other kinds of social structures.

RESEARCH ON COMMUNITIES AS WHOLES

Various holistic research emphases have in common the effort to understand the community as a totality. This does not mean that to be holistic one must try to describe everything, but it does mean that one should regard the community as an integrated whole and seek to understand what keeps it that way. Let us examine some varieties of holistic community research.

Community Ethnography: Description of the Round of Life

The anthropological tradition has produced many valuable case studies of American community cultures. The Middletown studies [5] may still be the most notable of these, even though subsequent researchers have been able to make use of improved research techniques and insights. The most obvious limitation these total community studies impose is that they can be made only in relatively small communities, where fewer and fewer of our people live. But it is still possible to study subcommunities within the big cities. [6] Some of the finest of the early Chicago studies were of this type, and include Wirth's study of the ghetto [7] and Zorbaugh's *The Gold Coast and the Slum*. [8] Subcommunity studies since the 1940's have paid even closer attention to ways in which subcommunities fit into the larger community matrix. Examples are Drake and Cayton's *Black Metropolis*, [9] Whyte's *Street Corner Society*; [10] works by J. Kenneth Morland and Hylan Lewis on the mill village and the Negro subcommunity of 'Kent' in South Carolina; [11] and still more recently, Herbert J. Gans's *The Urban Villagers*, on an Italian-American area in Boston. [12]

In a sense, the social diversity of modern communities does not prevent holistic analysis of fairly unified cultures as long as sub-communities rather than total communities are studied. But in addition to diversity of culture, modern communities large and small are characterized by an expansion in social scale. [13] The social relationships even of villagers extend far beyond the immediate localities where they live. More fundamentally, the forces which integrate modern communities are likely to lie in organizations, both private and governmental, centred outside the community, and any analysis which fails to take account of this has not really analysed the community social system as a whole.[14] Vidich and Bensman, in their study of an upstate New York village and township, build their analysis around this problem, showing how the local community is dependent on decisions made by outside organizations.[15] But if the integration of a community's activities is accomplished from outside, and if the community is divided into subcultural groups and special-interest groups which have relations, separately, to outside organizations but not to each other, it may be questionable whether a modern community *is* a unified whole in any real sense except that of geography. The moral may be that if the chief assumption of the holistic approach, that of the community as a unified whole, has become inaccurate, we should not put all our eggs in this basket though we need not give up the endeavour entirely.

Another difficulty with community ethnographies is that they tend to be noncumulative: each one is a case study of a single community. They usually show little attempt to build explicit theory, though one investigator may use concepts and insights developed by his predecessors. The answer to this charge is that many individual case studies can be drawn upon as sources of data for comparative analysis, and this can be cumulative and can lead to the establishment of generalizations about different kinds of communities. Maurice Stein, in his *The Eclipse of Community*,[16] for instance, shows that the work of Park and the early Chicago school, of the Lynds in Middletown, and of Warner and Low in their study of the Yankee City shoe strike reveal, respectively, the effects of urbanization, industrialization, and bureaucratization—three distinct processes which are hard to separate in a study of a single case because they tend to be found together empirically, but can be separated analytically by examining a wide range of studies.

Stratification Studies

These are anthropological in inspiration but focus on structural divisions of the community into social classes. In addition to describing the way of life in each class, they describe the relations between the classes. There have been many such studies, the best known probably being those by Warner[17] and by Hollingshead.[18] Recently Vidich and Bensman[19] have made a theoretical improvement over earlier stratification analyses by arguing that if classes are to be conceived as real entities—as status groups, to use Weber's term[20]—they must be conceived as two-dimensional rather than as a simple hierarchy. Vidich and Bensman note that communities have status groups which differ markedly in values and behaviour though they may be equal in social rank; leaders of the town and gown segments of a college town would illustrate this phenomenon. Accordingly, Vidich and Bensman arrange their classes vertically, by social rank, and also horizontally, by dominant values and behaviorial orientations. Taking this cue, perhaps future students should distinguish at the very least what Miller and Swanson[21] call the entrepreneurial and bureaucratic segments of the community. The nonvertical dimension of social class has been a central fact of history. The struggle between aristocracy and bourgeoisie, and the shift from a self-employed to a salaried middle class, are only two examples. It is time for sociologists to incorporate this commonplace knowledge into their systematic analyses.

The community stratification approach has died down somewhat. No stratification study in the past fifteen years has created nearly the stir in the field that followed the Warner and Hollingshead reports. Lenski[22] showed some years ago that people do not agree on the number of classes in a community; Lenski, Landecker, and others have shown that the different status attributes of an individual are often inconsistent with each other, so that the class placement of individuals is often ambiguous,[23] many writers have questioned the adequacy of Warner's and (by implication) Hollingshead's research methods.[24] These criticisms have won wide acceptance among sociologists. No one, however, seems to have produced a better general treatment of community stratification if we may judge by the decisions on topical coverage made by the writers of textbooks. Quite commonly the stratification chapter of an introductory textbook will indicate that no clear-cut stratification system exists in American communities, but will then present the Warner scheme in rich detail anyway.

If not much has developed in community stratification analysis except criticism for more than fifteen years, the reason may be that the traditional stratification approach becomes less applicable as the society becomes more urban and heterogeneous. The traditional approach assumes that the community as such has a class structure which unambiguously includes all or nearly all inhabitants, that people use the community as a reference group in their status-striving, and that most people agree on the criteria of rank and can classify each other by them. None of these assumptions is as true of cities as of small towns,[25] and none is as true in a society with diverse occupational and ethnic subcultures as in an occupationally and ethnically simple society. Therefore, while social ranking goes on in cities just as elsewhere, it is less likely than in the communities of the past to produce genuine social classes in the sense of socially unified status groups distinguished from each other by social rank.[26]

STUDIES OF COMMUNITIES AS TYPES

The effort in this kind of research is to explain a wide range of behaviour on the basis of a simple classification scheme. Once a concept like *Gemeinschaft*, or folk, is invoked, everything falls into place. The typological tradition can claim a long history of distinguished names: Maine, Tönnies, Spencer, Durkheim, Redfield, Odum, Becker, and others. Recently McKinney and Loomis[27] have surveyed the history of typological concepts, extracted some unities from the great morass of different words meaning the same things, and made use of their own refinements in a study of a Latin American community.

In addition to its use in studies of rural and folk communities, this approach is represented in theorizing about the Chicago studies by Louis Wirth in his 'Urbanism as a Way of Life,'[28] which may be the most influential article ever to appear in a sociological journal. This approach reappears in literature of the 1950's by William H. Whyte, Jr., and others, on the suburbs as a new community type combining urban and folk qualities.[29]

Unfortunately, it is the essence of typologies that they exaggerate the facts on which they are based. Several bodies of empirical work suggest that in the community typological tradition, the exaggeration may have gone too far.

William Foote Whyte, in *Street Corner Society*,[30] and Lazarsfeld and his associates and followers in their research on the two-step flow of information from mass communication media to opinion leaders to rank and file,[31] have 'rediscovered the primary group' in the city. As Katz indicates in comparing the Katz and Lazarsfeld research with rural sociologist's studies of diffusion of new farm practices,[32] the primary group communication networks seem to work about the same in both urban and rural settings. Studies of urban family life by Sussman,[33] Litwak,[34] Willmott and Young,[35] and others and of informal sociability in cities by Greer and Kube,[36] by Smith, Form and Stone,[37] and by Gulick, Bowerman and Back[38] suggest that rumours of the death of primary group life in cities have been exaggerated. Most city dwellers do not live in isolation. In addition, Kollmorgen and Harrison have questioned whether rural communities in the United States, with their pattern of isolated farmsteads rather than rural villages, have ever been the close-knit groups which are sometimes portrayed by rural sociologists and other incurable romantics.[39] All of these writings have created doubt about our traditional notions of the supposed differences between the quality of rural and urban social life.

The idea of the suburb as a distinct community type has also been questioned. Berger's study of a California working-class suburb suggests that workingmen do not suddenly start behaving like middle-class organization men simply because they have moved to a suburb. The Republicanism, upward mobility, *kaffeeklatsching*, and organizational joining of which we have heard so much in writings on middle-class tract suburbs were not prevalent among Berger's suburban factory workers.[40] Ernest Mowrer's research on the family in Chicago suburbs shows that the folksy, primary group quality of suburban life disappears after a few years of the suburb's existence; people then go back to their relatives and their specialized interest groupings and start ignoring their neighbours, like urban apartment dwellers (and like many farmers).[41] Meyersohn and Jackson reach a similar conclusion in their comparison of gardening norms in an old and a new suburb; the kind of hyperconformity Whyte has decried was found only in the new suburb where it would presumably disappear once people had lived there long enough to develop outside ties and stop worrying about what the neighbours might think.[42] William Dobriner in a survey of literature and a comparative study of several New York suburbs gives evidence that class and ethnicity, not suburban residence *per se*, explain many of the characteristics often attributed to suburbs.[43] Dobriner also finds reason to believe that a homogeneous, brand-new middle-class suburb like Whyte's Park Forest—Dobriner's suburb was Levittown —becomes less homogeneous in age, class and ethnicity after a few years.[44] These writings have cast serious doubt on the explanation of suburbanites' behaviour on the basis of community type.

The strongest attack on the typological approach may have been Oscar Lewis's critique of Robert Redfield's work on the village of Tepoztlán.[45] Lewis asserted that the characteristics by which Redfield distinguished folk from urban communities can vary independently from each other, so that a place can be very urban in some ways and decidedly 'folk' in others. Lewis's Tepoztlán findings suggest that instead of types under which many variables are subsumed, the separate variables ought to be the focus of study. The variables usually incorporated in the folk-urban distinctions fall into several clusters referring to (a) *interaction networks*: for instance, extensity of the range of close acquaintances, intensity of primary group ties; (b) *values and mental orientations*: for example, cosmopolitanism *vs.* provincialism, rigidity *vs.* flexibility of outlook, moral absolutism *vs.* moral relativism or tolerance, degree of attachment to traditional beliefs and resistance to changing them; and (c) *quality of interaction*: for example, intrinsic *vs.* extrinsic motivation to enter into interaction, expressivity *vs.* manipulativeness of orientation to other people. Parson's pattern variables[46] are a refinement of typological ideas into variables expressing the ways in which people relate to one another when they interact.

A good procedure might be to split up the global notions of the typologies into separate variables, examine their interrelationships through research, and then, insofar as possible, put them back together into theoretically coherent basic variables and perhaps (if the research findings warrant it) into new typologies. In this way the value of the typological tradition would be retained without our having to assume relationships which have not been demonstrated and may not exist. For example, instead of saying that in a folk community people lack secondary relationships, are provincial, and are resistant to innovation, the sociologist can take these characteristics as variables for research and see if they are in fact related. Does a lack of social contacts beyond the immediate primary group make people provincial? Do a provincial outlook and a lack of attachment to reference groups beyond the local community make people resistant to social change? These questions are raised in Daniel Lerner's study of modernization in the Middle East,[47] and also in the study by Emery and Oeser on the acceptance of innovations by Australian farmers.[48] Both of these studies try to see whether exposure to urban and nonlocal stimuli actually does broaden people's frames of reference, and whether a broadened frame of reference makes them more willing to accept change. (Both studies find that the answer to both questions is Yes.) These studies use insights from the typological tradition without trying to explain everything on the basis of global 'types'; for example both find great variation in the behaviour of different individuals within the same communities, one of them (Lerner's) quite backward and 'folklike'. These studies carry the process urged above half way; the variables are split up for use in research but are not recombined. Another use of typological characteristics as variables is that by Freeman and Winch.[49] They show that eight polar typological characteristics form a Guttman scale, which suggests that the characteristics change from folk to 'modern' in a predictable order as societies become increasingly complex.

A difficulty in the kind of revised approach we are suggesting is that it ultimately requires comparative community study, and in this kind of research it is not easy to isolate the variables empirically once the conceptual distinctions among them have been made. The logic of comparative study is the same as that of survey research, but surveys of samples of individuals are easier than comparative community studies. When it takes months or years to study a single small community properly, how can anyone get data on hundreds of communities so that their characteristics can be cross-tabulated to discover whether features of given communities are causally or only fortuitously found together? One answer is to use sources of comparative material like the Human Relations Area Files, or to do the same sort of comparative analysis less systematically but still using other people's work as data, as Stein did in *The Eclipse of Community*.[50] But the other people may not have gotten the data you need, because they may not have had your research question in mind. We will probably continue to rely in community research on less complete comparability of data than survey research can attain in order to keep the richness and depth which only intensive case studies can bring, and to count heavily on the creativity of the comparative analyst to classify the variables which parade under different names in different studies.

STUDIES OF COMMUNITY-SPECIFIC PROCESSES

The identification and examination of processes and dimensions which are specific to the community in the sense that they are not found in other social structures provide much of the rationale for regarding 'community' as a distinct area of investigation apart from stratification, family life, and other aspects of behaviour that may occur in communities.

Defining the Community as a Social Realm

The concept of community has suffered, like some other sociological concepts, from vagueness stemming from the vernacular rather than scientific origin of the term. Some progress has been made, however, in winnowing a workable sociological meaning from the many everyday meanings of the term.[51]

Harold F. Kaufman has given a clear portrayal of the community as a distinct social realm.[52] He regards the community as a set of locality-oriented interactions: as goal-directed interaction processes engendered by the fact of people's common residence in a locality. Thus, family life is largely noncommunity, and only some aspects of stratification are 'community' phenomena while most aspects of local government are 'community' phenomena. This view is logically sound, is rather easily applied, and leaves less room than most definitions for hair-splitting about what is and what is not a community phenomenon.

Sutton and Kolaja have developed a notion of 'community' almost identical to Kaufman's, and have worked out techniques for applying the concept in research.[53] To them, as to Kaufman, 'community' is not identical with 'local society' but involves only 'the policy-deciding, self- or identity-maintaining social system of families residing in a particular area which confronts collectively problems arising from the sharing of the area.'[54] Like Kaufman, they feel that such a view of community will be helpful in focusing research on the dynamics of action rather than on the statics of structure. Sutton and Kolaja have illustrated the feasibility of their approach by developing a scheme to measure the 'communityness' of events reported in local newspapers. To give an over-simplified example, the meeting of a committee of local citizens to petition for improved air service to the local airport would be community-relevant, while an article advising gardeners to spray rose bushes for bugs every three weeks would not be community-relevant.[55] They illustrate the technique by applying it to newspaper articles, but there is no reason why it could not also be supplied to other kinds of data on community events. They suggest that the overall degree of 'communityness' of the events taking place within a locality, and of the events deemed newsworthy, may be an important characteristic of the community.

George Hillery has examined a number of ethnographic and sociological studies to see what attributes communities have in common—what social structures, institutions, and other character-istics are found in all of them.[56] He contrasts villages and cities with prisons and mental institutions, because the latter are sometimes called communities. He shows that the social organization of villages and cities is integrated around three foci—space, co-operation, family—which are quite different from the foci of organization in what Goffman has called 'total institutions'.[57] Hillery concludes that to equate vills (cities and villages) with total institutions and call them all, indiscriminately, 'communities' loses sight of much that is important about cities and villages. This work, like Hillery's earlier efforts to find agreement in the definitions of community used by different writers and his earlier analysis of community characteristics,[58] should go a long way toward clarifying the nature of the community as an object of study. Like the writings mentioned previously, it is, however, just a beginning. These writings bring greater conceptual clarity, but the ways in which community research will be improved thereby will still need to be demonstrated.

In addition to the problem of defining what they mean by the community, sociologists who wish to analyse communities and systems face the problem of determining community boundaries:

where one community stops and the next one starts. This is not much of a problem in very small towns, in peasant societies where people go out to the fields from a central village, or—for some purposes— in metropolitan suburbs where school district lines and psychological identifications coincide with political boundaries. It is a problem in rural areas where farm homes are widely spaced, and in cities, except for some of their ethnic enclaves.

Efforts to delineate rural community boundaries have met with fairly good success. Galpin's pioneering techniques[59] have been refined, brought up to date, and used by rural sociologists such as Sanderson,[60] Sanders and Ensminger,[61] and Mayo.[62] Despite the ingenuity of these efforts, some nagging problems remain. Mayo finds in a southern county that the white and Negro community boundaries do not coincide; presumably the same is true wherever two relatively segregated ethnic groups are interspersed in an area. Trade area boundaries may not coincide with boundaries based on other criteria, and even trade areas are not always unambiguous as the area boundaries may be different for different kinds of purchases. The areas identified by the usual techniques may not coincide with political boundaries, and the latter must be taken into account in many types of action programmes.

The situation is still more complex in cities. Several studies have concluded that urban residents do not agree on the names and boundaries of the subareas where they live.[63] Ross,[64] in a recent Boston study, finds that people do tend to agree on the names and boundaries of local areas, and that the names of areas have a status-ascriptive function but do not coincide with trade areas except for local convenience goods like groceries which people buy very close to home; the small neighbourhood rather than the urban subcommunity or natural area seems to be the meaningful trade area for groceries, drugs and the like. Early Chicago sociologists noted that even in the 1920's, urban natural areas were already losing ground to specialized interest groupings which cut across spatial boundaries.[65] Paul Hatt, finding the same sort of conflicting boundaries based on different criteria which have bedevilled the rural sociologists, felt that the concept of urban natural areas had no meaningful empirical referent and should be abandoned.[66] But sociologists writing in the late 1950's and early 1960's have argued that meaningful subcommunities do characterize large cities; they point to homogeneity of demographic characteristics[67] and to locally based organizations and community newspapers[68] as evidence of the vitality of urban subcommunities.

From these conflicting arguments and partially successful attempts to identify community boundaries, it seems that for most Americans, except small town dwellers and some suburbanites, 'community' has no hard and fast empirical referent. Interaction, organizational membership, psychological identification and various types of service mapping produce differing community or subcommunity boundaries. Some of the most successful efforts to delineate communities are not congruent with the emerging definition of the community as an arena of goal-directed locality-based interaction exemplified in the writings cited earlier by Kaufman and Sutton and Kolaja. Despite its inevitable difficulties, however, the problem is important for both social theory and social action, and therefore should not be abandoned. How can we analyse something we cannot even identify? And how can we succeed in action programmes which fail to take account of people's behaviorial and psychological definitions of reality? Perhaps we should continue to attack the problem with old methods, until better ones are devised. If these methods bring success in identifying communities, well and good; if they do not, perhaps the locality under study simply is not a community with meaningful boundaries, and we should leave the matter at that.

Community Power Structure and Decision-making

This is a community-specific phenomenon *par excellence* by the Kaufman and Sutton-Kolaja definitions. The topic has received great attention from sociologists and political scientists during the past decade, since Floyd Hunter's *Community Power Structure*[69] was published. Unfortunately the subject has been dealt with increasingly as a dispute over research methods and over the differing theoretical implications of the competing methods.[70]

Hunter and many others following him have used the 'reputational' technique: go into the community and ask knowledgeable people who the leaders are. This technique seems to imply a monolithic power elite theory of power, or at least studies using the reputational method have tended to report that small cliques are said to run communities. Exponents of the method, some of whom have made useful refinements of it, include Alexander Fanelli,[71] Robert Agger,[72] Delbert Miller,[73] William D'Antonio[74] and Charles Bonjean.[75]

Robert A. Dahl and various others, chiefly political scientists among whom Dahl's former graduate students at Yale are prominently in evidence, argue that the reputational method incorporates a self-fulfilling prophecy: the sociologist goes into a community and asks who the bosses are, then comes out with the conclusion that the community has bosses.[76] This group prefers the 'decisions' approach in which an issue is traced from inception to resolution to see who brought influence to bear, and how, at various stages. Students using the decisions approach have tended to find a wider distribution of power; on any important community decision many people enter into the process at one time or another, and different decision-making groups are involved depending on the issue, rather than the same small group deciding everything.[77] A difficulty with this technique is that it captures only the overt manifestations of power. Without allowing 'reputation' to enter the picture it is hard to observe that a man who says nothing and does nothing may nevertheless be wielding power if those who make the decision tailor their actions to suit what they think he would accept. Another difficulty, noted by Anton,[78] is that those interested in maintaining the *status quo* sometimes do so by preventing any 'issue' from coming up for resolution, as in the case of the village board described by Vidich and Bensman.[79] Both of these situations—the tailoring of decisions to meet the perceived wishes of people who do not become overtly involved, and the suppression of potential conflicts so that no overt issue or decision arises—will show up in reputations but not always in identifiable decision-making events.

The topic of community decision-making is plainly of the highest possible significance, as a practical matter and for the theory of community organization. Therefore, it is to be regretted that the subject has become embroiled in polemics. The sanest course of action may be to do what Elaine Burgess did in her study of Negro power structure in a North Carolina city.[80] She used both main techniques and demonstrated that they are complementary rather than competing if they are skilfully used; in her study each revealed facts the other might have missed and they did not contradict each other in any essential way. A similar eclectic approach is used by political scientists like Edward C. Banfield and James Q. Wilson, who go after the facts of urban power without becoming overly concerned about the claims and counter-claims of alternative research strategies.[81]

An obvious next step, not yet pursued very far in a systematic way, is to see how decision-making structures vary in accord with other community characteristics. This makes power structure the dependent variable in comparative community study. Some efforts have been made in this direction. Ernest A. T. Barth, reporting a study of ten Air Force Base host communities, finds a pyramidal elite structure in the large, stable communities; a diffuse structure in smaller, rapidly growing communities; and an amorphous and poorly integrated structure in small, static communities.[82] Barth's findings seem, superficially, to contradict the results of David Rogers's analysis of published studies of community power. Rogers concludes that the more differentiated the social structure of a community is, the less monolithic its elite will be;[83] and one might suppose that Barth's large communities would tend to be more socially differentiated than his smaller though growing communities. Perhaps community size and rate of growth—hence, degree of social differentiation and rate of differentiation—need to be distinguished as variables influencing the shape of community power structure.

Studies of industrial communities by Hart[84] and McKee[85] lend support to Roger's hypothesis that social differentiation leads to power differentiation. They report that in the heavy industrial cities of Windsor, Ontario and Lorain, Ohio, the local business leaders must share power with representatives of absentee-owned big business, labour and the Roman Catholic Church. Their conclusions suggest that Hunter may have been led into overgeneralization by the relatively slight development of competing interest groups in Atlanta in view of its size. Negroes were weak, at least when Hunter's field work was done; the city was rather solidly Protestant and lacked sizeable ethnic minorities other than Negroes; and organized labour was weak. Small wonder, even apart from his research method, that he found a more monolithic and business-dominated power structure than one might find in, for example, Detroit or Buffalo.

A related study is reported by Amos Hawley,[86] who presents evidence that a city with numerous high status people can get things done more effectively than one whose class structure is weighted toward the lower end of the scale. Specifically, Hawley finds that cities with large percentages of relatively high status people have had the best success in getting urban renewal programmes into operation, the reason (he feels) being their readily available sources of elite leadership. Combining the Rogers and Hawley conclusions, one might infer that effective democracy—conflict resolution—is most likely where there is a large but differentiated elite representing differing interests and able to bring them into active controversy so that something will be done to resolve differences of interest one way or another.[87]

These studies are a promising beginning. More work is needed to explain the structure and dynamics of power, using it as a dependent variable in comparative research rather than as something simply to be described in one community after another. Of single-community power structure descriptions we may have enough by now, except as data for comparative analysis.

Ecology, Old and New

The old Park and Burgess ecology with its concentric rings[88] was an extremely useful descriptive rubric for Chicago and some other cities. But its assumption of subsocial (biotic) competition as the determinant of urban spatial structure was challenged by a number of writers, Alihan's and Firey's critiques[89] probably being the best known. Its generality for the United States was questioned by the sector theory of Homer Hoyt[90] and the multiple nuclei theory of Harris and Ullman.[91] An even more fundamental blow was struck at the concentric zone hypothesis by writers like Gist,[92] the Dotsons[93] and Sjoberg,[94] who showed that urban patterning is drastically different in foreign and preindustrial cities; the wealthy, for example, tend to live in the centre of preindustrial cities. The concentric ring style of ecology has become passé and has been replaced by two main variants which avoid its problems.

One brand of ecology, though its proponents do not call it that, is the social area analysis of Shevky and Bell.[95] It proceeds from different theoretical considerations but is somewhat reminiscent of early Chicago ecology in its treatment of urban social areas. One might hazard the guess that the main utility of Shevky-Bell analysis will be as a methodological aid in controlling certain social variables—class, family life style, and ethnicity—which cluster in areas within which other variables can then be examined. It is a form of 'contextual analysis' with the Census Bureau providing the data to construct the contexts. Analysis of this kind would fit under this paper's rubric of 'social life as affected by community settings.'

Another variant, which is self-consciously ecological, is the work of Otis Dudley Duncan and his associates and students. This deals with spatial attributes and distributions of social phenomena in the city. It makes use of available census data and modern statistical techniques to examine relationships among variables referring to aggregative community properties. Exponents of this brand of ecology besides Otis and Beverly Duncan include Leo F. Schnore,[96] Stanley Lieberson,[97] and Hal H. Winsborough.[98]

Duncan and his associates have strong ideas about ecology as an overall approach to sociology, very different from cultural, behavioral, social-psychological and traditional social organization approaches.[99] They castigate others who use cultural or social-psychological variables such as values or attitudes in their analysis. Fortunately, like many other exponents of special viewpoints, they do not always adhere rigidly to their own rules when they do research. For example, the Duncan report that clerical workers, despite their lower incomes, live in higher status areas than skilled craftsmen, and their explanation of this—though they avoid using the proscribed word—appears to be that clerical workers' values are different.[100] What the Duncan school's ban on cultural or social-psychological variables seems to boil down to, in practice, is that one should infer these variables indirectly from aggregative Census data instead of examining them directly by asking people questions about values or by observing behaviour at first hand.

Since these latter-day ecologists do not consistently adhere to their own strictures against the use of behavioral and cultural concepts in analysis, any more than did the early Chicago ecologists, their contributions to community sociology are already extensive, with the promise of more to come. They have focused attention on the importance of aggregative levels of analysis; they have developed, and used, highly efficient statistical techniques to deal with spatial distributions; and they have done pioneering work in comparative urban sociology and in the macro-analysis of national metropolitan structure.[101]

CONCLUDING REMARKS

Even this highly selective discussion of some leading kinds of community research makes it clear that the field is a broad one, and, if the rate of research activity is any sign, a healthy one. We will conclude with some evaluative remarks and suggestions.

First, comparative community analysis using variables and relationships among them should receive more emphasis than it has. In this way we can develop more theoretical propositions and test them and refine them on the basis of the tests. The logic ideally should be that of survey analysis, with variables controlled through cross-tabulation. This is less easily managed when the unit of observation is an entire community than when it is an individual with his attitudes and simple behavioral manifestations of them, but it should be kept in view as an ideal. If we comes as close to this as Max Weber did in his comparative analysis of societies—for example, in his *Protestant Ethic and the Spirit of Capitalism*, in which he roughly matched societies on social structure and technology and varied religion as an independent variable to explain economic systems as the dependent variable—then few will be inclined to criticize us for imperfection in our data.

For variables to examine in these kinds of studies, we can draw inspiration from the traditional typologies. These embody numerous distinct variables; Wirth mentions dozens in his characterization of urbanism.[102] Communities can be characterized in numerous ways derived from the folk-urban typologies and the ways in which these characteristics do and do not go together can be discovered, as grist for analysis, from available literature. Future ethnographic studies of single communities can be enriched if they have as an explicit goal the contribution they might make to comparative analysis.

Nevertheless, we should not abandon the traditional 'community study' as a type of research. Studies of communities in depth are not only the raw material for cross-community comparisons; they are valuable in themselves. Even if we take the construction of abstract theories as the major goal of sociology, an additional goal is to shed light on how people live, here and now, in a way that cannot be done without the insights of sociology. It is significant that a goodly number of community case studies have made their way into commercial paperback editions; this seems to indicate that the educated reading public outside the field accepts community studies as a contribution to social understanding in which sociologists excel in a distinctive way.

Some subjects which have customarily been investigated within single community contexts need not, however, be limited to this kind of research. Besides studying the power structures and class systems of individual communities, we need to classify them and explain them on the basis of other community characteristics. Some people, including Lloyd Warner himself,[103] have already attempted some of this, but the effort has not been carried forward systematically or cumulatively. Like sharpening the typological concepts, this is a task for comparative analysis.

Finally, we have made no mention of one very important and burgeoning activity of community sociologists: research and action programmes in community development.[104] We have left this area out of our discussion not because it is unimportant—clearly it is of major importance—but because it is, rather than a separate area of theoretical knowledge, an area in which different areas of knowledge intersect. Almost every one of the subjects of investigation mentioned earlier in this paper has some bearing on community development, though doubtless some more than others. Power structure, stratification, and networks of interpersonal influence would seem especially relevant. Like other practical concerns, community development programmes need to derive ideas from basic research; but in addition, they can contribute to basic knowledge if they are conducted and reported, as the best of them are, with this objective.

NOTES

1 Natalie Rogoff, *Recent Trends in Occupational Mobility* (New York: The Free Press, 1953).
2 Seymour Martin Lipset and Reinhard Bendix, *Social Mobility in Industrial*

Society (Berkeley and Los Angeles: University of California Press, 1959). This study includes analysis of effects of childhood community size on mobility opportunities, and therefore might be considered in part an example of our second-named research focus (below).

3 The best-known such study is reported in Clifford R. Shaw and Henry D. McKay, *Juvenile Delinquency and Urban Areas* (Chicago: University of Chicago Press, 1942).

4 For example, St. Clair Drake and Horace R. Cayton, *Black Metropolis*, vol. I (New York: Harper and Row, Publishers [Torchbook edition], 1962), pp. 174–213, esp. pp. 190–195.

5 Robert S. Lynd and Helen Merrel Lynd, *Middletown* (New York: Harcourt, Brace and World, 1929); Robert S. Lynd and Helen Merrell Lynd, *Middletown in Transition* (New York: Harcourt, Brace and World, 1937).

6 Holistic studies of urban subcommunities are urged by Conrad M. Arensberg, 'The Community Study Method,' *American Journal of Sociology*, LX (September, 1954), 109–124.

7 Louis Wirth, *The Ghetto* (Chicago: University of Chicago Press, 1928).

8 Harvey Zorbaugh, *The Gold Coast and the Slum* (Chicago: University of Chicago Press, 1929).

9 Drake and Cayton, op. cit.

10 William Foote Whyte, *Street Corner Society*, 2nd ed. (Chicago: University of Chicago Press, 1955).

11 J. Kenneth Morland, *Millways of Kent* (Chapel Hill: University of North Carolina Press, 1958); and Hylan Lewis, *Blackways of Kent* (Chapel Hill: University of North Carolina Press, 1955).

12 Herbert J. Gans, *The Urban Villagers* (New York: The Free Press of Glencoe, 1962).

13 The concept of scale was developed by Godfrey Wilson and Monica Hunter Wilson in *The Analysis of Social Change* (London: Cambridge University Press, 1945).

14 The dominance of local communities by outside organizations is shown in Albert Blumenthal, *Small-town Stuff* (Chicago: University of Chicago Press, 1932); and Kenneth MacLeish and Kimball Young, *Landaff, New Hampshire* (Washington, D.C.: Bureau of Agricultural Economics, 1942).

15 Arthur J. Vidich and Joseph Bensman, *Small Town in Mass Society* (Princeton, N. J.: Princeton University Press, 1958). See also Roland L. Warren, 'Toward a Typology of Extra-Community Controls Limiting Local Community Autonomy,' *Social Forces*, XXXIV (May, 1956), 338–341.

16 Maurice R. Stein, *The Eclipse of Community* (Princeton, N.J.: Princeton University Press, 1960), pp. 13–93.

17 The Warner studies include, among others, W. Lloyd Warner and Paul S. Lunt, *The Social Life of a Modern Community* (New Haven: Yale University Press, 1941); W. Lloyd Warner and Paul S. Lunt, *The Status System of a Modern Community* (New Haven: Yale University Press, 1942); W. Lloyd Warner and Leo Srole, *The Social Systems of American Ethnic Groups* (New Haven: Yale University Press, 1945); W. Lloyd Warner and J. O. Low, *The Social System of the Modern Factory* (New Haven: Yale University Press, 1947); W. Lloyd Warner and Associates, *Democracy in Jonesville* (New York: Harper & Row, Publishers, 1949); Allison Davis, Burleigh B. Gardner, and Mary R. Gardner, *Deep South* (Chicago: University of Chicago Press, 1941).

18 A. B. Hollingshead, *Elmtown's Youth* (New York: John Wiley & Sons, Inc., 1949).

19 Vidich and Bensman, op. cit.

20 Max Weber, 'Class, Status, Party,' in Max Weber, *From Max Weber: Essays in Sociology*, ed. and tr. by H. H. Gerth and C. Wright Mills (New York: Oxford University Press, 1946), pp. 180–195.

21 Daniel R. Miller and Guy E. Swanson, *The Changing American Parent* (New York: John Wiley & Sons, Inc., 1958).

22 Gerhard E. Lenski, 'American Social Classes: Statistical Strata or Social Groups?' *American Journal of Sociology*, LVIII (November, 1952), 139–144.

23 Gerhard E. Lenski, 'Status Crystallization: A Non-Vertical Dimension of Social Status,' *American Sociological Review*, XIX (August, 1954), 405–413; Werner S. Landecker, 'Class Boundaries,' *American Sociological Review*, XXV (December, 1960), 868–877.

24 Criticisms of the Warner approach are summarized and discussed in Ruth Rosner Kornhauser, 'The Warner Approach to Social Stratification,' in Reinhard Bendix and Seymour Martin Lipset (eds.), *Class, Status and Power* (New York: The Free Press, 1953), pp. 224–255. See also Milton M. Gordon, *Social Class in American Sociology* (Durham, N.C.: Duke University Press, 1958), pp. 85–123.

25 Gordon, op. cit. See also Neal Gross, 'Social Class Identification in the Urban Community,' *American Sociological Review*, XVIII (August, 1953), 398–404; Gregory P. Stone and William H. Form, 'Instabilities in Status: The Problem of Hierarchy in the Community Study of Status Arrangements,' *American Sociological Review*, XVIII (April, 1953), 149–162; and William H. Form and Gregory P. Stone, 'Urbanism, Anonymity, and Status Symbolism,' *American Journal of Sociology*, LXII (March, 1957), 504–514.

26 For a heuristic model of urban stratification which assumes an unambiguous rank order but does not assume clearly demarcated classes, see James M. Beshers, *Urban Social Structures* (New York: The Free Press, 1962), pp. 127–158. 'Horizontal' ethnic divisions are emphasized by Milton M. Gordon, *Assimilation in American Life* (New York: Oxford University Press, 1964); he expands on earlier analyses by Ruby Jo Reeves Kennedy, Will Herberg and Gerhard Lenski.

27 John C. McKinney and Charles P. Loomis, 'The Typological Tradition,' in Joseph S. Roucek (ed.), *Contemporary Sociology* (New York: Philosophical Library, 1958), pp. 557–582.

28 Louis Wirth, 'Urbanism as a Way of Life,' *American Journal of Sociology*, XLIV (July, 1938), 1–24.

29 William H. Whyte, Jr., *The Organization Man* (Garden City, N.Y.: Doubleday Anchor Books, 1957), pp. 295–434. See also Sylvia Fleis Fava, 'Suburbanism as a Way of Life,' *American Sociological Review*, XXI (February, 1956), 34–38. Prevailing views of the suburbs are discussed in William M. Dobriner, *Class in Suburbia* (Englewood Cliffs, N.J.: Prentice-Hall, Inc., 1963), pp. 5–28.

30 William Foote Whyte, op. cit.

31 See especially Elihu Katz and Paul F. Lazarsfeld, *Personal Influence* (New York: The Free Press, 1955); and Elihu Katz, 'The Two-Step Flow of Communication: An Up-to-Date Report on an Hypothesis,' *Public Opinion Quarterly*, XXI (Spring, 1957), 61–78.

32 Elihu Katz, 'Communication Research and the Image of Society: Convergence of two Traditions,' *American Journal of Sociology*, LXV (March, 1960), 435–440. On agricultural diffusion studies, see Everett M. Rogers, *The Diffusion of Innovations* (New York: The Free Press, 1962).

33 Marvin B. Sussman, 'The Isolated Nuclear Family: Fact or Fiction?' *Social Problems*, VI (Spring, 1959), 333–340; Marvin B. Sussman and Lee Burchinal, 'Kin Family Network: Unheralded Structure in Current Conceptualizations

of Family Functioning,' *Marriage and Family Living*, XXIV (August, 1962), 231–240.

34 Eugene Litwak, 'Occupational Mobility and Extended Family Cohesion,' *American Sociological Review*, XXV (February, 1960), 9–21; Eugene Litwak, 'Geographic Mobility and Extended Family Cohesion,' *American Sociological Review*, XXV (June, 1960), 385–394.

35 Michael Young and Peter Willmott, *Family and Kinship in East London*, (London: Routledge and Kegan Paul, 1957); Peter Willmott and Michael Young, *Family and Class in a London Suburb* (London: Routledge and Kegan Paul, 1960).

36 Scott Greer and Ella Kube, 'Urbanism and Social Structure: A Los Angeles Study,' in Marvin B. Sussman (ed.), *Community Structure and Analysis*, (New York: Thomas Y. Cromwell Company, 1959), pp. 93–112.

37 Joel Smith, William H. Form and Gregory P. Stone, 'Local Intimacy in a Middle-Sized City,' *American Journal of Sociology*, LX (November, 1954) 276–284.

38 John Gulick, Charles E. Bowerman and Kurt W. Back, 'Newcomer Enculturation in the City: Attitudes and Participation,' in F. Stuart Chapin, Jr., and Shirley F. Weiss (eds.), *Urban Growth Dynamics* (New York: John Wiley & Sons, Inc., 1962), pp. 315–358.

39 Walter M. Kollmorgen and Robert W. Harrison, 'The Search for the Rural Community,' *Agricultural History*, XX (March, 1946), 1–8. See also Walter L. Slocum and Herman M. Case, 'Are Neighbourhoods Meaningful Social Groups throughout Rural America?' *Rural Sociology*, XVIII (March, 1953), 52–59.

40 Bennett M. Berger, *Working Class Suburb* (Berkeley and Los Angeles: University of California Press, 1960).

41 Ernest R. Mowrer, 'The Family in Suburbia,' in William M. Dobriner (ed.), *The Suburban Community* (New York: G. P. Putnam's Sons, 1958), pp. 147–164.

42 Rolf Meyersohn and Robin Jackson, 'Gardening in Suburbia,' in Dobriner, *The Suburban Community*, op. cit., pp. 271–286.

43 Dobriner, *Class in Suburbia*, op. cit.

44 *Ibid.*, pp. 85–126. But see Reynolds Farley, 'Suburban Persistence,' *American Sociological Review*, XXIX (February, 1964), 38–47, for national data showing a tendency for the status levels of suburbs to persist.

45 Oscar Lewis, *Life in a Mexican Village: Tepoztlán Restudied* (Urbana: University of Illinois Press, 1951).

46 Talcott Parsons, *The Social System* (New York: The Free Press, 1951), pp. 46–51, 58–67, 101–112, *et passim*. See also Talcott Parsons, 'The Pattern Variables Revisited: A Response to Robert Dubin,' *American Sociological Review*, XXV (August, 1960), 467–483.

47 Daniel Lerner, *The Passing of Traditional Society* (New York: The Free Press, 1958).

48 F. E. Emery and O. A. Oeser, *Information, Decision, and Action* (Melbourne: Melbourne University Press, 1958).

49 Linton C. Freeman and Robert F. Winch, 'Societal Complexity: An Empirical Test of a Typology of Societies,' *American Journal of Sociology*, LXII (March, 1957), 461–466.

50 Stein, op. cit. The work of George A. Hillery, Jr., is another useful beginning in comparative community analysis. See especially his 'The Folk Village: A Comparative Analysis,' *Rural Sociology*, XXVI (December, 1961), 335–353; and 'Villages, Cities, and Total Institutions,' *American Sociological Review*, XXVIII (October, 1963), 779–791.

51 See especially George A. Hillery, Jr., 'Definitions of Community: Areas of Agreement,' *Rural Sociology*, XX (June, 1955), 111–124; and George A. Hillery, Jr., 'A Critique of Selected Community Concepts,' *Social Forces*, XXXVII (March, 1959), 236–242.

52 Harold F. Kaufman, 'Toward an Interactional Conception of Community,' *Social Forces*, XXXVIII (October, 1959), 8–17.

53 Willis A. Sutton, Jr., and Jiri Kolaja, 'Elements of Community Action,' *Social Forces*, XXXVIII (May, 1960), 325–331; Willis A. Sutton, Jr., and Jiri Kolaja 'The Concept of Community,' *Rural Sociology*, XXV (June, 1960), 197–203.

54 Sutton and Kolaja, 'Elements of Community Action,' op. cit., p. 325.

55 Sutton and Kolaja, *ibid.*, give less obvious examples and explain their classification of events on the basis of a formal scheme.

56 Hillery, 'Villages, Cities, and Total Institutions,' op. cit.

57 Erving Goffman, 'The Characteristics of Total Institutions,' in *Symposium on Preventive and Social Psychiatry* (Washington: Walter Reed Army Institute of Research, 1957), pp. 43–84.

58 Hillery, 'Definitions of Community: Areas of Agreement,' op. cit.; Hillery, 'The Folk Village: A Comparative Analysis,' op. cit.

59 Charles J. Galpin, *The Social Anatomy of an Agricultural Community*, (Madison: Wisc. Agr. Exp. Sta., Bull. 34, 1915).

60 Dwight Sanderson, *Locating the Rural Community* (Ithaca: Cornell University Press, 1939).

61 Irwin T. Sanders and Douglas Ensminger, *Alabama Rural Communities: A Study of Chilton County* (Montevallo: Alabama College, Quarterly Bulletin 136, 1940).

62 Selz C. Mayo, 'Testing Criteria of Rural Locality Groups,' *Rural Sociology*, XIV (December, 1949), 317–325; Selz C. Mayo and Robert McD. Bobbitt, 'Biracial Identity of Rural Locality Groups in Wake County, North Carolina,' *Rural Sociology*, XV (December, 1950), 365–366.

63 Roderick D. McKenzie, *The Neighborhood: A Study of Local Life in the City of Columbus, Ohio* (Chicago: University of Chicago Press, 1923); Svend Riemer, 'Villagers in Metropolis,' *British Journal of Sociology*, II (January, 1951), 31–43; Donald L. Foley, 'Neighbors or Urbanites?" (Rochester, N.Y.: University of Rochester, 1952 [mimeographed]); and Smith, Form and Stone, op. cit.

64 H. Laurence Ross, 'The Local Community: A Survey Approach,' *American Sociological Review*, XXVII (February, 1962), 75–84. Throughout this paragraph we are indebted to Ross's discussion.

65 For example, Zorbaugh, op. cit.; *cf.* Mowrer, op. cit., on the suburbs.

66 Paul K. Hatt, 'The Concept of Natural Area,' *American Sociological Review*, XI (June, 1946), 423–427. See also William H. Form, Joel Smith, Gregory P. Stone, and James Cowhig, 'The Compatibility of Alternative Approaches to the Delimitation of Urban Sub-Areas,' *American Sociological Review*, XIX (August, 1954), 434–440.

67 The mounting avalanche of urban studies using 'social area analysis' and related methods gives evidence of this. A few early examples are: Eshref Shevky and Marilyn Williams, *The Social Areas of Los Angeles* (Berkeley: University of California Press, 1949); Eshrev Shevky and Wendell Bell, *Social Area Analysis* (Stanford, Calif.: Stanford University Press, 1955); Robert C. Tryon, *Identification of Social Areas by Cluster Analysis* (Berkeley and Los Angeles: University of California Press, 1955); Maurice D. Van Arsdol, Santo F. Camilleri, and Calvin F. Schmid, 'An Investigation into the Generality of the Shevky Social Area Indexes,' *American Sociological Review.*

XXIII (June, 1958), 277–284. These writings, and our discussion, are concerned with the contemporary United States. Small homogeneous areas are also evident, perhaps more so, in preindustrial cities; see Gideon Sjoberg, *The Preindustrial City* (New York: The Free Press, 1960), pp. 80–107. It is also clear, though our discussion does not go into it, that unassimilated ethnic groups and lower class rural migrants very often form identifiable subcommunities with relatively clear boundaries, in both industrial and preindustrial cities. For recent studies showing this, see Erich Rosenthal, 'Acculturation without Assimilation,' *American Journal of Sociology*, LXVI (November, 1960), 275–288; and Janet Abu-Lughod, 'Migrant Adjustment to City Life: The Egyptian Case,' *American Journal of Sociology*, LXVII (July, 1961), 22–32. The existence and delineation of subcommunity boundaries become problematic when ethnic groups are not residentially segregated.

68 Morris Janowitz, *The Community Press in an Urban Setting* (New York: The Free Press, 1952); Scott Greer, 'Urbanism Reconsidered: A Comparative Study of Local Areas in a Metropolis,' *American Sociological Review* XXI (February, 1956), 19–25.

69 Floyd Hunter, *Community Power Structure* (Chapel Hill: University of North Carolina Press, 1953).

70 For concise nonargumentative sociological discussions of community power and decision-making, see Peter H. Rossi, 'Community Decision-Making,' *Administrative Science Quarterly*, I (September, 1957), 415–443; and Richard A. Schermerhorn, *Society and Power* (New York: Random House, Inc., 1961), pp. 87–105.

A fuller and also balanced treatment is that of Wendell Bell, Richard J. Hill, and Charles R. Wright, *Public Leadership* (San Francisco: Chandler Publishing Company, 1961). A general discussion which has things to say about the 'pluralist' approach of the political scientists (*vide infra*) is presented in Thomas J. Anton, 'Power, Pluralism, and Local Politics,' *Administrative Science Quarterly*, VII (September, 1963), 425–457: this article contains an extensive bibliography. For several papers arguing on both sides of the reputation *vs.* decisions controversy, see William V. D'Antonio and Howard J. Elrich (eds), *Power and Democracy in America* (Notre Dame, Ind.: University of Notre Dame Press, 1961).

71 A. Alexander Fanelli, 'A Typology of Community Leadership Based on Influence within the Leader Subsystem,' *Social Forces*, XXXIV (May, 1956), 332–338.

72 Robert E. Agger, 'Power Attributions in the Local Community,' *Social Forces*, XXXIV (May, 1956), 322–331.

73 Delbert C. Miller, 'Industry and Community Power Structure: A Comparative Study of an American and an English City,' *American Sociological Review*, XXIII (February, 1958), 9–15.

74 D'Antonio and Ehrlich, op. cit.; William V. D'Antonio and Eugene C. Erickson, 'The Reputational Technique as a Measure of Community Power: An Evaluation Based on Comparative and Longitudinal Studies,' *American Sociological Review*, XXVII (June, 1962), 362–376.

75 Charles M. Bonjean, 'Community Leadership: A Case Study and Conceptual Refinement,' *American Journal of Sociology*, LXVIII (May, 1963), 672–681.

76 Raymond E. Wolfinger, 'Reputation and Reality in the Study of Community Power,' *American Sociological Review*, XXV (October, 1960), 636–644.

77 Robert A. Dahl, *Who Governs?* (New Haven: Yale University Press, 1961); Nelson W. Polsby, *Community Power and Political Theory* (New Haven:

Yale University Press, 1963); Wolfinger, op. cit.; and Benjamin Walter, 'Political Decision Making in Arcadia,' in Chapin and Weiss op. cit., pp. 141–187. The basic theoretical ammunition for these assaults on Hunter was developed in Robert A. Dahl, 'The Concept of Power,' *Behavioral Science*, II (May, 1957), 201–215; and Robert A. Dahl, 'A Critique of the Ruling Elite Model,' *American Political Science Review*, LII (December, 1958), 463–469.

78 Anton, op. cit., p. 453.

79 Vidich and Bensman, op. cit., pp. 111–139.

80 M. Elaine Burgess, *Negro Leadership in a Southern City* (Chapel Hill: University of North Carolina Press, 1962).

81 Edward C. Banfield and James Q. Wilson, *City Politics* (Cambridge, Mass.: Harvard University Press and M.I.T. Press, 1963). This is only a recent example of the studies by political scientists, studies which probably number in the hundreds, many of which if examined with the present distinction in mind would turn out to have used varying combinations of the reputational and decisions approaches. Just as political scientists until recently ignored the many sociological studies of community power from *Middletown* onward, current community power analyses in both disciplines largely ignore the great wealth of material in earlier writings by political scientists and muckraking journalists. Big-city machines came in for an especially large amount of attention beginning with that of Lincoln Steffens. A recent study which compares different methods and, unlike Elaine Burgess, finds that the method makes a considerable difference in the findings, is Linton C. Freeman, Thomas J. Fararo, Warner Bloomberg, Jr., and Morris H. Sunshine, 'Locating Leaders in Local Communities: A Comparison of Some Alternative Approaches,' *American Sociological Review*, XXVIII (October, 1963), 791–798.

82 Ernest A. T. Barth, 'Air Force Base-Host Community Relations: A Study in Community Typology,' *Social Forces*, XLI (March, 1963), 260–264. See also Ernest A. T. Barth, 'Community Influence Systems: Structure and Change,' *Social Forces*, XL (October, 1961), 58–63.

83 David Rogers, 'Community Political Systems: A Framework and Hypothesis for Comparative Studies,' in Bert E. Swanson (ed.), *Current Trends in Comparative Community Studies* (Kansas City, Mo.: Community Studies, Inc., 1962), pp. 34–47.

84 C. W. M. Hart, 'Industrial Relations Research and Industry,' *Canadian Journal of Economics and Political Science*, XV (January, 1949), 53–73.

85 James B. McKee, 'Status and Power in the Industrial Community: A Comment on Drucker's Thesis,' *American Journal of Sociology*, LVIII (January, 1953), 364–370.

86 Amos H. Hawley, 'Community Power and Urban Renewal Success,' *American Journal of Sociology*, LXVIII (January, 1963), 422–431.

87 For a systematic treatment of the idea of democratic government as the development and resolution of conflict issues, see David B. Truman, *The Governmental Process* (New York: Alfred A. Knopf, 1951).

88 Ernest W. Burgess, 'Urban Areas,' in T. V. Smith and Leonard D. White (eds.), *Chicago, An Experiment in Social Science Research* (Chicago: University of Chicago Press, 1929), pp. 113–138. The concentric zone hypothesis was only a limited, empirical aspect of a broadly and theoretically conceived field of ecological investigation; but in its influence on research it may have been more important than the broader theoretical framework. For a discussion of classical ecological theory, see Robert Ezra Park, 'Human Ecology,' *American Journal of Sociology*, XLII (July, 1936), 1–15.

89 Milla A. Alihan, *Social Ecology* (New York: Columbia University Press, 1938); and Walter Firey, *Land Use in Central Boston* (Cambridge, Mass.: Harvard University Press, 1947). An excellent review of classical 'Chicago' ecology and of writings criticizing it on theoretical and empirical grounds is given in George A. Theodorson (ed.), *Studies in Human Ecology* (Evanston, Ill.: Row, Peterson and Company, 1961), pp. 3–126.

90 Homer Hoyt, *The Structure and Growth of Residential Neighborhoods in American Cities* (Washington, D.C.: Federal Housing Administration, 1939).

91 Chauncey D. Harris and Edward L. Ullman, 'The Nature of Cities,' *Annals of the American Academy of Political and Social Science*, CCXLII (November, 1945), 7–17.

92 Noel P. Gist, 'The Ecology of Bangalore, India: An East-West Comparison,' *Social Forces*, XXXV (May, 1957), 356–365.

93 Floyd Dotson and Lillian Ota Dotson, 'Ecological Trends in the City of Guadalajara,' *Social Forces*, XXXII (May, 1954), 367–374.

94 Sjoberg, *loc. cit.*

95 See the references in footnote 69. Wendell Bell gives a good brief presentation of the case for social area analysis in 'Social Areas: Typology of Neighborhoods,' in Marvin B. Sussman (ed.), *Community Structure and Analysis*, op. cit., pp. 61–92. Discussions of social area analysis, pro and con, are given in the Spring, 1962 issue of *Pacific Sociological Review*, V, 3–16, with articles by Wendell Bell and Scott Greer; Maurice D. Van Arsdol, Jr., Santo F. Camilleri, and Calvin F. Schmid; and Leo F. Schnore.

96 The following articles by Schnore are representative: 'Satellites and Suburbs,' *Social Forces*, XXXVI (December, 1957), 121–127; 'The Socio-Economic Status of Cities and Suburbs,' *American Sociological Review*, XXVIII (February, 1963), 76–85.

97 Stanley Lieberson, *Ethnic Patterns in American Cities* (New York: The Free Press, 1963).

98 Hal H. Winsborough, 'An Ecological Approach to the Theory of Suburbanization,' *American Journal of Sociology*, LXVIII (March, 1963), 565–570.

99 Otis Dudley Duncan and Leo F. Schnore, 'Cultural, Behavioral, and Ecological Perspectives in the Study of Social Organization,' *American Journal of Sociology*, LXV (September, 1959), 132–146; 'Comment' by Peter H. Rossi, pp. 146–149; 'Rejoinder' by Duncan and Schnore, pp. 149–153.

100 Otis Dudley Duncan and Beverly Duncan, 'Residential Distribution and Occupational Stratification,' *American Journal of Sociology*, LX (March, 1955), 493–503.

101 See especially Otis Dudley Duncan, W. Richard Scott, Stanley Lieberson, Beverly Duncan, and Hal H. Winsborough, *Metropolis and Region* (Baltimore: The Johns Hopkins Press, 1960). Related work without the accompanying ideological statements has also been done by a number of sociologists including Kingsley Davis, Jack P. Gibbs, and Walter T. Martin.

102 Wirth, 'Urbanism as a Way of Life,' op. cit.

103 Warner and Low, *The Social System of the Modern Factory*, op. cit.

104 For a useful overview of the field of community development, see the March, 1958 issue of *Rural Sociology* (Vol. 23), with articles by Irwin T. Sanders, Howard W. Beers, Christopher Sower and Walter Freeman, Robert A. Polson, and Charles R. Hoffer. See also the journal, *International Review of Community Development*, published in Rome, Italy, *passim*.

CHAPTER 29

Community Study: Retrospect and Prospect*

Conrad M. Arensberg and Solon T. Kimball

When more than three decades ago we were first introduced to the study of communities in complex societies, anthropologists were relatively little interested in that field. Sociologists did community surveys, but they were interested in social problems rather than in the characterization and comparison of ways of life. Cultural and social anthropologists were as yet little concerned with peoples other than the preliterate ones, and the subsequent inclusion of many European, Asian and Latin-American national cultures, of complex and developed civilizations, in the comparative analysis of institutions and culture patterns and in cross-cultural ethnology had not yet been effected. A beginning had been made in the appearance of the first of the Lynds' volumes on Middletown (in the Midwest) and in Warner's team study of Yankee City (in New England), but these were declaredly pioneer efforts, the first attempts to put anthropological field work, method, and whole-culture analysis to work on literate, complex communities.

Soon after our own work in Ireland, the war years choked off the momentum of these beginnings of the thirties which had inspired us. By then, indeed, studies had been completed in the American South, in Japan, in French Canada as well as in Ireland. But with the end of the near-decade of world war, community studies revived; the momentum of their use was regained and accelerated; and in recent years it has continued to proliferate. Each year the appearance of new studies, in new countries, extends the cross-cultural and geographic range of the extant descriptions and analyses of complex cultures undertaken by this method of anthropological investigation. In greater or lesser measure, as well, the proliferation has steadily increased the store of techniques and the depths of theoretical understanding in the science.

Of equal importance has been the gradual recognition that the community offers the most significant focus, the most viable form of human grouping, for directed innovation, for massive and

* Reprinted by permission of The University of Chicago Press from the *American Journal of Sociology*, vol. 73, 6, 1967–1968, pp. 691–705.

continuous stimulation of cultural change. The approach to change called 'community development' emerged at the end of World War II. It has grown into much vogue and some power, if not always easily or without failures. Programmes such as those of the government of India, Nigeria, Syria, Egypt, Pakistan, Bolivia, among others, efforts such as those of the United Nations in the movement, American foreign aid programmes geared in some countries to village development, such occasional brilliant successes as the Cornell University Vicos Project in Peru—all attest since then to the widespread use of the community as a focus for directed social change.

Since our work, and the pioneer community studies now force attention for their fundamental impact of community study, a collective result from so much scholarly and practical effort, seems to be a changed perspective in social science itself.

There are several explanations. Community studies now force attention for their sheer number and variety. Further, community studies represent a research method raising many interrelated questions at once, and they provide a method of exploring the interconnectedness of the answers to these questions. Community studies have thus taken part in the recent general movement of social science from the treatment of isolated data through the discovery of correlations to the analysis of systematic relationships among social facts. Such interconnectedness among the facts of social systems is challenging today both in the abstract and in the particular. It raises theoretical problems as to the nature of social and cultural phenomena; it requires our explanation of the nature of the different systems of collective restraints operating upon all men and of the integration of the socially supported goals, motives and values for individuals that combine in such different sociocultural systems. It raises particular problems as to the *raison d'être* of particular customs and social conditions, problems as to why in any one cultural and social system the facts take the form which they take.

The theoretical and the particular problems about social systems gain a common illumination today in community studies through their very multiplicity. With more cultures coming into analysis through such studies the variation of human social systems expands and the comparative interconnectedness of cultural and social data, from system to system, grow in intricacy. Community studies thus have shared in the gain to science which the growth of the comparative method has yielded. Throughout the human sciences interest has moved in recent decades from preliminary definitions of phenomena to analyses of structure among them, to the identification of differential functions among institutions, and to the exploration of the complex cultural integration interconnecting them.

If today's basic search is for principles in functional and systematic stability or of the dynamics of social, economic and cultural transformation, then the method of community study has strategic advantages which we shall spell out. The science is no longer content with definitions of cultural and social phenomena, or with typologies of these, or with the static properties of systems uniting them. Instead of analysing social and cultural phenomena for definitional recognition and classification, or for evolutionary classification, the social scientists of today, both in and out of community studies, wish to treat human behaviours, groups and values in vivo. That is, they wish to treat these things in the contexts in which they appear. Older, atomistic studies, not explorations of the community or social-structural matrix of the data, abstracted social and cultural data all too often away from their contexts in the complex interconnections determining their existence and force, denied social scientists a full view of their systemic relationships in particular cultures and of their differential possibilities of placement and connection in other, variant cultural and social systems.

Community studies seem to escape such distortion arising from artificial abstraction and suspension of data from real process. They do not remove the social and cultural data they encounter from the web of connections, functions, mutual supports, complementary placements, etc., they seem to have in the life of the people of the community undergoing study. They try instead to describe that web, to follow out its strands and stresses, to treat it for itself.

With the growth of community-study effort, indeed, even the common, now widespread functionalism of the modern social sciences has undergone a shift in nature. That shift is also, probably, part of the changed perspective in social science which has occurred since we began.

There is a difference in the functionalism of traditional sociology and that of those who have used the community study method. The difference is subtle, and it might easily escape notice, but it is real. The sociology and social anthropology that have come down to use from the thirties (from the founders of that time, Radcliffe-Brown and Malinowski) see the function of a custom or institution as its service to the support of society or, alternatively, its contribution to the management of the emotions, sentiments, needs and support of society's constituent individuals. In the codification of structure-function theory provided by Merton, and widely used in American sociology today, since the concept of function was taken from Radcliffe-Brown and Malinowski's earlier social anthropology, this employment of 'function' to mean service to society is explicitly developed and leads at once to an effort, as in biology, to evaluate the eufunctional and dysfunctional quality, or effect, of social and cultural phenomena. For us, however, who derive community study not only from social anthropology (in the above sense) but also from the comparative classificatory and evolutionary concerns with sociocultural systems, as wholes and as collections of rites, traits, rules and institutions whose *form* is to be explained in addition to any function they may have, such concerns rising prominently in continental ethnology and American cultural anthropology (even the nomenclature is different from the British 'social anthropology'), 'function' means, as it might in mathematics, congruent, configurational or systemic co-occurrence or emergence. Form and function must be separated, and indeed one form may have several functions, one functional need perhaps have several forms fulfilling it, and the questions community studies ask thus deal more with co-occurrence or emergence (as a systemic product or a historical vectorial resultant among forces) than with eu- and dysfunction.

Community studies proceed from quite different criteria. Even the emphasis upon functional analysis common between those who adhere to traditional sociological thought and those steeped in community study proves, on closer examination, to exhibit wide contrasts. The systemic view, inherent in the latter approach, sees function as interdependence within the context of the whole. Such a view is based on variability in relationships and not upon the contribution or utility of an item of behaviour, structure or value to some other item, although we grant the usefulness of such a view in some instances. For example, if criteria of benefit are the basis for judging some practice or institution, we could then see the justification for using the contrast of function and dysfunction. Our own inclination is to abandon such valued categorizations since they violate the principles of the inductive, natural-history method upon which community study is founded. The contrast is of course not complete, since a function can be both a congruent or resultant covariation and a contributor to or destroyer of something. But the questions are different ones, and the analysis of form and resultance is more complex, and more telling, than that of simple contribution to efficacy of operation. Indeed, it subsumes the other.

THE DIMENSIONS OF COMMUNITY

What we need to do now is to explore the relevance and relationship of the heritage of anthropological thought to community study. In particular, we wish to emphasize that perspective which seeks to explore the relationship between culture and society as it is manifested in the wholeness of community through delineation of the inter-dependencies of behaviour and institution within such wholes. This, then, sets forth the context in which one of us[1] described the perspective, the field, and the method of community study. In the brief recapitulation of the substance of this analysis which follows we restate our view of the current status of theory and method in this field.

There are two perspectives from which community may be observed. If one views it as an object or thing, then the questions which are asked will have as their objective the explication of its nature. The answers that one seeks will be those which establish identities, types, functions and the degree of success with which it meets the individual and collective needs of its inhabitants.

If one asks questions about the community as a field or sample 'in which to study something else than the community itself,' then the questions will be of a different kind. The criteria which must be satisfied and the other questions for which answers must be gained have as their objective the use of the results of community study for the purposes of social science. These are problems of comparison, variability and change; of the relationships between parts and wholes; and of the individual and group in their connections and life histories. There is also the need to establish the legitimacy of a procedure which views a particular community as a representative microcosm 'of the whole of, a society, culture, civilization or epoch.'

Those who view community as an object have been the most critical of the community-study approach. They ask: How does one determine that a community may serve as representative for a culture or society? How may you bound a settlement to ensure completeness? How inclusive of all aspects of behaviour and institutions must a community be? What level of cohesiveness must be evident? The answer to the questions of these critics can be gained in large measure if we state the multifactorial elements which a full community encompasses.

First, however, we must preface our answer by drawing attention to the numerous characteristics which animal and human communities share in common, and then to the distinctive and contrasting aspect of symbolically learned and transmitted behaviour found only among men. Basic comparability within these two types of community is established by delineating the territorial unit which provides the resources for support of a given population. But there are other parallels which Arensberg summarized as follows: 'Human beings, with culture, and animals, without it, equally well divide into communities, establish boundaries, trend toward exclusive member-ships; band together for mutual support, defence and mate choice;

establish rhythms of land use, travel and movement; throw up monuments of one physical sort or another to their co-residential, familial and communal livings; re-use and rework old settlements and their monuments into new shells for living; or, alternatively bud off new colonial and daughter communities duplicating old ones.'[2]

In addition to the distinguishing elements already enumerated, we must add still others. The population unit is no mere aggregate of undifferentiated individuals. It includes members of both sexes and an age range stretching from the newly born to those in the declining period of old age. Within such a range there occurs a differentiation of relationships, such as those of mother to infant, or old to young, which is one form of a hierarchy of status. In a human community this table of organization may be elaborated far beyond a purely biological definition to include possessors of the array of diverse skills which are learned. These are culturally transmitted within the setting of a community which in its range of individual variation is thus the chief repository of behaviours, patterns, and institutions. Each type of community possesses its distinctive social differentiations and exhibits a division of labour which must be perpetuated if it is to survive. Arensberg has formulated it thus: 'The community is the minimal unit table of organization of the personnel who can carry and transmit this culture. It is the minimal unit realizing the categories and offices of their social organization. It is the minimal group capable of re-enacting in the present and transmitting to the future the cultural and institutional inventory of their distinctive and historic tradition. And *from* it, *in* it, the child learns, from peers and the street as well as from parents and teachers, the lore of his people and what must be learned to become one of them.'[3]

The dimensions of community we have enumerated thus far include spatial (territorial), ecological (resources used), population (personnel), social (forms of grouping) and cultural (learned behaviour and its transmission). To these we must add one more—the temporal dimension. Communities, animals and human, exist over time. Each one of the several stages of an individual's life-span is represented in its membership at any one point of time. But the community extends backward and forward in time beyond the life history of any one individual. The biological expression of this transgenerational quality is generalized in the concept 'gene pool'. Its cultural expression is contained within the knowledge and behaviour generalized in customs, institutions, and values. Temporal succession, however, presents no smooth, unvarying pattern. The rhythms and periodicities of individual or group move within recurring cycles of altering relationships and the processes of natural history. Man, although unable to fully escape from the effect of diurnal and seasonal change and of the life cycle of the individual, has nevertheless created a ritualized temporality, and his *rites de passage*, and in his *rites of intensification*, in short, in the calendars of his religious and social activity.

These, then, are the dimensions of community. Their application permits us to answer the demands posed by sampling theory that require of a community as a sample of a society that it be a group or unit of that society which is itself representative, complete, inclusive and cohesive. We contend that any community in any society, properly chosen with due regard to these points of its character, meets sampling requirements in social science.

COMMUNITY-STUDY METHOD

The objectives of any study and the operations which are utilized in gathering and analysing data, however, have significant consequences for the results which emerge. It is for this reason that we must now turn to an examination of the concepts and methods which guide those who engage in community study. Since many of these are also utilized in other areas of social science research, we shall emphasize only those of greatest import.

The origins of community-study method can be found in the use, by anthropologists, of the natural-history approach to small and relatively simple tribal groupings. The isolated setting and the conditions of living permitted and forced the immersion of the researcher into the life of his group. His data were recorded from the day-to-day activities, the less frequent ceremonials, the verbally related accounts of past happenings of men and the gods, the observed techniques of tool making and use, the forms and membership of human groupings in the variety of domestic and field co-operative labours, and the practices associated with teaching and learning.

The raw data, won by observation and exploration, served no purpose beyond that of simple fact, however, until they became transformed through analysis and interpretation. From this ordering emerged the descriptions of groups, their activities and beliefs, and their relationships to the physical and social settings around them. Perhaps it was not inevitable, but the circumstances under which such field work was conducted led to the recognition of the value of describing the 'whole' and, eventually, as the perspective of anthropology shifted, of seeking explanation of functions and interdependencies rather than trait distributions alone. Although the researcher may have carried hypotheses into the field with him, their substantiation was established or disproved by the forced referral of his ideas back to the facts of situation or behaviour which he encountered.

The transference of this holistic method from the study of 'primitive', that is, small tribal societies, to the examination of 'civilized' communities in complex societies brought in its wake some new additions in technique and concept, oftentimes borrowed from other social sciences, sometimes freshly invented. From this older tradition community study has retained, as a basic goal, the search for those principles of behaviour and social structure which allow cross-cultural comparison and the formulation of general statements about culture and society, rather than emphasis upon the nature of the object itself. In this sense the community becomes the setting in which the exploration proceeds; the method encompasses those devices, conceptual and technical, which assist discovery, verification, and comparison. As Arensberg phrased it, 'Community study is that method in which a problem (or problems) in the nature, interconnections or dynamics of behaviour and attitudes is explored against or within the surround of other behaviour and attitudes of the individuals making up the life of a particular community. It is a naturalistic, comparative method. It is aimed at studying behaviour and attitudes as objects *in vivo* through observation rather than *in vitro* through isolation and abstraction or in a model through experiment.'[4]

Perhaps some additional elaboration at this time on the construction and use of models would assist in clarifying community-study method and in contrasting it with other approaches. Ever since social scientists discovered and borrowed from mathematics and the physical sciences the concept of 'models' there has existed an assumption, among some of them at least, that the use of such models has increased the scientific rigor and validity of their operation. (Kurt Lewin's transfer of field theory from physics to the study of groups can serve as an early example.) In those instances, however, where no clear distinction was made between the research design and the subject of research, and where the model was intended to represent, among other things, a hypothetical representation of that which was to be investigated, serious questions have been raised about the worth of such an innovation and the validity of the assumptions. There is no need for such doubts to arise in the case of the community-study method, as a real community and any model of social structure erected to describe it are always immediately separable. The misinterpretation which can result from the failure to keep these two things sharply separated can lead to dubious conclusions indeed, as exemplified in the Stein interpretations of American communities, to which we shall come shortly.[5]

For those who are partial to formal models, there is no reason why they should not think of the results of community studies as models of communities within their cultures and societies. Community-study method might be to them, then, the construction of specific, successive models for structuring local social relationships and local social and behavioral facts in the way best suited to depicting their real-life occurrences and interconnections. But those who prefer to start with either implicit or explicit models must beware of injecting a priori assumptions about the nature of their object of study, that is, the real life of the people in their community. They must try many models for best fit and best depiction; they must ride no hobby horses; they must hold free to try first this and then that identification of elements and arrangement of parts; structure this way and that way as the data, not their received concepts or favourite methods used elsewhere, require. For example, 'power structure', 'stratification', 'ecological system', 'social network', etc., are useful, modern concepts in social science, but to treat them as universal phenomena of all communities and societies, to seek their specific expression in each community used for study, or to generalize them without test from one to another, is to prejudge the comparative data before they have been gathered. Similarly as is so often true today, if all-too-plausible but simple contrasts are proposed, such as 'primitive' and 'complex', 'rural' and 'urban', or 'closed' and 'open', without test for their relevance to the real community before one, then, too, data are distorted before they are won and nature forced into reflecting art and theory, not reality.

If we can construct a living, moving model, both continuant and changing, of this life and structure of the real community of persons, then our imagery will approximate the reality. Certainly the creation of any a priori substantive model, deduced from hypothetical convictions about the nature of society, or culture, or *all human* groupings outside this one, deeply violates the empirical spirit of science and the canons of community-study method. Anthropology has let no received theory of human nature stand untested; certainly community-study method, even in complex society, can let no theory of social structure, of social and cultural change, or of institutional function overrule what it sees and what it hears in the life before it.

THEORY AND INTERPRETATION

Knowledge of the structure, function, and process of community and communities is won in quite other ways than deductive formulation of theoretical necessities. It comes from the laborious collection of the empirical facts in situ and from subsequent analysis of the regularities, similarities and concurrences among them. It requires an inductive approach for synthesizing social structure which contrasts with the logico-deductive procedure followed today in so much of social science.

As illustration of the contrast between such procedures and an approach which derives theory directly from the data, we propose to comment upon the monograph by Stein, previously mentioned, and to the summation by Frankenberg, entitled *Communities in Britain*, in which he makes eclectic use of various theories in his interpretation of several community studies.[6]

In his *The Eclipse of Community*, Stein draws upon studies examining numerous aspects and segments of American life to give us a provocative, sociological analysis of the direction in which American society is moving. It is not a treatise about community-study method, nor is it a comparative analysis in the ethnographic tradition. Its substantive purpose is to 'develop a theory of American community life' which is dependent upon 'the development of a framework for relating disparate community studies to each other.' Our interest centres upon his theoretical model, and we shall examine it as an example of the effect which such a definition exerts upon the selection of data and the conclusions.

Stein theorizes that the processes (also labelled social forces or pressures) of urbanization, industrialization, and bureaucracy are shaping American community life. In this view he finds himself in accord with 'general sociological theorists like Marx, Weber, Durkheim, and others.' His model of community is provided in the 'field-theoretical' postulate of Kurt Lewin, in which community is seen as 'an organized system standing in a determinate relationship to its environment.' Change is seen as the impact of forces on the system from which there emerges an alternating sequence of disorganization and reorganization. (Shades of Hegel!) 'The conceptual model rests on the examination of change and assumes that urbanization, industrialization and bureaucratization, as defined earlier, plot most of the key dimensions. In field-theoretical terms, the problem today is as much one of identifying the contemporary stages of urbanization, industrialization and bureaucratization through their manifestations as environmental pressures as it is of discovering the new patterns of community social structure that they call forth.'[7]

The 'case' material utilized by Stein included the sociological studies of Chicago under the inspiration of Robert Park to show urbanization;[8] the Robert and Helen Lynd report of *Middletown* (Muncie, Indiana)[9] to illustrate industrialization; and the Warner and Low study of the factory system in *Yankee City* (Newburyport, Massachusetts)[10] to demonstrate bureaucratization. As supplementary and supporting evidence, he examines another half-dozen studies, ranging from the slums and Bohemia to the suburbs. In his interpretation of social processes we encounter an unformulated but older theme appearing under a new guise—the assumption of implicit conflict between the individual and his society. This is exemplified in the impelling status quest accompanied by identity diffusion which afflicts the lives of suburban dwellers. Stein acknowledges that his views about the individual reflect the influence of Sigmund Freud and of Paul Radin, the latter holding to an individualist ideology amounting almost to anarchy. With the addition of a purely individualistic and psychological perspective, Stein provides a theoretically counterpoised closure in the symmetry of immutable historical processes at one extreme and individual life drama at the other.

Summaries such as this one can never fully catch the author's intricacies of thought and argument and must inevitably carry some distortion. They do lay the ground, however, for contrast with other views and thus can lead to further sharpening of intellectual apprehension. We think it helpful, however, if we make the general observation about the danger of confusing the process of change and its consequences. An elephant may be seen as a species representing a certain stage in the evolution of animals, but we can hardly explain the process of emergence as elephantizing. The generic process is found instead in natural selection. We think that the use of urbanization and other such terms as explanatory processes suffer from the same disability. Urbanization, industrialization and bureaucratization should be viewed as consequences, not as processes. We shall offer further comment about Stein's approach in conjunction with the analysis of Frankenberg's analysis to which we now turn.

The theoretical framework which Frankenberg utilizes to compare the results of several studies made on communities in Great Britain should be counted as a commendable effort to create an interpretive model which encompasses a wide diversity of community types. (That he has chosen to select as one of his examples our own study of Irish countrymen does us honour, although its inclusion was not central to his theoretical concern.) Frankenberg calls himself a model-building sociologist. As such, community studies provide him with the substantive data to verify and explicate social theory. His major concern is the construction of a morphological continuum on which the rural community stands at one end and urban society at the other. Each of the communities he summarizes may be placed at some point along the continuum as it approximates either the rural or urban model. Although he lists twenty-five themes in his model, for each of which he offers contrasting distinctions between rural and urban, the important differences are covered in concepts of community, role, network, class and status group, social conflict and social redundancy. This eclectic matrix is drawn from such diverse sources as Merton, Barnes, Marx, Weber, Durkheim and communication theorists.

The main substance of his argument can be presented quickly. At one extreme we have the face-to-face intimacy of rural communities, and at the other end of the continuum we find urban alienation and anomy. In such a theoretical construction of urban life we encounter once again the valued implicit assumption of separation and conflict between the individual and society. In rural areas, roles are few in number but possess a fluidity which permits a varied pattern; there are many inter-linkages and connections through others in the social network; the fruits of production remain primarily in the hands of the producers; class and status differentiations are minimal, and status is ascribed; and the language communication is redundant. In contrast, roles in the urban world are many but formal; the network of relations tends to be direct and bureaucratic; workers are alienated from the products of their labours; class distinctions and conflict appear, and status is achieved; and the language of behaviour tends to become a code.

These brief summaries of Stein and Frankenberg provide a contrast between the perspective, theory, and method, which they represent, and our own. The immediately apparent distinction is contained in their separation of the method of community study and the data of community from theory derived from within the data, and in their treatment of both as things which orbit quite independently of each other and without any necessary connection to the method of study. There are other differences. Frankenberg's continuum may serve some heuristic, definitional purpose in helping to clarify differences in social forms, but such a priori formulations can produce distorted categories, and they contribute little to understanding the process of social change. We are not opposed to creating typologies which permit comparison on the basis of process, structure or pattern, but we do not believe that comparison by polar opposition or dichotomization contributes very much to advance scientific understanding. Our criticism of Stein's designation of industrialization, bureaucratization and urbanization as processes is based upon somewhat the same premises. We grant that these terms may be made operational, but when they are used primarily as labels for supposed trends in community patterns we then suggest that the effort to identify variations and to model differences for themselves has been abandoned in favour of an all-too-easy dichotomization and polarization. *We suspect these authors have given up natural-history classification—which utilizes the internal data for its taxonomy—and the pain and effort of structural comparison based upon description of real specimens, for premature scalar quantification.* When Frankenberg offers us a continuum of two poles, with forced intermediate gradations, the beguiling ease of scalar quantification has taken over. No other model for presenting the relationships over other possible, better models of the connections the data may show has been presented. The hope of simple correlation is so strong that choice of model is not free, fit of various models never attempted, and a procrustean bed has been forced upon the still uncovered facts.

Although further analysis of the differences which separate our approach from that of others would be illuminating, we wish to draw immediate attention to only one additional aspect, namely, the perspective from which the individual and his interations with others is examined. Those who utilize role theory, as does Frankenberg, work with such concepts as role behaviour, role expectation, role-other, role-set, etc., as if these constituted the attributes associated with an assumed set of fixed positions such as one finds in a family, school, or other relatively stable institution. It seems to us that the individual, in such an approach, is either ignored entirely or becomes submerged as part of a position. We also believe that those who see the structure of society as consisting of sets of linked roles in inter-action cannot possibly develop principles which explain the processes associated with change, since role is not an empirical unit of observation.

The approach we favour is one which recognizes the intimate connection between the individual and the system (or systems) in which he participates with others but which also counts individual or system as separate focuses of reference in analysis. Basic data are always derived from observation of individuals in interaction with each other. We follow Radcliffe-Brown in considering each interpersonal event involving two persons as a reciprocal. Each individual's participation with others may be examined and categorized, and his 'social personality' is the expression of his participation in the various positions available. For example, individual A, who acts as father in one relationship, appears as son in another, as brother in another, as landlord in another, etc. Each relationship is viewed as reciprocal and in its specification, such as father-son, carries a cultural definition of appropriate behaviour which varies according to the situation. Data derived from observations from this perspective permit us to make statements about the individual, elicit a positional structure, and describe cultural practices. Only the referential fluidity which reciprocal analysis injects, however, permits a less static analysis than that which comes from role theory.

When we utilize the concept of reciprocals in interaction analysis, about which we shall have a great deal to say shortly, then our data permit us to specify the changes in both individuals and their relationships. For example, observation will establish that there are quantitative as well as behavioral differences in the relationship of an Irish farm father who directs a still immature adolescent son from that of a father to a son to whom the family land has been deeded and who is now its adult representative. When one takes into account such dimensions as age, etc., it can be seen that variation occurs in the reciprocal and hence function even though the positional definition of father-son still obtains. When you combine referential fluidity (any position or reciprocal may be chosen as the point from which the entire system is examined) and dimensional variability (time, space, personnel, etc.), then your data will yield explanations of change. The definitional basis of role theory does not seem so suited.

EXTENSIONS AND DEVELOPMENTS

In one sense, the methodological advances which have accrued with the proliferation of community studies represent elaborations and refinements inherent in the original approach. As we would expect, greater sophistication has accompanied their use and wider application. Furthermore, the self-conscious examination of field procedures and subsequent analysis has brought many of the underlying assumptions into conscious awareness and heightened the focus of theoretical considerations. In particular, the relationships between research method and substantive findings have become clear. In this area we acknowledge our debt to Bridgman for his formulation of the principle of operationalism. His insight gave us understanding of how the use of the tools of science affected the results obtained from any subject of study.

In another sense, however, there have been some major innovations, and there are three of these to which we wish to direct special attention. Their significance will be more deeply appreciated, we believe, if first we attempt to reconstruct a bit of the theoretical climate which prevailed when we were originally initiated into community study.

One of the objectives that time was the attempt to look beyond the particular individual or trait of culture as the basis for explaining social and psychological phenomena. Explanation was believed better to be achieved by ascertaining the functional connections between individual behaviours and items of culture or social institutional rules. As subscribers to this view, we were loyal adherents to the ideas of Durkheim, Radcliffe-Brown and Malinowski. Linked to the search for function was the need to establish social categories and the specification of the associated cultural behaviour. This taxonomic ordering is a first step in all scientific procedure. It gives us a framework or structure which helps to clarify differences and similarities and permits the placing of new elements in their proper niches. The delineation of a system of social class in the *Yankee City* study was one of the products of these early efforts. Once it had been formulated, one could ask about the manner in which social class was expressed in other parts of the community, such as institutions, or questions could be posed about the function of one social class in relation to another.

In retrospect, this ordering of the social environment was a necessary first step, but it was also a static one. 'Social system' or 'social structure' then referred to an arrangement of categories and their functions. Functional interdependence referred to the contributory effect or welfare of the parts to each other. There was no failure to recognize that the present was unlike the past, or that future changes might be expected to occur; it was only that the conceptual devices then available were inadequate to the task of specifying processes of change. Since then we have made considerable progress in overcoming these difficulties in three separate but related analytical approaches. These we call system analysis, interaction analysis and event analysis. Their use permits us to pose new types of questions and to begin to describe the dynamic aspects of community with greater precision. Although our own contributions to each of these areas have already been reported elsewhere, we shall offer a brief résumé of each one at this time.

System analysis assumes that the parts and relationships of each phenomenon are variable aspects of an identified whole. In the study of any group the first task is to decide what these basic variables are. Since community study examines groups in vivo empirical observation quickly establishes that individuals engage in repetitive activities of a solitary or co-operative nature and that they hold certain beliefs about these activities. Furthermore, we can establish that these activities exhibit regularities in time and space. Hence, the three initial classes of phenomena which we identify within a system include interaction between individuals from which we abstract structure; the behaviour which accompanies such interaction which in its standardized form we label custom; and the judgmental explanations which we call values. 'Thus a system is seen as composed of a number of *individuals* united by *ordering relations*, existing in *time and space*, each individual responding in a *customary* manner towards others within the system (or outsiders or events which impinge on the system), the nature of the *interaction* (ordered relations and customs) being an expression of the values affected by the situation or event which stimulated the response.'[11]

The question may properly be asked if this formulation is equally applicable to the community as a whole as well as to its parts. Can we explicate the interdependencies of all the varied behaviour in institutions and groups with the same facility that we analyse a school, a family, or the behaviour of young men who assemble nightly on some street corner? We believe that system analysis permits this since the problem is not one of size or complexity. For example, if we think of a community as a macrosystem and a family as a microsystem, what are the specific variables that are common to each? These are environment (the natural and technologically modified setting), population (individuals) social organization (categorical and relational groups), customs (forms of behaviour) and values (symbolic representations). It should be noted that each of these variables may also be examined systematically. Thus population may be treated demographically, the individual as a personality, values as logics, etc. In fact, interaction analysis and event analysis represent further elaboration of the principles of system analysis as applied to human behaviour.

Interaction analysis was born of the urgency to develop techniques which could measure the realities of social behaviour—the order of actions among individuals—and from such a base to construct the regularities and processes of change within institutions. Its discoverers, Chapple and Arensberg, have reported their scheme in its full content elsewhere.[12]

The condensed version which we shall present in the next few paragraphs is included primarily to give some taste of its nature to those who have not yet been introduced to this approach. Interaction, by the simplest definition, is an observed sequence of action. We can see that in the encounter between two individuals, one of them will initiate to the other, who in turn terminates by responding. Defined thus, an event is a time-measured sequence of action on the part of persons acting in a recordable order within each pair. The total of such events observed between any two persons represents the observed relation between them. In this manner we have a simple operational record of human relations. Relationships of status, reciprocity of personal ties and emotional bonds, legal and nonlegal, formal and informal, economic, political, religious or what one will, even those of antagonism, opposition and warfare, are all possible of reduction to a quantitative record of observed events.

The structure of the group is reached through the construction of a matrix of relations derived from the operations by which we describe, compare and generalize such events. One useful empirical model of the group is, thus, the collection of numerical formulas expressing the recorded number of events, orders of action, rates, and durations that characterize each relation between persons. Any relation of the collection is a numerical function of any and every other. The group is a function of its component relations, and they in turn to their total which describes the group as a record of the historical events of interpersonal activity, contact, communication and output. No matter what the group is, no matter what the activities of its members may be, or the events that mark the course of its life, it can be compared with any other group in this common analysis.

In this manner, interaction between individuals and the groups they form can be defined uniquely and quantitatively, yet in terms general enough to cover the whole range of human behaviour and human institutions. Operationally, thus, a group or an institution is a history of events involving the interactions of real persons, a history summarized in an explicit and unique description, but permitting comparative analysis. By using this method of specification and summation of interpersonal events, we can erect a classification of groups and institutions that is not at all merely a restatement of their normative, teleological and functional professions or expectations but one that is independent of these attributes and can be checked, correlated and matched with them independently.

Once the specification of a human group, institution or community, has been accomplished, several additional steps can follow. One of these is to erect a classification which is derived from the operation of recording and generalizing descriptions of the events of human interpersonal interaction. Within this classification of the structure of relations, a structure which includes patterns and sequential regularities, one then seeks for a taxonomy or a processual discovery of the kinds, and the connections among the kinds, of social action. The specification of the wholeness of the connectedness between and among groups viewed from the perspective of sequential process gives up a 'model' of a community derived from real life observation of individuals in interaction.

Some mention should be made of those who have applied this approach to their research and analysis. The use of the order of events of interpersonal action in the industrial factory to define, describe and state the processual interconnections of occurrences in industrial relations has been achieved by Arensberg, Arensberg and Tootell, Horsfall and Arensberg, William Walker and Richardson, and Robert Guest in isolating and quantifying formal managerial line-authority, formal flow-of-work, formal in-plant, 'up-the-line' reporting, union-management grievance procedure, informal worker-worker and engineer-worker staff-line relationships, and formulating the dynamics of their determinacy of productivity, strikes, morale and solidarity. Outside the factory, in non-industrial anthropology and sociology, a similar use of the concepts of order-of-action within events among identified actors in time sequences was used by William F. Whyte, semi-explicitly, in establishing the nature and the function of the street gangs of *Street-Corner Society*,[13] and by Douglas Oliver, in isolating the social control and the societal integration performed on Bougainville by the *muni* or pig-feast competitors of the Melanesian villages.[14] Still further use of the comparison and structuration of differential orders of action was used by Arensberg in ordering and generalizing the data on comparative, ethnographically diverse primitive economic systems reported in Polanyi, Arensberg and Pearson's *Trade and Markets in the Early Empires*.[15]

In some of the examples cited above the use of events as the basis for analysis is clearly evident, and it is legitimate to ask if interaction analysis and event analysis are not really the same thing. The emergence of event analysis to conscious formulation came somewhat later and clearly reflects the influence of the former. It seems to us, however, that at this juncture in the development of our science a separation between them is fully justified. There is a difference between specifying the hierarchies of interaction built from observation of pair-events and set-events within them and the naturalistic description of the events-of-action and results-of-action of sequential events in the life of either simple or complex groups and of their interconnections, recurrences and rhythms. The latter is the subject matter of event analysis. Furthermore, event analysis gives greater emphasis to the conditions within which happenings occur and to the natural history cycle.

Event analysis subsumes all that is inherent in both system analysis and interaction analysis. In fact, it might be regarded as a joining of these two but with a somewhat different perspective and emphasis. Its data are the activities of individuals in assemblage and dispersal in sequence and place. It elicits from such data the structure and pattern of institutions within the dimensions of time and space and in similar fashion traces out institutional interconnections. The natural history of individual, group or community is observed in the context of changing conditions.

In fact, the significant questions become those associated with transformation—the socialization and enculturation of the individual; the reshaping of institution or pattern; and the modification of values. The creation of what is meant by community through examination of events leads one to see community as process based on the activities of individuals in events rather than as a thing of set structure and pattern.

The concept of event analysis was an after-the-fact formulation. In this regard it resembles other discoveries made by those who follow the inductive, natural-history method of science, a procedure dramatically exemplified in Darwin's development of the theory of evolution. Some explanation of the circumstances which gave birth to the idea may be helpful. For a two-year period in the early 1950's a team of researchers from the University of Alabama worked alongside a group of citizens in a small Alabama town as the latter organized and carried to completion a health inventory which has been reported in *The Talladega Story*.[16] The researchers hoped to develop an understanding of community process from observing who was involved with whom in what activities as well as the sequence of action and consequences. The nature of the problem shaped the research strategy in a direction other than that associated with a traditional community study. Emphasis was on recording the actual happenings within the numerous events which accompanied the activity. Only as we were working through our materials after the completion of the study did we realize how our research methods had yielded a new perspective of community. It was then that we learned how fully the course of events we had recorded had been shaped by a pre-existing structure of relationships, patterns of behaviour and values. In effect, through watching an event of near community-wide spread, we had not only been able to abstract some generalizations about community process but had gained a perspective of community structure that might not have been otherwise possible. A full exposition of the method has yet to be made although at the time it was reported upon briefly.[17]

As so often happens, when the literature was re-examined to discover others who had used events as their basis of analysis several instances were uncovered. Many anthropologists have adduced exemplifying incidents to illustrate some point, but this practice does not qualify as event analysis. In Van Gennep's study of *rites de passage*, however, he examined events that appeared with rhythmic regularity in the life cycle of the individual. His important discovery was not the near universality of such rites, a fact of great significance, but that from the analysis of their internal structure he could extract a *schema* which showed the processes associated with sequential transformations. Van Gennep was quite explicit that his discovery did not arise from any a priori formulation but was yielded by the data themselves from application of the comparative method of ethnography.

A few British social anthropologists have used a case history or dramatic incident to provide the data for their analyses. There appears to be, however, a significant difference between what we mean by 'event analysis' and this other approach, a difference which resides primarily in theoretical perspective. Frankenberg offers us a brief account of this development in *The Social Anthropology of Complex Societies*, edited by Michael Banton.[18]

There is still much about the use and potentialities of event analysis that we do not know. Until we have completed several community studies in which this method is utilized, we cannot test some of its possibilities, especially those which explore comparative analysis. 'Models' of communities drawn from within the data, and including both temporal and spatial dimensions, should yield understanding of both structure and process and the relationships between them in a fashion that has yet to be realized. Once this step has been taken it seems probable that social science will have advanced still further in understanding the organizational forms of animal life and of human culture and of their congruencies.

These three innovations then—system analysis, interaction analysis and event analysis—stand as methodological tools which have been explicitly formulated since our own first introduction to community study. They give greater precision in observation and analysis than was previously possible. Furthermore, they permit construction of theories of human organization and behaviour from connections discovered within the data themselves rather than depending upon a priori formulations, which may have been borrowed from other sources, to explain the structure and function of groups and community.

NOTES

1 Conrad M. Arensberg, 'The Community as Object and as Sample,' *American Anthropologist*, LXIII, No. 2, Part I (1961), 241–264; and Arensberg, 'The Community-Study Method,' *American Journal of Sociology*, LX, No. 2 (1954), 109–124. Reprinted as chaps. i and ii in Conrad M. Arensberg and Solon T. Kimball, *Culture and Community* (New York: Harcourt, Brace & World, 1965).

2 Arensberg, 'The Community as Object and as Sample,' op. cit. (see n. 1 above), p. 250.

3 Ibid., p. 253.

4 Arensberg, 'The Community-Study Method,' op. cit. (see n. 1 above), p. 110.

5 Maurice R. Stein, *The Eclipse of Community: An Interpretation of American Studies* (Princeton, N.J.: Princeton University Press, 1960).
6 Ronald Frankenberg, *Communities in Britain: Social Life in Town and Country* (Harmondsworth, Middlesex, England: Penguin Books, Ltd., 1966).
7 Stein, op. cit. (see n. 5 above), p. 107.
8 Robert E. Park, E. W. Burgess and R. D. McKenzie (eds.), *The City* (Chicago: University of Chicago Press, 1925).
9 Robert and Helen Merrell Lynd, *Middletown* (New York: Harcourt, Brace & World, 1929).
10 W. Lloyd Warner, J. O. Low, Paul S. Lunt, Leo Srole, *Yankee City* (New Haven, Conn.: Yale University Press, 1963).
11 Solon T. Kimball and Marion Pearsall, *The Talladega Story: A Study in Community Process* (University: University of Alabama Press, 1954), p. xviii.
12 Eliot D. Chapple and Conrad M. Arensberg, 'Measuring Human Relations: An Introduction to the Study of the Interaction of Individuals,' *Genetic Psychology Monographs*, XX, No. 1 (February, 1940).
13 William F. Whyte, *Street-Corner Society: The Social Structure of an Italian Slum* (Chicago: University of Chicago Press, 1955).
14 Douglas L. Oliver, *A Solomon Island Society: Kinship and Leadership among the Siuai of Bougainville* (Cambridge, Mass.: Harvard University Press, 1955).
15 Karl Polanyi, Conrad M. Arensberg and Harry W. Pearson, *Trade and Markets in the Early Empires* (New York: Macmillan [Free Press], 1957).
16 Kimball and Pearsall, op. cit. (see n. 11 above).
17 Solon T. Kimball and Marion Pearsall, 'Event Analysis as an Approach to Community Study,' *Social Forces*, XXXIV (1955), 58–63.
18 Michael Banton (ed.), *The Social Anthropology of Complex Societies* (London: Tavistock Publications, 1966).